DEGREE MILLS

The Billion-Dollar Industry That Has Sold Over a Million Fake Diplomas

ALLEN EZELL AND JOHN BEAR

UPDATED EDITION

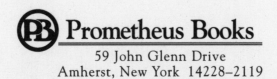

Prometheus Books

59 John Glenn Drive
Amherst, New York 14228–2119

Published 2012 by Prometheus Books

Cover image © 2012 Media Bakery
Cover design by Liz Scinta

Inquiries should be addressed to
Prometheus Books
59 John Glenn Drive
Amherst, New York 14228–2119
VOICE: 716–691–0133
FAX: 716–691–0137
WWW.PROMETHEUSBOOKS.COM

16 15 14 13 12   5 4 3 2 1

Library of Congress Cataloging-in-Publication Data Pending

ISBN 978–1–61614–507–1 (pbk.)
ISBN 978–1–61614–508–8 (ebook)

Printed in the United States of America

*To all those who pursue the facts and truth about
academic credentials and institutions.
Always be vigilant and may your quest be successful.*

*And to our wives, Donna Ezell and Marina Bear, for your
support and your guidance and for patiently listening to all
those degree mill stories over the years.*

DEDICATION FROM ALLEN EZELL

In honor of United States District judge Robert D. Potter, Western District of North Carolina, Charlotte, North Carolina, who died on July 2, 2009, at the age of eighty-six. Judge Potter was known as a no-nonsense jurist, humble and caring, who believed there was a price to pay for committing a crime. He was honest and fair, and was affectionately known as "Maximum Bob" based on the length of sentences he gave to defendants appearing before him. (He disliked this nickname.) He once commented to me, "If you will do your job, I will do mine," and so he did. It was an honor and pleasure to be in his court. During the FBI's DipScam operation, one individual sold the FBI a counterfeit diploma from Judge Potter's alma matter, Duke University. This particular defendant was later arrested and decided to plead guilty in California rather than personally appear before Judge Potter in Charlotte. We will always remember Judge Potter fondly and miss him greatly.

CONTENTS

PART 1. THE BASICS

PART 2. INFORMATION, OPINIONS, AND STORIES

PART 1

··

THE BASICS

··

PREFACE:
A MAJOR WORLD CRISIS

There is a major crisis in the world of higher education: the large and growing number of fake universities and fake degrees.

Many people are either unaware of the situation, don't know what a huge problem it is, or don't appreciate how it is affecting them, their institution or employer, and society at large.

Consider, for instance, these five things:

- There are more than 3,300 unrecognized universities, world-wide, many of them outright fakes, selling bachelor's, master's, doctorates, law, and medical degrees to anyone willing to pay the price. No nation is immune from the problem.
- One international diploma mill, with offices in Europe and the Middle East and mailing addresses in the United Kingdom, run by Americans, has sold more than 450,000 degrees—bachelor's, master's, doctorates, medicine, and law—to clients worldwide, who did nothing more than write a check. Their revenues exceeded US $450,000,000.
- The number of earned PhD degrees in the United States is 40,000 to 45,000 each year. The number of fake PhDs bought each year from diploma mills exceeds 50,000. In other words, more than half of all people claiming a new PhD have a fake degree.
- Fake medical degrees are an urgent problem. It is easy to buy a medical degree from a fake school, or a counterfeit diploma in the name of a real school. Twenty-five years ago, a Congressional committee calculated that there were over 5,000 fake doctors in the United States, and there are many more now. People have died because of these fakes.

- The Government Accountability Office looked for fake degrees among employees of less than 5 percent of federal agencies and found enough to suggest that more than one hundred thousand federal employees have at least one, many of them paid for by taxpayers not to mention resulting higher pay and increased retirement benefits.

And if we needed another reminder, just before this book went to press, Allen Ezell received a call, made from New York City, by the registrar of Amhurst University, whose "campus" is a mail forwarding service in Colorado. Ezell was offered an MBA for $2,400, no questions asked, with a free bachelor's degree thrown in. After a short pause, the price came down $400 "because you're a veteran."

No wonder Ezell has been heard to mutter, "Oh, if only I still had my badge!"

Both authors have been working for more than thirty-five years to expose and close down these dangerous fakes. We begin our book with the biggest phony ever.

ACKNOWLEDGMENTS

FROM ALLEN EZELL

My thanks go to all those FBI employees who participated in, or supported, DipScam, from investigation through prosecution, especially those at the Charlotte, North Carolina, office. DipScam would not have been possible, or a success, without their dedicated efforts. Special thanks goes to the White Collar Crime Supervisor and to the Special Agent in Charge of the Charlotte, North Carolina, office. Investigative initiatives like this do not happen by accident and take the support of the entire office. Special thanks also go to the Assistant United States Attorneys (AUSAs), Western District of North Carolina, who prosecuted these cases. Additionally, I will always be appreciative for the support given to the FBI and DipScam by officials of American Association of Collegiate Registrars and Admissions Officers (AACRAO), Washington, DC. We continue to have an excellent relationship with AACRAO today.

I am grateful for the support and encouragement my wife Donna and my daughters Cindy and Pam have given me in these endeavors.

FROM BOTH AUTHORS

Grateful thanks to Professor George Gollin, who came to this field late but soared to the front with his copious research, writing, and dedication to making the problems known.

For their general support and helpful writing on degree mills, in print, on news forums, and in personal communications, thanks to George Brown, Ann Koenig, Steve Levicoff, Rich Douglas, Gus Sainz, Chip White, and Vasco Dones.

We are grateful to all the state and federal people who have addressed the problems in the past and, we hope and trust, will continue to do so. We are pleased by the attention that Sen. Susan Collins (Maine) and Rep. Tom Davis (Virginia) have brought to the problem of degree mills in recent years. Thanks also to Rep. Betty McCollum (Minnesota) who, in 2007, introduced a bill that would have been the first federal law addressing degree mills (a tiny part of which ended up in the Higher Education Act Reauthorization of 2008; more on this later), and to Rep. Timothy Bishop (New York) who, in 2011, introduced a new bill (H. R. 1758), which, if passed, will refine the earlier bill and specifically address accreditation mills. Cong. Howard P. "Buck" McKeon's Subcommittee on 21st Century Competitiveness also helped bring attention to the problem through a hearing addressing degree mills.

We have said many times that if every state had a state attorney like Jeffrey Brunton of Hawaii and a regulator like the recently retired Alan Contreras of Oregon, the degree mill problem would diminish promptly and dramatically.

Hundreds of people in the media deserve the thanks of the authors and of society in general for discovering and reporting on degree-mill operators and their schemes. Mike Wallace of *60 Minutes* was the first to do a major national report. J. W. August of ABC San Diego returned to the topic again and again in the early years to great effect, as did Greg Hunter, when he was consumer editor of *Good Morning America*. Tom Bartlett, reporter for the *Chronicle of Higher Education*, has written frequently and forcefully on the problem. Bill Morlin, staff writer for the Spokane, Washington, *Spokesman Review* covered the huge St. Regis University scandal in depth, resulting in years of page-one stories.

We appreciate the good work of our agent, Laurie Harper, and our editor and copyeditor at Prometheus, Steven L. Mitchell and Julia DeGraf. And, for reasons only he will know, we thank the man we know as J. J. Doe.

INTRODUCTION: ANOTHER DAY AT THE OFFICE

For Nicolas Tanasescu, it's just another day at the office.[1]

He takes the trolley from his flat at the western edge of Bucharest, Romania, and gets off at Calea Victoriei. He walks half a block down a nondescript street in the business district of the Romanian capital city and turns left into a narrow passageway, Pasajul Victoriei. Number 48 is an old red-brick two-story building. Downstairs is a bar, "TZ's Cotton Club," and a modeling agency called Top Model. Nicolas climbs an unmarked wide staircase leading to the upper floor.

It is nearly 10 p.m., and there is a steady stream of men and women climbing those stairs for their night's work. The office runs twenty-four hours a day, seven days a week, but the 10 p.m. to 6 a.m. shift is the busiest, with about fifty people—Romanians, South Africans, and a scattering of other nationalities—sitting at computer terminals in what they call the DL Room: an array of small drab cubicles.

Most are in their twenties and thirties. All of them speak excellent, if slightly accented, English. Like most of the others, Nicolas earns just over a dollar an hour. That's not a great wage even in this economically depressed country, but with unemployment around 10 percent, he is glad to have work.

He fits a telephone headset and microphone apparatus to his head, adjusts the small computer screen, and settles in for his night's work: telephoning potential customers all over North America.

The office manager, who is also the owner of the business, strolls up and down the aisles, amiably nodding and smiling at his employees.

He is a short, plump, bald American who looks to be in his sixties and sports a white beard and always wears an American baseball cap. He is, in fact, a rabbi from Boston, Massachusetts, who divides his time between Romania and another branch of his business in Jerusalem, where the office closes for the orthodox holy day at sundown on Friday.

On an average day, he earns more than $150,000. A million dollars a week. Fifty million dollars a year. And he's been doing this for many years.

His business is selling fake university degrees, by telephone, to people all over the United States and Canada. More than two hundred thousand degrees have been sold to date, including bachelor's, master's, MBAs, doctorates, law degrees, and medical degrees in every possible specialty, from neurosurgery to pediatrics.

What's going on here?

This is one of the most recent and most ambitious manifestations of a business that has been around since at least the fourteenth century: the selling of university degrees to people willing to pay the price and to take the risk.

Nicolas dials his first client, a businessman in Cleveland who has responded to an unsolicited e-mail by leaving a message on an answering machine somewhere in New York City. "Hi, this is Nicolas. I'm a registrar with the University Degree Program. I apologize for my European accent. We just wanted to contact you to tell you that, because we have some spaces left in our program, we reduced our registration fee by more than $2,000. What I am going to tell you is very important, so if you don't understand everything I say, just let me know. If now is a good time for you, I'll explain our new program and answer any questions that you might have."

The odds are one in three that within the next fifteen minutes, Nicolas will make a $2,000 sale, perhaps more if the man in Cleveland decides to buy two or three degrees complete with transcripts and a degree-verification service.

Just another day at the office.

～✦～

We estimate that Nicolas's employer has sold more than $450 million worth of fake degrees to Americans and Canadians. And he is employed by just one of many sellers of fake and worthless degrees, each of whom is earning many millions of dollars a year.

We know these numbers through a combination of methods: unhappy "deep throat" employees who supply the information, detective work of various kinds, and the most accurate means, the inspection of the evidence collected in those cases when federal search warrants are executed. (There has been no search at Nicolas's employer.)

For example, the California-based degree mill called Columbia State University, which pretended to be in Louisiana and sold its PhDs by return mail for $3,000 each, made bank deposits of well over $10 million, perhaps as much as $72 million, during its last four years of operation. An employee of Columbia State testified before Congress that her employer took in more than a million dollars a month over one six-month period in 1998.

When the FBI executed a search warrant at LaSalle University in Louisiana (not to be confused with the real LaSalle in Pennsylvania), they found evidence of $36.5 million in recent bank deposits and were able to seize $10.75 million that had not yet gone toward the lavish lifestyle of the university's founder.[2]

And a most interesting window into the world of these entities opened a crack with an advertisement for the sale of Almeda University, self-admitted seller of "bogus . . . degrees." The ad, run in a Boise, Idaho, newspaper, offered the "university" for sale for up to $5 million, saying that annual revenue exceeded $3 million, and, rather candidly, said that the reason for selling was bad press in Florida from cops that got caught with bogus Almeda degrees.

In 2011, we estimate the worldwide sales of fake degrees at $300 million per year or more. Over the last decade, fake degree sales have easily exceeded a billion dollars. At an average cost of $1,000 per degree, a low estimate, this suggests at least one million customers.[3]

Is this selling of degrees something new? Not at all. It has been identified as a major national problem for nearly one hundred years. Here's a brief overview of the history of the problem; these matters will be discussed in more detail in the next chapter.

In the 1920s, there were dozens of page-one degree-mill stories in the *New York Times* alone: "Diploma Mill Facts Laid before Senators," "Says 15,000 Have Bought Bogus Medical Diplomas," "Spiegel Held for Selling Fake Law Degrees," "3,000 Fake Diplomas Obtained in Chicago," and so on.[4] US Senate hearings on degree mills were held in 1924, but no action was taken.

This pattern—problem, concern, publicity, demand for action, and then nothing—was to repeat itself several times in the decades to come, roughly in twenty-year cycles.

In the 1940s, the National Education Association established a Committee on Fraudulent Schools and Colleges and launched a "crusade" against degree mills, publishing articles in their journal with titles such as "Degrees for Sale."

In 1950, Benjamin Fine, the distinguished education editor of the *New York Times*, stated that there are "more than 1,000 questionable or outright fraudulent schools and colleges in the United States."

In 1959, US Secretary of Health, Education and Welfare Arthur S. Flemming stated in a US Office of Education press release dated October 29, 1959, that "Degree mills have become such a blight on the American educational scene that I have come to the conclusion that the Department of Health, Education and Welfare has a responsibility about them."

A year later, Flemming wrote that

> I am not so optimistic as to believe that we have uncovered all degree mills since public attention was drawn to this situation five months ago. Therefore . . . we will continue to make known the existence of degree mills whenever we find them operative. It is in the public interest for us to create a national and international awareness of the inadequacy and utter worthlessness of degree mills.[5]

Twenty years later, Allen Ezell's DipScam task force in the FBI marked the first and, still, the only time that a government agency seriously dealt with the problem. But with Ezell's retirement in 1991, DipScam ended.

In 1985 and 1986, Rep. Claude Pepper's Subcommittee on Diploma Fraud concluded that more than five hundred thousand Americans were currently using fake degrees, more than five thousand of them medical degrees.

In 1998, Ezell and John Bear addressed a group of federal personnel officers and federal background investigators, giving information on the growth and seriousness of the degree-mill problem. A good many people left that auditorium in Pittsburgh seemingly determined to *do something* about this national problem.

In the summer of 2003, Ezell and Bear were invited to Washington by the Office of Personnel Management as principal speakers in two four-hour workshops on degree mills.[6] Nearly five hundred HR and security officers left that hall seemingly determined to *do something* about the problem.

In 2004, a diploma-mill summit was held in Washington, where representatives of the FBI, the FTC, the Government Accountability Office, the Office of Personnel Management, the House of Representatives, and the Senate vowed to "protect the federal workforce" from the scourge of fake degrees.

Later that year, the Office of Personnel Management held two more workshops on degree-mill issues for hundreds more HR and security officers. In May, the US Senate Committee on Governmental Affairs, chaired by Sen. Susan Collins of Maine, held two days of hearings titled "Bogus Degrees and Unmet Expectations: Are Taxpayer Dollars Subsidizing Diploma Mills?" In July, the Council for Higher Education Accreditation held a two-day workshop, focusing both on degree mills and accreditation mills.

Is Washington really waking up to the problem? Or is this just another cyclical resurfacing of concern that will fade away just as it did in the twenties, the forties, the sixties, and the eighties? Have things gotten so out of hand—like Nazism in the thirties, civil rights abuses in the fifties, or drugs in the seventies—that this time it cannot be easily ignored?

As we have both watched and participated in various events up through 2011, we have grown increasingly pessimistic. Perhaps the most telling thing about Senator Collins's hearings was that there was absolutely no presence of any law enforcement agency.

No speaker urged the participation of the FBI, the postal service, the Secret Service, or any other enforcement agency to help with the problem.

No one suggested asking the US Attorney's office to initiate a criminal investigation.

No one suggested impaneling a federal grand jury, which could subpoena the records of the less-than-wonderful schools that refused to furnish such information to the committee.

No one noted that the fake-degree service called Degrees-R-Us, from which Senator Collins purchased two degrees more than three years earlier, was still in business and still selling fake degrees.

Two senators present, both former attorneys general, joked that if they were still in office, they would know how to handle the degree mills.

And when Congressman Howard P. "Buck" McKeon's Subcommittee on 21st Century Competitiveness subsequently held a hearing titled "Are Current Safeguards Protecting Taxpayers against Diploma Mills" (one-word answer: "no!"), he reminded the public that an earlier investigation determined that federal Head Start funds, intended for early childhood education programs, had been used to purchase fake degrees—and that, astonishingly, it was still not illegal to do this.

Maybe good things will happen. Maybe there will be some significant changes. But change often requires outrage. A woman might spend years petitioning for a traffic light on a busy corner, but nothing happens until a child is killed by a speeding car. Attempts to launch a health-care program for the elderly were ineffective for half a century until enough people got sufficiently angry that Congress finally listened and Medicare came into existence.

It is not just the occasional user of such degrees discovered by an employer, the media, or a law enforcement agency. It is truly a national, indeed an international, epidemic in which hundreds of thousands, very likely millions, of people are using degrees they did not earn.

But unlike a medical epidemic, in which one can observe large numbers of people suffering from smallpox, measles, and so forth, these fake degree cases are uncovered one at a time, often far from the glare of publicity. And when there *is* publicity, it is generally local at best and quickly forgotten.

Infrequently, a fake-degree case gets national attention, as happened in 2003 with the newly hired and almost instantly fired Notre Dame football coach who didn't have the degree he had been claiming to have for years. Generally, when the media do address the issue—a *60 Minutes* degree-mill segment in 1978 and a second one in 2005, a *20/20* segment, and three *Good Morning America* reports in the early 2000s—they seem to be in the category of just another nine-(or fewer) day wonder: the buried Chilean miners, the landing of a jetliner in the East River, a pop star's latest antics . . . and, oh yes, here's a prominent politician, business leader, minister, or professor with a fake or useless degree.

In rare instances, the media have had a major impact, but only, it seems, if they pound away at the issue until it truly cannot be ignored. One of the rare instances of success was in 1983 at a time when many suppliers of fake degrees had moved from California to Arizona. The largest newspaper in the state, the *Arizona Republic*, assigned its two top investigative reporters, Rich Robertson and Jerry Seper, to the story, and what emerged was a devastating report, featured on page one for four consecutive days under the headline "Diploma Mills: A Festering Sore on Arizona Education."

A crusading newspaper can have a dramatic effect. This four-day page-one series in the Phoenix newspaper brought about public outrage followed by new legislation. Every one of the state's many degree mills either closed or moved elsewhere.

To show readers, and the legislature, how easy it is, the paper even founded its own university and accrediting agency.

Now the issue could no longer be ignored in Arizona. Under mounting pressure from the public and the educational establishment, the Arizona legislature promptly took action, and within a matter of months, every one of Arizona's several dozen active phonies had either closed or, more commonly, moved on to Louisiana, Utah, Florida, Hawaii, and other states that at the time had no laws to prevent this sort of thing.

Much more common, alas, was the response of an editor at a major Honolulu newspaper, when we notified him that a notorious diploma mill operator, Edward Reddeck, had just set up shop in Hawaii. "We report the news," he said. "We don't *make* the news." Many months, and untold victims later, the postal inspectors closed this place down, and *then* it made page-one headlines.

What will it take to make these matters a national concern and a national priority? Clearly it needs to be more than "just" people like these with fake degrees:

- the founder of a popular sex therapy clinic in upstate New York who bought his PhD for $100
- the fake MD in North Carolina convicted of manslaughter when a child he took off insulin because "she did not need it" died
- the head of engineering for a major city's transit system
- the superintendent of schools for California's second-largest school system
- the coaches of two major university sports teams and the head of the US Olympic Committee, discovered within weeks of each other
- the fire chief for one of our largest cities
- generals in the Pentagon, scientists at NASA, and high-ranking officials in the Department of Defense, the Department of Homeland Security, and even in the White House Situation Room, all with fake degrees: all publicly noted, occasionally written about, and pretty much dismissed as isolated and presumably rare incidents.[7]

We don't have a single "magic bullet" solution, although we do have many recommendations, set forth in chapter 19. We only hope it will not require a major and dramatic incident to bring about the needed awareness and changes: a pilot with fake credentials who crashes his jumbo jet, a scientist with fake credentials who sets free a plague virus, or the havoc that could be wrought by one of the many "engineers" with fake doctorates in nuclear engineering safety.

WHAT, EXACTLY, IS A DEGREE MILL?

It is generally advisable to define the "beast" before going out to attempt to slay it. In the case of degree mills, this turns out to be an elusive task.

Let's begin with the most basic words: *degree* and *diploma*.

A *degree* is the title one earns from a legitimate school or simply buys from a fake one: Bachelor of Arts, Master of Science, Master of Business Administration, Doctor of Philosophy, Juris Doctor (law), Doctor of Medicine, and scores of other titles.

A *diploma* is the certificate—the piece of paper or parchment—that signifies that a degree has been awarded.

Schools award *degrees*. And then they present the graduate with a *diploma*, which is, in effect, an announcement, a proclamation of the degree that has been awarded.

Degree mills issue diplomas. Diploma mills sell degrees. We can live with either word, but we have selected "degree mill" as our term of choice since it refers to the entity *awarding* the degree and not just to the decorative announcement framed and hung on the wall.

Different people define these words differently, depending on their intention. There is far from unanimous agreement on just what a degree mill is.

Almost no one would deny that a "university" operating from a mailbox service that grants the PhD in three days is a degree mill. But what about an institution that operates legally in a state with minimal regulation and requires three months and a thirty-page paper in order to earn its PhD? What about one that requires six months and sixty pages? How about twelve months and one hundred twenty pages? One person's degree mill may be another's innovative new-style university. Clearly more definition is needed than just time and work required.

Until now, only three books have been devoted entirely or largely to degree mills. Here's how each of them define the term.

In 1963, Robert Reid wrote that "degree mills are those institutions that call themselves colleges or universities which confer 'quick-way,' usually mail-order degrees on payment of a fee. These institutions turn out . . . degrees without necessarily requiring the labor, thought, and attention usually expected of those who earn such degrees."[8]

In 1986, David W. Stewart and Henry A. Spille wrote, "Basically a diploma mill is a person or an organization selling degrees or awarding degrees without an appropriate academic base and without requiring a sufficient degree of postsecondary-level academic achievement."[9]

In 1990, Steve Levicoff, realistically acknowledging that no single definition can work in every situation, offered a list of sixty-two characteristics sometimes exhibited by degree mills, and he suggested that each reader would have to decide how many of these characteristics it would require before calling a school a degree mill.[10]

In Allen Ezell's presentations to academic and business groups, he often uses this definition adapted from several publications of the US Office of Education: "Degree mills are organizations that award degrees without requiring [their] students to meet educational standards for such degrees. They receive fees from their so-called students on the basis of fraudulent misrepresentation and/or make it possible for the recipients of its degrees to perpetrate a fraud on the public."

It would be wonderful to have an infallible and undisputed test of what is a mill and what isn't, but clearly there is no perfect definition that works for every person in every case. We offer in chapter 2 our list of ninety-two things that schools do to fool people. If a school has eighty or ninety of these characteristics, almost no one would deny it is a mill. But what about sixty-three? Or forty-two? Or seventeen? Some would say yes and some would say no or maybe. The important thing is to be clear about why you say something is, or is not, or probably is.[11] In general, it seems to us, identification as a degree mill comes down to consideration of these five crucial issues:

a. degree-granting authority,
b. credit for prior learning and experience,
c. amount of new work required,
d. quality of new work required,
e. who makes the decisions.

Let's look at each of these issues in a bit of detail.

a. Under what authority are the degrees granted? Who has given the school permission to grant degrees? How have they made that decision?

Authority to award degrees needs to come from an independent entity, almost always a government agency. Some mills claim to give themselves the authority through their corporate charter, but no legitimate school does this.

We are talking about well over three hundred government agencies, and that means more than three hundred different policies and procedures. There are the 192 members of the United Nations, a few dozen countries that haven't joined the UN, and dozens of territories, colonies, and protectorates. There are countries where some or all of the school decisions are made one step down from the national government: the fifty US states, of course, as well as the Canadian provinces and territories, the Swiss cantons, and others.

Some government agencies have a comprehensive and responsible method for determining who can grant degrees; others are little more than rubber stamps or have a simple and trivial process. And a great many are somewhere in between, thus subject to various interpretations, depending on who is doing the interpreting and for what purpose.

b. How much credit is given for prior learning, and how is that decision made?

It is an academically valid and well-accepted practice to give credit for learning experiences that took place prior to enrollment. A typical example is skill in a second language. If an American student takes four years of French in college, she will earn about twenty-four semester units and achieve a certain level of competency in the language. But what if she reached exactly the same level of competency on her own, whether through taking a Rosetta Stone course, living in that country, or learning from her grandmother? Many schools will award credit, although not necessarily those twenty-four units, once the competency has been demonstrated on a meaningful written and/or oral examination.

Credit is responsibly given for a wide range of prior learning, ranging from an Army map-reading course, to an IBM in-house training program, to earning a multiengine pilot's license, to extensive independent study in Buddhist philosophy, to achieving a high score on the Graduate Record Examination in math.

While each school makes its own decision on how much credit to give, many rely on recommendations made by the American Council on Education's (ACE) College Credit Recommendation Service, described at http://www.acenet.edu/calec/corporate. ACE evaluates thousands of learning experiences and publishes its recommendations on how much credit to give for each experience in several large volumes each year.

While there can be a considerable range in the amount of credit given for the same experience, the bad and fake schools regularly abuse this process by making outrageous credit awards. For instance, a good score on the ninety-minute College Level Evaluation Program (CLEP) test in history is worth one or two semester units at many schools and as much as five or six at a few. But degree mills have been known to give forty or fifty semester units, or even the entire bachelor's (typically 120 units), master's, or doctorate degree, for one CLEP test.

Again, we have a continuum, with the least-generous legitimate school at one end and the degree mills at the other. If the amount of credit awarded for a Navy music course ranges from three units at School A to one hundred twenty units at School Z, where does one draw the line between "good school" and "bad school" and perhaps another line between "bad school" and "degree mill"? And, most significantly, *who* draws that line?

c. How much new work is required to earn the degree?

While there are three regionally accredited US schools that will consider awarding their bachelor's degree totally based on prior learning (if there is a great deal of it), the vast majority of schools require at least one year of new work, no matter what the student has done before.[12]

At the master's and doctoral level, giving credit for prior learning is minimal and rare. We know of no school with recognized accreditation that will award its master's degree for anything less than one academic year (eight or nine months) of new work. The doctorate typically requires at least two years of new work, but usually three to five.

It is a common approach for degree mills to look at an applicant's CV or resume and say, "Ah, yes, you've been selling life insurance for three years. That is the equivalent of an MBA," or "We have determined that your five years of teaching Sunday school can earn you a Doctor of Divinity degree."

Once again we have a continuum. At one end are the schools that require a great deal of new work after enrollment, and at the other end are the degree mills that offer any degree, including the master's or doctorate, entirely or almost entirely based on the resume.

Is a three-page paper and one short open-book quiz sufficient for a master's degree? A thirty-page paper and a one-hour unproctored exam? Ten thirty-page papers and five two-hour proctored exams? Where does one draw the line, and, again significantly, *who* draws it?

d. How does one judge the quality of the work done?

Even more complicated than evaluating the quantity of work done to earn any given degree is the *quality* of that work. A brilliant thirty-page thesis might be considered more worthy of a master's degree than an ordinary hundred-page one or a poorly done three-hundred-page one.

Once again we have a continuum from A to F (or 4.0 to 0.0) grades, and we have the complicated issue of who makes those grading decisions and on what basis.

The quality of work done has been used in courtroom trials and other public situations to help prove that a given school is a degree mill. A high school teacher with a dubious PhD sued his school district, which had refused to pay him at the doctoral scale as the union contract required. The district had acquired a copy of this man's seventeen-page doctoral "dissertation" directly from his alma mater, an unaccredited California university. The arbitration committee was clearly not impressed with this work, which the committee said was nothing more than a book report, and denied the claim.

That situation turned out well. But what if the three arbitrators had "voted" two to one? What if the lawyer for the defendant had found three professors who said that the work *was* adequate? What if the degree holder had hired an academic writing service (and there are plenty of them) to write a good dissertation for him, *after* his degree was challenged?

e. Who makes these decisions? How do they do so?

Gatekeepers and decision makers must decide where to draw all these crucial lines: how much credit for life experience, how much work to earn a degree, and what quality of work. Whenever possible, they will make use of external examiners: scholars from other schools and agencies, who will review the processes and determine that they are valid and equivalent to what their own institutions do.

All of this means that there is no short, simple, universally accepted definition of a degree mill. The complexity of the current educational situation precludes that.

OUR DEFINITION OF "DEGREE MILL"

A degree mill is an entity in which

- degree-granting authority does not come from a generally accepted government agency,

- procedures for granting credit for prior learning, and for determining the amount and quality of work done to earn the degree, do not meet generally accepted standards, and
- those who make the decisions on credit, and on quantity and quality of work, do not have the credentials, experience, or training typically associated with people performing these tasks.

THE DEPARTMENT OF EDUCATION'S DEFINITION OF "DEGREE MILL"

The Higher Education Reauthorization Act of 2008 introduced the concept of "diploma mills" into federal law for the first time. It's not a wonderful law, and it was watered down dramatically between introduction and passage (more on this later), but at least it is a start.

In its original form, House Resolution 773 of 2007, this was the definition:

> The term "diploma mill" means any entity that—
> (A) lacks valid accreditation by an agency recognized by a Federal agency, a State government, or the Council for Higher Education Accreditation as a valid accrediting agency of institutions of higher education; and
> (B) offers degrees, diplomas, or certifications, for a fee, that may be used to represent to the general public that the individual possessing such a degree, diploma, or certification has completed a program of education or training beyond secondary education, but little or no education or course work is required to obtain such a degree, diploma, or certification.

In the final version (the actual law), this is how it reads:

> DIPLOMA MILL.
> The term "diploma mill" means an entity that—
>
> (A)   (i) offers, for a fee, degrees, diplomas, or certificates, that may be used to represent to the general public that the individual possessing such

a degree, diploma, or certificate has completed a program of postsecondary education or training; and

  (ii) requires such individual to complete little or no education or coursework to obtain such degree, diploma, or certificate; and

(B) lacks accreditation by an accrediting agency or association that is recognized as an accrediting agency or association of institutions of higher education (as such term is defined in section 102) by—

  (i) the Secretary pursuant to subpart 2 of part H of title IV; or
  (ii) a Federal agency, State government, or other organization or association that recognizes accrediting agencies or associations.

The big potential problem here is that phrase "or other organization or association." These are not defined, as they were in the original wording of the bill, and that leaves the door wide open for fraudulent organizations, in the United States or elsewhere, that are set up to recognize fake accrediting agencies.

And the second big problem is that nothing is said about fake or bad schools outside the United States: those that are owned and run from the United States but use addresses in other countries, and those that are non-US-owned but sell their degrees to people in the United States.

The content of this book has been shaped by these definitions of "degree mill" or "diploma mill," the attendant problems with the definitions, and by these three additional factors:

1. *The continuum concept.* While we have our own clear ideas on where to draw lines on the continuum that runs from "degree mill" to "legitimate school without recognized accreditation," it is equally clear that many others have *their* clear ideas, and they are different from ours. A school whose degree can qualify you to take the bar or a state licensing exam in California can get you arrested on a criminal charge in Oregon. Every decision maker and gatekeeper draws his or her line in a different place.

2. *Our litigious society.* In this great democracy of ours, anyone can sue anyone else, and except in the rarest instances of wildly frivolous actions, the courts accept these suits. In the

mid-1990s, LaSalle University (Louisiana) sued John Bear for a seven-figure amount because he had identified the institution as a degree mill. The following year, the proprietor of LaSalle was indicted on eighteen counts of mail fraud, tax fraud, and other charges; pleaded guilty; and was sent to a federal prison. But before this happened, John Bear had to spend thousands of dollars to respond (successfully) to this action that he believed to be both frivolous and vengeful.

In the late 1970s, Allen Ezell, John Bear, and a whole bunch of others (including CBS, the FBI, and some state attorneys general) were sued for $500 million by an already-imprisoned degree-mill operator, claiming libel, slander, and a conspiracy to put him out of business. We were content to let CBS and the others speak for us, but a lot of attorney time was booked before the courts eventually threw that one out.

And a few years ago, the Canadian publisher of John Bear's book on online degrees was sued by an unrecognized Canadian school unhappy because it *wasn't* listed in the book.[13] Eventually, again after time and expense, the Canadian court declined to accept the case.

But we also want to point out, in passing, that things might have been different if media peril insurance ("libel insurance") were available and affordable, and/or if the US courts were (in this respect) more like those in some Commonwealth countries. When our colleague George Brown, an Australian, was sued in Australia by a "school" allegedly in England that he had called a degree mill, the plaintiff was required by the Australian court to put up a multi-thousand-dollar bond. When the "school" did not press the suit, presumably because it would have meant revealing the names of the owners and its location, the court canceled the suit and gave the bond money to Dr. Brown.

3. *The fact that information and opinions on degree mills are readily available.* Anyone who needs to decide whether a given school is a degree mill (based, of course, on where he or she decides to draw the line on that continuum) will find plenty of information available in places ranging from government sites (such as the ones run by the states of Michigan,

Oregon, and others, which identify hundreds of illegal schools by name) to news forums, such as DegreeInfo.com and DegreeDiscussion.com, where responsible people call many institutions degree mills (often we agree with them, but choose not to use those words) to companies in the business of checking academic credentials and issuing opinions on the legality and legitimacy of schools.

In chapter 14, we provide the official long list of schools whose degrees cannot be used in the states of Michigan and Oregon, the two most thorough and up-to-date such lists.

Add to these the recognition of the speed with which situations change as the Internet and other advanced technologies make it increasingly easy for degree mills to launch, move, change their names, and cover their tracks, and you can see why this is not a reference book with an annotated list of several thousand school names. It is, rather, a consumer awareness work. With the information in this book, any intelligent reader can, at the very least, recognize the red flags that signal a less-than-legitimate enterprise and can develop sufficiently sensitive degree-mill "radar" to know when questions need to be asked and of whom to ask them.

Chapter 1

....

THE SORDID PAST

....

A *History of Degree Mills from the Middle Ages to the Present Day*

T he history of fake degrees and diplomas is logically divided into three eras: the period from ancient times up to the start of DipScam in 1980; the DipScam era, including the Congressman Claude Pepper hearings (1980 to 1991); and the period since then.

THE FIRST ERA: 700 (OR EARLIER) THROUGH 1979

Perhaps the earliest use of what we would call diplomas is found in western Europe among the Merovingian and Carolingian people. As J. M. Wallace-Hadrill writes, these "diplomas . . . were official instruments, couched in an elaborate form of words and authenticated in several ways, whereby kings made known their gifts and grants to communities or individuals, and did so in what seemed to them the safest and most permanent manner."[1]

And yet, the author explains, "[i]n spite . . . of all precautions, it was not very difficult for medieval scribes to forge diplomas well enough to deceive rivals. . . . So there are many bogus diplomas" from that era.

For all we know, there may be older fake diplomas in clay pots by the Dead Sea or daubed onto papyrus in the tombs of ancient Egypt, but at least we know that fake diplomas have been a problem for a minimum of thirteen hundred years.

The first legitimate academic degrees were awarded in Europe in the eleventh century at the University of Bologna and soon after at Oxford and the University of Paris (the Sorbonne). It seems safe to suggest that fake diplomas—and fake schools—followed closely on the heels of the real ones.

In his massive book *The Universities of Europe in the Middle Ages*,[2] Professor Hastings Rashdall devotes more than a thousand pages to detailed descriptions of several hundred institutions, from the 1100s through the 1400s. Intriguingly, three Italian authors[3] made the claim, in 2010, that included in Rashdall's book are twenty-three degree mills: "establishments which various contemporary and later authorities claimed to be universities, but for which no adequate evidence existed."

One of those may well be a "university" in the French city of Albi, where, in the thirteenth century, the bishop excommunicated everyone living in Albi because, he said, they falsely claimed to have established a university. The excommunication was reversed, on appeal, but the popes around that time played fast and loose with the issuing of commands to open or to close universities. Not only that, but they had the power to grant academic titles (like "Doctor") without requiring any work. The titles they thus issued allowed recipients to call themselves "Dottori," but they were pretty much the laughingstock of the academic world. They were often identified as "Doctor Bullatus," one who was made a doctor pretty much automatically, by a notary, for a very modest fee.

By the fourteenth century, according to Barbara Tuchman, diplomas from Oxford or Cambridge served, in effect, as the "library cards," necessary to gain admission to the research facilities of the University of Paris.[4] As a result, there was quite an active traffic in the buying and selling of fake diplomas. It was also the case that it required as much as fifteen years of study beyond the master's degree to earn a doctorate, a fact that may have motivated some younger scholars to acquire the doctorate by faster means.

In this period, so many new universities opened, the University of Paris begged the pope to stop them, in part because some of the newer ones, more interested in making money than offering education, got into the business of first selling admission to the highest bidders, and eventually to the selling of degrees themselves.

Further, degrees were in such demand that the alumni of some of the established universities went into business selling fake or counterfeit diplomas from their own schools. Indeed, in the late 1400s, one major university (Avignon) lost at least two-thirds of its students—some to war or disease, but most simply purchased their degrees and departed.

Similarly, the year before Columbus sailed, one major Italian university (Padua) formally accused three others (Parma, Piacenza, Ferrara) of selling Padua degrees at a very low price.

Because legitimate doctorate degree programs cost a great deal more than lesser degrees, it was common for would-be teachers to do their lower degrees at a prestigious university, and then either buy or do an easy doctorate at a less-than-wonderful school. One of these was the University of Cesena, which became well-known for its cheap and easy degrees, and was sarcastically called the "university of the two hams." (Graduates in those days were expected to provide a lavish and expensive feast for their entire faculty, but at the bad schools, it was said that two hams would be sufficient.[5])

Fake schools may have arisen in the United States long before the American Revolution. The earliest mention is a tantalizing reference in an 1883 treatise.[6] The author, in the midst of complaining about "[t]he bogus degrees [that may] claim to have issued from some university which is nonexistent," says that the sale of degrees was commonplace at least since the year 1730. The tantalizing part is that he does not name any names, nor has any other scholar yet discovered which fakes he may have been referring to.

In his 1963 doctoral dissertation on degree mills, Robert Reid reports that the earliest date associated with a known fake is 1797, the year on the seal of the Colonial Academy.[7] However, as Reid correctly points out, it has always been common for degree mills to lie about how old they are.

Because of this proclivity for lying, we cannot know if the "honor" of being the first American degree mill goes to the Colonial Academy, to Milton University of Maryland (claimed to have been founded in 1847 and definitely incorporated as a university in 1909), or to Richmond College (claimed to have been chartered in Ohio in 1835 and definitely soliciting students in 1876).

Certainly by the 1880s, there were quite a few fake colleges and universities in operation and often in legal trouble. Reid cites American University in Philadelphia (charter revoked by the courts in 1880), Livingston University of America (charter repealed by West Virginia in 1881), and Western University (chartered in Illinois in 1897). The US Commissioner of Education at the time, John Eaton, referred each year in his annual reports (1876 through 1881) to the "scandal and disgrace" of degree mills in the United States.

During the early years of the twentieth century, fake medical schools proliferated,

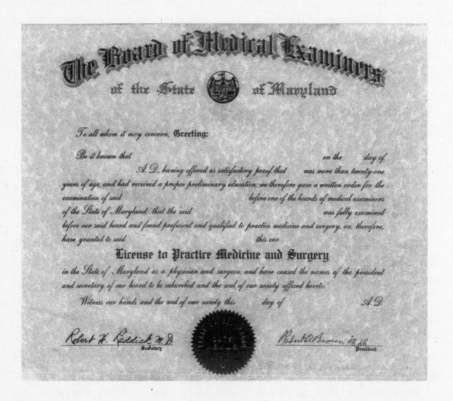

Along with their fake medical degrees, one degree mill provides a realistic-looking license to practice medicine in the state of Maryland.

leading to the first US Senate hearings ever held on the matter of fake degrees. The report of the Subcommittee of the Committee on Education and Labor, chaired by Sen. Royal Copeland of New York, himself a medical doctor, suggested that there were "at least 25,000 fraudulent doctors, doctors who have fraudulent . . . medical diplomas, practicing in the United States."[8] But no action was taken, and it would be eighty years before the Senate again looked even briefly at the fake degree problem.

One curious (by twenty-first-century standards) recommendation of this subcommittee was in fact implemented, amending the postal laws to make it illegal to grant degrees for work done entirely by correspondence. Needless to say, this law was never enforced, and today it is commonplace for legitimate degrees to be earned entirely by distance or online learning.

According to a German scholar fascinated by American degree fakes, the 1930s were the "golden age" of degree mills, fueled in part by the depression and the wish for inexpensive degrees.[9]

In 1950, the distinguished education editor of the *New York Times*, Benjamin Fine, wrote that there were "more than one thousand institutions operating unethically, of which "at least one hundred of these [are] diploma mills where one can buy . . . a high-sounding doctorate for less than $50."[10]

Fine's article upset so many people that the large and powerful National Education Association launched a well-publicized effort to identify and outlaw degree mills. But they were unable even to agree on what sorts of laws should be enacted, and their efforts faded away. By 1957, the dubious Association of Home Study Schools, which Reid says "represents many of these phony colleges and universities," were claiming that total enrollment in "their" schools was 750,000 students, paying an annual tuition of $75 million.[11] Based on the Consumer Price Index, that would be $581 million dollars in 2011.

Reid's excellent research and writing on degree mills, culminating with his 1963 doctoral dissertation at Columbia, was clearly designed and intended to stir things up among the regulators, the state legislatures, the media, and the public, but it was not to happen. John Bear wrote Reid a "fan letter" after discovering his work in the seventies and received this rather despondent reply. "Sometimes I think the Kennedy assassination, the Vietnam era, and the whole cold war thing diverted the attention of the decision makers in Washington and in the state capitals away from degree mills, but I can tell you, it has been extremely discouraging to see how little has been done over the past two decades. Perhaps the 1980s will bring about a turn for the better."[12] Sadly, they did not.

In 2006, the authors, along with colleague George Gollin, made a pilgrimage to the Columbia University library in New York to examine the archives that Reid had deposited there: three cartons of materials that had gone pretty much untouched for forty years.

THE SECOND ERA: PEPPER AND DIPSCAM

The 1980s did indeed go a long way to fulfilling Reid's hopes. Between the FBI's DipScam operation and Rep. Claude Pepper's hearings on degree fraud, the topic of fake degrees had more government attention and public awareness than at any time before or since.

The Pepper Hearings

In the course of far-reaching hearings relating to fraud against the elderly, Congressman Pepper's subcommittee on health and Rep. Don Bonker's subcommittee on consumer interests discovered in 1985, that the problem of fake degrees and credentials extended far beyond the fake medical doctors, nurses, and other health-care practitioners. Indeed, one of their most popular witnesses was then-imprisoned degree salesman Anthony Geruntino, who said that although he had sold thousands of fake degrees, he did not sell medical degrees, since that "would be unconscionable." (Geruntino's conscience did not stop him, however, from selling engineering degrees to people at Three Mile Island and Westinghouse Nuclear or degrees, including doctorates, in aerospace engineering to people at NASA's Johnson Space Center and Kennedy Space Center.)

The subcommittee staffs did good and comprehensive work in looking into both the fake schools and the people using fake degrees. To demonstrate the ease of operating in the fake-degree world, and with an unerring sense for getting publicity, they invested $1,800 of taxpayer money in buying a PhD in psychology for Mr. Pepper from Union University in Los Angeles, thereby making him "Doctor Pepper."[13] Then they established and ran advertisements for their own fake school, the Capitol Institute of Advanced Education.

Their numerical estimates are scary indeed: "[A]pplying the rate of bogus [health] credentials . . . to all other occupations, there would be as many as 2 million bogus practitioners in this country. . . .

"The American Council on Education estimates there are . . . about 400–500 diploma mills in operation around the country. . . .

"The National Council for Accreditation of Teacher Education estimated [that] fully one sixth of all [doctorates] in education were phony. If one generalizes from this estimate to all doctorates granted [in the past five years], this would translate to nearly 40,000 Americans holding bogus doctorate degrees alone."[14]

Pepper concluded with these recommendations:

1. "With the release of this report, I am calling upon the Federal agencies to investigate the qualifications of employees."
2. "I am asking that they provide the Subcommittees with a statement of the actions they have taken to verify the authenticity of those employees' academic credentials."
3. "I am also requesting that they take appropriate action where necessary to ensure that these sensitive posts are occupied by . . . genuinely qualified individuals."
4. There should be a "computerized national clearinghouse on fraudulent credentials," accessible to government agencies, businesses, and consumers.[15]

Pepper was a well-liked and powerful politician and a skilled power broker who genuinely was concerned about fake degrees, but on those four recommendations, he had almost no success.

The FBI's Operation DipScam

One evening in 1980, some FBI agents in Greenville, South Carolina, were watching *Monday Night Football*. Howard Cosell was extolling the virtues of Houston running back Charles "Boobie" Clark, who, he reported, had just earned his degree from Southeastern University in Greenville. The FBI agents looked at each other and said, in effect, "Hey, wait a minute. This is our town. We don't have any such university here."

Around the same time, a resident of Charlotte, North Carolina, was able to purchase a bachelor's, master's, and doctorate from Southeastern University without doing any work. This information reached an FBI white-collar crime specialist named Allen Ezell, based in Charlotte. It was clear that something phony was going on. Ezell took the information he gathered to an assistant US attorney, who saw harm to society, and authorized Ezell to begin a mail fraud and fraud-by-wire investigation.

That Charlotte resident introduced Ezell (by telephone) to Dr. Alfred Jarrette of Southeastern University. Mail does not have to cross a state line to constitute a federal violation, whereas a telephone call is a violation of federal law only if it crosses a state line. Since Ezell was in North Carolina and the school was in South Carolina, they had their case.[16]

Ezell negotiated for the purchase of a bachelor's, master's, and doctorate, all backdated. He did no work at all, sent Jarrette the money, and in due course received the diplomas and transcripts.[17]

It was after the investigation had already begun that he learned about the "Boobie" Clark *Monday Night Football* story.

After the sale of degrees to another FBI agent, they were invited to come to Greenville to be photographed in caps and gowns. The two new graduates were offered one-third of the revenues if they would raise money for the school.

Since Southeastern also claimed a religious connection, to show *that* was bogus, a third agent arranged to purchase a degree in theology for $5,000 to be picked up in person.

The FBI's DipScam operation began after Allen Ezell was able to purchase this diploma from Southeastern University.

With the cooperation of North Carolina National Bank, now Bank of America, the agents ostensibly applied for jobs. The bank wrote to Jarrette to verify the degrees, and he wrote back a glowing letter confirming them. This showed how far he was willing to go.

On the appointed day, Ezell and two other agents went to Jarrette's home, but now as FBI agents with a search warrant, which was served at the door.

Jarrette sat quietly while the agents went about their work, collecting many Southeastern student records. He had been expecting to sell a $5,000 degree, and instead he got three feds with a warrant.

The agents gave Jarrette a receipt for the confiscated materials, reassured him that this was not the end of the world, and headed back to Charlotte. But for him, it was the end. That night, he had dinner with a lady friend, gave away some of his possessions, and then committed suicide with a .38 revolver.

In analyzing the seized papers, the FBI learned that Jarrette had sold 620 degrees, including 171 to federal, state, and county employees. *Parade* magazine later discovered even more graduates, including a fairly high official at the US Department of Education who had purchased his PhD in criminal justice for $1,800.

The seized materials also showed that Jarrette had traded degrees with a man named James Vardaman Kirk: two Southeastern degrees for Kirk, backdated to 1974 and 1975, in exchange for a law degree from Kirk's school, backdated to 1978.

This was the first we heard of Kirk, then of the University of San Gabriel Valley, later to found Southland University (California), International University (Louisiana), and LaSalle University. We started paying attention to Kirk's activities, and he later went to prison for his fake LaSalle University.

This, then, was the start of the FBI's DipScam program, the longest-lasting and most effective effort by any government anywhere to deal with the degree-mill problem. Over the next ten years, forty fake diplomas were purchased, sixteen federal search warrants were executed, nineteen Federal Grand Jury indictments were returned. More than twenty perpetrators were convicted, most of them pleading guilty when they recognized the case against them, and five others after a long and complex trial in federal court. The FBI identified more than 12,500 "graduates" of these institutions from school records, including more than a few federal, state, and county employees.

Both for historical interest and as an indicator of the kinds of things that are still being done, in chapter 6, we look at many of the specific DipScam cases.

By the end of DipScam, most of the big degree-mill cases had been resolved, and with the growing savings-and-loan scandals unfolding, Ezell was spending less time on degrees and more on these other crimes. He retired from the FBI after thirty-one years in December 1991, and, following a thirty-six-hour "retirement," began his next career in banking, working in fraud and special investigations for nineteen years, then retiring again.

During the eleven years of DipScam, forty degree mills were "dismantled," with total sales into the many tens of millions of dollars.

The general feeling was: Now the word is out. The schools were put on notice. The FBI never lost a case, and a bunch of bad guys ended up in prison. It seemed as if the problem was largely abated.

And along came the Internet, and it was a whole new ballgame.

Chapter 2

···

THE SELLERS

···

Fake Schools, Accreditors, Counterfeiters, and Visa Mills

There are five distinct categories of schools, businesses, or individuals who offer degrees that do not meet what is sometimes called the GAAP standard. Just as accountants talk about their GAAP, Generally Accepted Accounting Principles, so, too, do educators refer to Generally Accepted Accreditation Principles. Not mandatory, not universal, but, simply, generally accepted.

THE FIVE CATEGORIES OF NON-GAAP DEGREES

Category 1: Too new or too unusual. Schools that are either too new or too unusual or innovative to qualify for recognized accreditation. Recognized accrediting agencies typically want an applicant school to have at least two years of successful operation before applying. Academic models and fields of specialty are flexible concepts, and so what is potentially accreditable can change from time to time. Less than fifty years ago, there were official government warnings that any school offering degrees 100 percent by distance learning had to be a fake. Now, of course, there are many hundreds of properly accredited universities that do this. In the same vein, there have been times when there was no recognized accreditation for schools specializing in acupuncture, naturopathic medicine, cosmetology, funeral service education, midwifery, or leisure studies. Now each of these fields has its own recognized accrediting agency.

Category 2: Geographical Issues. There are schools that operate

45

from, or have a token presence in, states or countries that have less stringent school legislation. These range from places with moderately rigorous systems of oversight (such as California state approval) to places that let just about anyone do just about anything in the way of offering degrees (such as the state of Mississippi and the island nation of the Grand Caymans).

Category 3: Religious Issues. This category includes schools that have, or claim to have, some sort of religious exemption. There are hundreds of such institutions, ranging from one-man Bible schools to large campus-based universities that do not believe in the concept of accreditation and/or licensing.[1]

Category 4: Degree Mills. There are degree mills that pretend to be legitimate schools but simply sell their degrees to anyone, man or beast, based on little or, in most cases, no work.

Category 5: Counterfeiters. These are the "services" that make and sell copies of diplomas of real schools, sometimes alarmingly well done (with signatures, gold seals, ribbons, and security devices such as imbedded magnetic stripes), sometimes ludicrously inaccurate (and yet, how many people know what a diploma of some small and distant state university "should" look like?).

A small number of people find something that meets their needs in schools in categories one, two, or three, but many people have difficulty in knowing exactly where to draw the line between legitimate (or acceptable) schools and degree mills.

There are unaccredited schools whose degrees qualify people to take the bar or various licensing exams in some states, which some employers accept and pay for. And yet those very same degrees are illegal for use in some other states and have little acceptance in the academic world.

Over the years, we have identified roughly three thousand degree-granting schools that fall in one or more of the first four categories. But readers will need to decide for themselves what to call a "degree mill," what to call "acceptable" or "adequate" or "meets our standards," and what to put in between. We offer detailed guidelines for the ways and means of making that decision and, a bit later in this chapter, a detailed list of ninety-two things that some dubious or less-than-wonderful schools do to mislead people.

While many fake diplomas are sold on eBay, this was an opportunity to buy an entire diploma-counterfeiting company for a mere $10,000.

But we are well aware that if we asked one hundred readers (registrars, HR people, school seekers, alumni, law enforcement officers, news media, etc.) to sort one hundred schools into those four categories, we'd have responses all over the map.

FIVE REASONS THAT PEOPLE HAVE PROBLEMS WHEN DECIDING WHAT TO CALL A DEGREE MILL

The term degree mill (or *diploma mill*) is a real pejorative. It is not a term to be used lightly. One can call a school "dreadful" and "dubious" and "nonwonderful" and "suspicious" and "unsavory" (and so on), and that is just a matter of opinion. But if one calls a school a degree mill, a phony, or a fake, especially if one bases a decision, policy, or news story on those words, one must be very confident of the ground on which one is standing.

Here are five factors with which we have seen people struggle when they are attempting to identify and describe degree mills or unacceptable schools in the course of developing personal, business, media, government agency, or legislative guidelines on the problem— in other words, where to draw the line on their own particular continuum.

It is appropriate to explain and discuss these reasons in some detail, since they provide insight into the degree-awarding and degree-selling situation as it is today.

1. That Pesky Church-State Situation

Most states are terrified about doing anything that might be construed as restricting the right of a church to do just about anything it darn well pleases, including starting and running a university and handing out degrees of all kinds.

The Universal Life University in California has "awarded" hundreds of thousands of degrees, including the PhD, for "donations" of $10 and up (for many years, their PhD cost $100), and the state Supreme Court has decreed that this is all quite legal *as long as they award only religious degrees* (Doctor of Divinity, Doctor of Theology, etc.).

There are two problems with this reasonable-sounding rule.

One problem is that people don't wear badges saying what their degree is *in*. When a high-school dropout calling himself "Doctor" was busted in upstate New York for running an illegal sex therapy clinic, his *only* degree was a perfectly legal PhD in religious science from the Universal Life people.

A second and equally serious problem is that not every state says that religious schools can grant *only* religious degrees, as we believe they should. In other words, even though a school may operate entirely through a religious exemption, in some states it can award degrees in physics, psychology, political science, or anything it wishes. Not surprisingly, the church-operated schools that do this sort of thing are rarely associated with mainstream religions— Catholics, Lutherans, Jews, and so forth—but are typically a one-man (or one-woman) church founded by the school owner and existing primarily as another line on his or her home telephone.

One such institution, Hamilton University, operated legally (under Wyoming's minimalist regulations) from a former motel building in Evanston, Wyoming.

Hamilton University, with a staff of two, operated from this former motel in Evanston, Wyoming, population, 12,000.

It is run by the not-exactly-mainstream Faith in the Order of Nature Fellowship Church. Hamilton made big news in the summer of 2003 when a reporter for Government Computer News discovered that a high-ranking executive in the Department of Homeland Security in Washington had "earned" her bachelor's, her master's, and her PhD in computer-related fields from Hamilton University.

The Hamilton doctorate, which can take as long as ten days to earn, requires nothing more than producing a four-page paper (on ethics, believe it or not), and, of course, the ability to sign a check or credit card voucher.

Laura Callahan's account of her involvement with Hamilton University and the aftermath appears as an essay in chapter 10.

It is clear from the findings of the Government Accountability

Office that a great many other federal employees have degrees from Hamilton and from dozens, perhaps hundreds, of unrecognized and often fake schools. Hamilton is just one drop in a very large bucket.

All degrees are religious degrees because God created everything: How LaSalle University of Louisiana parlayed that argument into selling more than $35 million worth of degrees

For many years, Louisiana was one of the states that did not regulate religious schools as long as they granted only religious degrees. The state's assumption was that this would allow church-run schools to train their own clergy in a setting where academic quality was less important than doctrinal soundness.

Along came LaSalle University, prepared to drive its eighteen-wheeler through the loophole in that law. (We refer, of course, *not* to the legitimate LaSalle in Philadelphia but to the operation that had been "invited" to leave California, then Arizona, Florida, and Missouri and finally headed south to the then-friendly bayous of Louisiana.)

As the official university of the Trinitarian Church, later the World Christian Church, a religious entity existing only in the mind of owner James Kirk (also known as Thomas Kirk and Thomas McPherson), LaSalle was exempt from state licensing, as long as it gave only religious degrees.

So it did.

With a straight face, presumably, it declared that because God created everything, *all* degrees had to be religious degrees. God created the elements, so chemistry degrees were religious. God created the mind, so psychology degrees were religious. God created numbers, so math degrees were religious. And so on.

Could anyone in his or her right (God-created) mind take this seriously? Fortunately, the feds didn't. Following a surprise visit to the campus with search warrants in hand, agents of the FBI and the IRS and the postal inspectors found evidence of fifteen thousand students, a grand total of one faculty member (who had only LaSalle degrees), and more than $35 million in bank deposits made over the previous four years.

Following an eighteen-count grand jury indictment for mail fraud, wire (telephone) fraud, tax evasion, and money laundering, LaSalle owner Kirk/McPherson pleaded guilty and was sentenced to the maximum possible term in minimum-security federal prison— five years—by an angry judge who said he wished it could have been longer.

As mentioned earlier, within days of Kirk/McPherson's arrival at the federal prison camp in Beaumont, Texas, advertisements began appearing in *USA Today* and other national publications for Edison University. Edison's literature was almost identical to that of LaSalle. Indeed, in the promotional video telling us what a fine place Edison is, one can see, on a shelf in the background, a framed photo of Kirk's children.

While the "campus" of Edison University was in fact a mail-forwarding service in Honolulu, Hawaii, the catalogues bore the postmark "Beaumont, Texas." And the director of admissions and registrar of Edison University, Natalie Handy, had become Kirk/McPherson's wife while he was in prison. We've heard of many instances of "university without walls." This would clearly seem to be a case of "university *behind* walls."

Edison University was promptly accredited by an unrecognized, but still thriving, agency called the World Association of Universities and Colleges. Then, when the real Edison in New Jersey got an injunction, the name was changed to Addison and finally to Acton University.

Kirk/McPherson served his time and became a free man a few years ago. Can you guess what he's doing now? If you answered, "Affiliated with a new university in Mississippi," you win an honorary doctorate in the field of your choice.

2. The Four-Inch-Square Campus

In the course of our more-than-three decades of checking out new and suspicious schools, there have been numerous occasions in which one of us arrives at the campus address to discover a mailbox rental store, a secretarial service, or one of those office-services companies that rents cubicles and conference rooms by the hour.

More often than not, this official address of the university is in a state that either has weak licensing laws or doesn't seem to care what people do as long as they aren't defrauding the citizens of *that* state. So the crack they have fallen through is this: state A, where such schools would be illegal, says, "We don't care, because they're really run from state B—just look at their mailing address." And state B says, "We don't care because all they have here is a rented mailbox; they are really run from state A; it's *their* problem."

Once in a while, a state will impose some minimal requirements on a school it knows is really operated from its own state, even though the "campus" (i.e., the mailing address) is in another state or even another country. Often, the only requirement is that the school cannot accept students who live in the state from which it is *really* run.

Thus, for instance, the attorney general of California said to the very large Kennedy-Western University, run from California but whose "campus" was, at the time, a small office in Wyoming, "We don't care what you do with people in the other forty-nine states or in other nations, but you can't deal with people who live in California."

Authorities in Idaho and Alabama have, at times, also ordered several dreadful universities not to enroll people who live in the same state as the school.

It goes without saying (but some people need it said anyway) that when a school tells a potential student, "Sorry, we cannot accept applicants living in your state," there is quite a large red flag waving, even for students who live in a different state or country.

Of course, most schools in this situation don't mention this geographical problem. They wait until a potential student supplies an address, and *then* the telemarketer (that is to say, the admissions counselor) makes the explanation. And even then, of course, the "counselor" doesn't say, "Sorry, even though we say our campus is in South Dakota, our location there is actually a four-inch-square box, and we are run from Florida, but the attorney general in Florida has told us that if we accept one Florida student, we're off to prison." No, the telemarketer will, if pressed, provide an elaborate explanation of how the state laws are unfair or restrictive or don't allow innovative schools like theirs to operate or, in the case of an Idaho wonder, that it would "cost millions of dollars" to go through the state licensing process (not true), and so, reluctantly, the school has this policy.

A few states have attempted to be compassionate in writing laws that allow legitimate but low-budget start-up schools to operate from within their borders. They want to see something more than the four-inch-square mailbox "campus"—but not a whole lot more.

Hawaii, for instance, says that an unaccredited school can operate legally if it has at least one full-time employee in the state. But when a tabloid television program, *American Journal*, visited the official Hawaii address of the heavily advertised Pacific Western University that claimed to have more than twenty-five thousand graduates, the TV program found a nearly empty room and a secretary at the law offices next door who apparently was the entire Hawaii employment force of this really-run-from-Los-Angeles university.

California used to have an innovative law that encouraged unaccredited schools to operate while ostensibly maintaining some level of consumer protection: a new university needed to own at least $50,000 worth of property in order to get a state license. While this may possibly have prevented some fly-by-night schools from opening in California, it also served to encourage the better-funded fakes, whose operators would simply put their homes in the university name.

In the case of the notorious California Pacifica University—the school whose owner was caught by *60 Minutes*'s camera selling Mike Wallace a PhD for $3,000, no questions asked—owner Ernest Sinclair bought one hundred used high school textbooks and found a corrupt accountant who appraised them at $500 each, thus meeting the state's $50,000 law. When Sinclair went to prison, and for at least a year thereafter, this phony was listed in the official California directory of state-authorized schools.

California Pacifica at least had a two-room office with its name on the door. But some of the people with those four-inch-square mailbox campuses make it as hard as possible for a reporter, a law enforcement official, or a potential student to check them out.

First, they make it sound as if their tiny campus is a real one by using an address designed to deceive. If they rent mailbox forty-seven at their local UPS Store, they might refer to "Suite 47" or "Building 47" or even "47th floor" in their address.

They can also say anything they darn well please before the box number. When John Bear visited St. John's University, at "University Center" on "University Drive" in a tiny rural Louisiana town, he found them in a small building at the end of a one-lane road, across from a fence with a hand-painted sign reading "Bad Dog."

One of our favorite examples of chutzpah is a degree mill run from a mailbox address whose impressively designed literature and website invite potential students to visit the registrar's office, "located on campus in the Office of Institutional Advancement, at the top of the stairs to the right of the Chapel." Presumably one of those extra-large two-story mailboxes.

Another thing some institutions do to obfuscate the no-real-campus situation is to rent their mailbox in a place so remote that they hope that no student, reporter, or sheriff will ever make the effort to visit. A major Canadian start-up, for instance, although apparently run from Toronto, established its mailbox campus in Whitehorse, in the Yukon Territory, which is a mere four-day drive from Yellowknife.

Those accommodating Canadians offer another interesting option for using smoke and mirrors in the matter of a school's actual location. When the owner of the fake Kansas-based Monticello University attempted to escape the authorities who were after him in Kansas and South Dakota, he moved his university to Canada, where he provided what looked like a real street address. But it turns out that in Canada, if you have a post office box, you can use the street address of the *post office* as part of the address, so that "123 Maple Street, Suite 63" is actually box sixty-three in the post office located at 123 Maple.

3. Schools That Are Undeniably Legal—Legal, That Is, in Some Place You May Never Have Heard of

The islands that aren't quite countries

There are a number of islands on our planet—most of them in the South Pacific or the Caribbean—that aren't exactly countries, but they behave like one in some ways, and they seem quite happy to have universities set up on their land or their Internet domain. Consider, for instance, Niue, a tiny dot in the South Pacific most people have never heard of. This "self-governing parliamentary democracy" with a population of 1,400 has its own Internet abbreviation—.ni—and is the legal home to at least five less-than-wonderful universities: a ratio of one university for every three hundred inhabitants!

Norfolk Island, Puerto Rico, the British and the US Virgin Islands, Turks and Caicos, Barbuda, Sark, and the Isle of Jersey are also not-quite-countries that are or have been home to unaccredited universities.

The champion is Ascension Island in the South Atlantic, whose .ac Internet abbreviation is much in demand, since it is easily confused with the British .ac designation used by academic schools. Several dozen "universities" call this rock outcropping with a permanent population of, well, zero their home.

Indian reservations

The argument goes like this: If an Indian nation can run gambling casinos without any interference from the state in which it is located, and sell cigarettes without paying state sales tax, then why can't they accredit and run their own university without fretting about annoying little things like state approval, much less accreditation?

A California unaccredited university in trouble with the state gave it the old college try by claiming full accreditation from a small Nevada-based Indian tribe. The university did not operate from Nevada, but the tribal council produced an official "letter of accreditation." By the time the laughter in the academic world had died down, that institution had moved: first to Montana, and then to oblivion.

The special cases of Liberia, Malawi, and St. Kitts

There are currently at least three countries that have been granting their accreditation to various United States–based institutions that, in some cases, have little or no presence in those countries. This practice has proven troublesome to some gatekeepers and decision makers, who are uncertain how to deal with degrees from such schools.

These troubled decision makers include the publishers of the *International Handbook of Universities* (a UNESCO-related publication), college registrars, human resource professionals, and indeed the authors of this book. For years, such people have said that if the highest education authority in a sovereign nation approves a school, there must be *something* there. But recent developments have caused significant dilemmas in this regard.

Liberia

In 2003, a representative of the government of Liberia, widely regarded at the time as a corrupt, unstable, and nearly bankrupt country, wrote to a number of unaccredited and less-than-wonderful universities offering them the full accreditation of the Liberian Ministry of Education in exchange for a payment of $1,000, later raised to $10,000, and then $50,000 down and $20,000 a year. In short order, more than a dozen institutions, most of them run from the United States but claiming campuses in various other countries, were proudly showing off their certificate of accreditation, apparently signed by the Minister of Education of a country that is undeniably a full-fledged member of the United Nations.

This situation caused much consternation at the United Nations office in Geneva, which publishes the huge, expensive, and generally reliable reference book called the *International Handbook of Universities*.

UNESCO's mandate is to accept whatever the highest education officer of a member-nation says and does. They are not in the business of evaluating the accrediting or licensing procedures of individual countries and saying to some, "You don't meet certain standards, so you can't be in the book." *Everyone* goes in.

Presumably, no one at UNESCO anticipated that there would ever arise a situation in which a UN member would be openly selling its accreditation, willy nilly, to any school willing to write a check. Being responsible professional educators, how can they possibly put schools into the *International Handbook* that offer ten-day PhDs, sell honorary degrees of all kinds, and appoint anyone as a professor on payment of a fee?

They know what that will mean to the reputation of their book and its usefulness as a reference source in the worlds of education, business, and government. On the other hand, how can they be put in the position of having to say that one UN member is not being treated the same as other UN members?

This particular dilemma seems to have turned out well when it became known that the Liberian higher education system had been "hijacked" by the Americans who ran the fake St. Regis University, as described in some detail in chapter 7. The editor of the *International Handbook of Universities* thereupon wrote that neither St. Regis nor any of the other schools who purchased Liberian accreditation would be included in the next edition of that book.

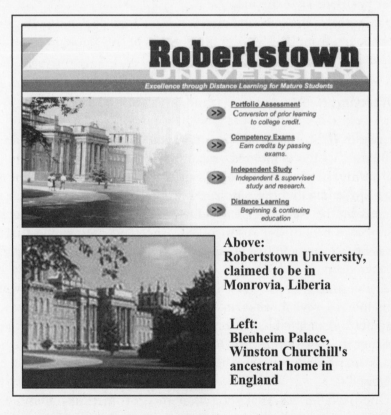

Above:
Robertstown University,
claimed to be in
Monrovia, Liberia

Left:
Blenheim Palace,
Winston Churchill's
ancestral home in
England

The fake Robertstown University claimed to be in Monrovia, Liberia. It bears a remarkable resemblance to Blenheim Palace, Winston Churchill's ancestral home in England.

Malawi

Malawi is a mostly agricultural nation of about 10 million people in southern Africa. Because the country has only two universities and one college, all government-run, there has been no need for a system of higher education accreditation. Then, inexplicably, Columbia Commonwealth University, an unaccredited institution then operating from a small office in Missoula, Montana—which also had a Wyoming license to operate, and a California-based chancellor— declared that it was fully accredited by the Republic of Malawi. Why a small, poor African nation accredits only one university in the world, and one that is not in Malawi but in Montana/Wyoming, has never been clearly explained.

Once again, the question arises: how are the decision makers and gatekeepers, from UNESCO to the authors of this book, to know how to deal with this situation?

St. Kitts and Nevis

The nation of St. Kitts and Nevis consists of two small islands in the Caribbean, with a combined area a bit larger than Washington, DC. Berne University, an American-owned school that at the time was run from a small office in rural New Hampshire, although not licensed by that state, began holding an optional four-week summer session at a beachfront resort on St. Kitts and proclaimed that the university was now fully accredited by the Ministry of Foreign Affairs and Education.[2]

At the time, and for years after, the ministry was either unwilling or unable to reveal what its rules, standards, or procedures for accreditation might be. On one occasion, when a reporter for the Portsmouth, New Hampshire, Record inquired, he was told, "We have just as many votes in the United Nations as you do. What's your problem?"

One problem was that soon after this, St. Kitts also granted full accreditation to something called Eastern Caribbean University, an institution that issued doctorates based entirely on study of a few

James Bond films and was run from the home of its owner, a teacher in Smithville, Texas.

A few years later, St. Kitts passed a law formalizing the accreditation process and describing a reasonable set of criteria for granting accreditation. As a result, Eastern Caribbean University and Berne University (which changed its name to Bernelli and opened offices in Virginia and West Virginia) are no longer accredited, but seven others, including five medical, veterinary, and nursing schools, are.

4. The Matter of Having Hundreds of Sets of Laws

Each state and each country has its own body of laws, and they often conflict with those of other states or countries. A man having four wives? OK in Saudi Arabia but illegal in Connecticut. Driving eighty miles an hour on the interstate? OK in Nevada but illegal in Minnesota. Owning an assault rifle? OK in the United States but illegal in Canada.

It is when people from one place end up in another place that problems may occur and lawyers start earning their fees. This is as true in the area of degrees as it is in bigamy, speeding, or gun ownership, a fact that clouds the issue of which schools can properly be called degree mills.

Consider a person who earns a degree from an unaccredited but entirely legitimate distance-learning school that is officially approved by the state of California. Many people in California and worldwide have and use that degree. The law degrees of this university enable graduates to sit for the state bar exams, and the psychology degrees may qualify students to take state licensing exams. So of course we would never consider calling such a degree mill.

And yet if an alumnus of this university takes up residence in Oregon, New Jersey, North Dakota, Nevada, or Illinois and uses that degree, then he or she technically becomes a criminal. Use of a California-approved but unaccredited degree (as well as most other unaccredited degrees) in those states is a criminal offense, punishable by a stiff fine and up to six months in prison. So while Oregon puts hundreds of such schools on its official state site, some of those illegal-in-Oregon schools would be legal elsewhere. We find it inappropriate to call such schools "degree mills"—but others do so.

There is, in effect, a continuum of strictness of school laws, from places like Liberia, Hawaii, and Mississippi, where just about anything goes, to places like Oregon, New York, and Canada, where things are very strict indeed.

5. *Who Makes the Decision as to Whether a School Is Good or Bad, Legal or Illegal, Degree Mill or Not?*

The question of whether any given school is a "good" school is one that has been debated for many years. We are not referring to the classic debates that rage in clubs, locker rooms, and the pages of *U.S. News* as to whether Harvard is better than Yale, Cal is better than Stanford, or Michigan is better than Michigan State. Those debates are mostly over reputation. No one challenges the legality, legitimacy, and value of such schools and their degrees.

When the issue at hand is whether to call a school a degree mill, things get more complicated. We provide our definition of "degree mill" in the introduction, but it has a lot of flexibility, a lot of "wiggle room" in it. And we discuss the methods that bad or fake schools use to fool or mislead the public later in this chapter.

Whenever anyone publishes a list *called* "Degree Mills," as the US government did in 1959 and many others have since, there are always people who disagree with those lists in *both* directions: believing that it includes schools that it shouldn't have or that it *doesn't* include schools that it should have. It is up to each reader to decide whether any given school meets his or her definition of *degree mill* or *innovative educational provider* or anything in between.

THE KINDS OF SCHOOLS THAT SOME PEOPLE CALL DEGREE MILLS

They run the gamut from modest "mom and pop" (or just "mom" or just "pop") operations run from the family home to huge international cartels.

The DipScam case histories presented in chapter 6 give a taste of the kinds of people and schools that were in operation at that time. The main changes since are that many of the entities have grown bigger (dozens of, even a hundred or more, employees) and are using advanced technology, aggressive marketing (on the Internet as well as the "old-fashioned" ways), and their sales are in the many millions of dollars each year.

The People Who Run the Schools

We're talking about a very small number of people here, in the general scheme of things. All the people who have run unrecognized schools of any kind in the past half century wouldn't even fill a single lecture hall on a university campus, so it is hard, perhaps impossible, to generalize.

Many people who run schools that we believe are bad or fake are "loners," working by themselves, or with some hired hands to stuff envelopes, enter data, or take messages.

Some are friendly, likeable, affable, even charming. Others are hostile, angry, and abrasive. Some are so secretive that literally nothing is known about them. Others are genial, even jolly. Ernest Sinclair lit up like a Christmas tree when *60 Minutes*'s Mike Wallace walked through his door at California Pacifica with the cameras rolling. Ronald Pellar (Columbia State University), while officially a federal fugitive, welcomed ABC's *20/20*, after the show found him living on his yacht in Mexico and gave quite a charming interview.

Some are career criminals who add selling fake degrees to a resume already filled with other scams and even violent crimes.

There is an interesting subset of academics gone bad: people with earned doctorates from properly accredited schools who end up running their own dubious or fake institutions. There are even a few cases where they played both sides of the street simultaneously.

When authorities finally discovered who was running the fake Pacific Northwestern University, it turned out to be an officer of a traditional university in Seattle. And it was the Rector of Villareal, a traditional Peruvian university, who set up a fake school with the same name to offer bogus PhDs to Americans.

And some are simply opportunists who seem to see selling degrees, or counterfeit diplomas, as just another way to earn a living by supplying something that people want and are willing to pay for.

Most mill operators practice what might be called a "hands-on" management style. They simply don't trust other people to run their business. There have been, however, more than a few family-run operations, involving either a husband and wife or extended family members.

There are many more men than women who start and run degree mills, but there have been a handful of women-run ones. Many of the operators are middle-aged, but there have been some quite young ones (the founder of the dreadful Ratchford University was in his twenties) and some well into their dotage. Ronald Pellar of Columbia State University was in his seventies when he was indicted for that fraud, and "Bishop" Lyon of Thomas Edison University (and others) was past eighty at the time of his last arrest.

In North America and Europe, most of the people who start degree mills are Caucasians, but at least three have been run by African-Americans and a few by Chinese-Americans. Most of the many degree mills in Africa, India, and Asia are run by people from the region in which they operate.

The Different Kinds of "Campuses"

There is a very wide range of kinds of "campuses." Some ambitious fakes have actually purchased buildings, sometimes former school buildings. Southwestern University had a very large building in Tucson, even if only two or three people worked there. At the time that LaSalle's founder was indicted, the "university" had four large and attractive buildings in a New Orleans suburb.

At the other end of the location scale, the Internet has made it possible for a degree mill literally not to exist in any physical space other than the mind of its owner. With a website and an electronic banking arrangement using credit cards, online payment services such as PayPal, or Western Union, there does not need to be an office or even a telephone. Many are somewhere in between: typically a few

rented rooms or even a small house. When John Bear visited Ray-
mond Chasse's multischool operation in New Orleans, he found a
tiny house, with one university in one bedroom, a second university
in the other bedroom, and four or five others on the dining table in
between.

It is also common for mills (as well as some legitimate schools) to
operate from so-called executive suite facilities, which can function
just as mail, phone, and Internet handlers or can rent little cubicles
by the month or conference rooms by the hour.

How They Get Their Customers

Selling degrees is a business with many things in common with traditional, legitimate businesses. You have a product to sell. You have
to figure out who your potential customers are. You need to make
them aware of your product. You need an infrastructure in place, so
they can reach you and place an order. You may need salespeople to
encourage them to buy. You need a fulfillment function, to get them
what they ordered, and possibly a follow-up "customer service" function to assure that they are happy with what they bought.

While the Internet is clearly the tool of choice, the tens of millions of people who are *not* online, or have limited use, are not being
neglected by the degree sellers. We'll look first at the "old-fashioned"
methods, then the electronic ones. Any given degree mill may use a
combination of approaches.

The "Old-Fashioned" Methods

Print advertising

The "old-fashioned" methods are still selling degrees. The surest sign
that advertising works is if it is regularly repeated. Although fewer
than in pre-Internet days, the number of ads for unaccredited
schools appearing in major consumer, military, and business publications is holding strong. The smallest classified ad in USA Today
costs about $300 a day. A one-third-page color ad in a major airline
magazine (which some of these guys have used) costs more than

$10,000. You can work out how much business they need to do to keep those ads running.

Of course, not every advertisement comes from the "bad guys." On many occasions, we've seen a Harvard ad and a degree mill ad side by side in *The Economist* and other well-regarded publications.

Direct mail

Before spam, there was "junk mail": unsolicited letters and brochures, sometimes sent to "Occupant" and sometimes meticulously personalized, as "Dear Mr. Ezell." Names can be acquired from list rental companies for about ten cents each, and they can be carefully selected by age, sex, income, religion, occupation, education, and so on. If you want names of men in their thirties with no bachelor's degree and living in middle-class neighborhoods, there are hundreds of thousands available. Even if most letters are thrown away unopened, the institution only needs to make one sale per thousand letters to show a profit.

One degree salesman told us his most productive mailing lists are people called "self-improvers"—people who have already bought weight-loss gimmicks, get-rich schemes, and find-inner-peace programs, and now they might like to have a degree or two. Mailing packets of advertising postcards, with one advertiser on each card, is another form of direct mail used by these people.

Telemarketing

"Inbound" telemarketing (they call you) is little used in the era of the national "don't call" list, but it has been effective in the past. One operator of unaccredited schools reported that a skilled salesperson working on commission and making "cold" (unsolicited) calls to people in carefully chosen neighborhoods can make two or three sales a day, more than enough to make the practice pay. "Outbound" telemarketing, where skilled telephone salespeople call those who have returned coupons or left messages on machines, is very popular and very successful. An "insider" at one large degree mill told us that one-third of people who are called back after leaving a message end up buying a degree. A telemarketer for Kennedy-Western (later Warren National) University testified before Congress that the callers in the "boiler room" he worked in were required to call 120 to 125 prospects a day, earning $15 if the prospect signed up and $100 more if they actually paid.

Bogus referral services and misleading reference books

Elsewhere we have described the seemingly impartial degree referral services that only refer clients to one fake school (their own) and the mostly reliable school guides that nonetheless include some less-than-wonderful schools.

Resales to old customers and alumni referrals

There's an advertising adage that "your best new customer is an old customer." Some mills routinely mine the names of their alumni, offering special deals on higher or different degrees. In the same vein, alumni are invited to tell their friends and associates about the degree opportunities available and are sometimes offered a referral fee or commission or even another degree for themselves for so doing.

Miscellaneous methods

Signs on buses, trains, and train stations; radio spots; flyers put under windshields at malls; billboards—they've all been tried, although not often. The one thing we haven't seen is a television "infomercial" for a degree mill, but somehow it seems inevitable.

The Internet and Electronic Methods

Unsolicited e-mail

Some of the biggest schools, real and fake, send "spam" in huge quantities, even millions a day. Anyone can hire a spam-sending service, many of which are in central Europe, Asia, or other less-regulated places. The cost can be as low as $100 per million messages sent. At that rate, even if there is only one customer for each five million spams, the business is profitable. The actual rate of success is probably a good deal higher: perhaps one customer for every ten thousand spams. The spams are not designed to sell but only to encourage the recipient either to go to a website or to make a telephone call to ask for more information, and then the skillful telemarketing comes into play.

Another creative use of e-mail is the "letter from home," sent either to or from "mom and dad" about how wonderful the given school is, a letter that someone sent "in error" to the spam recipients.

Banners and pop-ups

Anyone who uses the Internet is well aware of the "banners" that regularly appear at the margins of the page you really wanted to look at, and pop-ups—screens full of something other than what you wanted, which you have to close manually or choose to ignore. (Ignoring is difficult when they are flashing or otherwise annoyingly competing for your attention.) Real and fake schools are major users of these banners and pop-ups, paying to have them appear either randomly or on pages related to education and degrees. The companies that sell and place banners pay little or no attention to the content. One of the most inappropriate events imaginable happened when USA Today ran quite a good article on the menace of degree mills. And when one read that article online, there were two large degree-mill advertisements flashing away on the same page.[3]

Search engine advertising

Much the same thing as banners and pop-ups, the major Internet search engines routinely sell advertising that will appear on the same page as your search results. The more ethical ones, like Google, at least clearly identify the paid advertising as such. But even if you search for Harvard, Yale, or Oxford, you may well see bad or fake schools advertising on the same search screen.

Search engine placement

While advertising at least usually looks like advertising, many people seem not to realize that advertisers can pay the search engine companies to appear near the top of the list, just as publishers pay bookstores to put their books in more prominent locations. When we searched in Google for "MBA by distance learning," we found more than nine million sites. Obviously, no one is going to look at even 1 percent of those, so there is a great advantage to being in the top ten. As it happened, in our Google search, the top ten included six properly accredited schools and four others: two gray-area ones and two degree mills, all of them probably paying for that preferred location.

WHAT IS REQUIRED TO GET A DEGREE-MILL DEGREE?

The majority of degree mills require no work whatsoever, although they often talk about certain requirements, which can then be waived for a given student because of his or her excellent life experiences. Each of these customers may well believe that nearly everyone else is required to do work, but they are not.

A few mills have very minimal requirements, perhaps so the customers will feel they have done *something* to earn the degree. A common method is to require a book report. Some mills send customers a book in (or related to) their field, telling them to read it and write a ten-page book review, which no one ever reads.

Since many mills use the artifice of basing the degree on career experience, they will ask for a resume or for customers to fill out a form telling about their life. No matter what they say, whether fifty words or five thousand, they will be complimented on their excellent achievements and told they have qualified for the degree they wish. Some mills add a bit of apparent authenticity to this process by asking a question about the resume: "How many years did you work at [such-and-such a place]?" or "What were your duties?"

Testing

There are legitimate accredited universities where a bachelor's degree can be earned entirely by taking examinations. The University of London, for instance, requires thirty to forty, or more, hours of exams. Some mills say they have adopted this well-accepted procedure and give exams of their own. University of Illinois professor George Gollin, intrigued with this process, reported on the news forum at http://www.degreeinfo.com (August 19, 2003) that he had taken the online multiple-choice degree exams of several schools claiming Liberian accreditation. It turned out that a score of twenty-six out of one hundred on the absurdly easy test, which required about ten minutes, was enough to be offered the degree. He cheerfully pointed out that a pigeon, pecking randomly at such a test, would have achieved a similar score and "earned" the degree.

Pay

The only certain requirement to get a degree-mill diploma is that payment must be made, although there have been some schools, such as the Clayton Institute in California and another in the state of Washington, that would award the degree for free, but then you would have to pay to get the diploma and transcript.

From the sophisticated telemarketing script used by the University Degree Program in Romania (see chapter 7), it is clear that prices are highly negotiable. If the salesperson senses hesitation, the price is likely to come down. The Romanian degrees have had a $3,000 price, which is reduced in various ways, including an instant $500–$600 scholarship and ultimately the offer to allow four payments of $600 each, with the diploma and transcript sent after the first payment, knowing full well that no one will make the later payments.

NINETY-TWO DECEPTIVE TACTICS

Degree mills have come up with an extraordinary number of ways in which they attempt to fool the public, ranging from the absurdly simple (choosing a name that can be confused with that of a legiti-mate university) to the fiendishly complex (claiming accreditation from another country and then setting up a large and elaborate coun-terfeit website pretending to come from that country).

In attempting to decide if a given school is a degree mill, some of these tactics are of the "all or nothing" sort. When a school offers to backdate the diploma to the year of your choice, there is no gray area, no "in between" possibilities: that school is unequivocally a fake. But many of the tactics are on a continuum from "definitely fake" to "probably OK" and even include things used by legitimate and well-known schools, some of which are extremely aggressive in their advertising and marketing.

For instance, when a school claims its accreditation from an agency that is not recognized by the authorities in Washington, it could be a sincere and reasonable accreditor that has not yet been recognized, a nonexistent accreditor that is just another button on their telephone, or something in between.

No one entity will use all of these tactics, of course, but it is not uncommon for dozens, even scores, of red flags to be waving from the same flagpole.

The annotated list that follows is as complete as we could make it. Yet hardly a week passes in which some new tactic or a variation on an old one appears—a reminder to be thorough, to be careful, and if there is some possible evidence of chicanery, to delve deeper until the truth is known. At the end of this section, we offer a checklist of the ninety-two items in condensed form, which can be copied and used to help evaluate schools.

Accreditation Claims

1. *Accreditation is claimed from a fake or unrecognized agency.* In the United States, accreditation is useful only if the accrediting agency is recognized by the US Department of Education (http://www.ed.gov) and/or the Council for Higher Education Accreditation (http://www.chea.org). Unfortu-nately, many popular press articles on choosing schools men-tion the importance of accreditation but fail to point out that

there is such a thing as fake or worthless accreditation. That we have identified more than two hundred unrecognized accreditors suggests that this may be the most popular way in which degree mills pretend to be legitimate.

2. *The fake or unrecognized accreditor also accredits or recognizes legitimate schools.* A common tactic is for such accreditors to claim to accredit traditional universities such as Harvard and Stanford, so that their list of members might include many well-known schools, thus camouflaging the appearance of one or more degree mills on the list.

3. *The accreditor offers a confirming telephone service, website, or "hot line" to assure people that a given school is accredited.* Some people presumably are reassured if they can reach the accrediting agency by telephone and are told that yes, such-and-such a school is indeed accredited. Some fake accreditors take messages and return calls; others have an outgoing message that says, for instance, in the case of one large mill, "We are proud to accredit such fine schools as Notre Dame, Yale, and Columbia State University."

4. *The school claims that, as a global or international university, it doesn't require accreditation and/or government approval from any single government agency.* Every legitimate school has some form of recognized accreditation and/or government approval from the country, state, or region in which it operates.

5. *The school explains at length why accreditation is not important or is relevant only for student loans.* Some mills correctly state that they are not accredited, and then go on to explain, sometimes for two or three pages, why accreditation isn't all that important anyway, unless a student wishes to apply for a federal student loan.

6. *The school claims that Harvard and Oxford aren't accredited either.* Harvard is indeed properly accredited. Oxford was founded in the eleventh century under a Papal Bull, predating introduction of the royal charter. Nonetheless, each constituent college of Oxford has its own royal charter, the British equivalent of accreditation.

7. *Accreditation is correctly claimed but from a place where the word is used in quite different ways.* One example is Australia, where the word "accreditation" refers to a self-study process schools may go through, which has nothing to do with approval from an outside agency. When a school based in Australia, or one of its territories or protectorates, says, "We are accredited," it means only that they regard *themselves* as worthy. Outside recognition there comes from the Australian Qualifications Framework.

Another example comes from Great Britain, where one university, or department within a university, can accredit another university, even in another country. All this means that the university will accept the credits or degrees of the second school. But because the word accredited is used, there have been situations in which, for instance, a US institution claimed British accreditation after one department in one British university agreed to accept the American institution's credits.

8. *The school claims that accreditation is impossible because of the separation of church and state.* Some religious or church-owned "schools," especially those that also award nonreligious degrees, maintain that accreditation is impossible for them because religious schools can't qualify for accreditation. This is nonsense. Not only are there four properly recognized religious school accreditors, but also the regional accrediting agencies routinely deal with church-owned or operated institutions, ranging from Notre Dame to Southern Methodist to Yeshiva University.

9. *The school lists approval or accreditation from a fake or unrecognized country.* From time to time, people or groups establish what they claim is a new sovereign nation, whether for political, social, or nefarious purposes. When they do, one of the first things that often happens is the establishment of a university, either run by or recognized by said "country." Recent examples include:

- The Dominion of Melchizidek, located either in central Europe or an out-island of Fiji or both, established, according to an article in the *Economist*, primarily to sell bank charters that the magazine called "worthless" but also to operate its own "university," Dominion University, and to give its blessing to others, such as a "Russian" university run from California.
- New Utopia, home of the International University of Advanced Studies, ostensibly located on a seamount beneath the waters off Honduras but actually run from a dryer location in Texas.
- Seborga, a northern Italian area with about three hundred citizens, declared its independence in the 1960s and was ruled for half a century by a self-styled prince addressed as "Your Tremendousness." It has been home to at least seven universities: DiUlus, Miranda, Monroe, Trinity, King's, Marquis, and Riviera.
- Hutt River Principality, created in 1969 by some renegade wheat farmers on Australia's west coast, is home to at least five universities, Southern Pacific, Pebble Hills, Johnson Davids, Australasia International, and Hutt River University.
- Sealand, a World War Two installation in the North Sea off Britain, occupied and claimed by "squatters" decades ago, whence come postage stamps, passports, and the degrees of the University of Sealand.

Other not-exactly-real countries with universities include the Republic of Anodyne (Anodyne International University) and the Washitaw Nation (City University Los Angeles).

10. *Dubious accreditation is claimed from a real country or national agency.* In 2003, impressive-looking websites appeared, claiming that they were official sites put up by Liberian and Russian authorities. These sites confirmed and described the accreditation of various universities. It subsequently turned out that the sites of the Liberian National Board of Education, the Liberian Embassy, and the Russian Academy of Sciences were not the real sites but had been established by people associated with the various unrecognized schools.

11. *The school claims accreditation and the right to confer degrees due to wording in the school's articles of incorporation.* A common tactic is for a school to incorporate as a business in a place where one can say anything one wants in a corporate charter, which turns out to be almost anywhere. Thus the school bestows upon itself both accreditation and the "right" to award degrees. And then it advertises that it is "chartered" to grant degrees. Sometimes it adds the name of the country of incorporation for added credibility: "We are chartered by the Republic of Ireland as an accredited university with the power to grant degrees."

Other False or Misleading Claims

12. *The institution is certified by disreputable or incompetent credential checking services.* There are several dozen legitimate and reputable credential evaluation services where people can learn about the validity and equivalency of credits and degrees from both non-US and US schools. These services, described on page 179 (This section is on pp. 464-466, under the heading "Credential Evaluation Services"), are nongovernmental and unregulated, and there are some bad apples in the basket. Whether run by the fake schools, or just cooperating with them, they will confirm the legitimacy of the dreadful schools.

13. *The school misuses the concept of state licensing.* There are a few US states that will license or permit just about any school that applies, with no evaluation involved. The bad guys make statements of the form, "We have met all legal requirements set for private universities by the state."

14. *The institution points to inclusion on an impressive-looking compiled list of universities.* There is a gag item one finds in gift catalogs: a poster titled "The World's Ten Best Golfers." The well-printed list includes the names of nine famous golfers and, usually at number six, the name of the person buying this item or his designee. The bad or fake

schools will create such a list of the "best universities," either in print or on what looks like an impartial Internet site, always with an impressive title at the top, for instance: "The International Association for Quality Education," with their own name appearing, probably at number six, between Princeton and Stanford.

15. *The "school" lies or misstates its age.* Since longevity is felt to be reassuring to customers, some phonies just out-and-out lie. Created in 2010, they will fabricate a story of offering quality education since 1927. Others, more creatively, build on a shred of truth. One, in a southern California building that was on a Spanish land grant, said "Since 1843." Another that rented an old church for its graduation invited people to "come join us, where people have gathered since 1829."

16. *An institution writes about an earlier use of its building as if it were its own.* An Australian-owned "university" rented a building that had once been used by Oxford University. In what may well be the most creatively misleading such statement ever made, the university wrote: "It is here on [our] terraced lawns that some of this century's great innovators have conceived great thoughts. Mahatma Gandhi, Bertrand Russell, Albert Einstein, Madame Curie, Bernard Shaw, H. G. Wells, Gilbert Murray, and many others, have all walked the halls, and found a place of inspiration amongst [our] 13-acre woodland campus."

17. *The school confuses the city with the university.* Some well-known universities take the name of their city: Cambridge, Princeton, Chicago, and so forth. And so a school that rents a room or a building in that city may say, for instance, "Come to Oxford. Come to [our] college." When a US state attorney successfully sued this place, he had found students who genuinely believed they were enrolling in Oxford University.

18. *The school provides information about the legitimacy of awarding life/work experience credit then abuses that process.* Many unrecognized schools correctly explain that schools like Thomas Edison State College award credit and even degrees based entirely on experiential learning, and

"just like Edison, we follow that process." But while Edison might give three semester units for a given experience, the bad guys will offer an MBA or even a PhD.

19. *The institution claims that its critics (individuals, websites, and authors of books) are out to get it because they are run by fired employees or by people who secretly own fake schools and are afraid of the competition.* John Bear is regularly accused, in print and on Internet news groups, of being a disgruntled former employee of criticized schools or the secret owner of "dozens" of degree mills. The man who founded a website that exposes degree mills (http://www.degreeinfo.com) has been accused of being a wanted criminal. In an extreme manifestation of this phenomenon, the owner of a fake California school sent hundreds of telegrams to the media claiming that his fine university was called a degree mill in *Bears' Guide* because he had rejected the author's homosexual advances.[4]

20. *The school pretends to be bigger than it is.* The catalog or website has long lists of staff. The only real person involved calls himself "vice chancellor" or "vice president," as if there were a chancellor or president. Dozens of e-mail addresses or phone extensions are given using different names but all going to the same place. Some low-budget or noncreative mills have the same distinctive voice at each of many extensions: "The dean is busy with students"; "The registrar is on another line."

False or Misleading Memberships and Affiliations

21. *Membership in real organizations—but ones that don't screen members.* It is common for mills to list memberships in a long list of legitimate and relevant-sounding organizations, suggesting there is some approval process here, when in fact the organizations have open membership. Even some recognized accrediting agencies have a membership option open to all.

22. *The school implies legitimacy through United Nations–*

related organizations. There are many nongovernmental organizations (NGOs) that have a tenuous affiliation with the United Nations for educational, scientific, or humanitarian purposes. Some of these have open membership or do not screen members carefully, leading the mills to claim that they are "affiliated with" or even "approved by" the United Nations.

23. *The institution claims affiliations with real schools.* Degree mills love to be able to associate their names with those of legitimate schools. Sometimes they simply lie about being, for instance, a member of the (fictitious) Northeast University Alliance, along with Harvard, MIT, and Dartmouth. Sometimes they make a small donation to a legitimate school's scholarship or building fund, and, when they appear on a list of donors, they state that their institution "is featured prominently in the literature of Stanford University."

24. *The institution cites membership in nonexistent or bogus organizations.* Some degree mills put out long lists of organizations to which they claim to belong. While they always have impressive-sounding titles ("The International Alliance of Universities," "The World Society of Scholars"), in reality they rarely can be located.

25. *The school rents space from an organization, then implies an affiliation.* Many legitimate colleges rent out their buildings for special events. So a bad or fake school that rents space for a day may claim that its graduation ceremony has been held "in association with the University of London." One unrecognized accrediting agency once advertised an event "at the United Nations in New York," but it turned out they had simply rented a room at the unaffiliated United Nations Plaza Hotel.

26. *The school puts out a list of businesses and agencies that have accepted and paid for its degrees.* Some schools simply lie; it is not easy to confirm this information, even if a prospective student tried to. But others report the truth. When the fake LaSalle University in Louisiana published such a list, it turned out that many of the companies had

confused it with the real LaSalle in Pennsylvania, while others were misled by the fake accreditation claim and did pay for employees' degrees. Some mills have offered their graduates a small cash bonus if they can get their degree or transcript accepted by a traditional school.

Fake or Meaningless Documents

27. *Use of Apostilles and notarized statements of all kinds.* Apostilles are simply a form of federal notarization, and notaries validate only signatures, not the content of the document. Many mills claim that their Apostille shows that their school is approved by the government of the United States, which is simply untrue. Some go even further and charge their students as much as $700 for the Apostille statement, which costs less than 10 percent of that.

28. *Claims to have International Standards Organization 9001 or 9002 certification.* A small number of schools, accredited and otherwise, promote their certification under the rules of the International Standards Organization (ISO). Even if the original ISO distance education standard hadn't been written by an unaccredited California school, it holds no weight in the world of higher education.

29. *Misstatement of nonprofit status.* Because of the belief that the public has more trust in a nonprofit organization, and because the Internal Revenue Service has not always been as careful in policing matters as one might wish, some degree mills and at least one major unrecognized accrediting agency have falsely claimed to be nonprofit section 501(c)3 entities.

30. *Misusing the certificate of incorporation.* Some mills show a small picture of their certificate of incorporation, complete with gold seal and ribbons, as they state that they are "Officially chartered by the State of California, as shown by this document signed by the governor."

31. *Misusing other kinds of certificates.* Almost every city council, board of supervisors, chamber of commerce, and even congressional office will issue a handsome certificate of

honor or thanks, when asked, especially by a member, donor, or politically connected person. An entire wall of the little office of a dubious university in Los Angeles was covered with such documents. They were also shown in the literature as evidence of quality and acceptance.

32. *Misusing a "certificate of good standing" (CGS).* A part of many "graduation packages" from bad schools is an actual "CGS," which affirms only that a corporation or business may be in "good standing" in terms of a corporate charter or business license—but has nothing to do with the quality or legality or usefulness of the degrees awarded.

Misleading Recommendations and Links

33. *Better Business Bureau membership.* Some completely phony schools have joined the Better Business Bureau and benefited from promoting that affiliation. Many other unaccredited and less-than-wonderful schools have also been accepted as members.

34. *BBB imitations.* Schools that either cannot or choose not to join the BBB have created their own sound-alike entities, such as the American Business Bureau, which, in turn, gives them a glowing testimonial.

35. *Business organizations.* It is not uncommon for degree mills to join otherwise respectable business organizations that often have few membership requirements other than holding a business license or a corporate charter. Thus, some mills trade on the good reputations of chambers of commerce, Rotary, Kiwanis, Civitan, and other such groups by mentioning their membership in their literature.

36. *Inclusion in "official" directories that list everyone.* Being included in the directory of the government's National Center for Educational Statistics sounds impressive, until one realizes that at one time this directory listed everything that called itself a college or university, regardless of legality. It was as much of an achievement as being listed in the telephone directory.

37. *Inclusion in the official Norwegian Higher Institution Registry.* In a classic example of how a well-intentioned plan can go wrong, the Norwegian Ministry of Education, in turn affiliated with the United Nations, posted an online directory of distance-learning schools worldwide. Those trusting Norwegians permitted any school not included to add itself to this Higher Education Institution Registry. Predictably, more than a few degree mills did this and promptly advertised their inclusion and, by association, their UN affiliation. Thankfully they don't do that anymore, but some fake schools still display screenshots of their "official" listing.

38. *Fake referral services.* Over the years, some degree-mill operators have discovered the scam of setting up an allegedly independent school referral service. But when well-meaning clients fill out the necessary forms, they are told that the only school on earth that precisely meets their needs is the degree mill run by the same people. First to use this method was Tony Geruntino, whose Vocational Guidance company in Columbus, Ohio, referred all clients to his fake Southwestern University in Arizona and several other schools where he had an interest. Others have included an allegedly impartial referral service in Kentucky linked only to a dubious school in Hawaii, and another such service in Chicago linked only to a dubious school in Wyoming.

An added problem is that some publications that have set up good defenses against accepting advertisements for bad *schools* have accepted ads for these spurious *services*, not realizing their true purpose.

39. *Bogus or self-interest reference books.* It seems most ambitious to publish an entire comprehensive-appearing school guide solely to promote one school, but this has happened at least four times. The owners of the degree mills called American International University, Columbia State University, and the University de la Romande each produced and sold or gave away their own guides to distance learning, 99

percent copied from John Bear's books, with 1 percent devoted to what they called "the best school in the United States," which was, of course, their own. A currently sold book comes from a man associated with two now-operating dreadful schools.

A variation on this theme is to produce a single page featuring one's own "school" and make it look as if it had been copied from a book. A variation on the variation is to take an unfavorable listing from a legitimate book and rewrite it to make it positive. This was done, for instance, by a widely promoted unaccredited university in southern California, which rewrote its listing in *Bears' Guide*, printed it to look like the real pages in that book, and distributed it to prospective students, stating that it had been copied from *Bears' Guide*.

40. *Offering legitimate certifications along with fake degrees.* There are companies such as Microsoft that license other schools or companies to offer training courses, available from third-party vendors leading to certification, for instance, as a Microsoft system engineer. Some bad schools have gained permission to run these certification courses and feature those in their advertising, to give legitimacy, by association, with their useless degrees.

41. *Testimonials.* Testimonials from happy customers are a tried-and-true marketing tool. Degree mills make frequent use of testimonials in four ways:

- from co-conspirators—comments from colleagues, partners, or people who knew they were buying a fake degree.
- from fooled people—customers who may not yet have realized that their degree is fake and may possibly even have benefited (albeit temporarily) from it. One mill offered huge cash prizes for the "best" testimonials submitted, undoubtedly inspiring buyers of the fake degrees to write fake stories. Fittingly, the offer of prizes *also* turned out to be fake.
- from nonexistent people—glowing endorsements from names plucked from thin air, accompanied by smiling faces cut from clip art collections.

- from real people, but they didn't really say that—statements from well-known people who might never know what they were supposed to have said (one phony concentrated on Nobel laureates) or even from recently deceased celebrities.

42. *Posting positive comments on Internet newsgroups.* The operator of a mill, a colleague, or a graduate joins an Internet news-group or forum, sometimes lying low or making innocuous comments, but as soon as someone says he or she is looking for a certain kind of school, the so-called "shill" or "troll" awakens with a glowing recommendation of his degree mill.

Degree-mill operator Les Snell was a master of the "multiple personality" approach. Under one name, he would ask, "Hey, has anyone ever heard of Monticello University?" (One of his mills.) Under a second name, he would reply, "Yes, they're terrific," and in a third voice he would add, "I got my degree there, and my employer paid for it all," and so on.

Some forums are carefully moderated, so this kind of behavior is difficult or impossible. Some, such as http://www.degreeinfo.com and http://www.degreediscussion.com, are moderated *after* items are posted, so objectionable messages can be removed. A few have no moderation at all, and needless to say, the degree-mill operators thrive there, badly confusing and misleading the well-meaning people who stumble onto such sites. The huge educational publisher Peterson's once operated such an unmoderated site, and when the degree-mill people began to dominate it, the publisher took it down rather than try to sort the bad from the good.

The People Involved in These Schools

43. *The faculty.* All legitimate schools and many fake ones provide a list of their faculty members, often with credentials—their degrees and the sources of them—and some biographical information. If no faculty information is provided, or if most or all of the faculty members have their degrees from the school in question, that is probably all one needs to know.

Five kinds of faculty can be found in degree-mill literature.

- Co-conspirators: people who are either owners or otherwise share in the revenues. Some may well have legitimate credentials of their own. An ivy league degree is no more a guarantee of honesty in education than in business or politics.
- Real but naive: A common degree-mill tactic is to run help wanted ads, offering lower-level faculty at legitimate schools the opportunity to earn a good side income as adjunct faculty. In reality, they rarely, if ever, are given students, but they have given permission for their names to appear on the faculty list.
- Ones who don't know they are on the faculty: Another degree-mill tactic is to run enticing help wanted ads, receive many applications, never respond, but add the responders to their faculty list, hoping they won't find out or won't pursue legal action if they do. Since the ads are often "blind" (no school is mentioned), these people may only learn they are listed as faculty months or years later, if at all.
- Hijacked faculty list: simply copied from the catalog of a legitimate school.
- Made-up names: Since most of their other "facts" are fiction, why not the faculty list. Some mills choose common names ("Douglas Ford," "Robert Wilson") to frustrate Internet searches for such people.

44. *Administrators.* The chancellors, deans, provosts, vice presidents, trustees, and such, are typically found in the same five categories as just listed for faculty. A few quirky mill owners seem to enjoy throwing down the gauntlet by selecting obscure but once-prominent names. For instance, the fake Calgary Institute of Technology was ostensibly run by a man identified as a Canadian hero of World War One, while Columbia State University identified its president as Austen Henry Layard, who was in fact a prominent nineteenth-century anthropologist. And when the state of Missouri established its own fake school, as part of a sting operation to entrap a dubious accrediting agency, their spurious

Eastern Missouri Business College listed a faculty of Moe Howard, Curley Howard, and Larry Fine, better known as The Three Stooges.

Advertising and Marketing

45. *Paid search engine placements, often appearing along with legitimate schools.* When one does an Internet search for a degree program ("MBA" or "PhD in psychology," for instance), the result will be hundreds or thousands of "hits." No major search engine makes any effort to weed out the bad and fake schools, so you will get them all, mixed together. Adding "accredited" to the search is useless, since most of the fakes claim to be accredited.

Compounding the problem is that the search engines (Google, Yahoo, Bing, etc.) sell top-of-the-page advertising to anyone willing to pay. While such ads are often, if subtly, identified as such, it is also the case that the search engines sell placement, so that any school, real or fake, willing to pay will show up in the top ten or twenty-five listings. Even if you search for a very specific program, such as "MS in engineering, CalTech," the search engine, seeing what you *think* you want, may entice you with ads or banners for bad or fake schools that offer the same degree, but cheaper, faster, and easier.

46. *Banners, pop-up ads, and spam.* Once a person has been electronically identified as a possible degree seeker, whenever she is "surfing," she will see banners and pop-up ads from good schools and bad, and of course her e-mail box will be getting offers to "become the envy of your friends" by acquiring a degree.

47. *Advertisements in prestigious magazines (and use of "as advertised" labels elsewhere).* As we lament in chapter 19, more than a few prestigious magazines gladly accept advertising dollars from fake schools as well as real. While some bad guys advertise in almost every issue of *The Economist*, for instance, others may just run a small ad once and then be

able to say and show, in all future promotional materials, "As advertised in *The Economist*."

48. *Stating that the university is not a diploma mill because "diploma mills are illegal."* It is the mark of many scam artists to warn their intended victims, while setting themselves apart. "Some used-car dealers turn back the odometer and put axle grease in the transmission, but here at Honest Eddie's. . . ." Some degree mills go out of their way to warn people not to deal with degree mills but only with fine schools like theirs. One currently advertising referral service, which refers clients only to a degree mill, says "Watch out for diploma mills. . . . We help you obtain a degree from an accredited school with a full campus. No classes required."

49. *Persuasive and aggressive telemarketing skills.* Read a portion of the actual degree-mill telemarketing script in chapter 7 and marvel, with us, at the skill these people have in using the telephone as a sales tool.

50. *Offering a long menu of opportunities—the package deal.* Some mills offer not only a choice of two or more schools and up to five accrediting agencies but also a credential-evaluating service, transcript service, verifying services in case an employer tries to check, guaranteed letters of recommendation, and, if you want some evidence of your achievement, a term paper or thesis writing service. The fake Sussex College of Technology even used to offer its diplomas in three designs, two sizes, and a choice of English or Latin wording.

51. *The "loophole."* Many scams suggest that the purveyor has found some long-lost or secret or clever way to cure the disease, remove stains, buy gold at bargain prices, and make the engine last a million miles. Similarly, some mills hint or simply say that they have found a legal loophole that can be exploited to earn a medical, law, or other degree.

52. *Photographs with prominent people.* Many politicians and celebrities are willing to have their photographs taken with people they don't know or don't know enough about. One large unaccredited California school invited a well-known congressman to speak to a luncheon meeting of European

businessmen, each of whom was photographed shaking his hand. The congressman did not know that the Europeans had paid $5,000 for a weekend in California, during which they would visit Disneyland, be "awarded" their degree, and have their picture taken with a genuine US congressman.

A man associated with Southwestern University in Arizona was photographed presenting a certificate to the mayor of Tucson, and that picture was subsequently used to promote the fake university. And the proprietor of an online university promoted in Asia used photographs of himself standing next to what was clearly a cardboard cutout of the US president.

Misleading or Fake Internet Presence

53. *Flaunting the ".edu" extension.* The company called Educause has fallen asleep at the wheel (and down on the job). Not only are the dozens of bad and fake schools permitted to keep their ".edu" that they managed to get before Educause took over the process in 2002, but also new and dreadful unaccredited schools are still being granted the ".edu" extension. We have thus far identified seventy-one schools using the ".edu" suffix that would not qualify to have it if the rules were followed. So of course those that have it flaunt it, and unless retroactive standards are initiated, the ".edu" will never be a guarantee of quality or legitimacy.

54. *Fake .edu and fake .ac addresses.* Because the public has some awareness that ".edu" is supposed to be an indicator of legitimacy, some of the newer phonies are coming up with misleading but legal alternatives, such http://www.School-Name-edu.com. Another variant is registering in a country that does not regulate the ".edu" and ending up, for instance, with http://www.SchoolName.edu.li. A third variant is sticking an "edu" after the school name, as "http://www.SchoolNameedu.com." And a fourth variant is for a defunct school that already has an ".edu" designation to sell it on the

open market. Even though this is prohibited, it happens, with asking prices as high as $40,000.

The other suffix that is associated with recognized schools is ".ac," which, in Great Britain, means "academic" and is restricted to legitimate schools. However, ".ac" is also the Internet suffix for the Ascension Islands, which aggressively advertises the "highly sought after" ".ac" domain name. As a result, this tiny outcropping in the South Atlantic ocean has an indigenous population of zero but dozens of universities.

55. *Spoofed websites.* "Spoofing" is computerspeak for creating a website that looks like something legitimate but is in fact an imitation or counterfeit. Degree mills have created spoofed sites that look like the sites of countries, agencies, or accreditors, which, in turn, say positive things about them. Links to the spoofed sites are provided on the school's site.

56. *Names similar or identical to real schools.* Degree mills routinely select names that are either identical to those of real schools (there have been fakes named LaSalle, Stanford, Harvard, and the University of Wyoming), slight variations (Stamford, Cormell, and Berkley, for instance), and slight variations in wording (e.g., the fake "Texas University" instead of the real "University of Texas").

57. *Setting up fake discussion forums and chat rooms.* They look like legitimate sites, with impartial-seeming names, but they exist to lure well-meaning potential customers who get dangerous advice from school operators and apologists.

58. *Selected legitimate links to convey respectability.* Many links are offered, typically to ".gov" sites, where there are lengthy explanations and articles on experiential learning processes, accreditation, and so forth. The degree-mill site surrounds the real links with misinterpretation and misrepresentation, just in case anyone actually does read them.

The Trappings of Real Schools

59. *School paraphernalia.* Traditional items with the school logo, including T-shirts, coffee and beer mugs, and, typically, school rings "made by Jostens, the same company that makes school rings for many prestigious universities." Some of the schools have their diplomas printed by the same companies that do the work for major universities and make them available with the same leather or leatherette holders (at additional cost, of course).

60. *Scholarships offered.* Even at a legitimate school, awarding a scholarship rarely means that money is given to the student, only that tuition is reduced. The telemarketers for degree mills almost always have the option of offering "scholarships" to hesitant customers, sometimes being authorized to settle for an amount that is 20 percent of the original price. The mill still makes a handsome profit.

61. *Fake course lists.* Degree mills typically offer their degrees in dozens, even hundreds, of fields of study. To back this up, they sometimes show long lists of courses, these lists typically copied verbatim from the catalogs of legitimate schools.

62. *Map to a nonexistent campus.* Legitimate schools often provide a map showing how to find their campus. Carrying deception in a new direction, some mills, such as Concordia College and University, actually provide a fictitious map to their nonexistent campus.

63. *Claim to offer a student loan program.* Many mills feature what they call a student loan program. In reality, this simply means that they offer the opportunity to pay on the installment plan. Some, such as LaSalle, have required students using their loan program to send in a bundle of twenty-four to sixty checks made out to the school and dated at one-month intervals. The checks are cashed one per month. Because the checks in schemes like this are typically written on federally chartered banks, the schools may call this process a "federal loan program."

64. *Detailed accounts of campus life.* To support the fiction that there really is a campus, some degree mills provide glowing descriptions of campus activities, fraternities and sororities, community involvement programs, the chapel services, the university theater, and the sports programs.

65. *A nonexistent "on-campus" option.* Again, to support the fiction that there is really a campus, some mills offer the option of earning the degree through residential on-campus study, knowing full well that no one will (or could) take them up on this opportunity.

66. *Nonexistent alumni association and alumni gatherings.* The prospect of joining an alumni organization and participating in its events is held out as a further indicator of the legitimacy of the school.

67. *Picture of the diploma and transcript.* While a few legitimate schools show a picture of the diploma in their literature, this is rare. On the other hand, the majority of bad or fake schools do so, often accompanied by a picture of the transcript, to show the potential customer what a fine product they are acquiring.

68. *Support for charities.* A few of the currently operating bad guys hope to attract students by claiming that a portion of tuition received goes to charitable causes.

69. *Unnecessary follow-up questions.* Some mills ask applicants some gratuitous questions, such as providing the phone number of an employer or the address of a school, simply to show that the application is really being evaluated (which, of course, it isn't).

70. *"Branch campuses" worldwide, which are really alumni homes.* Some schools offer international graduates the opportunity to establish a "branch campus" in their home country, at best by putting a small sign on the door of their home or office.

Links with Well-Known People

71. *Claims of famous alumni.* There are three ways in which degree mills associate themselves with well-known people or ostensibly well-known people:

- Real people who don't know they've been given a degree. The mills actually send a diploma to prominent people, and unless they get a letter of rejection (which rarely happens), they go ahead and state that that person is a graduate of their "school." In this way, a non-wonderful school in Los Angeles claims Ethel Kennedy, Coretta Scott King, and Muhammad Ali as alumni, while others have listed Jonas Salk and various Nobel laureates.

During the 2008 presidential campaign, one fake school, the University of Berkley, offered a degree to candidate Rudolph Giuliani, who responded to them, writing, "I am delighted for the honor bestowed upon me by your institution." We tried, without success, to alert Mayor Giuliani to this problem, and in 2011, this fake school's website still leads off with a picture of Mr. Giuliani's diploma.

- False claims. Knowing that it can be very difficult for a skeptic to get in touch with some famous people, the mills simply list some celebrities as graduates, hoping they won't be caught lying, and knowing that if they are, there will almost certainly be nothing more than a demand to remove Prince Charles, Bill Cosby, or whomever from the list.
- Fake people with impressive titles. Since it is the titles not the names that are designed to impress, sometimes names are not even used: "A senior vice president of General Motors." "Two Saudi Arabian princes." "An Olympic gold medal winner." And so on. Hard to check and unlikely to be protested.

72. *Inviting (and paying) a prominent person to speak at a gathering or graduation, then misstating the connection.* After paying a speaker, they say things like, "Yale University sent a delegate to address our convocation." An unaccredited

California institution once hired a former British prime minister to speak at its graduation and dined off that for years.

73. *Big names as chancellors.* It is common in British universities to have a well-known person in the largely honorary role of chancellor. Some unrecognized institutions in Britain and in the United States have discovered there is apparently no shortage of naive, impoverished, or senile (or possibly all three) titled people willing to accept this job. That is why various lords, ladies, barons, duchesses, and so forth, have been listed as the chancellor of some less-than-wonderful institutions.

Misleading Acceptance of Degree Claims

74. *Lists of businesses and organizations who have "accepted" the school for tuition reimbursement.* Some did in error; some never did. In some large companies, degree acceptance is a local option, so that a branch manager might accept and pay for a degree that the home office would never recognize.

75. *Misusing the Sosdian and Sharp study.* In 1978, the National Institute of Education published a study that demonstrated the obvious fact that regionally accredited undergraduate degrees had a high level of acceptance in the business world and that graduates were happy with these degrees. Dozens of schools have misinterpreted the findings of Carol P. Sosdian and Laure M. Sharp, claiming that their *unaccredited* degrees through the doctoral level have this level of acceptance.

76. *Claims of reciprocal, automatic recognition due to being a dependent territory of the motherland.* Degree mills and other unrecognized schools have claimed that because they are located or have an address in a dependent territory, they are "automatically" recognized by the home country. The claim has been made, for instance, that institutions associated with Turks and Caicos, Barbados, and Barbuda have recognition in the United Kingdom; that Norfolk Island licensing is concomitant with Australian licensing; and similarly that the US Virgin Islands is just the same as the United States. For schools in British dependencies, the claim is sometimes

made that their incorporation grants "derivative full European Union acceptance of the degrees."

Misleading or Fake Physical Evidence

77. *Fake pictures of the school's building(s).* In these times of easy-to-copy Internet images, it is commonplace for degree mills to "borrow" photographs of real universities and other impressive buildings and claim them as their own. A university that claimed to be Liberian, whose "campus" was a mailbox service, depicted Winston Churchill's stately home in England as its campus. Columbia State University, run from a California warehouse, depicted Lyndhurst, a historic mansion in Tarrytown, New York, as its main building.

COLUMBIA STATE UNIVERSITY
INFORMATION CATALOG
3500 North Causeway Blvd.
Suite #160
Metairie, Louisiana 70002
(504) 455-1409

The catalog of America's biggest degree mill, Columbus State University. Right inset: the mansion in Tarrytown, NY, that bears a striking resemblance to the university. Left inset: the actual "campus" of the university.

78. *Doctored photos of real buildings.* By making use of computer photo-editing techniques, it is possible to change the look of an impressive building to make it appear as one's own. A California-approved university once showed a photograph of a large office building with the university's sign at the top. When a colleague visited that building and found no such sign, the school, which actually did rent a small office in that building, claimed the sign had not yet been installed, and the doctored photo in their catalog was "anticipating it."

79. *Prestigious-sounding address.* The postal service essentially looks at the last two lines of an address and doesn't worry about what comes before it. A school in rural Louisiana informally named their driveway "University Circle" and made that part of their address. A mill whose mailbox was in the North Point district of San Diego referred to their "North Point Campus."

80. *A private mailbox (PMB) presented as "suite" or "floor" or "building number."* Businesses renting private mailboxes are required to use "PMB" as part of their address, but some say things like "Suite 210" instead of "PMB 210."

81. *Facilities rented once, or rarely, portrayed as the campus.* A currently operating Swiss school rents a city-owned castle for some meetings and shows it in the school's literature as if it were the campus. One dubious school, run from the suburban basement of its owner, rented a cathedral in Washington for a graduation ceremony and showed only that picture in their catalog. In an almost charming case, a degree mill called the College of Applied Science in London was asked to stage a graduation ceremony for a wealthy industrialist who had bought his PhD. The degree mill rented a fancy girls' school for a day, rented costumes portraying dukes and duchesses for their friends, and staged an impressive ceremony.

82. *Depicting a large building in which the school either rents one room or uses a mailbox or an "executive suites" service, as if it all belonged to the school.* Sometimes the school name is pasted onto the photograph to make it seem as if it really is its building.

83. *Illegal activity associated with a legal school.* There have been instances when dishonest employees or executives at a legitimate university had a degree-mill sideline associated with their school. For instance:

- A dozen faculty and administrators of the regionally accredited Touro College in New York were arrested for selling grades, transcripts, and diplomas to students.
- A medical school in the Caribbean was sending four-year-trained MDs out the front door at the same time as it was selling MDs to unqualified people for $28,000 out the back door.
- A traditional South American university signed up more than one thousand Americans for a $10,000 nonresident doctoral program, but it turned out to be run by an executive of the university without the knowledge or permission of the school.
- A fake doctor in California turned out to have bribed a computer room employee at a major university to alter all the records to make it appear as if he had earned the degree. The university believed there were no other such cases but could not be certain.

Misleading Policies

84. *Claiming exclusivity: stating that only 5 percent of applicants are accepted.* With degree mills, the actual number is generally 100 percent.
85. *Not specifying which classes are required or how many units are required to graduate or saying that "rare exceptions can be made."* The mill might list dozens of "required" courses but then tell every applicant that because of his or her extraordinary experience, the course work has been waived.
86. *Backdating diplomas.* No legitimate school backdates diplomas. Degree mills regularly do the date of the client's choice, sometimes using the argument that the diploma can be dated as of the time the knowledge was actually gained.

87. *Selling graduate honors and the GPA of choice.* Some degree mills charge extra if the client wishes to graduate "with honors" or "summa cum laude." One mill, Westmore, will increase a customer's "standard" 3.2 grade point average for $10 per point. The "summa" or "magna" designation is also sold for masters' and doctoral degrees, a practice rarely if ever done in the real world. Amusingly, while mills offer to make the fake transcript up showing any grade point average the customer wants, they often recommend against a perfect 4.0 as being too suspicious, suggesting instead a more modest 3.79. Some even charge more for higher grades on the fake transcript!

88. *Assuring the customer that "we'll always be here for you."* Mills typically offer a "degree verification service," suggesting they will always be available to answer employers' inquiries and confirm the "earning" of the degree. In reality, the way many innocent victims learn they've been had is when they attempt to make contact with their alma mater a year or two later and find it is no longer there.

Sometimes the "verification service" takes the form of a secure website listing the names of graduates, so that employers can go there directly to confirm the degrees.

89. *Using names of real universities no longer in existence.* An average of a dozen or so properly accredited colleges and universities go out of business each year. Mill operators sometimes "harvest" those names—Eisenhower University, Nasson College, Beacon College—for their own purposes and even claim or imply that they are a legitimate successor to the original school. One Louisiana operator of many schools listed a legitimate defunct school in the telephone book, then fielded calls and fabricated transcripts for alumni, who didn't realize they were dealing with an interloper.

90. *More than one degree at a time.* Some mills offer package deals: a bachelor's, master's, and PhD at the same time for a single payment, backdating them to different years so that it does not appear all three degrees were "earned" on the same day.

91. *Multilevel marketing combined with a degree mill.* The "deal" is that one buys a bachelor's degree. Then, when one signs up another person for a bachelor's, he gets a "free" master's, and so on. Georgia Christian University offered a multilevel faculty scheme: with your degree came appointment as assistant professor. When you signed up three people to buy degrees, you became an associate professor. When your "down line" people signed up others, everyone rose in rank: full professor, dean, and so on up the academic ladder.

92. *"Order by midnight tonight."* Big discount if you sign up quickly. The telemarketer offers a special discount for people who buy their degrees immediately, "before this special offer expires." More than a few legitimate schools also use this kind of marketing. Some fake schools offer to send a courier to the door to pick up the tuition check—quite possibly the same courier who will deliver the diploma a week or so later. To date, no "university" has offered miracle-blade Ginsu® steak knives with every diploma, but we will not be surprised when it happens.

On the following pages, we summarize these ninety-two red flags into a single checklist, which can be copied and used as a means to help evaluate any given institution.

CHECKLIST: 92 THINGS BAD AND FAKE SCHOOLS DO TO MISLEAD PEOPLE

Accreditation Claims

☐ 1. Accreditation is claimed from a fake or unrecognized agency.

☐ 2. The fake or unrecognized accreditor also accredits legitimate schools.

☐ 3. The accreditor offers a confirming telephone service or "hot line" to assure people that a given school is accredited.

☐ 4. The school claims that, as a global or international university, it doesn't require accreditation and/or government approval from any single government agency.

☐ 5. The school explains at length why accreditation is not important or is relevant only for student loans.

☐ 6. The school claims that Harvard and Oxford aren't accredited either.

☐ 7. Accreditation is correctly claimed but from a place where the word is used in quite different ways.

☐ 8. The school claims that accreditation is impossible because of the separation of church and state.

☐ 9. The school lists approval or accreditation from a fake or unrecognized country.

☐ 10. Dubious accreditation is claimed from a real country or national agency.

☐ 11. The school claims accreditation and the right to confer degrees due to wording in the school's articles of incorporation.

Other False or Misleading Claims

☐ 12. The institution is certified by disreputable or incompetent credential checking services.

☐ 13. The school misuses the concept of state licensing.

☐ 14. The institution points to inclusion on an impressive-looking compiled list of universities.

☐ 15. The "school" lies or misstates its age.

☐ 16. An institution writes about an earlier use of its building as if it were its own.

☐ 17. The school confuses the city with the university.

☐ 18. The school provides information about the legitimacy of awarding life/work experience credit then abuses that process.

☐ 19. The institution claims that its critics (individuals, websites, and authors of books) are out to get it because they are run by fired employees or by people who secretly own fake schools and are afraid of the competition.

☐ 20. The school pretends to be bigger than it is.

False or Misleading Memberships and Affiliations

☐ 21. Membership in real organizations—but ones that don't screen members.
☐ 22. The school implies legitimacy through United Nations–related organizations.
☐ 23. The institution claims affiliations with real schools.
☐ 24. The institution cites membership in nonexistent or bogus organizations.
☐ 25. The school rents space from an organization, then implies an affiliation.
☐ 26. The school puts out a list of businesses and agencies that have accepted and paid for its degrees.

Fake or Meaningless Documents

☐ 27. Use of Apostilles and notarized statements of all kinds.
☐ 28. Claims to have International Standards Organization 9001 or 9002 certification.
☐ 29. Misstatement of nonprofit status.
☐ 30. Misusing the certificate of incorporation.
☐ 31. Misusing other kinds of certificates.
☐ 32. Misusing a "certificate of good standing" (CGS).

Misleading Recommendations and Links

☐ 33. Better Business Bureau membership.
☐ 34. BBB imitations.
☐ 35. Business organizations.
☐ 36. Inclusion in "official" directories that list everyone.
☐ 37. Inclusion in the official Norwegian Higher Institution Registry.
☐ 38. Fake referral services.
☐ 39. Bogus or self-interest reference books.
☐ 40. Offering legitimate certifications along with fake degrees.
☐ 41. Testimonials.
☐ 42. Posting positive comments on Internet newsgroups.

The People Involved in These Schools

☐ 43. The faculty.
☐ 44. Administrators.

Advertising and Marketing

☐ 45. Paid search engine placements, often appearing along with legitimate schools.
☐ 46. Banners, pop-up ads, and spam.
☐ 47. Advertisements in prestigious magazines (and use of "as advertised" labels elsewhere).
☐ 48. Stating that the university is not a diploma mill because "diploma mills are illegal."
☐ 49. Persuasive and aggressive telemarketing skills.
☐ 50. Offering a long menu of opportunities—the package deal.
☐ 51. The "loophole."
☐ 52. Photographs with prominent people.

Misleading or Fake Internet Presence

☐ 53. Flaunting the ".edu" extension.
☐ 54. Fake .edu and fake .ac addresses.
☐ 55. Spoofed Web sites.
☐ 56. Similar or identical names to real schools.
☐ 57. Setting up fake discussion forums and chat rooms.
☐ 58. Selected legitimate links to convey respectability.

The Trappings of Real Schools

☐ 59. School paraphernalia.
☐ 60. Scholarships offered.
☐ 61. Fake course lists.
☐ 62. Map to a nonexistent campus.
☐ 63. Claim to offer a student loan program.
☐ 64. Detailed accounts of campus life.
☐ 65. A nonexistent "on-campus" option.
☐ 66. Nonexistent alumni association and alumni gatherings.
☐ 67. Picture of the diploma and transcript.
☐ 68. Support for charities.
☐ 69. Unnecessary follow-up questions.
☐ 70. "Branch campuses" worldwide, which are really alumni homes.

Links with Well-Known People

- [ ] 71. Claims of famous alumni.
- [ ] 72. Inviting (and paying) a prominent person to speak at a gathering or graduation, then misstating the connection.
- [ ] 73. Big names as chancellors.

Misleading Acceptance of Degree Claims

- [ ] 74. Lists of businesses and organizations who have "accepted" the school for tuition reimbursement.
- [ ] 75. Misusing the Sosdian and Sharp study.
- [ ] 76. Claims of reciprocal, automatic recognition due to being a dependent territory of the motherland.

Misleading or Fake Physical Evidence

- [ ] 77. Fake pictures of the school's building(s).
- [ ] 78. Doctored photos of real buildings.
- [ ] 79. Prestigious-sounding address.
- [ ] 80. A private mailbox (PMB) presented as "suite" or "floor" or "building number."
- [ ] 81. Facilities rented once, or rarely, portrayed as the campus.
- [ ] 82. Depicting a large building in which the school either rents one room or uses a mailbox or an "executive suites" service, as if it all belonged to the school.
- [ ] 83. Illegal activity associated with a legal school.

Misleading Policies

- [ ] 84. Claiming exclusivity: stating that only 5 percent of applicants are accepted.
- [ ] 85. Not specifying which classes are required or how many units are required to graduate or saying that "rare exceptions can be made."
- [ ] 86. Backdating diplomas.
- [ ] 87. Selling graduate honors and the GPA of choice.
- [ ] 88. Assuring the customer that "we'll always be here for you."
- [ ] 89. Using names of real universities no longer in existence.
- [ ] 90. More than one degree at a time.
- [ ] 91. Multilevel marketing combined with a degree mill.
- [ ] 92. "Order by midnight tonight."

VISA MILLS

In 2011, federal agencies raided a California-approved university, which they called "a sham university" that admitted a large number of students from India, gave them a convenience address (553 students were listed as living in the same two-bedroom apartment) and, most significantly, a visa to come to the United States.

Several months later, the founder of Tri-Valley University, Susan Xiao-Ping Su, was indicted by a federal grand jury on thirty-three counts of wire fraud; mail fraud; visa fraud and conspiracy to commit visa fraud; use of a false document; making false statements to a government agency; alien harboring; unauthorized access to a government computer and money laundering.

According to the indictment, Su cleverly manipulated the government's Student and Exchange Visitor Information System (SEVIS) to secure F-1 visa documents. Students were not required to go to classes, and their "training" program typically consisted of menial jobs at Wal-Mart and 7-Eleven. In return, they paid fees resulting in more than $3 million, which Su laundered and kept.

This is by no means the first or only "visa mill." Indeed, earlier, the Immigration Customs and Enforcement agents arrested Pastor Samuel Chai Cho Oh, founder of California Union University, who charged Korean students up to $10,000 to enroll in his state-approved school and get the necessary visa forms. Oh was said to make $50,000 a month from this scheme. In one affidavit, a student told how Oh put on a bogus graduation ceremony, where students in caps and gowns laughed as they were handed their phony diplomas.

It is important to note that both of these schools were California-approved at the time they were running these major frauds. Insiders suggest that more than a few of the several hundred other California-approved schools are engaged in similar behaviors.

In England, where the problem has been known for many years, Immigration Minister Liam Byrne has estimated that 25 percent of the registered English-language schools in Great Britain are in fact visa mills. A BBC investigation suggested that upward of fifty thousand people are using such schemes to stay in England illegally.

In Canada, the Border Services Agency says that there are so many people, and so many fake schools, scamming the system that they can investigate only 5 percent of the cases. In just one province, Canada Border Services Agency has only three officers dealing with a backlog of more than five hundred visa scam cases, with dozens of new ones coming along every month.

In 2011, Sen. Charles Schumer of New York called for a federal crackdown on sham colleges handing out student visas to potential criminals and terrorists. They "are nothing more than fronts for people like the 9/11 terrorists who pay to enter the United States illegally," he said. Recall that it was a visa fraud situation that persuaded the US Secret Service to become involved in shutting down the fake St. Regis University, as described in chapter 7.

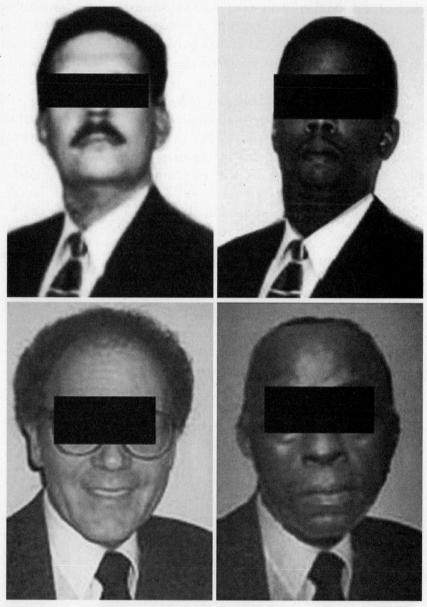

When the fake St. Regis University, presenting itself as an African school but actually run from Spokane, Washington, got questions about why an African school had mostly Caucasian faculty, they solved the problem by pasting (not very well) photos of Africans onto the bodies of Caucasians. George Gollin discovered the chicanery.

Chapter 3

···

THE BUYERS

···

WHY ACQUIRE ANY DEGREE?

L et's start with the broader question of why people would spend the time and the money to acquire any degree, real or fake, and then look at the reasons someone might choose "fake" instead of "real." Legitimate degrees typically represent one of the three or four most expensive and most time-consuming things a person will do in a lifetime. There must be persuasive reasons to consider doing this, and indeed there are.

Years ago, John Bear ran a consulting service, offering advice to people who wished to earn one or more degrees. That process began with a questionnaire asking, among many other things, the reason that the client wished to have a degree. The multiple-choice question had these six options:

1. My employer/potential employer says I must have a degree.
2. I plan to look for a new job, and the degree will help.
3. I would like to advance/get higher pay in my current job.
4. I wish to learn more about my field of interest.
5. I plan to start or expand a business, and I want my customers or clients to have more confidence in me.
6. For personal satisfaction, and/or to earn the respect of others.

The responses, based on several thousand clients, were pretty evenly distributed among the six choices, with a fair number of people checking two or more boxes.

The first three are all pretty much different ways of saying the same thing: many jobs either require degrees or reward degree-holders with higher pay and the possibility of promotion. That, of course, is a persuasive reason to want a degree. And for some people, it is a persuasive reason to short-circuit the process by purchasing a degree in the hope of getting away with it. (The matter of people who are, themselves, genuinely fooled by a degree mill will be discussed later in this section.)

The fourth choice is usually combined with one of the other choices, since a person who *only* wants to learn more about a subject, whether business or astronomy or Greek history or whatever, could simply take one of the thousands of online or home study courses available from hundreds of legitimate colleges and universities, without the need to commit to a full degree program.

Choices five and six are both concerned with image: being seen as a person with certain credentials and the level of knowledge that it suggests to friends, family, business associates, or potential clients. While a marriage counselor doesn't *need* to have a doctorate in most states, or a financial planner an MBA, or a contractor a degree in engineering, the fact of those degrees may attract more customers and inspire confidence in them.

One of the especially scary subsets of the matter of image, or being seen as an expert, is the matter of expert witnesses. Some courts have been quite remiss in verifying the claimed credentials of a proposed expert witness. To the best of John Bear's knowledge, almost no one has ever checked to see if he has the credentials and publications he has claimed.[1] But sometimes attorneys for the "other" party *do* check, and so John Bear has done expert witness work in cases where he was not relevant to the main topic but was only there to help discredit an expert witness for the other party. One case, for instance, involved a tree expert, calling himself a forensic arborologist, whose only degree was a doctorate from an unrecognized British school.

Other so-called experts who were found to have bogus degrees include

- a self-styled automotive engineer who testified on behalf of an auto manufacturer that the brakes "could not have failed" in a fatal accident. This man was exposed on the witness stand as having bought his engineering degree from a notorious degree mill.

- an asbestos removal "expert" whose degrees in environmental sciences came from a worthless source.
- a burn expert, who always seemed to conclude that horribly disfigured burn victims had somehow brought it on themselves through carelessness and that his corporate clients were in no way responsible. When his fake PhD in safety was exposed, it triggered a review of many decisions in which his testimony had been a factor.

There are these two general categories of people who buy degrees from degree mills:

- Category one consists of those who hope and plan to use them with employers and potential employers.
- Category two consists of those who simply want to impress other people.

An essential difference between these two categories is that in the first, the person knows that a third party is going to have to approve the degree, while in the second, the person concerned is not only the one who wants the degree but also the one who finds a supplier and decides whether to go ahead—deciding whether any given school and degree is likely to meet his or her needs.

This suggests that people who know that the degree will have to get past a gatekeeper—another person or a committee—may be less likely to deal with a degree mill.

But people in both categories *do* deal with degree mills. In asking why they do so, it is appropriate to ask the crucial question that every human resources person, law enforcement agency, potential customer or client, and even the media, should ask when people with degree-mill credentials are discovered: Did they know it was fake, or were they genuinely fooled?

DID THEY KNOW IT WAS FAKE,
OR WERE THEY FOOLED?

Give us an infallible mind-reading machine for just a few minutes and we would use it to get to the heart of one of the most perplexing and, sadly, unanswerable questions of all: What is really going on in the mind of the person who purchases a degree from a degree mill? There really are only these two possibilities:

1. They knew exactly what they were doing, and they bought the fake degree for the sole purpose of using it to fool others.
2. They genuinely believed they were earning a legitimate degree from a legitimate institution that recognized their excellent career achievements and said those achievements were equivalent to a degree. (After the fact—after a degree mill is exposed or the person gets in trouble—there are some who will say that they really did have some concerns or doubts but decided to go ahead anyway. There may well be a small subset of such people.)

To be sure, there are people in each category. But is it 90–10 percent, 10–90 percent, or somewhere in between? Our hunch is that it is nearer to the former than to the latter. Common sense tells us that most people with an IQ higher than room temperature must at least suspect that a doctorate that can be earned in two weeks, no questions asked, or a bachelor's degree that can be backdated to the date of one's choice, cannot be legitimate.

And yet, when a place like Columbia State University with its twenty-seven-day degrees or Concordia College and University with its twelve-hour degrees is exposed, inevitably we will hear from some people who sound absolutely truthful and genuinely astonished. One victim wrote, "I can't believe I did this. I earned a master's degree from the University of Wisconsin. I know what graduate school is like. But these sellers were so persuasive, so soothing on the phone, and of course I really *did* believe that I had the knowledge and skill of a person with a doctorate in my field."[2]

If we were sitting on a jury, we'd probably give some of these people the benefit of the doubt, but not a whole lot of them. And, in our experience, the more people talk about what they did and why they did it, the deeper the hole they dig. Consider the following case history for a textbook example.

Case History

John Bear was an expert witness for one state's department of professional regulation in a case involving a psychologist who worked for the state prison system in a job that did not require a PhD but had a significantly higher salary for people who did have doctorates. The employee in question had a legitimate bachelor's and master's degree, and then he purchased his PhD for $600 from the University of England at Oxford, one of the many fakes started and run by the notorious Fowler brothers of Chicago and Los Angeles. Allen Ezell had earlier helped bring them to justice in a trial where John Bear testified as an expert witness.

This psychologist, predictably, had insisted that his colleagues and underlings call him "doctor." He started out on the witness stand by expressing astonishment that this school could be anything other than the excellent long-established institution they claimed. Why, he even wrote and submitted a doctoral dissertation, he said.

The prosecutor introduced the school's badly designed and poorly printed little six-page catalog. Was the defendant familiar with graduate school catalogs? Yes. Have you seen one for the state university where you earned your master's? Yes. Did it look anything like this? No.

The prosecutor pointed out that the university had no telephone and operated from a post office box. Does that sound like a real university? The defendant mumbled that he had never had any need to telephone the school. Do you mean you earned a Doctor of Philosophy degree without ever speaking to anyone from the university, even once? Yes.

Next, the prosecutor noted that the "university" offered to backdate the diploma to any date of the graduate's choice. Have you ever heard of any school that will state that you earned their degree years before you even heard of them? Does that seem right to you? Well, when you put it like that. . . .

Then the prosecutor asked what sort of due diligence the defendant had done before choosing his school. Had he looked it up in any directory? No. Had he asked any friends or colleagues about it? No. Had he checked with the registrar of any of the state universities to see if the degree would be acceptable? No.

Finally, the prosecutor explained that he had had the defendant's doctoral dissertation read by several experts in the field. They all agreed that it was at best at the level of a high-school term paper. There was a strong suspicion that he had cobbled it together *after* he had been subpoenaed to appear, or possibly purchased it from one of the many "services" that write academic papers to order.

The outcome was that the defendant lost his license to practice as a psychologist, despite his tearful appeal that this was literally his meal ticket, his only way to earn a living.

And the office of the attorney general was seriously considering a criminal suit, based on the fact that this man had "stolen" tens of thousands of dollars from the state, by collecting, for years, the much higher salary paid to psychologists with a doctorate, as compared to those with a master's degree.

Another Case History

In 2011, John Bear testified in a case in which two men had invested a seven-figure sum in a start-up "dot com" business, based largely on the master's and doctorate in business and engineering claimed by the founder. After the business failed, they learned that both of the founder's degrees had been purchased from the fake University of Palmers Green. The founder's response was that he now agreed that his degrees were fake, but that he, too, had been fooled, and in any event, the investors should have done more "due diligence."

Bear's role was to persuade the jury that the "university" in question was so blatantly fake, it would be almost impossible to be fooled. The jury agreed, and voted for the investors, but in sentencing, the judge pointed out that the investors were not entirely blameless. If the degrees were so clearly fake, then the investors should also have taken note. As a result, the amount of the judgment was decreased.

While there may not always be a clear answer to the "Did he or she know?" question, in many situations *either* a yes or a no answer can be useful and provides a course of action for the person asking the question.

If he *did* know that he was buying a fake degree, then what else does one need to know?

And if he genuinely *didn't* know, what does this say about the intelligence, judgment skills, and decision-making ability of that person?

HOW PEOPLE RATIONALIZE BUYING DEGREES: THE ISSUE OF SUMPTUARY LAW

No one would challenge the notion that robbing banks or shooting people is a criminal act, deserving of punishment of some kind. But we still hear a lot of people saying, with regard to their fake degrees, "Well, what harm is really being done here. I already knew how to do the work; I just needed that piece of paper to get the job." Alternatively, the argument goes, "This job did not require that particular degree. I just wanted the self-satisfaction and the respect that went with being identified as a master or doctor in my field."

When we try to understand their motivation and explain their behavior, we move into the realm of sumptuary law.

Sumptuary law relates to matters of law that attempt to regulate human behavior, typically on social, religious, or moral grounds. The concept arose in ancient Greece and Rome, dealing with everything from dress codes (slaves must not wear clothes similar to that of their masters) to behavior in public places.

In the twentieth and twenty-first centuries, we have seen numerous attempts to regulate human behavior in areas such as gambling, drugs, prostitution and sexual behaviors, clothing (as with high school and college dress codes), and of course the "great experiment" of Prohibition, making alcohol illegal in the United States during the 1920s.

The simple fact is that all of these activities survive and often thrive, despite attempts to regulate them, because of the law of supply and demand. If enough people want those products or services and are willing to take the risks involved, then they will somehow become available. As a sarcastic advertisement of the 1970s said, "Drive over fifty-five. Cheat on your income taxes. Smoke marijuana. If you don't like a law, ignore it. It's the American way."

All of this is relevant to degree mills because the simple if distressing fact is that they survive and prosper *solely* because there are enough people who want and are willing to pay for their product and are either unaware of the risks or willing to accept them.

"I will drive ninety miles an hour on the freeway because I am a good driver, and I am late for an important appointment."

"I will use cocaine because I know I can handle it, and anyway I'm so discreet that I'll never get caught."

"I will buy a PhD and call myself 'doctor' because it will help my career, and I already know a great deal in my field, and I don't have time to go back to school."

That is why we acknowledge, with sorrow, that the scourge of fake schools and fake degrees and diplomas, a problem since at least the eighth century, will probably always be with us no matter how stringent the laws, no matter how widespread the publicizing of dangers and prosecutions, and no matter how effective the "gatekeepers" or decision makers on degree acceptance may be.

There is no better evidence of the willingness of people to buy degrees—even people who know the dangers—than what happened on CBS television in 1978. That year, *60 Minutes* did its first segment on degree mills, focusing on a major phony then operating in Los Angeles. Mike Wallace visited California Pacifica University and was shown on camera buying a PhD for $3,000. While the cameras were rolling, the sheriff arrived with an arrest warrant for school owner Ernest Sinclair and took him away.[3] After the program aired on Sunday evening, according to segment producer Marian Goldin, more than eight hundred people telephoned CBS to learn the address and phone number of that school so they could buy a degree "just like Mike Wallace did."

Oh, dear.

WHY PEOPLE DEAL WITH MILLS:
SOME ACADEMIC RESEARCH

The academic world has been surprisingly apathetic in looking at degree-mill matters. Searching academic records for the last half century, we found only three doctoral research projects and one master's thesis specifically addressing the issues: a historical look at the problem (done in 1963 and discussed in chapter 1), a 2003 survey of what human resource managers know about degree mills and how they deal with them (discussed in chapter 19), an in-depth look at whether three "virtual universities" operating in Australia are "a guise for degree/diploma mills to thrive,"[4] and the only experimental study—some charming if modest introductory research by Robin Calote for her doctorate in education in 2002, under the title "Diploma Mills: What's the Attraction?"

Dr. Calote's purpose was to look at the effect of four factors on the decision to choose a degree mill: time (degree mills are fast), credit for life experience (degree mills are exceedingly generous), tuition on a per-degree basis (degree mills are cheap), and institutional licensure (degree mills rarely have a license to operate as a degree-granting school).

Her experimental subjects were students enrolled in an accredited community college. Each was asked to view web pages created by Calote for sixteen fictitious colleges. They varied only in the presence or absence of the four variables: time, credit for experience, cost, and licensure.

After viewing each web page, the subjects were asked to rate their likelihood of enrolling in the college on a five-point scale. Then they were asked to reflect on their choices and to rate the effect each of the four variables had on their decisions.

There was no relationship between the variables of time, credit for life experience, or tuition and the decision to choose that institution. But there was a statistically significant relationship between the assertion that an institution was licensed and the decision to choose it.

Intriguingly, the subjects *believed* that they had been influenced by all four variables, but in fact only licensure really influenced them.

The results offer a persuasive argument why so many bad and fake schools choose locations, from Alabama to Liberia, where they can claim to be licensed and even approved or accredited. It also points out why such places are doing a real disservice to the public through their weak licensing laws and regulations.

In her dissertation, Calote concludes that "accredited colleges should partner with the media to build public awareness of diploma mills as a form of consumer fraud. In addition, academic counseling should include instruction regarding the meaning of accreditation, the difference between accreditation and licensure, the definition and legal status of diploma mills, and the professional risks taken by those who acquire diploma mill degrees." We could not agree more.

THE RISKS

Human beings take risks all the time. Nearly every aspect of human behavior involves some risk, whether or not we think about it at the time.

There are high-risk behaviors, such as smoking, climbing Mount Everest, or unsafe sex, and there are low-risk behaviors, including driving, flying, and walking down the sidewalk (even though people have been killed by falling debris).

Then there is the matter of results or consequences.

A high-risk activity can have very small consequences. Most tax cheats, if caught, get relatively minor penalties. Playing the lottery is extremely high risk, but for most people the downside means only losing a few dollars.

A low-risk activity can have very big consequences. Not many people are hit by lightning on the golf course, and most people who drive fifty miles an hour through a school zone don't have incidents. But for the golfer who is hit by lightning, or the driver who kills a child, the consequences are extreme.

The two important questions, then, are these: Is buying a diploma from a degree mill a low- or a high-risk activity? And are the consequences small or large?

Is Buying a Degree High Risk or Low Risk?

It comes down to a matter of odds. If one knew that 98 percent of people who fiddle their taxes get caught, they'd be crazy to try. But if it were 3 percent? Or 17 percent? Might be worth the risk.

Our best answer is that buying and using a fake degree *used* to be very low risk. Nearly thirty years ago, the Pepper Subcommittee estimated there were half a million people with fake degrees. How many of those have suffered? Very few, indeed. But we believe the winds have shifted. Fake degrees are getting more and more attention. Human resource people, law enforcement people, and the media are paying closer attention than ever before.

People who buy a degree are truly putting a time bomb in their resume. More time bombs have exploded in the last few years than ever before. Every one that *hasn't* exploded is ticking away. There are no exceptions, no other categories.

Bottom line: we believe this formerly low-risk activity is well on the way to becoming high risk.

What Are the Consequences?

As with the risk level, we think things are changing. Thirty, twenty, even ten years ago, people found to be using fake degrees were often seen as amusing scoundrels at worst. Some degree abusers achieved the status of folk heroes. There have been popular books and movies about fake degree users Ferdinand Waldo DeMara (*The Great Imposter*) and Frank W. Abagnale (*Catch Me If You Can*).

Things seem to be changing, although not as quickly as some of

us may wish. When a popular television advice guru who called herself "The Love Doctor" was found (by the media) to have a degree-
mill PhD, she was promptly fired. When a college professor in
Michigan had his fake degree exposed on *Good Morning America*, he
was promptly fired. When a fairly high state official in Colorado was
found to have a fake degree, not only was he fired, but also his "green
card" was revoked and he was deported to his native country.

In addition to the obvious matter of general embarrassment and
humiliation, the risks of fake degree use would seem to be:

- loss of job (or reduced chance for advancement)
- loss of professional license or security clearance
- deportation
- criminal prosecution

The first three are clear and are persuasive reasons not to take a
chance. The fourth seems to be an area of growing risk. While any
state can theoretically prosecute a fake degree user under general
fraud statutes, it is only recently that some states have begun to
address the precise problem by passing laws specifically punishing
the use of unrecognized or fake degrees.

Will what began in Oregon and has now spread to a dozen other
states become a national trend? Even if no one is actually imprisoned on the offense of fake degree use in North Dakota, for instance,
the very fact that people *could* be is a major deterrent to using such
a degree or indeed to hiring an employee with one.

Yet people *are* imprisoned. An extreme example, yet not a unique
one, happened a few years ago when a senior public television executive was found to have a fake degree. He was fired, indicted, tried,
convicted, and imprisoned, all in a matter of a few months.

How Do People Feel, and Behave, after They Are Caught?

Social scientists are fascinated by what people do when something
they really thought was true turns out not to be (for instance, that
smoking is relatively harmless or that Richard Nixon was a totally

honest politician), or when an event they truly believed was going to happen didn't happen (such as the religious leaders who name an exact date for the end of the world and go onto a mountain top with their followers to see it happen).

Since the category of "I really believed it was a legitimate university" fits here as well, the findings on how these people react has relevance here.

Essentially, in most cases, the "aftermath" can be fitted into one of these four categories:

Acceptance: I see now that I was fooled. I shall renounce and stop using my degree(s); apologize to all concerned, make amends to colleagues, coworkers, and clients; and seriously consider pursuing a legitimate degree program.

Denial: There simply is no way Lexington University can be a fake. I have seen photographs of the campus. I have talked to the dean. I have confirmed its accreditation. This is an attempt by [villain of choice: "my political enemies," "the left-(or right-) wing press," etc.] to discredit me. When the facts are known, I will be vindicated.

Rationalization: Well, the accrediting agency may not be recognized, but accreditation is voluntary anyway, and they are state licensed, and at least two famous authors have degrees from there, and my employer paid for it, so what's the problem?

Dysfunction: No comment. This topic is off limits. The facts speak for themselves. There is nothing more to say.

Needless to say, we believe the first category of response is the only healthy and realistic one. But people who have fake or dubious degrees, and others who must deal with such people, should recognize that responses might fall into any of these categories.

Chapter 4

··

THE LAW

··

What's wrong with buying a degree from a degree mill?

How should employers and others think about and deal with this issue, both legally and ethically?

From the employer's point of view, these two questions are not quite as simple as they might seem at first glance. There are, for instance, many cases in which the buyer of the degree is performing well, sometimes in a job that does not require that particular degree. But at the same time, there may well be legal, ethical, and public relations issues to consider.

A well-publicized case is that of Laura Callahan, a senior employee of the Department of Homeland Security, discovered in 2003 to have fake degrees. Her response to her employer was fivefold:

- She did not seek out this fake but responded to an advertisement for a school referral service, not knowing it was secretly linked only to one fake school.
- She believed she was dealing a properly accredited school, apparently not knowing there were such things as fake accrediting agencies. She even used a "degree-mill checklist" to avoid being a victim.
- The job she held did not require any college degree.
- No one denied that she was doing a good job.
- She had listed the three degree-mill degrees on her official resume for several years.

An essay by Callahan relating to this situation appears as chapter 10.

Is there an issue here? Is there, in fact, a problem if the person with the fake degree is doing a good job?

Many people would suggest there are two factors to consider in formulating an answer:

- What the degree purchase says about that person, and his or her judgment.
- What is the possibility of causing problems for the employer?

Some feel that it is situational: dependent on the person, the field of endeavor, and the circumstances. A psychotherapist, however competent, with a fake doctorate in psychology, is inappropriate, while a successful real estate broker with a fake MBA may not be as much of a problem.[1]

This topic was addressed in depth in a paper by Creola Johnson with the splendid title *Credentialism and the Proliferation of Fake Degrees: The Employer Pretends to Need a Degree; The Employee Pretends to Have One.*[2]

These issues are regular fodder for coffee shop discussions and for ethics classes. Would you rather have your jet piloted by a man who flew jumbo jets for the Air Force but then bought a fake bachelor's degree in order to get his airline job, or man who barely scraped through at an accredited aeronautics school? Would you rather have a compassionate marriage counselor with a fake degree or a less-caring person with an Ivy League doctorate?

These issues arise commonly in the workplace, often causing anguish among the decision makers, who are uncertain how to find the best answer: whether to take drastic action, punitive action, or no action at all.

These three different options—major penalty, some penalty, or no penalty—were each exercised in recent cases involving the top officers of three large corporations. Each was found to have a fake MBA degree. None was accused of doing a bad or unsatisfactory job.

At Veritas, a billion-dollar software company, now merged with Symantec, the chief financial officer was summarily fired.

At Bausch and Lomb, the chief financial officer was penalized more than a million dollars by having his promised bonus withdrawn, but he was allowed to keep his job.

And at the third company, whose situation never reached the

public eye, the chief financial officer was neither fired nor penalized, and no public announcement was ever made.[3]

With increased public and media awareness of degree mills, and with new public disclosure rules and practices in the post-Enron era, it is probably wise for any organization to have in place a policy to deal with newly discovered fake degrees and to try to keep the problem from arising in the first place.

WHO IS HARMED BY USE OF FAKE DEGREES?

It saddens us that the question even needs to be asked. But when we wrote to a reporter for a Boston daily newspaper to alert him to a school psychologist with a fake PhD in his area, and he replied, "And I should care because?" we were reminded there is a problem here.

In fact, that "So what?" response comes all too often, as in the case of the publisher of *The Economist* magazine who, when alerted to the fact that the magazine has run hundreds of advertisements for degree mills, replied, "Our readers are smart enough to make their own decisions."

Who, then, is harmed by degree mills?

- The truly innocent victims who unknowingly acquire a degree from an illegal university, perhaps one they saw advertised in the *Economist*, *USA Today*, or an airline magazine, and then get in trouble with their employer or with the law.
- The employers who have potential liability for bad publicity and for damages attributed to employees with fake degrees.
- The customers or clients of bogus doctors, lawyers, therapists, architects, accountants, and so on. When someone defiantly declares that no one is being harmed, as longtime degree-mill operator Ronald Pellar said to ABC's *20/20* a few years ago, we point, among many others, to patients at Lincoln Hospital in New York who were treated by an accountant who bought a medical degree and was employed as an emergency room physician, or the couples who divorced following their "treat-

VNIVERSITAS HARVARDIANA

CANTABRIGIAE IN REPVBLICA MASSACHVSETTENSIVM

QVONIAM

IOANNES BEAR

studio diligentiore et specimine erudeirionis idoneo adhibias
Professoribus Artium et Scientarium

persuasit se penitus pernoscere

CHIRURGIA CEREBRUM

Praeses et Socii Collegii Harvardiani Ordine Professorum
illorum commendante atque consentientibus honorandis et
reverendis Inspectoribus dederunt et concesserunt ei gradum

DOCTOR MEDICINUM
et omnia insignia et iura quae ad hunc gradum pertinent.

IN cuius rei testimonium nos Praeses et Decani auctoritate
rite commissa de Domini 14 Martius 1989
Collegiique Harvardiani
Vniversitatis sigillo muntis nomina subscriptsimus.

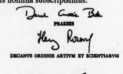

PRAESES

DECANVS ORDINIS ARTIVM ET SCIENTIARVM

DECANVS ACADEMIAE SVPERIORIS

THIS IS A REPRODUCTION NO SCHOOL CREDIT OR DEGREE STATUS IS GRANTED OR IMPLIED

John Bear's Harvard medical degree was sold for $39 by Alumni Arts, the Oregon-based counterfeiter raided and closed by Allen Ezell.

---

ment" at a New York "sex therapy" clinic run by a high school dropout whose only degree was a PhD purchased from a California degree mill.

- The taxpayers who are paying the salaries of federal, state, and local government employees with unrecognized degrees, from teachers and principals to elected officials to military officers to a former senior undersecretary of defense.

WHAT TO CONSIDER IN DEALING WITH FAKE DEGREES

1. Legal Issues

Can hiring or harboring an employee with a fake degree cause legal problems for the employer, quite apart from any problems the employee may face? There are at least two areas where this is a possibility.

One relates to an organization's potential liability for things done by employees with fake degrees or even things that have not yet caused evident problems. Consider bridges built under the supervision of people with fake engineering degrees, therapy from people with fake psychology degrees, medical treatment from a fake MD, and so on.

When we looked at resumes posted on Monster.com, we found thousands of people with fake degrees who should give corporate officers and their insurance companies cause for alarm: a quality control officer at a controversial tire plant, a safety official at a nuclear power facility, the head of a clinic for a national health-care organization, a missile control officer for the army, and so on. Every person listed in the extensive "Time Bombs" section (chapter 8) was or is a potential insurance disaster.

One relevant area of the law in this matter is the rule of *respondeat superior*, or "let the master answer." It says that an employer is liable for harm done by employees while acting within the scope of their employment.[4]

The second legal issue deals with the way various federal regulations may be interpreted, especially in the "full disclosure" post-Enron era. Such matters have not been clearly resolved in the courts, but one attorney for a Fortune 500 firm, wrestling with the problem of a senior officer discovered to have a fake degree, expressed concern that the company's filings with the Securities and Exchange Commission, including the credentials of this officer, could be construed as a violation of Sarbanes-Oxley Public Accounting Reform and Investor Protection Act of 2002.

2. Financial Issues

Discovery of a fake degree problem can have a significant, even a dramatic, impact on the value of a company. The stock of three large American companies where a degree scandal surfaced declined sharply in the aftermath, and in Hong Kong, Richard Li, the tycoon often called "the Bill Gates of Asia," saw the value of his companies drop by a billion dollars after his fake degree was revealed.

Sales can be affected through loss of confidence in the company, as can possible mergers and acquisitions. In what was known as the Fermenta Affair, a several-hundred-million-dollar sale of an industrial company to Volvo was canceled when the fake degrees of the seller became known to Volvo.

There is also the matter of companies that pay tuition for employees to acquire degrees from fake schools and pay them higher salaries once they have their degrees. Degree mills often publish lists of companies that pay tuition for their employees, and many of these claims turn out to be correct: the companies had simply failed to do the most minimal "due diligence" in checking whether a given school was properly accredited.

3. Publicity Issues

Public disclosure of a fake degree, especially when it is a person in a high profile and responsible position, has the potential to be a public relations nightmare.

Publicity can affect reputation, which can result in losing customers or clients, even if the person or people with fake degrees are dismissed. A big-city daily newspaper suffered a decline in readership and advertising revenue when the fake law degree of its publisher was disclosed by a rival paper. A national organization of health-care professionals lost members after its national director was found to have her highest degree from a California mill.

4. Business Development Issues

There are many thousands of people with fake MBA degrees. How many of these, as employees or consultants, may have produced flawed business plans, whether for small-business clients or departments within large organizations?

5. Logistical and Personnel Issues

As a practical matter, a person with a degree-mill degree, as well as most other unaccredited degrees, faces the risk of prosecution if he or she uses that degree in Illinois, New Jersey, Oregon, and other states, whether by working there or possibly attending a convention or sales meeting there.

There are the practical matters of whether such degrees should be included on personnel records, either with comment or without, and, if the employee keeps his or her job, whether the degree should be mentioned when a potential employer asks for references.

6. Ethical Issues

What about whistle-blowing? Should other employees be encouraged to report possible bad or fake degrees or even be rewarded for so doing? What about members of the public? When we have reported particularly egregious fake degree use to executives of organizations, sometimes we receive grateful thanks, and sometimes, as with a division of Brunswick that had paid for at least three fake degrees, we are told to mind our own business.

Sometimes, of course, it is unclear whether a person has been punished for blowing a whistle for other reasons. A few years ago, the chief scientist in a study that led to new California policies on diesel fuel emissions, Hien Tran, falsely claimed a PhD from the University of California. He had in fact purchased his degree for $1,000 from a diploma mill called Thornhill University. The head of the California Air Resources Board, Mary Nichols, knew about the degree fraud but did not tell her board until after the new policies had been adopted. (She later apologized for this.)

The whistle-blower who exposed this information, Professor James Enstrom, was let go from his job at UCLA after thirty-four years, but not, UCLA said, because of his whistle-blowing. In 2011, he was appealing the decision. Tran was suspended for sixty days but still has his job, as does Nichols.

The role of an ethicist in these matters. Sometimes people who are faced with the decision of whether to fire, punish, or ignore a person with a fake degree turn to professional ethicists for advice and counsel. Marina Bear, coauthor John Bear's wife, earned her doctorate in philosophy from Vanderbilt University and has helped clients work through these issues. Here, for instance, is one of those cases.

Case History

In a medium-sized American city, the job of school principal unexpectedly became available after the death of the incumbent. The school board decided to appoint a woman who was several years from retirement to reward her for many years of outstanding service. The problem was that the job required a master's degree, and this woman did not have one.

The school board apparently "looked the other way," while the woman purchased a master's degree from a degree mill operating from a mailbox rental address in another state. The degree, ostensibly based on her life experience, cost her about $1,000 and was delivered ten days after she applied.

After the new principal had served successfully for a year, the local newspaper discovered her fake degree and ran a story on it. At that point, a teacher in the district who had a legitimate master's degree, and had been in line for the job of principal, brought a suit against the school board, claiming it did not act appropriately.

The attorney for the woman who brought the suit was troubled. He was required to oppose a woman who was well liked, who by all accounts was doing a good job as principal, and who seemed to believe she was fulfilling the school board's wishes in acquiring this degree.

The attorney engaged Marina Bear's services to help him work through the complex ethical situation surrounding these matters. An abridged version of the report is provided in chapter 13. It offers a detailed and useful way to look at and deal with the issues involved.

SHOULD JOB DESCRIPTIONS EVEN INCLUDE DEGREE REQUIREMENTS?

Many employees or job seekers feel they are compelled to deal with a bad or fake school in their desperation to secure a job where the degree is a requirement. Whether many job descriptions should have a degree requirement is a big and complex matter, beyond the scope of this book.

Certainly there are some situations where a degree is *essential*: a psychology degree for a therapist, a business or finance degree for a financial planner. But there are also many situations in which people have the necessary knowledge and skills without the benefit of a degree. It is these latter situations that often motivate people, such as that school principal, to deal with degree mills.

A landmark Supreme Court decision, *Griggs v. Duke Power Company*, established that it is illegal to set an unnecessary job requirement, including a degree, solely to exclude certain people, typically minority groups, from applying.

The big question, then, is, just what is an "unnecessary" degree requirement? An important study by Ivar Berg, charmingly titled *The Great Training Robbery*, suggests that the degree requirement may be regularly abused.[5] Berg looked at jobs where some employers require degrees and others do not, ranging from air traffic controllers to operators of a fabric-cutting machine at a clothing factory. People without a degree were found to perform as well as, or better than, those with the degree. Berg suggests many employers have inappropriately been persuaded that degrees should be rewarded with higher salaries.

Why do so many jobs either require or reward degrees, forcing employees or job seekers to earn legitimate ones, or buy fake ones? There are four principal reasons.

- Reassurance that there is likely to be a certain knowledge or training level. If a job pool at a brokerage firm included fifty applicants with Ivy League MBAs and fifty with no master's degree, the probability is high that most of the former group, and a much smaller number of the latter group, would be capable of doing the work. So why take chances? It is probably much more efficient to shortlist a subset of the MBAs and reject the others.

For every accomplished non-degree-holder, from Harry Truman and Eleanor Roosevelt to Bill Gates and Steve Jobs, there are many more who simply don't have the skills or training of a person with the appropriate degree or credential.

- Simplifying the recruitment process. If one can reasonably expect hundreds of applications for a given job, it is much more efficient for the employer to reject automatically those persons who do not meet a certain criterion. It is illegal in most places to reject people based on their race, religion, or gender. However, one can have a degree requirement, as long as it can be defended as desirable for a given job.

Things have reached the point where many major employers use automatic resume-scanning software, and so the person without a degree may get the rejection letter without a human being even having looked at their otherwise impressive CV. But the software is not nearly as likely to "know" that Trinity University can mean either the real one in Texas or the bogus ones that operated from South Dakota.

Case History

John Bear once surveyed the personnel or HR departments of twenty airlines, all of which, at that time, required that pilot applicants have at least a bachelor's degree, although most did not specify that the degree be in a field related to aviation, science, or engineering. As one non-degreed applicant so charmingly put it, "I've flown four-engine jets for the Air Force for ten years, and I'm passed over for a Cessna-flying kid with a bachelor's degree in English poetry."

- It makes the selection process faster and more efficient. If there are a great many applicants for an advertised pilot job, it is much simpler (although, of course, not necessarily fair) to reject automatically all those with no degree, since there will almost certainly be enough qualified people among the degreed subgroup.
- Earning *any* sort of degree, even one in poetry, shows a certain level of gumption, of ability to follow instructions, play by the rules, and complete a major endeavor; as one personnel officer put it, "a demonstration of 'stick-to-it-iveness,' which is a quality we like in pilots." Of course, a degree in avionics or mechanical engineering might be a bit of icing on this particular cake.

Note: Not surprisingly, in times of major airline growth, and concomitant pilot shortage, these degree requirements tend to be removed or overlooked.

The bottom line here is for employers to look seriously at any degree requirements that are written into job descriptions and employment and union contracts, and for employees and potential employees to resist going out and buying a "time bomb" solely to meet some employer requirement, no matter how inappropriate or unfair it seems to be.

Chapter 5

....

THE ENFORCERS

....

HOW CAN DEGREE MILLS CONTINUE TO EVADE THE LAW?

This is a question we hear all the time. As John Bear once said in a speech at an accrediting agency convention, "If you hold up a convenience store for $50, you'll probably be in prison before your Slurpee melts. But if you steal millions of dollars from thousands of people by selling fake degrees, no one seems to be able to do anything."

That's a bit exaggerated, perhaps, but there is almost always a triage situation going on in law enforcement. With a limited budget and limited personnel, which crimes or potential crimes are going to be dealt with? Degree mills often don't make the cut because they are much less visible and rarely involve violence or urgent matters of life and death. Further, there are at least these four other factors:

- the complex issues of federal versus state jurisdictions, as well as the international complications;
- problems of enforcement, especially across state or national borders;
- issues of overlapping agency functions: the notion that degree mills have been dealt with by state attorneys general, other state and even county and local consumer protection agencies, the FBI, the FTC, the postal inspectors, the IRS, the Secret Service, and others. Who makes the first move? Do they work together?

The US Department of Justice's Prosecution Manual suggests that prosecutions of mail and wire fraud "should not be undertaken if the scheme employed consists of some isolated transactions . . . involving minor loss to the victims. . . . Serious consideration, however, should be given to the prosecution of any scheme in its nature which is directed to defrauding a class or persons, or the general public, with a substantial pattern of conduct."[1] This is presumably why the FBI, the FTC, and the postal inspectors only choose to get involved if there is a likelihood of a large number of victims.

- The potential time and effort required to convince a judge to issue a search warrant, a grand jury to issue an indictment, or a jury to convict.

Here's an extreme but relevant example. The degree mill called Dallas State University began operating in the early 1970s. State officials in Texas took many years to shut it down. But the mill reopened almost immediately as Jackson State University in California. The postal service eventually shut off its mail, whereupon the school resurfaced as John Quincy Adams University, with an Oregon address. And on and on and on. It was nearly two decades, and millions of dollars in revenues, before the FBI finally brought the perpetrators to justice. Nowadays, neither the FBI nor any other agency seems to have the time, the budget, or even the interest to pursue situations like this.

This became sadly clear when Allen Ezell discovered a flagrantly illegal degree mill operating in his then-home state of Florida. He collected a good deal of information and shared it with the appropriate regulatory authorities in the state capital who said, in effect, "Yes, we agree it is a degree mill, but we simply aren't going to be able to do anything about it at this time." A year later, the phonies were still in business.

WHICH LAWS ARE BEING BROKEN?

This is not a law textbook, and we will not go into great detail here. It is emphatically the case that there are ample laws on the books in every state and federal jurisdiction to deal with the selling, buying, and using of fake degrees. While not every jurisdiction has laws that specifically mention either degree mills or degrees, they all have laws dealing with fraud and other deceptive practices.

Laws Relating Specifically to the Selling of Fake Degrees

All fifty states have some laws governing school licensing and degree-granting behaviors, although a few are notoriously weak or vague. And a handful of states have laws relating specifically to the buying and using of degrees, and we suspect an ever-growing number of states will move in this direction.

What About a National Law Addressing Degree Mills?

We almost had a good one, but somehow we lost it.

For decades, legislators and higher-education officials had been clamoring for federal legislation that would outlaw degree mills. The US Commissioner of Education practically *demanded* such a law in 1960.

Finally, in 2007, it looked as if something was about to happen. Congresswoman Betty McCollum of Minnesota introduced legislation via House Resolution 773, the Diploma Integrity Protection Act of 2007, that would have, among many other things,

- instructed the Department of Education to create a list of accredited institutions and valid accreditation associations for immigration and federal employment and hiring purposes,
- formed a task force of higher-education and law enforcement experts to develop a "strategic diploma integrity protection plan,"
- encouraged states to take similar steps, and

- empowered the Federal Trade Commission to crack down on diploma mills.

Essentially the same wording was carried over into H. R. 4137, a much broader bill, which was passed overwhelmingly by the House of Representatives in February 2007 (354 to 58). The Senate had already passed its own broad education bill without any degree-mill clauses, but Washington insiders generally believed that adding those clauses would be a mere formality; how could anyone be in favor of degree mills?

But five months later, that is exactly what happened. By the time the bill was passed by the Senate, and again by the House, just about everything relating to degree mills had been removed, with the exception of a watered-down definition of the term "diploma mill," which we quoted earlier.

So now at least we have a federal law that acknowledges that there are such things as degree mills and that provides a definition that might be helpful in some enforcement situations. But it accepts federal, state, or (here's the joker) "other organizations" that recognize accrediting agencies, and it says nothing about US-run "schools" that use mailbox addresses in other countries. Disappointing, to say the least.

Perhaps this is, at least in part, why, two years after the official definition of "diploma mill" was available, not a single federal agency (or anyone else that we know of) has taken a single step to identify holders of fake degrees.

In 2011, a new and stronger bill, H. R. 1758, was introduced in the House of Representatives by Cong. Tim Bishop of New York, which will now spend the next year or two moving in and out of various committees—Oversight and Government Reform, Energy and Commerce, Education and the Workforce, and the Judiciary, very likely to be modified often, if it survives at all. A copy of that bill, as introduced, appears in chapter 11. We wish it a better fate than McCollum's bill.

In the meantime, what have we got? For starters, all states and the federal government have laws dealing with fraud in general, which can include fraudulent behavior with regard to selling, buying, or using fake or misleading degrees.

As one example of this, there is a section of the United States Code that deals with fraud by wire (which includes telephone and Internet).[2]

Other general fraud provisions are found in sections dealing with unfair or deceptive acts and practices by individuals or businesses that affect commerce in any way. The Federal Trade Commission has made good use of this concept in its May 2003 action against a seller of fake degrees, part of which said:

> Defendants provide to others phony academic degrees, including but not limited to, doctoral degrees in medical related fields, and associated verification and backup materials, including, but not limited to, university transcripts, letters of recommendation, and other verification materials.
>
> These materials are used to facilitate deceptive activity, including, but not limited to, falsely representing that the recipient has completed and shown proficiency in a curriculum recognized as necessary to earn the academic degree, and that the diplomas are issued by established colleges or universities. By providing the academic degrees and associated verification and backup materials, Defendants have provided the means and instrumentalities for the commission of deceptive acts and practices.
>
> Therefore, Defendant's acts and practices, as outlined above, constitute deceptive acts and practices in violation of Section 5(a) of the FTC Act, 15 USC § 45(a).

Since there are no strong federal laws regulating degree mills per se, following is the "shopping list" from which an investigator, regulator, or prosecutor can choose where fake-degree selling or usage fits into the body of the frauds described. All but the last listing are sections of the United States Code, title 18:

section 2, Aid and Abet
section 371, Conspiracy
section 1028, False Identification
section 1030, Computer Fraud
section 1030, Mail Fraud
section 1341, Fraud by Wire
section 1343, Criminal Forfeiture

section 982, Money Laundering
section 1961 and 1963 (forfeiture 3554), RICO
    (Racketeer Influenced and Corrupt Organizations)
section 2320, Trademark Violation
    United States Code, title 26, section 7201, Tax Evasion

SHOULD ALL DEGREE BUYERS BE PROSECUTED?

If there were a simple answer that all could agree on, of course we would not need lawyers or juries. But many people write about the law as part science, part art; part objective and part subjective. We like the answer that a scholar of these matters posted on an education forum when the question arose.

> If I buy a jar of pickles, then I own a jar of pickles. If I wanted to, I could *call* it a jar of diamonds, but that wouldn't make it anything other than pickles. It would be a stupid, but harmless thing to do. However, if I try to sell my pickles as diamonds, I'll be doing something dishonest. Buying a $500 jar of pickles that sits on a shelf in the garage is stupid. Buying a $500 doctoral diploma that sits on a shelf in the garage is stupid but not a fraud. But if I hang it on my office wall, and it plays any kind of a role in solicitation of business, then I would argue that both I, and the seller of my diploma, are in violation of the fraud provisions of the US Code.

HOW TO CHECK OUT A SCHOOL

The good news is that in a great many cases, the work has already been done, and one can rely on other people's research and opinions. The extent of checking depends largely on the purpose at hand: Is it simply a matter of whether to accept a given degree by an employer or other decision maker? A decision whether to consider a business venture with a school? Whether to recommend it to others or to enroll oneself? Whether to consider writing about it or prosecuting it?

Relying on others may be sufficient for most purposes, but doing one's own due diligence can be satisfying and, at times, especially informative.

Information Already Available

- *Other people's lists.* As we have made clear throughout this book, there are institutions we choose not to call degree mills, but others do. In chapter 14, we tell how to find these.
- *Ask a professional.* We often point out that many people who claim to have been fooled by a degree mill could have done the necessary "due diligence" for free in about one minute by telephoning the registrar or admissions office of any nearby college and asking if they accept the credits or degrees of such-and-such a school.

One can also hire, at modest cost, an expert: one of the reliable degree evaluation services that are members of the National Association of Credential Evaluation Services (NACES, http://www.naces.org) or use the services of the American Association of Collegiate Registrars and Admissions Officers (AACRAO, http://www.aacrao.org), or one of the private commercial services that do this kind of evaluation, such as Accredibase (see chapter 18).

- *DegreeInfo.com and DegreeDiscussion.com.* These two free Internet forums have more than one hundred thousand postings relating to schools good and bad. They have good search functions, and they are also places to ask questions. While the information is usually reliable, there are, of course, no guarantees.
- *Agencies, directories, and reference books.* The legitimate agencies and reference books provide information on legitimate schools but rarely offer information or opinions on the others.

Agencies

Each state has its higher education agency or equivalent. Agencies rarely comment on the quality of schools, only on whether they are properly licensed, but there are exceptions. A complete list, with all contact information, can be found on the US Department of Education site at http:// bcol02.ed.gov/Programs/EROD/org_list.cfm?category _ID=SHE or by typing "State Higher Education Agencies" into a Google search box.

We call various state agencies fairly often. We have found that once we get through the voice mail, the basic answers are generally correct but often incomplete. A lot depends on who happens to answer the phone.

For instance, one time when we called Alabama to check on a dubious school operating there, we were told, "Oh, we've been trying to close them down for years. At least we got them to agree not to accept students from the state of Alabama." But on another call to the same office, we were told (by a different person), "The state of Alabama has no official position with regard to this school."

In another example, we called the proper California agency to ask about a school that we had heard had just lost its state approval. The helpful person on the phone confirmed this and gave us the exact date it had happened. But then we found out, a few days later, that the school had gone to court and secured a writ that prohibited the state from enforcing its decision until further hearings were held, and thus the school continued legitimately in business.

The inconsistency from state to state, the level of knowledge of state personnel, and the volatile situation with regard to many schools and many laws makes our job a harder one—and yours as well.

Reference books

The reference book we use the most is the *Higher Education Directory*, which lists every school with recognized accreditation, as well as all the recognized (by the Council for Higher Education Accreditation [CHEA] and the Department of Education), accreditors, the state agencies, and hundreds of higher education associations. A new edition comes out every October or November.

A list of all recognized accrediting agencies can be found on the website of the Council for Higher Education Accreditation, http://www.chea.org. A list of nearly three hundred unrecognized accrediting agencies can be found in chapter 15.

Developing Your Own Information

- *Hunches, intuition, and experience.* It may not easily be teachable, but we know with certainty that people who regularly check on educational claims develop a very strong sense of whether a school is likely to be good or bad, based on some combination of its name, location, the way it presents itself, the kind of address it has, and so on. It is not to be relied on as a sole reason for a decision, but it is an interesting and useful skill. Reviewing and becoming familiar with our list of ninety-two things degree mills often do and say is one good way to start.

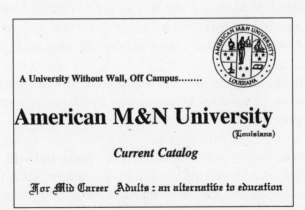

A University Without Wall, Off Campus........

American M&N University
(Louisiana)

Current Catalog

For Mid Career Adults : an alternative to education

We are especially fond of the inadvertent slogan of the fake American M&N University: "an alternative education."

- *Telephone the school.* If there is nothing but an answering machine during business hours, that is a clue. If a sleepy person answers when you phone at three in the morning their time, that is a clue.

- *Determine who owns or manages the website.* This can be a very rich source of information, especially when the information conflicts with information the school publishes about itself. Two reliable sources of ownership of URLs are http://www.betterwhois.com and http://www.whois.net.
- *Determine what is at the "campus" address.* While a visual inspection is nice, it is often not essential. Typing the complete street address into the Google search box very often provides information on whatever is at that address. If it is a mailbox service or "executive suite" service—or, in the case of one especially dreadful school, a Holiday Inn hotel—you know what you need. If the listing is for a university, it still can be anything from one shared room to a major campus. Google Earth® and Google Satellite View® are both very helpful in learning more about what is at a given address. Degree mill expert Steve Levicoff writes that local fire departments can be very helpful in telling what is to be found at a given address.
- *Use reverse telephone information.* Typing a telephone number, with area code, into a search engine will often produce the name or names of the school (or person or business) with that number. This is how we learned, for instance, that the Calgary College of Technology was actually a pizza parlor.

The search engine at Google.com works well for this, and sometimes the free site at http://www.reversetelephonedirectory.com or http://www.whitepages.com work even better.

- *Business information.* Most schools, good and bad, are incorporated, and incorporation is a public action, with information available, usually online, from each state's secretary of state or comparable office. Some states' corporate records can be searched by name of people as well as organizations, which is how we learned, for instance, that one of our favorite scoundrels was involved, either as an officer or a director, with a couple of "schools" we'd not heard of before.

CURRICULA OF THESES AND AWARDS

CALGARY COLLEGE OF TECHNOLOGY
Caisse Postale 5481
Chinook Ridge
Calgary, Alberta, Canada
T2H 0L0
Tel: (403) 242-0444

When one telephoned the Calgary College of Technology in Canada, the phone was answered, "Hello, Spiro's Pizza."

- *Consulting a "time machine."* The majority of things that were ever posted on the Internet, going back fifteen or more years, are probably still accessible, one way or another, and can provide valuable information about good and bad schools, and the people behind them. Most of this information is archived at the huge site (over 150 billion pages) called, appropriately, archive .org, where their "Wayback Machine" can show you many versions of a school's old websites.

- *Consulting old and diverse Internet forums.* Often we have learned things about people associated with degree mills by seeing what they may have posted on the Internet, not just on education forums and sites, but the full gamut of interests and activities, ranging from chess to travel to quasi-legal activities.

People and their postings, going back to the mid-1990s, can be found via a search in Google Groups®.

What If There Is No Information Whatsoever Available?

In the very unlikely but not impossible event that none of the eleven steps just described result in learning anything whatsoever about a given school, you may well be the first person ever who wishes to check it out. This sometimes happens. If it does, here are two suggestions.

1. Learn more (or try to) about the school

If you have already learned that the school is not known to the relevant accrediting agencies or state or national departments of education, that very likely is all that you need to know. However, if it is important to know more about who the school is and how it operates, here are some questions you may wish to ask. It is safe to suggest that no legitimate school would decline to respond to such questions.

- *How many students are currently enrolled?* Curiously, quite a few schools seem reluctant to reveal these numbers. Sometimes it is because they are embarrassed about how large they are, as, for instance, in the case of one less-than-wonderful school that at one time had more than three thousand students and a faculty of five! Sometimes it is because the school is embarrassed about how small it is, as is the case with one heavily advertised school that had impressive literature, extremely high tuition, and fewer than fifty students.
- *How many degrees have been awarded in the last year?* Some bad schools are embarrassed, either because there are so many (typically with few or no faculty), or so few.
- *What is the size of the faculty? How many of these faculty members are full-time and how many are part-time or adjunct? From which schools did the faculty members earn their degrees? From which school(s) did the president, the dean, and other administrators earn their own degrees?* There is nothing inherently wrong with faculty staff members

earning degrees from their own school, but when the number doing so is 25 percent or more, as is the case at some institutions, it starts sounding a little suspicious.

- *May I have the names and addresses of some recent graduates in my field of study and/or in my geographical area?* Most, but not all, legitimate schools will supply this information.
- *May I look at the work done by students?* Inspection of masters' theses and doctoral dissertations can often give a good idea of the quality of work expected and the caliber of the students. But you may either have to visit the school (not a bad idea) or offer to pay for making and sending copies.
- *Will your degree be acceptable for my intended needs (state licensing, certification, graduate school admission, salary advance, new job, whatever)?* This sort of information is often specific to the state or country where the student lives and/or the field of study.
- *What exactly is your legal status, with regard to state agencies and to accrediting associations?* If accreditation (or candidacy for accreditation) is claimed, is it with an agency that is approved either by the US Department of Education or the Council for Higher Education Accreditation? If not accredited, are there any plans to seek accreditation? Is the school listed in any major reference sources used by registrars and admissions?

No legitimate school should refuse to answer questions like these. Bear in mind, however, that alternative education does not require all the trappings of a traditional school. Legitimate schools may not have a big campus with spacious lawns, an extensive library, or a football team.

You definitely cannot go by the website, the catalog, or other school literature alone. Some really bad schools and some outrageous degree mills have hired good writers and designers and produced very attractive catalogs that are full of lies and misleading statements.

2. Ask us

One of the ways we learn about new degree mills and other dubious schools is when people ask us.

If you have failed to learn about a new school after doing appropriate due diligence, as just discussed, *including pursuing the matter on* http://www.degreeinfo.com and http://www.degreediscussion.com, then please let us know, and we'll do what we can. If you e-mail us, tell us what steps you have already taken to try to learn more. Write to us at mailto:info@degreemills.com.

HOW TO CHECK OUT A PERSON WITH A SUSPECTED DEGREE

There are many variables to consider in this situation. The flow chart below makes the various paths clear.

The first variable is whether you want people to know that you are checking up on them.

If it is all right that they know, then of course, you can simply ask them. If they don't answer or are evasive or reluctant, this is useful information.

We are aware of more than a few situations in which a person simply declines to answer your questions. When John Bear asked the president of the unaccredited Somerset University (and several other schools) the source of his PhD, he replied, "That's for me to know and you to find out."[3] So not all "refuse to say" situations refer to fake degrees; some might just be embarrassing.

There is an interesting subset of prominent politicians who have properly accredited doctorates yet seem reluctant to reveal this in public. Most of the public seemed unaware, for instance, that Newt Gingrich, Phil Gramm, George McGovern, Woodrow Wilson, and others had legitimately earned doctorates. Perhaps there is something to columnist Herb Caen's hypothesis that many people won't vote for someone they think may be smarter than they are.

FLOWCHART FOR CHECKING A DEGREE

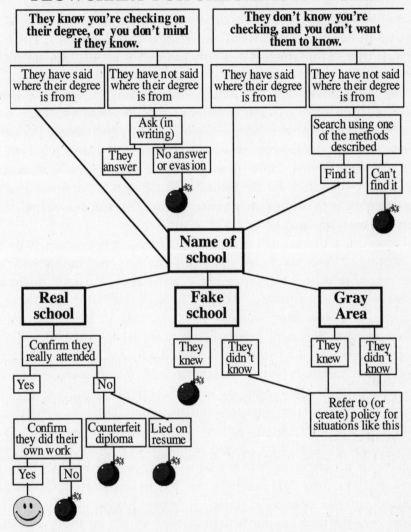

There is no simple way to find out where someone other than a well-known person earned her degree. A search of the Internet, or of the LexisNexis database of newspaper articles, may discover a news story or press release or governmental document that lists the school.

While the LexisNexis database is huge, it is also rather pricey. An excellent free alternative is the news search feature at http://news.google.com. The good news is that it searches millions of articles in nearly five thousand newspapers and magazines. The bad news is that at this time, it can only search for articles appearing in the past sixty days.

Another option is to use one of the relatively inexpensive document search services. For instance, http://www.knowx.com can search records of professional licensing, DEA registrations, Dun and Bradstreet reports, Experian business reports, and a large database of executive affiliations. There is no guarantee that degree sources will be given, but they could be. KnowX will tell you if the name you're checking on is in any of their sources, but then the actual information will cost between $5 and $10 in most cases.

In asking a person where he got his degree, it is prudent to do so in writing. There are more opportunities for miscommunication, intentional or otherwise, in speech. For instance, a person might be heard to say the legitimate "Western Reserve," when in fact there is a fake school run from Canada, also claiming to be in Cleveland called "Weston Reserve." Similarly, there are fakes called "Concoria" (not Concordia) and "Stamford" (not Stanford). And we read one report of someone replying "Southern Cal," which means "University of Southern California" to nearly everyone in that state, but which referred to the unaccredited but state-approved "Southern California University for Advanced Studies" in this instance.

Further in this vein, some people use initials intending to deceive. If a person in Arizona says a degree is from "ASU," it is assumed to be from Arizona State but may in fact be from the unrecognized American State University. An extreme case of deception by initials was the man in a medical profession whose business card said "John Smith, BA, MD." When authorities came for him, he explained that the listing really meant that he had earned his BA degree from the University of Maryland, the state whose official abbreviation is "MD."

Once the name of the school is known, from whatever method, the next step is to decide whether the school is real, fake, or in a gray area.

If it is either a degree-mill or a gray-area school, then the next question is whether the person knew or suspected it was fake.

If the school is legitimate, then the next step is to determine whether the person really attended and earned the degree(s) claimed.

Next, one may wish to get a copy of the transcript. Most registrars and many HR people will no longer accept a transcript that comes from the graduate. With technology ranging from white-out fluid and color copiers to complex computer programs, it is all too easy to modify or create a transcript. Most decision makers ask that the transcript be mailed directly from the registrar's office of the school.

Some fake transcript "services" (and there are many of them) are so sophisticated that they can reproduce most or all the forgery-preventing devices that are often used. Common ones are special-quality paper with a distinctive watermark, use of ostensibly noncopiable colors, a metallic strip embedded in the paper, use of microprinting (as on US currency), "secretly" embedded individual serial numbers, embedded holograms, and whatever new technology the transcript printers have come up with to try to defeat the forgers and have revealed only to their clients or, in some cases, to no one outside the company.

Other fake schools and counterfeiters *claim* to be using this high technology, and presumably charge extra for it, but in fact they don't.

It is common practice to save and file the envelope in which a transcript arrived, first to make sure it was postmarked in the city where the school is located and sometimes even to go as far as analyzing the postal meter indicia to learn if the serial number matches that of the meter actually used by the school. This also serves as proof that the US mails were used.

Inspect the diploma itself. This does not necessarily provide useful evidence, since there are so many "services" that sell counterfeit diplomas, and it is so easy for people to make changes in their own legal diplomas and then have them rephotographed or copied on a digital copier.

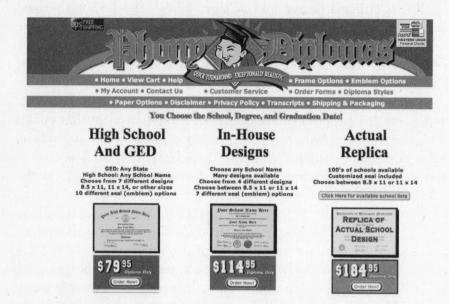

"Phony Diplomas" offers a cafeteria of choices: high school diplomas, degrees of their own design for $115, and authentic relicas for $185.

In one case, for instance, a man who had been practicing law in California for quite a few years turned out never to have gone to law school, but he did take the nice certificate he was given after doing a weekend workshop on the law for businesspeople, pasted on new wording giving himself a law degree, and had a good color copy made of the finished product.

Ask the school. Nearly all legitimate schools will give out what is called directory information, which can include name and degree awarded and year. But some don't even do that without permission of the student or the student's Social Security number or a letter explaining the reason for the request. Some need to know the year the degree was awarded in order to confirm whether a given person received one.

If there is no apparent record of the degree, there could be an issue of a name change, whether through marriage or another reason, or a computer or clerical error. Some schools have lost records through fires or war-related events. Hundreds of legitimate, properly accredited schools have gone out of business. In most cases, they will have deposited their alumni records with the state education agency or, in the case of religious schools, with another school run by the same church or religious order, but there are exceptions.

Finally, a reminder that no detection method is perfect, and there are scoundrels with great skill or great luck who break through the defenses. One such example is the staff physician at a prestigious university's campus hospital who had never been to medical school but had the same name as a distant relative who had a legitimate medical degree. He was able to secure an authentic diploma and have authentic transcripts sent to his employer. He got away with it for years, until an uncomfortable family member reported him.

WHAT (IF ANYTHING) TO DO WHEN YOU FIND A PERSON WITH A FAKE DEGREE

This is a very complex issue, with legal, interpersonal, psychological, and other ramifications. And it is generally beyond the scope of this book. People who work for, or have involvement with, an organization and discover a "time bomb" in that organization are often in a different situation from members of the general public, because they need to think about the welfare of the organization as well as the common good. At least two questions merit consideration:

- Is the person with the bogus degree a danger to others or society, such as a medical practitioner or therapist or a mechanical engineer?
- If so, is the danger immediate, because he or she is seeing clients or flying the plane or building the bridge right now?

Even when the common good does not appear to be a major factor, as with discovery of an accountant or a warehouse manager with a fake degree, there is still the factor that ensuing publicity could affect the employer's reputation and possibly, if a publicly traded company, its share value.

It is essential to be on very firm ground when making an accusation, to avoid recriminations or legal repercussions. Conduct a *thorough* investigation before making any public accusations. Some whistle-blowers have themselves been criticized or even attacked for meddling in something that was not their business.

Finally, many whistle-blowers are disappointed by the nature or lack of response from the employer of a person with a questionable degree or the news media. We have that feeling all too often. How can anyone fail to be concerned about a NASA scientist, an engineer at Three Mile Island, or a senior army officer with a fake degree? But it happens all too often. Discouraged, we march on.

PART 2

....

INFORMATION, OPINIONS, AND STORIES

....

Chapter 6

··

THE FBI'S OPERATION DIPSCAM

··

I n chapter 1, we described the formation of Operation DipScam, the FBI diploma-mill task force founded and run by Allen Ezell from 1980 through 1991, and the initial operation with Southeastern University. Here are descriptions of other major DipScam cases, presented in Allen Ezell's own voice, based on interviews conducted by John Bear.

After the Southeastern University case, the FBI office in Charlotte, North Carolina, learned of advertisements by the Johann Keppler School of Medicine. We consulted the AUSA (Assistant United States Attorneys), then initiated our investigation. Later on, as we learned of more and more diploma mills, we discussed the entire landscape with the AUSA and established investigative criteria. DipScam (Diploma Scam) began.

Once it had been named, DipScam started getting special attention: publicity, press releases, an article in *US News*, and a spot on the *CBS Evening News*. This was all orchestrated not from Washington but by my special agent in charge (SAC) in Charlotte. Initially, degree fraud was just a part of my normal white-collar crime work, which included bank fraud, embezzlement, bankruptcy fraud, and so on. But before too long, degree cases were occupying about 80 percent of my time, and other agents were brought in as well.

L. Mitchell Weinberg, the Medical Schools in the Briefcase

The fake Johan Keppler School of Medicine, mentioned above, was run by a man named L. Mitchell Weinberg. Weinberg claimed his medical school was in Zurich, Switzerland, but in reality he used various post office boxes in New York State and actually ran the school from his room at the Greystone Hotel in New York City. Wherever his briefcase was, there was the medical school.

In addition to medical degrees, Weinberg sold transcripts, wallet ID cards, memberships in his World International Medical Association (claimed to be in Panama), PhDs from the North American University of Canada, and certificates from the Arkansas Board of Natural Therapeutics and Northwest London University.

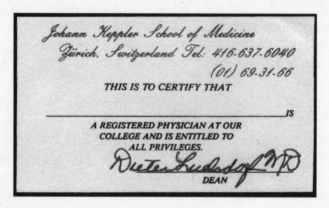

Johann Keppler School of Medicine
Zürich, Switzerland Tel: 416-637-6040
(01) 69-31-66

THIS IS TO CERTIFY THAT

_____IS

A REGISTERED PHYSICIAN AT OUR
COLLEGE AND IS ENTITLED TO
ALL PRIVILEGES.

DEAN

This fake medical school issued wallet identification cards so its graduates could secure hospital privileges and write prescriptions.

Weinberg also operated under the identity of Dieter Luelsdorf, effecting a fake German accent as an administrator of the Keppler School. When I came to realize that Weinberg and Luelsdorf were the same person—they had an identical stutter—I arranged to be on the phone with "Dieter" at the same moment another FBI agent went to Weinberg's room at the hotel. On the tape, you can hear Dieter talking to me in his fake German accent, then a knock at the door, and then Weinberg's normal voice explaining to the other FBI agent that there is no one else there.

Based on this and other information, we secured a search warrant and found diplomas, seals, and other evidence in his magic briefcase. Weinberg kept almost no records. While it was clear he had sold dozens of medical degrees at $1,900 each, most of his customers were unknown, probably even to him. One significant exception was a man running a clinic in Orange County, California, with his Keppler degree. His specialty was determining whether women were predisposed to getting cancer by doing cervical examinations.

Weinberg, who was also connected with "Bishop" George Lyon's fake United American Medical School, pleaded guilty and was given three years at the Federal Correctional Institution at Danbury, Connecticut.

Bishop George Cook Lyon, Thomas A. Edison College, United American Medical College, Palm Beach Psychotherapy Training Center

We got onto George Cook Lyon and his various activities as an offshoot of Weinberg and his fake medical school. Weinberg had also offered the degrees of Lyon's United American Medical College.

Before we got involved, Lyon had been convicted of running a degree mill in Florida, had been fined $10,000, and had spent about six weeks in jail. On his release, he headed for Arkansas, and we got in touch with him there.

Another agent and I each purchased degrees from Thomas A. Edison College. We told him we might be interested in doing business together, and we flew to Little Rock for a meeting.

As I came down the escalator at the airport, there at the bottom was this tiny little man, in his late seventies, no more than five-foot-two. He was wearing cowboy boots, black pants, a black shirt with a purple clerical collar, and a big silver cross on a silver chain under his white beard. He was wearing a huge amethyst ring that would have choked a horse. Looking past him, we saw a large dark green Rolls-Royce parked just outside the glass doors. We soon learned he also had a bright red Mercedes parked in his driveway in Benton, Arkansas.

It was my first and only ride in a Rolls-Royce, and on the way back to the airport after lunch, he hit us up for gas money, so we gave him a couple of bucks. It was a fun day. While visiting Lyon, I told him the MD degree that he had previously sold me, signed by Lawrence Weinberg, had been damaged in the mail. And so, in our presence, Lyon took out a blank United American Medical College diploma, forged Weinberg's name on it, and handed it to me. It was a great piece of evidence for court later.

UNITED AMERICAN MEDICAL COLLEGE

UNIVERSITY MEDICAL CENTER
POST OFFICE BOX 248   OAKVILLE, ONTARIO
CANADA L6J-5A2

TRANSCRIPT OF PERMANENT RECORD

LAST NAME   OTHO ALLEN EZELL, JR.

IDENTIFICATION NO.	BIRTHDATE	SEX
7076	8/24/41	Male

PRIOR DEGREES

DEGREE	SCHOOL	DATE
Ph.D.	TAEC	7/21/76
M.S.	"	7/21/73
B.S.	"	7/21/71

CODES
P   Pass
F   Fail
Cbt   Credit by Transfer
CbA   Credit by Audition
CbE   Credit by Examination

A total of 1840 (Resident) Hours are transferred on (UNITED AMERICAN MEDICAL COLLEGE) transcript from previous attained studies towards (Doctor of Medicine) Degree as follows:

PHASE I — Basic Science Subjects   CBT

I. Anatomy — includes gross anatomy, embryology, and histology. .... 640 Hrs.

II. Physiology — includes physiology of blood and lymph, circulation, respiration, excretion, digestion, metabolism, endocrine, special senses and nervous system. .... 320 Hrs.

III. Chemistry — Inorganic, Organic, Biochemistry and Nutrition — includes physical chemistry, chemistry of foods, digestion and metabolism. .... 320 Hrs.

IV. Pathology — includes General and Special Pathology. .... 180 Hrs.

V. Bacteriology — includes Parasitology and Serology. 320

VI. Hygiene and Sanitation and Public Health — includes sanitation and hygienic procedures and regulations and the prevention of disease. .... 60 Hrs.

TOTAL BASIC SCIENCE .... 1840 Hrs.

PHASE II — Clinical Subjects

I. Physical, Clinical, Laboratory and Differential Diagnosis. .... P

II. Gynecology, Obstetrics and Pediatrics. .... P

III. Roentgenology. .... P

IV. Geriatrics, Dermatology, Toxicology, Psychology, and Psychiatry. .... P

V. Jurisprudence, Ethics, and Economics. .... P

TOTAL CLINICAL	2080 Hrs.
Principles	880 Hrs.
Practice	1200 Hrs.
Required elective	80
TOTAL	4000 Hrs.

COMMENTS

Passed, qualifying Examination for the degree of DOCTOR OF MEDICINE.

M.D., Degree Awarded September 17, 1978.

All work Validated.

Honorable Dismissal Granted.

DEGREE(S) AWARDED

DOCTOR OF MEDICINE (M.D.)

E. M. Lindberg, M.D.

I certify that this is a true copy of the student's record. Not an official transcript without a signature and university seal.

Sept. 17, 1978

This is the transcript that accompanied the diploma granting Allen Ezell a Doctor of Medicine degree. The medical school was run from a suitcase in a New York hotel room.

After our undercover visit to Lyon's operation in Arkansas, we had probable cause for a search warrant. When we returned to execute the federal search warrant in the old church he'd bought in Benton, we found and took documents of Edison, the medical school, and thirty-eight other entities, sixteen of them his and the rest from other mills that he was representing.

Lyon was indicted on thirteen counts of mail and wire fraud. He was seventy-eight years old at the time. He entered a Rule 20 guilty plea, which meant he wouldn't have to go back to North Carolina, where the indictment was issued, but would appear before a federal judge in Little Rock. He did so, showing up in cowboy boots, red-and-white checkerboard pants, a red sports coat, and that big silver cross around his neck.

He told reporters, "I have not done anything illegal or improper at all. I never offered a diploma of Thomas A. Edison College. I call it entrapment. It is my word against the person who set me up."

The evidence suggested he had sold between three thousand and four thousand degrees at an average of $500 each, meaning total sales between $1.5 million and $2 million. He also sold State of Maryland medical licenses, which gave the holder permission to practice medicine and perform surgery.

At age seventy-nine, he was fined $2,000 and sentenced to a year in prison, which he served at Fort Worth, Texas. He was a feisty old guy, very sharp. At the end, he declared, "I am being persecuted. My background is without blemish. This is a dirty rotten deal, and I hope God takes care of me."

Alumni Arts, One of the Early Counterfeiters

The FBI received a letter from a concerned citizen about an advertisement in *Soldier of Fortune* magazine, offering a so-called lost diploma replacement service in Grants Pass, Oregon. The ad, which also had run in many other newspapers and magazines, read:

COLLEGE DIPLOMA—1 DAY

Has your diploma been lost or damaged? Most schools available.
Beautiful exacting reproductions including seals & colors. All
inquiries confidential. Color catalogue $3.

At the time the Alumni Arts Business in Oregon was closed by Operation Dip-Scam, they had an inventory of thousands of accurate blank diplomas from hundreds of real universities.

Alumni Arts (an address in Grants Pass, Oregon)

I ordered degrees in two names other than my own—one of the first times I had permission to do that—and as things turned out, I'm glad I did, since the perpetrator had a DipScam newspaper clipping, mentioning my name, tacked to his bulletin board. One diploma was from the University of North Carolina, which I felt would be of special interest to the North Carolina grand jury, where we would seek an indictment.

Based on information I had collected, I prepared an affidavit for a search warrant, flew to Oregon, at which time it was reviewed by the assistant US attorney. Then I appeared before the US Magistrate in Eugene, Oregon, who issued two search warrants, one for a private home and one for a commercial printer, both in Grants Pass, Oregon. The warrants specified exactly which documents could be taken.

It is important that multiple search warrants be executed simultaneously, and it is desirable to cooperate with local law enforcement. As I knocked on the door of an old Victorian house in a residential neighborhood—so residential there were actually goats grazing in the front yard—an FBI agent from Oregon was walking into the print shop. We were each accompanied by local deputy sheriffs.

The first thing you do on any search warrant is secure the premises. First, are there any firearms? Second, is anyone else present? Clearly this was a family home. There was a computer on the kitchen table, and hundreds of shrink-wrapped bundles from the printer lining the long hallway of the house: schools A through M down one side, N through Z up the other side. There was a light table, photonegatives, and various seals, ribbons, and lettering devices: all the paraphernalia needed by a counterfeiting service.

We ended up taking more than thirty-two thousand blank diplomas representing more than three hundred legitimate colleges and universities, including all of the "big names"—Harvard, Yale, Princeton, Stanford, and so on—as well as military credentials (Bronze Star, Air Medal, etc.), and certificates for the American Society of Clinical Pathologists. Some, but not all, of the diplomas had a line of tiny print at the very bottom edge, reading, "No degree status is granted or implied."

From the man's computer records, we found evidence of 2,311 clients, so he had major growth plans based on those thirty-two thousand blanks.

The perpetrator, in his late thirties, had no prior record. He was indicted by a grand jury in August 1984, pleaded guilty in December, and was sentenced in February 1985 to five years of probation and 120 hours of community service. Local publicity for the case had caused considerable humiliation to the man's wife and children. To the best of our knowledge, he never engaged in crime again. He later declined an offer to testify before Congressman Pepper's subcommittee.

What kind of a man was he? We had occasion to talk over coffee when I returned to Oregon to oversee destruction of all the confiscated goods. He seemed a very likeable sort of guy. Printing diplomas was simply his job; it was what he did. He'd found a niche, and felt, as illogical as it sounds, that he was filling a need and doing no harm.

His wife, who surely knew what was going on, was never charged, nor was the printer who clearly should have paid closer attention to the things he was being paid to print.

The one interesting "loose end" here is where this man got the originals of the diplomas he copied. At the time, we simply didn't know. The perpetrator talked about picking things up at yard and estate sales and getting them from "some guy in California," whom we could not identify at the time. As it happened, new evidence came to light in 2004, and now the source is known but unlikely ever to be prosecuted.

American National University

A California chiropractor named Clarence Franklin, also using the name John Caraway, operated the fake school of this name, advertising regularly in *Psychology Today*, *Popular Science*, and other publications. Accreditation was claimed from the National Accreditation Association, incorporated in Maryland by Franklin. Degrees were sold for $2,000 and up, including $2,495 for a combined master's and doctorate.

I answered one of the ads and applied for an MBA. I was asked to write a twenty-page paper, but when I said I didn't have time, I was told that a job description would do. I sort of left out the fact that I was with the FBI. I also ordered a class ring from the university's "jewelry department," which turned out to be the office of a fake degree broker in Miami, Stan Simmons, who represented American National and three other phonies, including American International University, run by Edward Reddeck, where Franklin had once worked. (Simmons would surface twenty-five years later, operating a fake high school that provided diplomas to high school athletes whose real grades were not high enough to allow the students admission into college.) Within two weeks, I received my MBA diploma and my class ring. I paid a friendly visit to the office in Phoenix, saying I was on a business trip and wanted to have a look at "my" alma mater. I was given a tour of the offices and invited to attend the graduation ceremony later that month.

Back in North Carolina, I prepared three search warrant affidavits, for American National, North American University, and their broker Stanley Simmons's "Off-Campus University Programs" business in Miami.

When I showed up in Phoenix, now as an FBI special agent, with a search warrant and a truck, the office manager wistfully said, "I guess you're not coming back for the graduation ceremony next week."

Following their indictment, Franklin and Simmons each pleaded guilty to one count of mail fraud. Simmons went to prison, in part because of his involvements with other schools; Franklin received a suspended sentence and did not go to prison.

Anthony Geruntino, American Western University, Southwestern University, and Others

I responded to an advertisement run by Vocational Guidance Services of Columbus, Ohio, which offered to find the perfect school for me, based on a questionnaire I filled out. When I sent in the questionnaire, they replied that because of my "unique situation and credentials, I have taken the opportunity of contacting American Western University, in Tulsa, Oklahoma, and have been advised that you already have the qualification for the MBA degree."

I purchased the MBA for $485, $25 for a transcript (I earned straight As), and $97.50 for a class ring. Almost immediately after this, I received an unsolicited offer from Southwestern University in Tucson, Arizona, and purchased a master's in business management and two transcripts.

I then contacted proprietor Anthony Geruntino in Columbus, telling him I was an accountant with interest in this business, and could I stop by when I was next in the area. He took me on a tour of the operation, and then he offered me a job helping him find clients. "Don't look at this as a job," he said, "but as a way to get rich." He told me I would make $100,000 in my first year. So that is what I put in my affidavits for search warrants for the premises in Ohio and Arizona. When I walked into the "university" in Tucson with several other FBI agents and a search warrant in hand, Tony was there. "I thought you were too good to be true," he sighed.

We had an immense amount of data to review—a fourteen-foot truck full. Two staff members took months to put all the "student" records into a database so that we could ask FBI agents all over the country to interview Geruntino's clients, focusing on federal employees and others in the public sector, such as school principals. There were people with the Federal Bureau of Prisons, the Department of Justice, the Joint Chiefs of Staff, an Undersecretary of State, and so on. We were building what is called a prosecutive case to take to a federal grand jury. We found clear evidence of twenty-two hundred people who bought degrees, with revenues of $1.8 million.

While study of his materials was going on, Geruntino had not yet been charged with anything. However, because of Arizona's new laws governing private postsecondary institutions, he moved his operation to St. George, Utah. He advertised that he would be transforming Utah in general and St. George in particular into a major worldwide educational center.

Many people in St. George seemed enthusiastic about Tony's plans. But some people had concerns about this man, and so a well-attended public hearing was held to discuss issuing the business license for which he had applied. People spoke for and against him. When the hearing was over, he stepped outside and was arrested based on a thirty-one-count indictment handed down earlier that day by a federal grand jury. He was taken to the local jail and the next day was taken before the US Magistrate at Salt Lake City. He made bond and was released from jail.

After he entered a guilty plea in US District Court, Western District of North Carolina, in Charlotte, but *before* he was interviewed and sentenced, he moved Southwestern University from St. George to the address of an answering service in Salt Lake City. He actually put on a graduation ceremony in Salt Lake City.

Geruntino was fined $5,000 and sentenced to five years in prison. We were on pretty good terms with him. He respected what we did and saw why we did it. While in prison, he testified in a forth-right and repentant manner before Congressman Pepper's hearings on degree fraud. A couple of years after his release, he declined a newspaper request for an interview and has been working quietly in Ohio ever since.

Edward Reddeck, American International University, North American University, Dallas State University, and Others

American International was one of the fraudulent activities of a man who appears over and over in the world of fake schools and degrees, Edward Reddeck, also known as John Palmer, John Polmar, and many other names. Reddeck has been imprisoned at least three times for his various fakes. His affiliations include North American University (Utah), the University of North America (Missouri) and Coast University and Gold Coast University (Hawaii), Dallas State University, the Global Church of God, the International Accredita-tion Association, Success International, and the American Freedom Foundation. He also worked with degree-mill agent Stanley Simmons in Florida.

I interviewed Reddeck in 1983 when he was in Terminal Island Federal Correctional Institution following his conviction for selling the fake degrees of Dallas State University. He called himself the "grandfather of nontraditional education in America" and said that he could be a huge asset to the FBI in identifying fake schools, but his "fee" would be having all the perceived "wrongs" done to him by the United States government taken care of.

Later, he was indicted by a federal grand jury in Utah for North American University: mail fraud, fictitious name abuse, money laun-dering, forfeiture, and aiding and abetting. He claimed, among other things, that it was all a government frame-up.

After his conviction and imprisonment, he filed a lengthy ram-bling suit against John Bear, me, and state officials in Washington and Utah, asking for $1.5 billion (with a *b*). Another suit was filed against the Attorney General of Missouri, citing a "rain [*sic*] of terror" against him.

Reddeck is out of prison again, following his Gold Coast and Coast University convictions, still writing long angry letters, filing *pro se* law suits, and I wouldn't be surprised to learn that he is running yet another so-called school.

Some degree sellers, like Geruntino, Jarrette, and Bishop Lyon, were likable enough, with just a touch of class, but there is nothing charming about Reddeck. He is an angry, hostile man, a con man with no class, all rough edges.

Doc Caffey, National College of Arts and Sciences, Northwestern College of Allied Science, American Western University, South Union Graduate School, Northwestern College of Allied Science, and Others

In 1980, a social studies teacher from New York knocked on the door of the National College of Arts and Sciences in Springfield, Missouri. He was there because of a concern he had about the National College degree being used by his school superintendent. The door was opened by a man in a bathrobe: the Right Reverend Dr. James Robert Caffey, the founder and president of all the above-named institutions.

Caffey first learned about the world of fake schools and degrees while in prison. As one newspaper article at the time put it, "His fondness for cocaine and other people's property earned him several years in the Missouri State Penitentiary at Jefferson City."

In prison, he served as editor of the prison paper, the *Jefftown Journal*. When he got out, he headed for Tulsa, where he opened three diploma mills, and he opened five more in Missouri.

Before Caffey was indicted, convicted (along with Geruntino and others), and sent back to prison for five years, he sold a National College degree to a man named Wiley Gordon Bennett, who was soon to go into the degree-mill business himself.

Wiley Gordon Bennett, Sands University and Great Lakes University

Bennett used a mailing service in Yuma, Arizona, for his fake schools, but everything was run from his Consulting Specialists Inc. business in Memphis. His literature all had the slogan, "Knowledge Today is Success Tomorrow." Degrees, including the PhD, were offered in eighty-one listed subjects, and if you didn't like those, the literature said that he would "be happy to grant the PhD in any subject you want," and with any date.

I bought a Master of Education degree from his Great Lakes University, and two months later, an MBA from Sands University which cost $580. When we got a warrant and searched his premises, we found evidence of 527 customers. He kept meticulous records. The federal grand jury returned an indictment on eleven counts of mail fraud and wire fraud, and an arrest warrant was issued.

When Bennett learned of the warrant, he checked himself into the psychiatric ward of the Veterans' Administration hospital in Long Beach, California, but since he had done this voluntarily, we were able to arrest him there. Like so many of the others, he never resurfaced after this episode was over. He was a pleasant enough fellow.

Roosevelt, DePaul, Northwest London, and Metropolitan Collegiate: The Crook Who Stole from Other Crooks

In 1983, a man in South Carolina, who happened to be the brother-in-law of the local police chief, copied some pages from the literature of other degree mills and started selling them as his own, operating under the name "External Study Program."

He must have had problems keeping things straight, because when I ordered my degree from Roosevelt University, the diploma I actually received was from Northwest London University.

His lawyer claimed that these $940 diplomas were just an expensive novelty and that his buyers knew just what they were doing, which somehow made it all right. He was indicted on six counts of mail fraud; pleaded guilty to one count of title 18, section 1341; and was sentenced to three years' probation and restitution of $1,700 to the US government.

The Fowler Family, Roosevelt, Cromwell, Lafayette, DePaul, John Quincy Adams, Dallas State, Loyola, Southern California University, and Others

The Fowler family, operating from Chicago and Los Angeles, ran one of the more complex and far-flung degree-mill empires and ended up in the only full-fledged courtroom battle of the DipScam era. Brothers Norman, Arnold, and Randall Fowler; their mother; their sister; and her husband operated all of the above-named degree mills, along with three fake accrediting agencies, using a wide range of addresses in England, France, the Netherlands, Belgium, Germany, and the United States.

Both the FBI and postal inspectors responded to several advertisements placed by "External Degree Program" and purchased degrees from this operation. Later, members of the Chicago police department, in an unrelated criminal investigation, searched the apartment of Arnold Fowler, and in his safe they found evidence of the sale of degrees, which they turned over to us.

The Fowlers had been operating for up to twenty years, taking in millions of dollars. Selling degrees was the family business. They had annual family gatherings, where they would each brag about how well their various "branches" were doing.

The FBI worked with the postal inspectors on this case, each agency buying a variety of degrees in business, law, music, and pulmonary physiology. This was one of the few cases where the phonies had no office, no telephone, and not even a claimed faculty.

We didn't ask for a federal search warrant because we had no place to search in the United States for which we had sufficient possible cause, so we took possession of no records. Even if records had existed, they might have been at any number of locations, in and outside the United States. So we did everything through the "backdoor" approach, rebuilding business records through study of bank evidence.

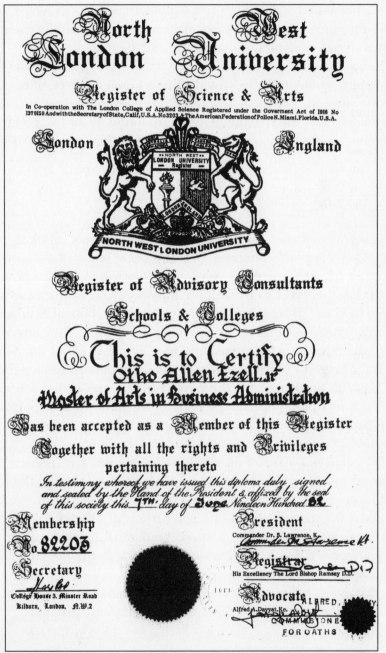

The Fowler brothers of Chicago and Los Angeles made millions with one crude and simple school catalog, changing the name of the school every few years.

We presented our findings to a federal grand jury, which returned a twenty-nine-count indictment against the seven family members on mail fraud, conspiracy, and aiding and abetting.

Following quite a complex ten-day trial, with 110 witnesses from the banks, mailing services, and others (John Bear testified as an expert witness), the judge dismissed all charges against two lesser defendants, and the remaining five were found guilty by the jury on all counts and sentenced to prison terms ranging from two to seven years.

Rabbinical Academy of America

We generally stayed away from religious schools, sticking with "middle-of-the-road" phonies, but this one really wasn't even a school at all, just a service. Several people from a congregation in North Carolina came to us with the message "Our cantor is a ringer; please help us." His credential was from the Rabbinical Academy of America (RAA), ostensibly in Brooklyn, New York. They advertised regularly in the Jerusalem Post and in a New York Hebrew paper.

We asked an FBI agent who was fluent in Hebrew to give them a call, and he negotiated for the purchase of a credential. After submitting a one-page paper and a copy of his junior-high report cards from Israel, he received his ordination as a rabbi by return mail. FBI agents visited the RAA in New York.

We retrieved a list of all their graduates and sent them a form letter asking what work they did for their degree or ordination, how long it took, how much it cost, and how it had been used. We were flooded with letters and phone calls from all over the world, the great majority of them from these graduates' lawyers. When the academy closed down, the decision was made not to pursue matters any further.

Of course, when people used a religious shell to hide a diploma mill, as in the case of LaSalle, that was a different matter.

John Jacob Gordon, the Presidential Candidate

This was a meat-and-potatoes case. The man, who claimed to be a candidate for president of the United States, was wanted for wire fraud for unrelated issues and had tried to run over an IRS agent, and now his picture was hanging in the post office. When we learned that he was helping support his life as a federal fugitive by selling degrees, we reached out to him. He'd always call collect. When he phoned me to sell me a degree, it was from a pay phone in New England. We sent an FBI agent to drive twenty miles in each direction from that phone booth, hitting every motel. At the last motel in the twentieth mile, the desk clerk looked at the picture and said, "Room Fifteen." Gordon pleaded guilty, but then he claimed that he had been kidnapped by Russians and was a political prisoner. He had bumper stickers made that said "Free Jake Gordon."

Because of jail overcrowding, Gordon was held in jail in Rutherfordton, North Carolina, a town of fewer than five thousand people. The matter was heard by Judge Woodrow Wilson Jones in Rutherfordton. Gordon had an observer monitoring his court proceedings and announced he had found judicial misconduct and prosecutorial fraud. Gordon held a press conference on the courthouse steps, where he announced that he liked this area so much that he was going to return and live in Rutherfordton when released from federal prison. Judge Jones was not amused.

Lynetta Gail Williams, Elysion College

Ms. Williams was one of the few women to run a fake school. She apparently inherited her degree mill from her father, Lane Williams, who had operated Elysion and Williams College from Arizona, Idaho, and other locations. Elysion degrees were being sold through a mail drop a few blocks from her apartment in San Francisco.

We didn't make a buy, but Williams was served with a federal grand jury subpoena to produce all the Elysion records. In the apartment house, tenants put their trash into a large cabinet that the manager emptied. The manager called the FBI and said, "You fellows might want to come back." He noted that Williams had deposited twenty large bags of trash in this cabinet right after the subpoena was served.

He surrendered the trash, the courts having ruled that garbage no longer belongs to a person once she has put it in the trash. Pursuant to a federal grand jury subpoena, Williams called the FBI and surrendered all the Elysion records—about twelve pages. But we already had twenty bags of college records. Following our analysis of the Elysion material, Williams was indicted on the charge of obstruction of justice. She pleaded guilty to this charge and got a suspended sentence, since there was no evidence she was selling degrees but only tidying up after her late father. Yet twenty bags of trash suggest that a fairly sizeable business had been in operation.

James Kirk/Thomas McPherson/Thomas Kirk/James McPherson, LaSalle University, Southland University, and International University

We first encountered James Kirk as a graduate of Southeastern University, since he had traded a degree from the University of San Gabriel Valley with Dr. Alfred Jarrette (mentioned in chapter 1) for a Southeastern degree.

By the time we turned our attention to Kirk, he had incorporated Southland University in Louisiana in 1979 under the auspices of the Trinitarian Church. He had been working at the University of San Gabriel Valley in California, which he left, along with its president's wife, and opened Southland University of California in Pasadena in 1980, as a state-authorized school. We were unable to purchase a degree from Southland. We executed a search warrant in 1983, but while we found some irregularities, including claimed faculty members who said they had never worked there, we didn't have enough for the grand jury at that time. At the time, Southland qualified to have its students take the bar exam in California, the last remaining state that permits students from unaccredited law schools to take the bar exam.

After our visit, Kirk moved Southland University to Arizona, along with a fake accrediting agency, the Arizona Commission of

Non-Traditional Private Postsecondary Accreditation. The *Arizona Republic* newspaper exposed that activity promptly. Then we received information that Kirk was setting up shop in Florida. We immediately notified Florida authorities, and they didn't even last a week there. Around the same time, Kirk's wife and mother were incorporating International University in Louisiana.

When Arizona invited him to move on, Kirk opened up in a St. Louis suburb shortly after. By then, both he and his school had a new name. He was Thomas McPherson, and the school was LaSalle University. Following certain activity in the Missouri state capital, LaSalle closed in Missouri suddenly one Friday and opened in Louisiana the following week.

Kirk's schools generally had an affiliation with a church of his devising: first the Trinitarian Church, and then the World Christian Church. When the state of Louisiana questioned the legitimacy of the World Christian Church, Kirk/McPherson built a chapel on his land in Louisiana and scheduled some services.

Later, I was happy to be able to cooperate with FBI agents in New Orleans in supplying information that they could use in requesting a search warrant for LaSalle. In addition to the "usual" charges of mail fraud, wire fraud, aiding and abetting, and conspiracy, the New Orleans agents added two new statutes: money laundering and forfeiture, which meant the government could keep the $10 million plus discovered in executing the search warrants, until the case was resolved.

Kirk professed his innocence, claiming the ruthless government was attacking his little church school. He made this claim in a full-page $70,000 advertisement in *USA Today*. But following an eighteen-count indictment by a federal grand jury, Kirk pleaded guilty to one count. Part of the agreement was that Kirk's partner, Stanley Foster, plead guilty to obstruction of justice and tax evasion.

The judge seemed irritated by the agreement and gave Kirk the maximum sentence possible for the one count, five years. Kirk went to the federal prison camp in Beaumont, Texas, and within weeks, literature of the brand-new Edison University, with Kirk's wife as registrar, was being mailed from Beaumont, Texas. (Following complaints from the real Edison in New Jersey, the name was changed to Addison and then Acton.)

Acton University came on the scene just after LaSalle University's James Kirk was sent to federal prison in Beaumont, Texas. While the "university" used a mailbox in Hawaii, it did not require major detective work to determine that Kirk was running Acton from his prison cell.

Kirk served four years. Since his release, he has had involvements with several unaccredited universities in Louisiana and Mississippi.

LaSalle was allowed to continue in business as long as there were new directors unaffiliated with the World Christian Church. It operated legally for a short while, changed its name to Orion College, then closed for good.

Because of the many millions of dollars recovered, the US Attorney's office wrote to all LaSalle students and alumni, offering them the opportunity for a refund of their payments. They had to surrender their LaSalle diploma to get the refund. A large number of people chose to keep the diploma and, presumably, continue using the degree.

Bruce Copen, Sussex College of Technology, Brantridge University, and University of the Science of Man

Sussex was one of the longest-surviving British degree mills. We thought we should give it a try, since people in the United States were using these degrees on their resumes, and Sussex/Brantridge had used mail drops in both Louisiana and Hawaii.

We had no jurisdiction in England, of course, so the odds of getting prosecution were very low, especially since British authorities were well aware of what was going on there and had done nothing. Still, we felt it would at least be good to have a file on them, to make things easier when their degrees came up in other cases. This is just what happened in the case of the fake medical doctor, Gregory Caplinger, who claimed several of his seven doctorates from Sussex.

I sent Bruce Copen my enrollment form, a cashier's check for $372, a five-page paper I'd written for another purpose on the psychology of the embezzler, and a resume of sorts. I must have fallen short of his high expectations because when I got my degree and my transcript nineteen days later, it showed that I'd gotten four Bs along with my fourteen As.

University Novelty and Engraving Company

One of the last DipScam cases was one of the few disappointing ones. Knowing I was being transferred from Charlotte to Tampa, I entered into communication with this Tampa-based company, which sold counterfeit diplomas. I bought a University of South Florida degree, a BS in elementary education, and another agent bought a University of Florida degree in electrical engineering. I thought that subjects relating to teaching children and possibly working at a nuclear power plant would get the attention of a grand jury and judge.

I obtained a federal search warrant and executed it with the assistance of a postal inspector. We took everything, including the proprietor's outgoing mail, which the FBI can't touch, but a postal inspector can. The woman in charge had been selling degrees for at least eight years and had many, many customers. Hers was the first operation where we found a lot of metal seals with the names of major universities for making imprinted gold seals.

But when we looked at her customer lists and conducted some interviews, we didn't find the clear cases of harm to society that we had elsewhere: the teachers and the government employees. Bottom line: even though we'd made our buys and had plenty of evidence, the US Attorney's office declined to prosecute the case. Still, she was, in effect, put out of business, and as far as I know, she's never done this sort of thing again.

There were other DipScam cases, but that covers many of the highlights.

Chapter 7

···

THREE CASE HISTORIES

···

Here we will look in depth at three major degree-mill opera-tions that have flourished in recent years. They are very dif-ferent from each other, yet they all have the end result of selling degrees of all kinds to the public.

The first case is an amazing story of hijacking an entire country to sell degrees. The second is the biggest degree mill ever, run by an American in Europe, at one time taking in a million dollars a week. And the third, apparently run by a disgraced politician from his prison cell, is still going strong, but the FBI is working to try to put a stop to it.

A. THE ST. REGIS UNIVERSITY SAGA

During the years 2001 to 2011, a most extraordinary drama played out in the world of degree mills. The cast of characters included eight criminals from the state of Washington, including a child pornog-raphy collector, some high-level Liberian diplomats, the US Secret Service, a fictitious Middle Eastern bomb expert, and a University of Illinois professor of physics named George Gollin.

Dr. Gollin used the term of a Guggenheim Fellowship to write a book about, as he describes it, "the nine-year trajectory and spec-tacular immolation of St. Regis, and the resulting increase in inter-national attention to the problem of diploma mills."

We invited Dr. Gollin to write an overview and summary of the St. Regis saga for our book, and we were quite overwhelmed by his generosity in providing a very long and, we felt, well-written and grip-

173

ping account of some aspects of the story. We decide to include all of it but have rendered it a bit less scholarly by removing his long explanatory footnotes, which thoroughly document every statement he makes. They are likely to reappear with the entire story in his forthcoming book with the working title "A Dream of Serpents: How a Physics Professor and a Law Enforcement Task Force Buried Saint Regis."

BURNING ST. REGIS
George Gollin
Professor of Physics, University of Illinois
© 2011 George D. Gollin

Introduction

They gathered an hour after sunrise in a meadow north of Spokane, some in ballistic vests labeled USSS, CID, IRS; others in jackets with the more obvious "U.S. Secret Service," "Sheriff," "U.S. Marshal," and "Police." They carried guns and handcuffs, had sledgehammers in their cars, and knew the fastest routes to an emergency room. These agents, along with five other teams at rally points near targets in Washington and Idaho, waited for the "go" signal that would come after the seventh team called in from Arizona.

Richard Novak was the bagman for the woman who bought Africans. He had invited a business associate, the owner of a university that would never exist, to come to his home near Phoenix to finalize the details of an upcoming trip to Monrovia. Novak would travel there in the company of a corrupt Liberian diplomat to negotiate the purchase of government recognition for the fictitious school. He was confident of success, having already bought his way into Liberia's Ministries of Education and Justice.

But Novak's associate was the leader of the seventh team, a United States Secret Service agent working undercover who brought a search warrant, rather than a cashier's check to their meeting. He was part of the task force that would seize the business records and web servers of the network of bogus universities, fake government agencies, and supporting infrastructure that surrounded "St. Regis University." In 2005, three years after Novak paid the first bribe to a Liberian diplomat and two years after his employers came after me, the Department of Justice rolled up the criminal organization that had sold ten thousand degrees to customers in a hundred countries, earning Dixie and Steve Randock, the couple who owned St. Regis, millions of dollars.

The Randocks sold diplomas and transcripts from offices near Spokane to anyone with an internet connection and a credit card. By shoveling money into Liberia, even before the end of its horrific civil war, they were allowed to pretend that St. Regis was based in Monrovia. At a time when the country's life expectancy was 39 years and a seventh of its children died in infancy, the Randocks controlled significant portions of Liberia's diplomatic corps and Ministry of Education.

On the day of the searches I was with my students in a beamline at the Fermi National Accelerator Laboratory, west of Chicago. I knew the raids had been scheduled—I had been working with the investigation for a year—and was too keyed up to concentrate. A rifle had been seen on the front porch of the Randocks' house, and the agents executing the warrants would be armed. So I waited for a call from John Neirinckx, the lead agent.

In 2002, when Richard Novak first knocked on the door of the Liberian Embassy, I was living quietly as a physics professor at the University of Illinois, teaching undergraduates and doing research in elementary particle physics. I knew nothing about diploma mills and never dreamed that they would sell degrees in any field the customer requested, even medicine and nuclear engineering. But then our computers became the targets of an insistent barrage of spam from the "University Degree Program." My office computer, the computers in my lab, and the ones in the physics department's classrooms all began receiving disruptive messages about "diplomas from prestigious non-accredited universities" whose "bachelor's, master's, MBA, and doctorate (PhD) diplomas" would be delivered "within days."

I could have blocked the ads by turning off the machines' alert message software, but it irked me that I might be driven by obnoxious spammers to reconfigure the tools I used every day. So I called the number in one of the ads, hoping to yell at whoever answered the phone.

Our lives can pivot around the smallest of decisions! If I had disabled the message utility I would have had a small story, forgotten by now, to tell friends at end-of-semester parties. But the phone call led to further investigation and then to a brawl with St. Regis that lasted five years. The threads of the story run through a dozen states, Washington DC, Paris, India, Ghana, and Liberia. There are heroes in the Secret Service, the Department of Justice, and the Society of Jesus, a smart federal prosecutor, and villains in a house full of guns. There are investigative reporters, offshore bank accounts, and payments to foreign officials, as well as internet servers stocked with fake universities and child pornography. The story ends in the archipelago of federal prisons in California.

In a single chapter I can only describe a small fraction of what happened. I won't tell you about the guns or the hand grenade, or Amy's monkey, or the fake doctor who murdered his patients to inherit their assets. I'll leave out how Allen Ezell and I were muzzled by a U.S. senator's office, and how a conference committee gutted anti-degree mill federal legislation. I won't write about the scoundrel who sold medical degrees and sued me, blaming me for the breakup of his marriage. Also missing will be the mid-engine Porsche, the stolen property bust, the meth bust, the post-taser car chase, and incineration of Dixie's Cadillac. I won't describe "Shower Girl" cavorting with an equally naked friend, or the "Syrian" bomb maker, or the eleven boxes grabbed by federal agents one night. And I won't tell you about the outlandish insurance claim for those boxes (which were filled with incriminating material), or the Society of Jesus, or perjury, or the land mine in a detective's testimony that blew the legs off a lying witness. We won't go to Bangalore, where the police roughed up a St. Regis salesman, or to Athens, where a vitriolic St. Regis "Dean of the School of Behavioral Sciences" ranted about child abuse, while thousands of child pornography images were cached in the servers that hosted the Randocks' diploma mill websites. I'll leave out the inability of Congressional committees to act on their intentions to destroy the diploma mill industry, even after listening to stark testimony during hearings.

The heroes of the piece are the law enforcement officers who stormed the house full of guns, and the gifted prosecutor who defeated eight defense attorneys in the most complex case his office had ever undertaken. But there is just too much material in all of this for a single chapter and I will say almost nothing about them, either.

What is here is taken in bits and pieces from a book about the St. Regis affair that I am finishing. I've selected material about the Randocks' invention of "St. Regis University," their hijacking of portions of the Liberian government, and the events that led to the multi-agency criminal investigation that brought them down. Even with this narrowed focus, I am leaving out significant parts of the story, such as the fake Liberian charter that said St. Regis would use the internet years before it existed.

The story of the investigation, the investigators, and the attorneys who buried St. Regis fills half my book, and is the part that I like best. Alas, almost none of it is in this chapter. Even so, the course of events that I have chosen to include continues to astonish me.

The Invention of St. Regis

Dixie Randock opened the "A Plus Institute" real estate training school in 1994 or 1995. It did so well that by February 2001 courses were available for realtors in Washington, Nevada, and Oregon, and the number of branch schools had grown to 75.

By 1998 the Randocks were using the internet for commercial purposes, promoting the services of the A+ Real Estate Institute through a web site and soliciting students and new staff through internet news groups such as alt.real-estate-agents. But they also ran a degree business, and used the newsgroups to post hundreds of announcements with subjects like "LEGITIMATE DEGREES for skills you have already learned in life." Many of the messages asked readers to visit the web site http://www.advancedu.org.

The Randocks used AdvancedU.org to sell degrees. Created in March 1999, five months after the internet domain for their real estate school, it was the first of their many web sites invented for this purpose. It advertised degrees from "Holy Acclaim University" and the "A+ Technical Institute," telling prospective buyers "No classroom attendance necessary!" Degrees were awarded in recognition of a customer's prior learning: "Our Peer Advisory can evaluate and match your life experience with traditional college curriculums to provide you a wide variety of 100 percent verifiable degrees, certifications, credentials, designations and awards for 'self-made' and 'self-taught' experts in all fields."

At first the Randocks claimed that they were not really issuing university degrees, but something else through a strange process the Randocks called "academic peer evaluation":

> The Academic Peer Advisory and the Academic Peer Evaluation Process IS NOT and DOES NOT CLAIM TO BE CONNECTED OR AFFILIATED WITH ANY UNIVERSITY or other SCHOOL. . . . If your background information qualifies you for an Academic Peer Degree, you are entitled to select or create a name to identify your Peer Advisory in your documents. . . . You may use words including "college," "university," "academy," etc., not as nouns, but as the lexis in the descriptive name that you select for your Academic Peer Advisory. The name you select will become the title of your Academic Peer Advisory. It is NOT a school.

Dixie performed the "peer evaluations" herself. Though she had not graduated from high school, she would issue "life experience degrees" at all levels in subjects such as engineering and education.

Since Holy Acclaim University was not really a university, it would not need a campus, faculty, programs of instruction, or accreditation. But even in the absence of courses, the Randocks would sell transcripts:

> . . . you will receive transcripts for each degree, showing courses that correspond to your experience as though you attended the traditional classroom setting. The transcripts show a traditional curriculum of courses that are the equivalent of the skills you have acquired as though you attended. There is no mention of "equivalency." The dates and grades and grade point average will appear.

The Randocks generated a transcript by doing an internet "search to determine the course work necessary to obtain such a degree legitimately . . . [then] "cutting and pasting" the courses [so] identified. . . ."

AdvancedU began attracting customers from all over the world. The very first client arrived from Scotland a week after the site opened. He spent $1,400 for BS, MS, and PhD degrees in computer science, backdated to 1993, 1997, and 1999, and later purchased a "Full Professor" certificate for $500. His PhD from Holy Acclaim University bore in fine print the disclaimer ". . . knowledge and proficiency has been demonstrated by completing and satisfying all requirements of the Evaluation & Endorsement Peers and the Advisory Chair and Directors." The diploma was signed "Stephen Frendock, D.D., Endorsement Advisory Chair." "Frendock" was the Randock family name before Steve's father changed it "to avoid discrimination earlier in the last century."

The Randocks' degree business was not much more than a cottage industry in 1999. They only attracted about a dozen customers that year and probably earned less than ten or twenty thousand dollars selling diplomas and transcripts.

Documents were created with Microsoft Word on a computer registered to Century 21 Randock, then printed by a staffer in the basement of the A+ Institute. In correspondence with customers they would describe their business as the "Advanced Education Institute Trust" with its "Evaluation & Endorsement Office" at the Mead, Washington, address also used by the A+ Institute.

AdvancedU enlarged its stable of non-universities in 2000, adding "Concordia Graduate Institute," "Audentes Technical Academy," "Cathedra Institute," "Primus Postgraduate College," "Valorem Academy," "Holmes University," and others. Dixie retooled the AdvancedU home page, rebuilding it with a more polished layout. By July the Randocks were using a mail drop in Coeur d'Alene for some (but not all) of their diploma mill correspondence, putting the Washington-Idaho border between the A+ Real Estate Institute and their growing flotilla of non-universities. Business picked up: they sold university credentials to over one hundred customers that year, earning more than $70,000.

In January 2001, all the while claiming to run non-universities, Dixie extended her product line to degrees bearing the names of real schools. The first was a "Geneseo State University of New York" degree, ordered by a customer living an hour north of the real SUNY-Geneseo. His diploma displayed the usual "Evaluation & Endorsement Peers" claptrap, but also bore the names of the actual Dean of the College and President of SUNY-Geneseo. Additional diplomas "from" Penn State, Clemson, Concordia, St. Paul's College, and other legitimate schools began flowing from AdvancedU.

The Randocks expanded their degree business infrastructure, building more web sites through which diplomas could be purchased, and offering document archiving services through facilities supposedly in Washington, D.C. The "Official Transcript Archive Center" was one of them, serving as a repository for customers' transcripts. OTAC's home page gave its address as 611 Pennsylvania Avenue SE, #211, and displayed images of the Capitol and the Cannon House Office

Building. But "Suite 211" was nothing more than a mailbox in a UPS Store near Capitol Hill, from which material was forwarded to the Randocks.

Their business improvements paid handsome dividends. In 2001 they sold degrees to over three hundred customers, earning more than $175,000. The AdvancedU web site continued to refer to their products as "Peer Advisory" degrees, somehow distinct from university degrees. But the Randocks were also selling diplomas bearing the names of real schools.

In late 2001 the Randocks stopped claiming that "Academic Peer Advisories" issued the credentials they sold, instead saying the degrees came from legitimate, accredited universities.

In September 2001 the Washington Higher Education Coordinating Board wrote to AdvancedU asking if it was issuing university degrees from inside Washington State. In response the Randocks rented a mail box in a UPS Store in Missoula, Montana from which mail was forwarded to them. They replaced references to Mead, Washington in their web sites with the Missoula address.

The sudden change worried at least one customer, an army staff sergeant who had mailed a money order to Mead, then became concerned that his payment had been lost. He had ordered a Texas A&M degree, which he would later use to gain entrance to Officer Candidate School, eventually rising to the rank of captain.

The Randocks sold their first St. Regis University degree in March 2001. The diploma bore the usual this-isn't-a-university disclaimer. But in November they created a web site for St. Regis, representing it for the first time as a legitimate university. The SRU home page touted the "solid reputation of Saint Regis University," the "acceptance [of its degrees] by HR managers and employers," and the "availability of nearly ALL fields of study." St. Regis was said to be an accredited postsecondary institution and a member of the unrecognized "National Academy of Higher Education." Terms like "Peer Advisory" were eliminated from the diploma templates. The Randocks claimed that St. Regis University was headquartered on the Caribbean island of Dominica.

By February 2002 Dixie had added a faculty roster to the St. Regis web site. Richard J. Hoyer, the owner of the unaccredited American Coastline University, was listed first. His biographical sketch said he had two master's and three doctoral degrees, but failed to mention his affiliation with the ridiculous International University of Fundamental Studies. Randock and Hoyer had met online the previous August when Dixie traded him a "Postgraduate Diploma in Teaching English to Speakers of Other Languages" and a "Post Graduate Certificate in Forensic Psychology" for free advertizing in Hoyer's "A College Degree in Your Spare Time" web site. There were only four other St. Regis professors on the faculty roster, three of whom were associated with IUFS. By June Dixie had added the clownish Hans Kempe to the faculty. He was a purveyor of quack cancer treatments, an IUFS yahoo, and a close friend of Richard Hoyer's.

That same month the Randocks created the "Interfaith Education Ministries Association of Academic Excellence," identifying "Rev. Dr. R. J. Novak" as its internet domain registrant. The IEM web site explained

> Founded in 1965, IEM was originally established to provide certificates of measurement and evaluation of the educational and professional credentials and practices of religious and other nontraditional schools teachers and students. . . . IEM is a private non-denominational accrediting body that accepts the universal good of the world's many religions and faiths.

In reality, IEM was a degree mill through which customers could purchase "International Educator Certificates," "Religious Degrees," and other academic credentials. The "Rev. Dr. R. J. Novak" was not a minister and had never gone to college. Richard John Novak was a friend of Dixie's from high school who had dated her for a time. After he settled in Arizona, Novak tried to earn a living selling cars, running "Novak Auto Wholesale" from home. Both Novak and his wife began working for Dixie after his business tanked in 2002.

The Randocks expanded their operation dramatically in May 2002, creating web sites for the "National Board of Education" and a dozen universities with names like "Stanley State University," "Hartland University," and "Blackstone University." Over time the schools' web sites came to identify each of them as Dominica-based "Official Branch[es] of St. Regis University."

By mid-2002 the Randocks had invented more than two dozen imaginary schools and were advertising in *Psychology Today* and *USA Today*. They sold diplomas in the names of real schools when asked, having already fabricated degrees from Wayne State University, the University of Illinois, the University of Tennessee, Penn State, Cal State Northridge, and others. They produced their first "Doctor of Medicine" diploma that summer, backdated to 1990. During the first half of 2002 they sold a half-million dollars worth of diplomas and transcripts, about three times what they had earned from the degree business in all of 2001.

The Randocks had no credible source of degree-granting authority to attach to St. Regis, since this can only come from a state or national government. To remedy this deficiency, Dixie told Richard Novak to buy her some Africans.

Hijacking Liberia

Novak traveled to Washington DC in June 2002 and took a taxi to the Liberian Embassy, hoping to gain an endorsement of the academic credentials sold by his ex-girlfriend. The embassy's dignified exterior belied the problems within, where Liberia's endemic corruption and factional hostilities, inflamed by a long civil war, played out in miniature.

By the time the Randocks sent Novak to Washington, a tenth of Liberia's population had perished in the ongoing civil war. Nearly a third of all Liberians had fled to refugee camps in other countries. Most of the schools were destroyed, the universities looted, the hospitals wrecked. Telephone service was unreliable at best, while the water and sanitation systems were in ruins. Electrical power was usually unavailable. Life expectancy at birth was thirty-nine years and the infant mortality rate was over fifteen percent.

Novak arrived at the Liberian embassy without an appointment and was introduced to First Secretary and Consul Abdulah Dunbar, the deputy chief of mission. There was no ambassador assigned to the embassy—Liberia barely had a government, much less one capable of managing its external affairs—so Aaron Kollie, the Chargé d'Affaires, served as chief of mission.

Dunbar was a portly, round-faced man who spoke English with an accent. Novak probably brought a letter of introduction, a Saint Regis University catalog, and a substantial amount of money to the meeting.

Novak told Dunbar that St. Regis was an online university based in Washington State and asked what needed to be done to obtain accreditation for the school. Dunbar said he would investigate and find out how much it would cost. After contacting Liberia, Dunbar told Novak that "he could get documents saying the school was accredited, signed by the commissioner of higher education for Liberia, a Mr. Bestman" for a price of $4,000. Novak, the former used car salesman, bargained the price down to $2,250. Dunbar was not interested in whether or not St. Regis actually taught anything, but only on the price and logistics for producing accreditation documents. Novak assumed the money was a bribe and that Dunbar would keep it for himself, but later learned that most of the payment had gone to Dan Bestman, a mid-level Ministry of Education official in Liberia.

Dunbar printed and signed a "notarial certificate" on embassy letterhead for the Randocks "certifying" that Dixie's National Board of Education could "establish and operate online and virtual Universities to grant college level degrees, based on assessment of prior learning, experiential learning, testing, independent study or coursework." The certificate was nearly identical to a document written on an A+ Institute computer a few days before. The two versions awarded the "National Board of Education" the conflicting powers of both accrediting and operating universities.

Novak returned to the Liberian Embassy in August to obtain two more attestation documents, signed this time by Boima Kiadii, Liberia's "Director, Division of Accreditation," Marcus Sokpah, "Assistant Minister for Teacher Education, Certification, & Accreditation," and Thomas Clark, "Acting Assistant Minister, Department of Instruction."

After Novak handed Dunbar $2,250 at the August meeting, the Randocks arranged to pay Dunbar a monthly retainer of $400, sometimes supplementing this with payments for specific tasks they would assign him. Over the next two and a half years he would receive $23,900 from the Randock organization, wired into his personal bank account. In a 2007 interview he admitted receiving money, but described it as payments "for services rendered" rather than bribes.

Dixie posted news of the recently purchased Liberian recognition on the St. Regis web site, leading with a quote attributed to Abdulah Dunbar. She (or her staff) also posted St. Regis ads with similar text, purportedly written by Abdulah Dunbar, to internet newsgroups.

References to Dominica as the home country of St. Regis were scrubbed from the Randocks' internet domains. Dixie posted the Liberian Embassy's contact information to her web sites, paying Abdulah Dunbar to vouch for her school whenever someone called to ask about the legitimacy of St. Regis University. But Dunbar was dismissed from his embassy post in June 2003, though he remained in the United States, so Dixie changed the phone number displayed below the embassy's address to a Maryland number, possibly Dunbar's cell phone.

To buttress further the illusion of Liberian recognition, the Randocks registered the internet domains http://www

.liberianembassy .com and http://www.liberia embassy.com,
loading them with material which might lead visitors to mistake them for official web sites of the Liberian Embassy. The
Education page on the imposter sites displayed a list of "Institutes of Higher Education Accredited under the authority of
the Ministry of Education, the National Commission on
Higher Education and the Board of Trustees." The contents of
the list varied with time; somewhat more than a year after the
Randocks began bribing Liberian officials the catalog of universities included the genuine University of Liberia and Cut-
tington University (though both had been largely destroyed
during the civil war) as well as St. Regis and two other Randock "schools." Below the list was the odd announcement
"More universities and polytechnics have been created
recently." The bottom of the page advised visitors "To inquire
as to the legal status of Liberian educational institutions contact mailto:gov@liberiaembassy.com." That was the email
address Dixie would use when she wrote to the University of
Illinois to complain about me in August 2003.

The purchase of Liberian credentials was good for profits.
During the second half of 2002 the Randocks sold more than
$900,000 in bogus academic products, nearly twice their take
from the first six months of the year.

Crashing the Peace Talks

The Randocks realized they needed more influence in Liberia
than they had been able to purchase through Dunbar. Dan
Bestman was inefficient and untrustworthy, and appeared to
be working for at least one diploma mill in direct competition
with St. Regis. Dunbar had left his embassy post in June and
was no longer able to speak as a Liberian official.

Richard Novak smelled opportunity in the ongoing civil
war, which continued in 2003 in spite of peace negotiations
underway in Accra, Ghana. Novak wrote Dixie in June 2003:
"I would really like to be at the hearings in Ghana, I think it
would help our standing. I believe I can meet the new interim

govt." Randock agreed—it would let her fling her well-funded paymaster at prospective Liberian officials clustered in Accra—so she promised to send both Novak and Abdulah Dunbar to Africa. In August 2003 Charles Taylor, Liberia's corrupt president agreed to resign and the violence in Monrovia began to subside, so Novak prepared to leave.

Novak described traveling to Washington before going to Africa, "with Steve and Dixie Randock staying in the same hotel [in Washington]. Steve and Dixie had a room about three doors down from Novak's . . ." After calling Dunbar to give him directions to the hotel, Novak "walked down to the Randocks' room where Steve Randock provided him with $4,000 . . . in U.S. currency. Novak brought the money back to his room and . . . paid Dunbar the $4,000 and walked with him into the hallway which was within 'earshot' of the Randocks' room (whose door was ajar)." Novak and Dunbar discussed "Dunbar getting into another political office and that he could be financially backed by Saint Regis University."

Dunbar and Novak took a KLM flight into Accra, arriving the 7th of August and checking into the city's Novotel Hotel. The Randocks wired $7,000 to a bank account in Paris a few days later, specifying the "Novotel Hotel, Accor, Ghana" as beneficiary. It is likely that Novak used the funds to provide incentives to officials during his visit. Novak took pictures of Liberians he met and kept a log of his activities so that Dixie could post an account of his trip to the St. Regis web site.

Novak met with Andrew Kronyanh, the Chargé d'Affaires of Liberia's embassy in Ghana. Kronyanh agreed to provide assistance; money changed hands, perhaps at their first meeting in Accra, but certainly later. According to Novak, "at Dixie Randock's request [he] arranged for Andrew Kronyanh . . . to receive a $400 monthly salary from SRU and also provided him with equipment (computers, fax, and copy machines). Kronyanh had an account in New York. The payments were wired to that account and then transferred to a bank in Ghana. The payments were made so that Kronyanh would answer questions regarding SRU [St. Regis University] and say they were 'accredited.'" Soon after Kronyanh was approached, Dixie posted his contact information to the St. Regis web sites below the legend "For telephone or postal verification accreditation, you may contact . . ."

One of the most significant connections Novak made was to Kabineh Ja'neh, an attorney who had been a leader in the LURD (Liberians United for Reconciliation and Democracy) rebel group which had helped depose Charles Taylor. Ja'neh would become Minister of Justice in the interim government and then an Associate Supreme Court Justice after Ellen Johnson Sirleaf was elected president. The men met at the Accra Novotel; Dixie posted photographs of them shaking hands and chatting to the St. Regis web site. According to Novak, he paid Ja'neh $1,000 at a meeting in the dining room of the Novotel. In an interview a few years later, Ja'neh's description of the meeting does not refer to a payment. "The first meeting [with Novak came] during the 2003 Ghana Peace talks when Novak introduced himself and requested that he and Justice Ja'neh be photographed together and with Abdulah Dunbar. Justice Ja'neh indicated that often people ask to be photographed with him and he thought little of it at the time."

The Randocks would assign Ja'neh to negotiate a credit-laundering deal between St. Regis and the University of Liberia. The arrangement, which did not seem to bear fruit, is described in an April 6, 2004 Memorandum of Understanding that appears to bear the signatures of Ja'neh and Novak. The MOU describes a "scholarship fund" to be established and entrusted to Ja'neh, then identifies him as "authorized to assist negotiate an Agreement with the University of Liberia for the establishment of mutual credits transfer policy between St. Regis University, James Monroe University, and Robertstown University and the University of Liberia." The document was faxed from Novak's home in Arizona to the Randocks.

Ja'neh later acknowledged receiving money from the Randock organization, but explained that this was "for services rendered," and that the payments were not bribes.

In all, Novak spent three weeks in Accra, eating fried rice and drinking local beer—he was afraid that other fare would make him ill—and meeting members of the Liberian political establishment. He accomplished a great deal in Ghana, establishing additional lines of influence for the Randocks into the Ministries of Education and Justice, as well as the Foreign Ministry which managed assignments of diplomats to embassies. Dunbar would be reinstalled at the Liberian embassy and, for a brief time, serve as Chief of Mission.

In the following months the Randocks would extend their influence further, paying another Liberian official to petition UNESCO to include St. Regis, Robertstown, and James Monroe in the International Academic Union's International Handbook of Universities. The Randocks and their associates would fool several legitimate universities into accepting St. Regis degrees for graduate admission. And they would take note of me and try to drop the University of Illinois on me like an anvil.

Mistakes Were Made

By the summer of 2003 the Randocks were selling degrees to about thirty-five customers per week. It was a surprisingly labor intensive business. For each customer there was a transcript to load with courses and a set of diplomas to create from templates. Someone would decide what other degrees should be offered to entice the customer to spend more money. A staffer would receive corrections from customers who had found errors in the "proofs" of their documents, PDF files which were sent by email. There were phone calls from prospective employers seeking to verify the award of a degree, who believed they were speaking to an Official Transcript Archive Center employee in Washington, DC. There were incoming payments from customers and outgoing payments to Dunbar, Kronyanh, and other Liberian officials. There were salaries and commissions to be paid to Dixie's employees.

Customers' transcripts were often copied from documents sold to previous buyers. But when a customer ordered a degree in a field that was unfamiliar to the Randocks, a staffer needed to fabricate an entirely new transcript. Dixie instructed her staff to do it this way: ". . . go to a search engine and type in 'degree' and 'construction' or whatever major you are looking for. It will take you to colleges that offer that kind of degree. Then check to see what courses they require you to take to get that degree. Make a copy of the curriculum and paste it into . . . a transcript and fix it up so the credits, years, etc. match up. Save it as a new transcript major. Hooray!"

Sometimes there were mistakes. David Brodhagen was a United States Marshal in Spokane who bought a St. Regis bachelor's degree in Criminal Justice in 2002. On his order form he wrote

> At this time in my career, I feel it is important to obtain a BA Degree. Without it, I will not be able to go further up in my career ladder. With only seven more years remaining before retirement, it is too late to go to the conventional route of a four year college. This is my primary reason for applying for a degree based upon my experience, training, and college education.

By paying $731 for his degree, Brodhagen was able to obtain a $16,000 per year increase in salary. But someone in the Marshal's office noticed that his transcript included the course "Self Defense for Women" (for which he received an A-) and burned him. Brodhagen was charged with a misdemeanor and fined.

The Worker Bees

The highest paid of the Randocks' employees was Dixie's daughter Heidi Lorhan, who worked from home using the alias "Advisor James" in emails to her customers.

Roberta Markishtum began working in the Randocks'

degree business in 2002, earning $9.50 per hour printing diplomas and transcripts. She corresponded with customers using the aliases "Jennifer Greene" and "Roberta Greene," and sometimes fielded calls from employers seeking to verify an employee's credentials. Once she posed as a University of Maryland employee by confirming that a (counterfeit) Maryland degree had been awarded to an applicant for a position at a Department of Veterans Affairs Medical Center.

Amy Hensley joined Dixie's degree business in 2000 and continued as a Randock employee until mid-2005. For a time Amy was married to Roberta Markishtum's younger brother, a "small business owner" with a tree service. Hensley served as the St. Regis bookkeeper and paymaster, but also as a saleswoman, corresponding with customers as "Advisor Tim" and deciding which degrees should be offered. Hensley submitted the wire transfers that moved funds into the bank accounts of Liberian officials.

Blake Carlson was the St. Regis stationer, manufacturing foil seals for diplomas and transcripts as well as rubber signature and logo stamps. He was also a salesman of degrees and religious ordinations through "World Chapel Ministries," created by Dixie as "the 'theological division' of 'Saint Regis University.'"

Carlson and Richard Novak were close friends while they were growing up. Like Novak, he knew Dixie in high school. Blake and his wife Carrie owned Northwest Business Stamp in Spokane, manufacturing rubber stamps, document foil seals, ID badges, and other specialty items. In 2002 he began selling Randock some of the paraphernalia needed to produce diplomas and transcripts, and probably manufactured the Liberian government logo stamps that she used.

Kenneth Pearson was the Randocks' information technology expert. Though Dixie became proficient at designing web sites, it was Pearson who managed the Randocks' web servers (which were kept in his house), office computers, and internet domain registrations. There are no indications that Pearson was directly involved in the sale of degrees, or that his wife played any role in the Randocks' businesses.

The Randocks' diploma mill was a family business. Dixie's daughter was involved, but there was more: Roberta Markishtum was Steve Randock's ex-stepdaughter, Hensley was Markishtum's sister-in-law, and Novak was Dixie's ex-boyfriend. Novak's wife sold degrees, while Novak and Carlson had been close friends for years. Only Pearson was an outsider. In spite of the personal connections among the Randock employees, Dixie was thought to direct considerably more income towards her daughter than the others. At one point Steve Randock told Carlson that Heidi "was making between $7,000 and $9,000 per month." Lorhan, who had lost her house to bankruptcy just a few years before, was suddenly earning a six-figure income.

Getting Beaten Up

By mid-2003, the Randocks' degree mills were the subjects of increasingly harsh criticism in internet discussion groups. In July 2003 AACRAO (the American Association of Collegiate Registrars and Admissions Officers) announced "[We] do not accept the recognition of Saint Regis University by the Ministry of Education of Liberia . . ." Even so, there was still nothing in the mainstream press about St. Regis, and sales were strong.

In August 2003 I noticed that the Branford Academy Preparatory High School, "a division of internationally renowned St. Regis University," hosted a "Degree by Exam" program in which prospective students could take a free 100-question multiple choice test to obtain a degree. I took the test twice, sending in scores of 26 percent and 21 percent, and receiving an offer of an associate's degree both times. I celebrated my academic triumph by posting the good news to a university web page; a week later I took the identical test at the Novaks' Interfaith Education Ministry web site, submitting only fourteen correct answers this time. My test results and contact information went to Jean Novak in her role as "Advisor Randall."

Jean wrote back that I had failed, inviting me "to study and take the [very same] test again at [my] convenience." I did so a few hours later, answering all the questions correctly to see what "Advisor Randall" would do in the face of such a large discrepancy.

Jean wrote to Dixie. "I sent Gollin the link to take the test. He took it and I got the score this morning. His score was 14 percent. I wrote him back and told him his score was too low to be granted a diploma from Branford. He took the test again, and this time his score was 100 percent. What should I do????" Randock sent Novak the text of a message to send to me. I was to be told I had scored 14 percent, then 100 percent, and would need to retake the exam in a proctored setting. But I was also instructed to "email [them my] full name, address, phone number, social security number and a clear copy of [my] driver's license or passport." Randock wondered if I would reply, writing to Novak "Think he will want to do this??? If so maybe we ought to post his ss# somewhere, or better yet, give his information to all the degree mills out there. They HATE him :-)."

After Dixie saw what I had posted to the web about the Branford Academy, the "Liberian Embassy Washington DC" sent emails to my university's president, chancellor, and vice president for academic affairs from the address "gov@liberiaembassy.com" to complain. I later learned that liberiaembassy.com was controlled by the Randocks: the protests weren't from the embassy at all, but from Dixie.

This scared me, but I had been paying attention to diploma mills as a faculty public service activity and thought the university would honor its obligation to protect me. In September 2003 I met with an associate provost, three university lawyers, my department head (who had always been supportive), and the deputy director of a campus unit that had been encouraging my investigations. To my surprise, the meeting was an ambush.

The associate provost said that what I had been doing might or might not be a good thing, but in any case it was not faculty public service. There was, the lawyers said, no source of funds to cover the costs of potential litigation. The associate provost thought the issue of costs was irrelevant since the university had no interest in participating in my defense if there were to be a lawsuit.

One of the lawyers turned to me and, as I remember it, said "Just so we understand what happens next, you're planning to remove the material from the web, right?" And I replied "I guess that's what I need to do." But then I said "You understand that messages from the 'Liberian Embassy Washington DC' were really being sent by a realtor named Dixie Randock in Spokane, right?" And he replied "That's what you say." Did he really believe I was no more credible than a dishonest realtor pretending to be a Liberian official?

That same attorney later described the latitude to be afforded professors in their choice of professional activities, comparing me to a windshield installer on an assembly line who asked his supervisor if he could work on a different part of the car for a while. The appropriate response would be "we pay you to install windshields, not do other things, so you're NOT going to do something else. We pay you to install windshields."

I left the meeting more angry than I have ever been in my life. In shock, I found my way home, took the material off the web, and sent up a distress rocket so that all my higher education colleagues would know what had happened. Alan Contreras, the head of Oregon's Office of Degree Authorization, contacted a reporter at the *Chronicle of Higher Education*, pitching the story to her as "Gutless major university refuses to defend value of its own degrees vs. scum-sucking, bottom-feeding, widow-bilking diploma mills," but cautioned "My attorney says she's not sure we can prove widow-bilking." When the reporter called me I agreed to send her a copy of my meeting notes, and the story ran a month later; a second story ran a few weeks after that. The university backed down, the provost apologized for what his associate provost had done, and my relations with the University of Illinois administration returned to normal. After that, the university ignored letters from Randock and Hoyer.

Better Than Lawyers, Guns, and Money

IS AN INVESTIGATIVE REPORTER

Bill Morlin, a reporter with the *Spokane-Spokesman Review*, and Gary Craig and Steve Orr, reporters at the Rochester, New York *Democrat and Chronicle*, learned of the diploma mill owners in their coverage areas and began writing stories.

Morlin's beat includes eastern Washington State and northern Idaho. He called me a week before Thanksgiving; I sent him the Branford Academy test, Dixie's email messages, and the Randocks' internet domain registration records. With an arsenal of hard data, he called the A+ Institute to ask Dixie for an interview, saying he was writing a story about her real estate school.

Randock refused to speak over the phone, but agreed to answer questions sent by email. The reporter began with a pair of innocent queries about the A+ Institute. But his third one must have startled Randock: "When did you begin operating Branford Academy?" She answered "I do not own or operate Branford Academy." He followed with "Earlier this week (I have the printout), you were listed as the 'registrant' for branfordacademy.com. Your office address, 14525 Newport Highway, Mead, WA, was also listed." Randock replied "I believe that information is pretty old. Since I am into distance learning and had computer equipment left over from the real estate business I helped a friend, Ken Pearson, set up a web hosting business. I don't get paid—I just help him with equipment and he is teaching me the business. Sometimes domain registration is included as well as my help with teaching others what I know about distance education. We help out new, struggling schools to set up a web presence. I like helping and it takes my mind off being a victim of embezzlement [the Randocks' bookkeeper had been convicted of embezzling funds from the A+ Institute]. Ken has at times used my PayPal account to register several domains for such clients (Branford was one of these). As everyone knows, lots of web hosts do register domains for their clients as a service. We host their site for a small fee, but I am sure you realize that web hosts have no ownership."

Morlin wrote "Now, after this newspaper began asking questions, the registrant is a man in Liberia? Why have we witnessed these sudden changes?" Randock replied "Hardly sudden. . . . Since it was pointed out that the registration information was inaccurate it was corrected, I assume by the actual owner." Curiously, even after the domain registration addresses were changed, some of the listed phone numbers remained those of the A+ Institute. Morlin next asked "How many high school and associate arts degrees has Branford Academy sold?" Dixie replied "You will have to ask them." When Morlin asked why Branford's exam was linked to "St. Regis University, described as a 'diploma mill' by experts we've interviewed," Dixie responded "As far as we know they are accredited by their country. But, you will have to ask them." She gave evasive replies to the rest of Morlin's questions.

The *Spokesman-Review* ran "Spokane a Hot Spot for Dubious Degrees" in its Sunday, November 30 edition. The article identified the Randocks, tying them to fake schools and suspect Liberian operations, describing the sale of Liberian accreditation through their National Board of Education, and revealing the sudden changes in domain registrations. Morlin wrote that his state's regulations were weak: "There are no laws in Washington or Idaho against selling, buying and using high school or university degrees from unaccredited institutions. Idaho does have a law making it illegal for unaccredited schools to specifically target Idaho residents. In Washington, the operations may violate 'unfair and deceptive business practices' provisions of the state's Consumer Protection Act, said Assistant Attorney General Steve Larsen. The act can include civil penalties. 'There is a red flag there,' said Larsen . . ."

Roberta Markishtum called Morlin after his story ran. Still upset with the Randocks after her divorce from Steve Jr., she told Morlin that Dixie was the web master for many of the degree business sites and that Heidi Lorhan handled the day-to-day operations of St. Regis, earning five or six thousand dollars per month. Markishtum described parties at the Randocks' residence where Heidi and Dixie would cackle about the money being made by the diploma mill. She told Morlin about suspicious aspects of the Randocks' 2001 bankruptcy filing, and about Dixie's younger daughter's substance abuse problems. Markishtum was a dream source, though her account of the operations of St. Regis would not be confirmed until later.

The story put the Randocks and St. Regis into the mainstream media and made it clear that they were in the business of selling degrees to unqualified customers. Morlin's next article appeared a week later, describing the head of a private high school whose St. Regis degrees could lead parents of prospective students to overestimate his qualifications. In all Morlin would write two dozen pieces about the Randocks, their customers, and their diploma mills during the next five years.

Steve Orr and Gary Craig, investigative reporters for the Rochester, New York *Democrat and Chronicle*, came to St. Regis from a different direction. In October 2003 they stumbled upon the tangle of bizarre online entities associated with Richard Hoyer. His "International College of Homeland Security" first attracted their attention, but the more they found, the more curious they became. Neither of them had heard of Hoyer before landing on his ICHS site; if his outlandish claims had been true, Orr was sure they would have known of him from media coverage of his wide-ranging activities. On December 6 the *Democrat and Chronicle* ran their stories "Diploma mills cast a shadow over valid distance learning," "N.Y. third state to question Irondequoit man's online diplomas," and "Hoyer's Internet Enterprises."

Orr and Craig learned that the New York authorities had ejected ICHS from the state, and that Hoyer then claimed it operated from Mariastein, Switzerland, where Hans Kempe lived. They found that Hoyer had registered a "State Duma Committee on Foreign Relations" website which "[purported] to represent an official committee of the Russian State Duma, the lower house of that nation's Parliament. Hoyer is listed as vice chairman for the United States; the other officials listed are his collaborators in other online ventures." But "Yevgeniy Khorishko, a press officer in the Russian Federation Embassy in Washington, DC, told the Democrat and Chronicle that Hoyer was misrepresenting himself. 'Yes, they (the Duma) have a committee on foreign relations, but he is not part of it,' Khorishko said." Orr and Craig saw that Hoyer claimed "two bachelor's degrees, two master's degrees and seven doctoral degrees, including two medical degrees from institutions in Russia" in his surprising curriculum vitae. Khorishko told them he "doubted the existence of one of the institutions and did not believe Hoyer received degrees from either of them." The reporters wrote about Hoyer's association with a pair of accreditation mills. Hoyer told them "he could not comment about ICHS or any of his past online activities. He said there was 'pending litigation' involving his online operations but would not identify his lawyer. He said he thinks court papers have been filed with the litigation but he would not say where those papers were filed. 'I'm at the mercy of the court system,' Hoyer said. Hoyer did not respond . . . about the inquiry into his use of medical degrees."

Two weeks later Orr and Craig wrote another pair of articles about diploma mills. One described the connection between St. Regis, Richard Novak, Hoyer, and Abdulah Dunbar while the other discussed in more detail the strange trajectory of ICHS as it fled from New York to Switzerland.

The Seeds of Their Destruction

In October 2003 I called an attorney at the Federal Trade Commission to ask if the FTC would consider suing St. Regis. During the university's 2003–2004 winter break I planned to write a long analysis of the degree business that I hoped to offer to the FTC as a guide to St. Regis. When it was finished, John Bear read it and offered corrections and organizational suggestions. I titled the report "Information about the 'National Board of Education,' Saint Regis University, and American Coastline University."

I described how Saint Regis and American Coastline sold diplomas based on "life experience" and how "NBOE also sells accreditation to unaccredited universities, with award of credentials guaranteed upon payment of a $50,000 fee." I wrote that customers of the Randocks and Richard Hoyer "use [their purchased degrees] to attract unsuspecting customers to their own businesses." I described the misleading use of their degrees by three of Hoyer's and eleven of the Randocks' clients. These customers were working as "international financial managers," clinical psychologists, security consultants, educators, translators, and engineers. And I showed, "through analysis of the internet manifestations of NBOE, Saint Regis, and American Coastline . . . that these organizations are operated by Dixie Randock, Steve Randock, Heidi Lorhan, Kenneth Pearson, and Richard Hoyer." There were links to web pages and archived files to support all of my assertions.

I sent the report to the FTC, Alan Contreras, and Washington State's Higher Education Coordinating Board; Contreras forwarded a copy to Christine Gregoire, Washington's Attorney General. I waited for news, but I had no leverage to encourage either the FTC or the Attorney General's office to take on another investigation. Nothing happened.

Shafiq

Frank ("Ishaq") Shafiq was a portly St. Regis professor who had earned a bachelor's degree from the University of Illinois in 1971, moved to Georgia, and gotten into trouble. "According to court records in Douglas County, GA, a jury convicted Shafiq in 1985 of first-degree arson for hiring three people to steal his car and burn it so he could collect insurance. That same year, he pleaded guilty of aggravated assault, serving time in the Douglas County Jail in 1985 and 1986.

Shafiq returned to Illinois, fleeing the wreckage of a bankruptcy and a failed marriage, his children, and a criminal record. He reenrolled in the University of Illinois, completing a master's in Urban Planning in 1991.

Shafiq contacted the Randocks in February 2003, hoping to shelter his "non-denominational Alexandria Theological Seminary" under their umbrella of fake schools. His "business plan" consisted of "attracting new students from our internet radio and TV network . . . [as well as] targeting African American individuals, Church groups and organizations. . . ." Shafiq was well-spoken and better educated than anyone else in the St. Regis orbit. Besides his Alexandria thing, he ran something called "Quantum III Consultants" out of his home in Illinois.

By the summer of 2003 Shafiq was selling St. Regis degrees to customers back in Georgia. He tended to communicate his business needs to Blake Carlson, whose role in St. Regis had grown from stationer to manager of some of Dixie's sales force. Shafiq wrote Carlson that he had "at least 6 students who have obtained SRU Doctor of Education degrees who are attempting to obtain pay grade increases with Georgia Professional Standards which is the certifying agency for the teachers in the State of Georgia." Shafiq sold more degrees to Georgia teachers; at least ten teachers and one building principal in Georgia ultimately received raises after buying St. Regis degrees through Shafiq.

Their raises were substantial. The salary of Sonya Mullings, who had been teaching in Gwinnett for a half-dozen years, went from $38,935 to $54,932. Detra Posey's salary jumped by $15,000. Ray Alley bought himself a $12,000 raise. Lisa Misiewicz received a $10,000 raise.

The building principal from Gwinnett "transferred into St. Regis from the Center of University Studies with the help of Liz Ross," paying $3,500 for his new degree. (In 2001 Texas had fined Sheila Danzig—the person whose business alias was "Liz Ross"—$213,000 for her unauthorized "Center of University Studies" activities.) The principal's purchase did not go smoothly. The first set of proofs Amy Hensley sent him were for a PhD in Criminal Justice instead of Educational Leadership.

Shafiq had sold a half-dozen advanced degrees into a single school system, without even distributing them over the three fake universities the Randocks were running. It worried Dixie that someone might notice this suspicious clustering of St. Regis customers and she complained to Novak that "Shafiq thinks it is just ducky to do these degrees in 'groups.' He brags about it. But when large groups from ONE place get SRU degrees it draws attention. I told him this would happen . . . but it [would be] worth it to me if we all made a killing."

In March 2004 Jaime Sarrio, a reporter for the *Gwinnett Daily Post*, received a tip from a Gwinnett teacher with a legitimate doctoral degree who had been angered by the dishonesty of his colleagues. Sarrio posed as a prospective customer, "enrolling" in St. Regis by listing her editor and another Post reporter as references, then taking a series of short multiple choice tests. Even though nobody contacted her references, Advisor James (Heidi Lorhan) offered Sarrio a whole raft of credentials: two different flavors of Education master's degrees and four kinds of certificates as either an education consultant or a guidance counselor. The *Daily Post* published "Teachers buy degrees, hike pay" on March 19th. Aileen Dodd, a reporter for the *Atlanta Journal-Constitution* had been doing her own investigation and wrote "Bogus degrees land teachers in woodshed," which ran the same day.

Randock thought she knew who was responsible for the bad press, suggesting to Novak that they use Liberia's Minister of Justice as a cudgel: "This asshole George Gollin has just gone too far. Someone—maybe Jannah [Kabineh Ja'neh] needs to step in and stop him. He will never stop this shit. . . . Can someone important do something to get him off us? . . . Can you see if someone can stop Gollin?" I had spoken with Sarrio, pointing her towards information about St. Regis, but she had begun her initial investigations after the tip from a Georgia educator.

Sarrio and Dodd published fourteen more articles over the next several weeks. Dale Gough, the Director, International Education Services for AACRAO (the American Association of Collegiate Registrars and Admissions Officers) told Dodd that "if Georgia officials had called his association about St. Regis, he would have told them, as he has told other states, that St. Regis was a diploma mill."

Six of the educators resigned almost immediately; in July a state ethics committee recommended that GPSC revoke the licenses of all eleven of the teachers. A member of the ethics panel told Sarrio "the teachers knew the degrees were fake when they accepted a boost in pay. 'In my heart, I know every single one of them knew what they were doing,' said committee member Terri DeLoach. 'They took money (in the form of higher salaries) . . . and they did it by misrepresenting the facts, and knowing of it the entire time.'" The Professional Standards Commission agreed and "voted 11 to 1 to exact its most severe punishment for violating the Code of Ethics for Educators, which amounts to banishment from working in Georgia public school. . . ."

By the middle of 2004 the news coverage of the Georgia mess began to subside. Dixie turned her attention towards Detroit, where Carlson and Shafiq were negotiating an enormous deal which would ultimately ruin her.

Selling to Chrysler

Blake Carlson and Frank Shafiq had learned of a United Auto Workers Union education fund that Carlson believed was valued at 30 billion dollars. It paid for union members employed by Chrysler, Ford, General Motors, and Harley Davidson to participate in programs such as the "UAW-Ford University," a cooperative initiative which sought "to facilitate the entrance of UAW-represented Ford Motor Company hourly employees into college degree programs."

If Shafiq and Carlson could enroll St. Regis as a UAW credit provider, they would all earn so much money that everyone could quietly disappear, never to work again. The role played by St. Regis would be to award academic credit through "prior learning assessment" of the training courses factory workers might have taken to improve their job skills. In reality, Shafiq would sell UAW members entire degrees (bachelor's, master's, and even PhD's) rather than limiting their awards to a handful of credit hours. Shafiq's UAW contacts seemed unaware of the Gwinnett train wreck so the deal moved forward.

It is possible that Carlson and Shafiq learned of the UAW fund through William Duncan and Teresa Williams. Duncan is an Indianapolis minister who runs both the Revival Temple Apostolic Church and the "Muskegon Bible Institute," an unaccredited degree provider located inside his church. He was also a "professor" for both St. Regis and Blake Carlson's World Chapel Ministry, first appearing on the SRU faculty roster some time before October 2003. Williams was a "local training facilitator" at an Indianapolis Chrysler plant scheduled for closure. She had obtained a degree from Duncan and had even been praised by Chrysler for doing this, receiving a "UAW-Daimler-Chrysler National Training Center Co-Chairs' Award" for "[demonstrating] a commitment to education" by earning a master's degree from the Muskegon Bible Institute [and] pursuing a doctoral degree there . . ." Williams' job included monitoring the education providers that partnered with UAW.

The discussions between St. Regis and the automotive industry began in mid-2003, not long after Shafiq became one of Dixie's salesmen. In September Shafiq phoned a member of the "Higher Education Learning Partnership" (HELP) steering committee which UAW and Ford had formed to guide the UAW-Ford "Prior Learning Assessment Initiative." Shafiq explained that "Quantum [was] working here in the States to bring degree opportunities to persons represented by the UAW" and asked how to proceed. The HELP advisor suggested a site visit to Quantum by observers from the National Programs Centers and sketched a possible agenda for the visit.

The entire St. Regis gang smelled money. Carlson told Novak "there is so much money on the table here. . . . We stand to make millions of dollars each your retirement, mine and the Randocks' is right here in view."

It does not appear that NPC officials ever visited the Potemkin Village of Quantum III Consultants that the Shafiqs could have erected inside their home. Even so, Carlson and Shafiq managed to keep moving the deal forward, obtaining some kind of preliminary approval for a few UAW employees at Chrysler to engage with St. Regis. And they were granted a one-hour meeting with UAW and Ford officials to pitch their grand plan for selling "Liberian" life experience degrees to auto workers. The presentation was scheduled for January 21, 2004 in Detroit.

Shafiq set about preparing the St. Regis proposal to UAW, requesting copies of the certificates and charters of corrupt origin that Dixie had plastered all over her fake schools. He retooled Dixie's St. Regis University Catalog, then sent the packet to Detroit.

The SRU catalog brings to mind Mary McCarthy's famous insult of playwright Lillian Hellman: "Every word she writes is a lie—including 'and' and 'the.'" The St. Regis document was thick with misrepresentations, lies, and fabrications. "Entry [into St. Regis programs] will be based on our detailed analysis of work experience and responsibility in positions held." (A valid credit card was all it took.) "St. Regis University . . . evaluates a person's proven qualifications objectively based on comparative analysis to standard curriculum requirements." (Dixie's gang of high school dropouts would "evaluate" customers for PhD's in physics.) "St. Regis is chartered (1984) by the National Legislature." (The legislature never saw the charter, which was fabricated by Dan Bestman in 2003.) "St. Regis University's homeland is Liberia." (Try Spokane.) St. Regis did not "operate with a code of ethics rooted in humanistic philosophy and psychology." The "Provost" didn't have a doctoral degree, or, for that matter, any other university degree. The "Executive Vice Chancellor" never earned a pair of doctoral degrees, having ended his studies after one year of college. The Liberian Embassy's telephone was not a Maryland cell phone.

Shafiq told Carlson and the Randocks that St. Regis had received preliminary approval from UAW, thanks to the catalog. The arrangement with SRU would probably be finalized at the January 2004 meeting in Detroit.

By November 2003 everything seemed to be in place for a first crop of customers. Teresa Williams assumed the role of liaison between the Chrysler foundry and St. Regis; the Randocks gave her a Doctor of Education for her efforts, referring to it in their business records as a "freebie." Dixie wrote Jean Novak that "Blake [Carlson] put together a great deal! It is Chrysler and he is expecting 200–500 degrees to come through in a week or two. If so, that is a LOT of money for us all. I have no reason not to believe it will not happen as Blake says it is a done deal and so does Shafiq and Sheila [Danzig, one of Dixie's business associates]. It is pretty exciting."

Shafiq reported to Dixie that his discussions with the automobile manufacturers were going well. He believed "SRU, JMU, and RU [will be able] to offer its degree programs to over 1 million potential students in the very near future and have their education paid for by their employer. From my conversations with the corporations today they are attempting to get SRU, JMU and RU on their approved university list within the next two weeks."

It really was going to be a lot of money, though ultimately less than they had expected, and slower in its arrival. The arrangement with Chrysler called for UAW to pay $2,000 for each bachelor's degree, $3,200 for each master's degree, and $4,000 for each PhD. There was some adjustment of this as the deal progressed—the price for a master's sold to some customers was reduced to $2,700—but UAW's cost per degree was still about twice as high as would be paid by a customer who purchased a degree directly from the main St. Regis web site. The Randocks agreed that Shafiq and his wife Sharon would keep half the receipts. Novak and his wife would receive 6 percent of the funds, Carlson and his wife 5 percent, and Roberta Markishtum 2.5 percent. Dixie and Steve would keep the remaining 36.5. percent.

Shafiq and Carlson organized the Detroit trip together. Carlson felt it was important to make a strong showing, with significant representation from St. Regis. He wrote Novak "I am as nervous as you are my friend but we must follow through with this meeting. It would be best if Dixie come too! Ford is an extremely visual company and it is extremely important that SRU shows with strength and in unity. It is odd but they need some white people to represent SRU." Each of the auto manufacturers would decide independently whether or not to partner with St. Regis, though it was likely that Ford's decision in January would influence Chrysler, General Motors, and Harley Davidson. Carlson hoped that Robertstown and James Monroe could serve as backup schools in case any of the companies rejected St. Regis. He wrote Novak "All the schools are waiting in the wings in case we should we loose [sic] one. We would probably happy with only getting one or two of them but shit don't you want them all?"

The discussions about who should represent St. Regis in Detroit burbled along in mid-January. Carlson suggested that a tame Liberian (Dunbar or Dan Bestman) be included. Dixie was concerned about revealing her identity to Shafiq, and to the UAW and Ford staff. She told Carlson "I will go as Dixie Dennis [her maiden name], and Steve will be Steve Randock and we will both be Trustees of SRU." The next day she changed her mind, realizing that she didn't want to appear subservient to Shafiq. She told Carlson "If I am going to this Ford meeting, I need to be 'somebody.'" She changed the alias she would use to "Desiree Jones." But as the date of the meeting approached, Dixie got cold feet. She wrote Carlson "I will be in Detroit, and I am willing to meet with Shafiq, but I will not be at the Ford meeting." Ultimately, Blake Carlson, Novak, and Shafiq (possibly accompanied by his wife) attended on behalf of St. Regis. The Randocks flew to Detroit and met Shafiq for the first time, but avoided the UAW and Ford personnel.

The meetings appeared to go well; the first face-to-face contact between the Randocks and the Shafiqs assuaged Dixie's concerns about revealing herself to them. Randock sent an unusually friendly note to Shafiq, expressing her pleasure and admiration: "It is not often that I meet people with your intelligence, integrity and ambition, traits I highly admire. Your warmth and grace made me feel a strong closeness to you both and I look forward to working with you for many years." She gave Shafiq her home address and phone number. The obsequious Shafiq replied "We find it difficult to find the words that adequately convey the tremendous joy it was for us to meet the both of you and Dr. Novak. We are looking forward to further developing the 'family' and business relationship." He reported good news, though with some exaggeration: "The Director of UAW Ford is very committed toward expediting the addition of SRU on its approved list of universities. As we mentioned to you both, they want to first get their entire staff degreed from SRU. And then begin the process of offering the degree programs to over 2 million of their members." At $2,000 per bachelor's degree, Shafiq appeared to be opening a four billion dollar market to the Randocks. But he was misrepresenting his ultimate intentions.

Shafiq wrote that he would travel to Indianapolis in a few days to "to begin the degree registration of the UAW Daimler-Chrysler employees." He said that there were already 60 who had "pre-registered" and that his goal was to raise that to 100 by the end of the following week.

Steve Randock explained to Novak the path to be taken by the Chrysler money: "Check comes from Ford, Chrysler, GM, etc. this check is sent to Frank & Sharon. They send check to you. Check is made out to St. Regis University. Since SRU is in Monrovia and we are in the US and do our banking here you will deposit this check in an account you have set up in the name of *St. Regis Accounting.* We will have Blake

make up a stamp for St. Regis University with probably
Jallah's signature. You will stamp the check St. Regis University by Jallah [one of the Randocks' Liberian lackeys]. Next
you will use your stamp *St. Regis Accounting* and deposit
the check in a bank account you have established in either
Arizona or Nevada. I would suggest this account is a LLC but
it could also be a corporation. I think the LLC is better-cost
less, etc. Once the check has cleared the bank of record (nor-
mally about 10 to 15 days for full clearance) you will break
down the funds and send checks to all concerned here in the
US." Of course, that wouldn't work if Shafiq cashed the UAW
checks and kept the money for himself.

Teresa Williams did some of the bookkeeping on the
Chrysler end, preparing at least one list of UAW members
who were in the process of obtaining degrees. By early April
2004 the UAW-DaimlerChrysler Tuition Assistance Program
had sent 31 vouchers to Shafiq. Each voucher carried a face
value of $2,000 and (save for one) listed the four courses
"Manufacturing Processes," "Work Methods," "Industrial
Safety," and "Quality Assurance." The vouchers identified
each course as worth four credit hours, but in reality, a St.
Regis bachelor's degree was issued to each Chrysler worker
who had received a voucher. Shafiq faxed the vouchers from
his home in Illinois to the Randocks.

To Dixie's alarm, she noticed that the vouchers listed her
school as "St. Regis University-Clayton," with a Missouri
address near the Shafiqs' home in western Illinois. By mid-
May Shafiq had sold 66 degrees to Chrysler workers, but the
Randocks had not received payment for any of the documents Shafiq had asked them to generate. They pressured
him for a complete accounting of his customers and the
degrees he had sold, which Shafiq refused to provide. The
Randocks believed Shafiq had taken in more than $150,000
from UAW-Chrysler, and was keeping it all for himself. Their
correspondence grew more heated and Shafiq finally sent
them a check for $27,000, claiming that this was all they
were owed. But Steve's calculations disagreed with Shafiq's,

and he again demanded that Shafiq open his books, and send them the remaining $51,800 they were owed. Shafiq stopped taking their calls.

Angry messages flowed back and forth for months. The Randocks discussed publishing the details of Frank's criminal record and looking for skeletons in his (marital) closet.

Ambush!

In March 2004 Sandra Chapman was part of an investigative news team at WTHR-TV in Indianapolis which solicited suggestions for stories using a telephone "tip line." Chapman recalls ". . . there was a tip that came in on March . . . somewhere around March 21st, 22nd of 2004 and the caller was from the Chrysler foundry in Indianapolis. He was concerned about a group of recruiters that had come to the plant signing people up to get degrees from St. Regis University without these folks ever having to go to class. And the best part of it was these degrees were going to be paid for with company funds. This tipster said there were bulletins and posters that had been put up around the plant and that there was even a small booth at one point where a couple of ladies were talking about St. Regis. He didn't remember their names, but these ladies came in to basically do recruiting, and he said about 10 percent of the folks [of the total work force at the plant] had signed up for these degrees. But all along he just didn't feel good about it and the thing that really got our attention he said that, you know, and this was his quote: 'It just shouldn't happen. It's criminal.' That's what he had told us."

Chapman began digging. She never learned the identities of the female recruiters in the St. Regis booth, and didn't know whether one might have been Sharon Shafiq. "We do know that Teresa Williams was there. . . . She was the contact person at the plant, actually who worked for the Chrysler foundry here in Indianapolis. So whoever it was came in through Teresa Williams. So they set up this booth and had the posters around and started recruiting people, because of course the foundry was going to be closing down . . . and all of these workers were going to be without jobs. . . ."

"I called Teresa Williams on several occasions. Once she knew what I was looking into she would not speak with me [and] not take any calls from me. . . . I never really got to have a good conversation with her at all. . . . My information was that Teresa had recently gotten some sort of a degree from a school at some point herself and I believe that when we started asking about how you can give degrees when people weren't attending any colleges or going to any classes or anything, how could that happen? I believe she knew that we were definitely looking at something that didn't appear to be right."

Chapman learned that Williams "took advantage of the tuition assistance program in 1991 once she got hired [by Chrysler] and that she had continued with her courses until July 2002, so it was clear that she had been involved in some of these 'programs' and she actually earned . . . here's what they say: 'earned her master's degree in theology from Muskegon Bible Institute.'" But Chapman took a look at Muskegon and concluded that it was just a church basement operation. "So, yes, I would say that she knew how this was working, and was very supportive of it and working along with whoever was—that she brought in to offer this to others."

Chapman and her cameraman tried to get inside the foundry. "We weren't allowed on the property. In fact we were escorted off by security. . . . We could be across the street . . . but there was a guard shack there and they would always say . . . 'You guys can't cross the line or be on our property.' We actually had gone into the parking lot to get some interviews and we got kicked out of there. So we visited quite a few times and did not get to get inside because they weren't willing to allow us in."

"The one thing that we got a copy of was actually their graduation flyer, a pretty curious little thing, basically telling them that . . . to order their caps and gowns, and the day they were going to 'graduate,' and how many people had signed up.

. . . That was the one that my tipster was able to get to me because he was just outraged that they were actually going to have a cap-and-gown ceremony, and telling everybody to order their caps and gowns and to get ready for this great thing that was going to happen. But of course once our stories ran that kind of changed the course of things."

Chapman tried to discuss what she was seeing with the Chrysler and UAW administrations. "My first contact was through . . . John Stallings [who ran the "Tuition Assistance Program" at the UAW DaimlerChrysler National Training Center] . . . I called John and he said OK, he'd get back with me. I was later then shifted to Ron Russell who was the Director of Communications at UC-NTC, and then later on nobody would talk to me. All of my contact had to go through Mary Beth Halprin, who was the [DaimlerChrysler] corporate communications person . . . in Detroit. Our back-and-forth with them went on until right after our piece aired." Halprin sent Chapman some material describing the Tuition Assistance Program. Tuition payments to workers were for programs at approved schools, which would need to be accredited. But then management stonewalled and wouldn't explain how the St. Regis fiasco had come about, or what Chrysler might do to prevent it from happening again.

She decided to see for herself whether "St. Regis University is . . . helping students achieve their maximum potential" or not. So Chapman asked "a WTHR administrative assistant with a high school diploma and two years of general studies courses" to apply for a degree. "On her application, she provided general job descriptions but no employment dates or other specifics. . . . Within 30 minutes, she received an e-mail response with authorization for two bachelor's degrees and four certificates. All St. Regis wanted was a payment of $895. . . . In this case, once our payment was processed, we received proofs of official documents, including a bogus transcript that gave her high grades for classes she never took. Her grade point average—3.35." The final versions of the documents arrived in May, with the shipping information identifying them as coming from Amy Hensley at the A+ Institute in Washington State, not Liberia.

Chapman interviewed Richard Novak for the story, but he was uncooperative. "When we finally got him on the phone, and he was defending St. Regis, and then started yelling, and eventually he hung up. (And we had that in the story as well.) But then he never answered the phone again, you know, for us. Unfortunately we never got a chance to talk to him again." Novak had told her that "St. Regis is not a university in the United States." When she asked "So what good is the degree for people here?" he replied "Oh, please. You think the United States is the only country that has the power to say who's right and what's wrong?" And then he hung up on an investigative reporter working a story in which he was a villain.

Chapman came to Champaign with a cameraman to film an interview with me. I got to tell the WTHR audience about taking a multiple-choice test for a pair of Branford Academy degrees, and make a joke about test-taking pigeons. She found Dale Gough from AACRAO at a conference in Las Vegas and let him tell viewers that "St. Regis is a farce that has no credibility in the United States."

The story, titled "Degrees of Deception," ran in two installments on May 11 and May 12. Robert Stefaniak, the "St. Regis University Humanitarian Affairs Director," called Chapman a few days before the stories aired, identifying himself as the St. Regis public relations director. He told her that hackers had gotten into the St. Regis computers and that was why degrees had been awarded to undeserving students.

Stefaniak was an ordinary man from Milwaukee who worked as a radio announcer. It is easy to believe he was frustrated by his own limitations and unsatisfied by the small rhythms of family and friends. The Randocks made him a professor and awarded him titles after he bought his PhD. Stefaniak became the St. Regis "Humanitarian Affairs & Public Relations Director" and the "Staff Faculty Advisor for students in mass communications, music, universal religions, and broadcasting arts." He posted messages to the St. Regis alumni forum when Dixie's customers grew restless, and participated in Liberian expatriate discussion forums to express his concern for the danger faced by those in-country before the civil war was over. And in his correspondence with Randock he expressed confidence in the St. Regis administration, and admiration for its noble mission of projecting postsecondary education into Liberia. He would write to Tia, Dixie's alias, that "SRU ROCKS!" Stefaniak drew satisfaction and a sense of his own importance from his position in the Randocks' empire. The small man wanted very much to believe he was a professor at a university.

Chapman learned that St. Regis would make a damage control visit to Chrysler on June 2, so she made another trip to the factory. "I didn't know . . . what I was going to run into when I got there, but when we first arrived and folks were realizing that we were there with a camera it was like mice scattering! That's the best way to describe it. There were some folks there who had signed up for these programs and they knew they weren't right, they knew that these were— these degrees were not legitimate. And I think they were trying to get away because they did not want to be seen as one of those who were trying to get these degrees. There were others that were very adamant, that they somehow deserved these. . . . Of course we couldn't go inside initially, so these folks were coming out and some of them were just running from us; others stood there and wanted to argue the point about how hard they had worked all their lives and they deserved to get these degrees. So it was kind of sad for them because they really felt like they somehow just should have been able to get these . . . [it's like we would] help them understand that these just weren't legitimate degrees, that. . . basically they were buying something and putting their names on it."

And then Ishaq Shafiq and Robert Stefaniak walked out of the plant, right into Chapman and her crew. "That was really fun. . . . Oh my gosh. . . . When I first laid eyes on Mr. Shafiq and Mr. Stefaniak, they were walking out and had their pull-carts or whatever, just little suitcases behind them, and trying to rush to their cars, and it was like 'There they are!' It was amazing. They had on sweatshirts that had 'St. Regis University' printed on them. And so we knew, there they are. . . . I had seen a picture of Shafiq. I had never seen Stefaniak, so I knew when I saw Shafiq, I knew who he was. . . . So we ran up on them with our cameras rolling, mikes out, and just started asking questions. And of course Mr. Stefaniak was denying they had done anything wrong, that we were the problem, that we somehow had convinced people that these were bogus degrees when they were not, and that we were in the wrong and that it was going to be proven. . . . It was very confrontational, and you know, I just kept saying 'Well, let's sit down and let's talk about it. Come on, let's go in and let's sit down and talk about it. I want to hear what you have to say.' And after about ten minutes of back-and-forth, back-and-forth, they finally said 'Fine, let's do it,' they said 'Fine, let's do it.' So we went in and we sat down at a table and we began to go through the issues one by one. And they sat there for—we probably sat there for 40 minutes or so. . . . First of all, I couldn't believe that they had agreed to do it. But second of all, just after they started talking it was even more unbelievable, you know, what was coming out of their mouths and what they were saying, as far as truth, and being a real university and . . . just trying to convince me that somehow they had done the right thing."

Chapman was unimpressed with Stefaniak. "To me, he came across as a wannabe. He wanted to be somebody really important and perhaps along the way, his own personal pursuits, he never attained that. So when someone was willing to give him a title, give him that position that he really wanted, that he really believed that he was doing his job and doing them all a favor. That's kind of how he struck me. . . . I could understand why you would say a stronger personality could lead him, could impact him, because that's how he struck me."

Shafiq was different. "Shafiq came across very confident. Very unapologetic, but also, if you didn't know the history behind what had happened, or if you hadn't done the research on what this university was like, almost believable. He was that passionate, and that straightforward about it, that if you didn't know better, you might walk away and go 'Hmm . . . maybe he is telling the truth. Maybe there is something to it.' He was saying things like 'if somebody's doing this they need to be prosecuted.' And in fact, I think I put that in the story. . . . The only thing he admitted to was that there were some problems with the system."

WTHR ran "Chrysler workers face St. Regis administrators" a few hours after Chapman ambushed Dixie's salesmen at the factory. Besides the footage of Shafiq and the unimpressive Stefaniak, the story included an interview with Jeff Weber, an official at the Indiana Commission on Proprietary Education. Weber was angry that a diploma mill had been allowed to drain funds from the pool intended to help workers in peril of losing their jobs. But he believed there was very little he could do, since St. Regis was, he thought, headquartered in Liberia.

I called Weber and showed him the trail that proved the Randock family was running St. Regis from Washington State. I suggested he write to Attorney General Gregoire, who was in the middle of a gubernatorial campaign that was going sour. Weber wrote a strong letter that used the word "prosecute" and sent me a copy on the sly.

I waited six weeks. It appeared that Gregoire was ignoring Weber so I sent it to Bill Morlin, who was not at all shy about blasting an attorney general for inattention to consumer protection issues.

Morlin did some digging and wrote a story a few days after receiving the letter. He learned that "the Washington attorney general's office had acknowledged receiving [Weber's] letter, but had taken no action." Morlin wrote that "Gregoire, who wants to be Washington's next governor, said through a spokeswoman that she's aware of the issue but wouldn't say why a consumer protection action hasn't been initiated or if one is forthcoming."

Alan Contreras passed word to the Attorney General that *60 Minutes* was doing a diploma mill story and that CBS might stop by to ask her about St. Regis. They really were working on a story—we were both helping a reporter and the producer— but Alan had no idea if the producer had ever considered interviewing Gregoire.

It was like playground basketball: pass, pick, pass, shoot. The four of us were helping gubernatorial candidate Gregoire understand why she had a stake in flattening St. Regis.

My report was not the first document about St. Regis to arrive in the Attorney General's office. In March 2004 attorneys for Georgia had written to Christine Gregoire to ask about the Randocks' diploma mill. Gregoire's office sent a bland reply, then forwarded the letter to Jack Zurlini, an Assistant Attorney General in the Spokane Office of Consumer Protection. I later learned that Jeff Weber's letter had finally propelled my report all the way from Olympia to Spokane, where it too landed on Zurlini's desk. Jack quietly opened an investigation in July 2004, using my report as a sort of Guide Vert, which he called "George's Bible." Bill Morlin wrote his unflattering *Spokesman Review* article a few weeks later, but the Attorney General and her staff were not at liberty to discuss the case, or even acknowledge the existence of an investigation.

The 2004 Washington gubernatorial election was one of the closest in history. In the initial count of 2.7 million ballots, Gregoire, the Democrat, lost by a scant 261 votes. A machine recount (required in Washington State in such close elections) again showed Gregoire losing, but by the even smaller margin of 42 votes. The Democratic party paid for a hand recount and, a few days after Christmas, saw Gregoire declared the winner by 129 votes. Perhaps a handful of the 109,000 Spokane County residents who voted against her had turned away from the Democratic candidate after reading Morlin's article.

In her stories, Sandra Chapman showed that Chrysler's management, along with the union that was supposed to protect the workers, had allowed—encouraged—a criminal organization to invade the foundry and prey on auto workers slated to lose their jobs. Chapman said "For me, what was the saddest part of it all was these were really hard working people in Indiana who really were looking for another opportunity. Their dream was bursting, basically, with the closing of this plant, and they were going to have to find another way to take care of their families, another way to make their other dreams come true. They were very open and very vulnerable, and looking for something. . . . For Dixie and her crew and all of those involved, to come to this foundry and offer them this empty promise of a piece of paper that said somehow you're going to be able to go bigger places, and be able to accomplish much with this—really it was all a lie, it was all something that they were just getting rich off."

The Randocks continued their scurrilous activities, unaware that Jack Zurlini's consumer protection radar had a lock on them. By then Dixie and Steve had earned more than $4.2 million from their degree business.

United States of America v. Dixie Ellen Randock, et al.

Zurlini opened an investigation, brought me in as an expert consultant in September 2004 (I did not charge for my time), and set Grant Collins, an investigator who worked with Zurlini, to digging into the Randocks' activities. We pitched the case to the FBI in October but they were uninterested, even though the Randocks were selling services to foreign nationals seeking H-1B visas to enter the United States. Collins began discussing the case with Jim Tilley, an investigator in the U.S. Attorney's office in Spokane. Tilley was interested, and helped Collins and Zurlini pitch the case again, in December 2004. The FBI still wasn't interested, but the U.S. Secret Service was. In January 2005 the case expanded to become a joint investigation mounted by six federal agencies,

Zurlini's office, and the Spokane Police Department. John Neirinckx, a Senior Special Agent with the Secret Service, was lead agent. Bryan Tafoya, a Spokane Police detective working fraud cases, joined the investigation soon after it began. Kevin Miller, the head of the Secret Service office in Spokane, worked the case as his time allowed, as did agents Greg Roberts and Paul Kemppainen. Shannon ("Sam") Hart came onboard from Immigrations Customs Enforcement, David Benscoter from IRS, and Darrin Gilbert from the Federal Protective Service. George Jacobs, a bright Assistant U.S. Attorney with one degree from Brown, another from Cambridge, and a law degree from Emory, came on as prosecutor. They named themselves the Operation Gold Seal Task Force.

The investigation stayed covert until August 11, 2005 when dozens of armed agents executed search warrants at seven locations in three states. On that day, investigators seized the computers, external drives and storage media, paper files, and degree-making equipment that had been used to project the illusion that the foul thing called "St. Regis University" actually existed. By the end of the day the Randocks' diploma mill empire was in ashes. On October 5 Jacobs filed an indictment for mail fraud and other felonies against the Randocks, Lorhan, Novak, Carlson, Markishtum, Hensley, and Pearson.

Carlson and Novak pleaded guilty in March 2006; the charges against Novak included bribery of foreign officials. Their early pleas, and the substantial assistance they provided to the prosecution, would help them at sentencing. Pearson pleaded guilty in October 2006, and Hensley did the same in April 2007. The indictment against Pearson included charges stemming from the collection of child pornography he had loaded into the St. Regis web servers.

The remaining defendants fought the case, filing June 2007 motions to dismiss the indictments and suppress the evidence seized in searches. The court heard arguments on the motions during eight days of hearings in October and November 2007; the transcripts of the hearings are more than

1,600 pages in length. In February 2008 the judge ruled for the prosecution, and all the air went out of the defendants' case. On March 26, 2008, Dixie, Steve, and Heidi pleaded guilty. Roberta Markishtum threw in the towel a few days later. A few months after that, a federal judge sentenced Dixie and Steve Randock to three year prison terms and Heidi Lorhan to a year and a day. Markishtum was sentenced to four months and Ken Pearson to four years, mostly for his pornography offense. Novak, Carlson, and Hensley were given terms of supervised probation, but no time behind bars.

At sentencing, George Jacobs offered a succinct description of Dixie Randock and her degree business: "Mrs. Randock is a high school drop out and former real estate agent who had no experience running a legitimate institution of higher learning. She was the mastermind of a sophisticated global Internet scheme that sold 10,815 degrees and related academic products to 9,612 buyers in 131 countries for $7,369,907. Mrs. Randock's scheme spread quickly outside of the United States into most areas of the world with the aid of the Internet. She developed and oversaw the scheme with passion. She pursued it enthusiastically and continued to develop ways to make money and the income generated in the scheme was hidden in various bank accounts including off shore accounts."

Publicity from the case against the Randocks led to new legislation, included in the 2008 "Higher Education Opportunity Act," that writes into law a federal definition of the term "diploma mill." There should have been more, but most of the text was removed at the insistence of a few members of the House-Senate conference committee that drafted the final version of the bill.

Liberia has remained at peace; President Ellen Johnson Sirleaf, the first woman to become president of an African country, has managed to move the country forward in spite of the damage from the civil war. The infant mortality rate has fallen to less than half what it was at the end of the war. To the best of my knowledge, the one or two diploma mills that still pretend to be Liberian universities are neither making much money at it, nor receiving cover from Liberian officials.

I continue to teach physics at the University of Illinois and do research in elementary particle physics. But I have added higher education policy to my areas of scholarship, and publish articles in the journals of that field. I was fortunate to receive a John Simon Guggenheim Foundation fellowship in 2009 to support the expenses of researching the book that has provided the source material for this chapter; the University of Illinois has also helped by providing me with a one-semester appointment as an associate at the university's Center for Advanced Study.

The agents and attorneys of Gold Seal have moved on, to other cases, sometimes to other agencies where they continue to work as investigators. I worked most closely with Neirinckx, Tilley, Collins, and Tafoya, but also came to know Miller, Zurlini, and Jacobs during the four years of the case. I liked all of them immensely, and came away from Gold Seal with a profound respect for these agents of civil society, who would put themselves into harm's way to protect our system of higher education. It has been an utterly remarkable experience for me, and I am grateful for it.

B. THE UNIVERSITY DEGREE PROGRAM: BIGGEST DEGREE MILL EVER

The biggest degree business the world has ever known was started by an American living in Bucharest, Romania. The business is the one described at the beginning of the introduction. Insiders estimate that total sales, since the mid-1990s, have been more than $400 million, representing sales of more than two hundred thousand diplomas, mostly to Americans and Canadians.

In 2002, we entered into communication with an unhappy employee of University Degree Program (UDP), working at the main offices in Romania. He supplied us with a great deal of information relating to the business and how it operated

Virtually everything is done by using the Internet. The Program begins by sending out "spam" messages by the millions. While the wording varies slightly, the messages nearly all begin, "Obtain a prosperous future, money-earning power, and the admiration of all." Recipients are invited to call a US telephone number, which is an answering service. More than one hundred different numbers in a dozen or more states have been used. The recorded message invites callers to leave their name and number. Within two or three days, they receive a telephone call. While the caller suggests or says that he is calling from England (or wherever the school currently featured is supposed to be), the calls are in fact made either from Bucharest, Romania, or from Jerusalem, typically either by natives of those countries or by South African immigrants living there.

The telemarketing call is extremely well orchestrated, with a detailed script, which is reproduced at the end of this section. Approximately one person in three ends up buying a degree during the phone call. A smaller "sideline" business involves selling counterfeit international drivers' licenses. More than three hundred fifty thousand of these were sold in the United States and Canada.

The school name is changed regularly; more than thirty names have been used. Sometimes names are changed when an earlier name gets some bad publicity; sometimes just for the sake of variety. The "degree package," as it is called, typically includes the diploma (date of one's choice), the transcript (courses and grades of one's choice), information on a degree verification service employers can call, and two extremely favorable letters of recommendation in which, for instance, Professor Bideman writes that this is one of the finest students he has ever had, and he cannot recommend her or him too highly.

The University of Ravenhurst is one of the many names used by the huge University Degree Program. Their professional-looking product, which they call the "degree package," consists of the diploma . . .

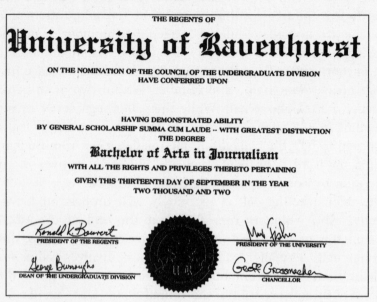

. . . the transcript

From the Desk of

Frederick Bideman

12 June 2003

Dear Sir or Madam:

was enrolled in several of my correspondence classes, in fulfillment of the core requirements for his major.

As proven by his work,   was diligent, well prepared, and absorbed new material quickly. Needless to say, his high marks in my courses reflect his outstanding performance on tests and written assignments.

I am confident that   has a bright future and will succeed in all his future endeavors.

Sincerely,

Dr. Frederick Bideman
Professor, University of Ravenhurst
Correspondence Address: Prinsengr 64
Amsterdam 1015DX Netherlands

. . . an effusive letter of recommendation . . .

UNIVERSITY OF RAVENHURST
CORRESPONDENCE ADDRESS: PRINSENGR 64
AMSTERDAM 1015DX NETHERLANDS

June 13, 2003

To Whom It May Concern:

graduated from our University with departmental honors.

As an honors student,   was responsible for supervising undergraduates through our distance learning tutorial program. Within a short time, he proved to be such a bright, astute, and accomplished student that we utilized his talents in many aspects of our academic program.

While with our University,   maintained constant contact with faculty members. His correspondence demonstrated knowledge, sensitivity, and intelligence in dealing with complex issues, earning him the accolades of our entire academic staff.

In sum, I unreservedly recommend   for any position suitable to his outstanding background, qualifications, academic achievement, and experience. He will be a valuable asset to any organization.

Very truly yours,

Professor Henry Clausdale, PhD

. . . and a letter attesting to the student's graduation with honors.

Brentwick University had an elegant Internet presence. The reality was a seedy secretarial service above a London laundry.

Ashford University
Bedford University
Brentwick University
Carrington University
Devon University
Devonshire University
Dorchester University
Dunham University
Glencullen University
Hampshire University
Harrington University
Kingsfield University
Lafayette University
Landford University
Northfield University
Parkhurst University
Parkwood University

Ravenhurst University
Shelbourne University
Shepperton University
Stafford University
Strassford University
Suffield University
Thornewood University
University of Palmers Green
University of San Moritz
University of Switzerland
Walsh University
Westbourne University
Western Ohio University
Westhampton University
Wexford University
Xavier University

There is persuasive evidence, as well, that some former employees of the University Degree Program have left and started comparable businesses of their own, from Israel and elsewhere.

Authorities in the United States, England, and Ireland (where the program uses mail-forwarding services); Israel (where the diplomas are printed); and Cyprus (where much of their banking is done) are certainly well aware of the business, as, of course, are the Romanians, but they seem either unwilling or unable to do anything about it, with rare exceptions.

In 2003, the Federal Trade Commission announced that it had "settled charges" against three companies and three individuals who appear to be the ones associated with this business. They agreed to pay $57,000 in penalties (or roughly eight hours of their revenues) and to refrain from selling diplomas. Their US-hosted websites were closed, but they simply opened others elsewhere. Intriguingly, the order says that "if they are found to have misrepresented their financial condition, a $5 million avalanche clause would become effective."

Three months after the order went into effect, we did not notice a decline in the number of "spam" messages offering the recipient the opportunity to buy a "prestigious university degree." It is conceivable these offers are coming from other sources, but it seems more than likely that they have just moved to Internet service providers in other places.

And perhaps most significantly, other than this minuscule fine—the equivalent of stealing $10,000 and being fined one dollar!—there has been no criminal prosecution by anyone, anywhere.

Here is a small portion of the actual telemarketing script used by University Degree Program. (The complete script is on our website, http://www.degreemills.com.) As you read through it, you may come to appreciate how one-third of the callers could end up buying a degree. Note that the caller is instructed to say that the school is a "nonaccredited diploma mill," but this is to be said quickly and softly. Not all callers say this. And, in our experience, if the person being called notices and says, "What did you just say?" then the caller hangs up. The boldface type, in brackets, are the instructions to the caller.

Hi, this is **[say your name]**.

I'm a registrar with the University Degree Program. I apologize for my European accent. We just wanted to contact you to tell you that, because we have some spaces left in our program, we reduced our registration fee by more than $2,000. What I am going to tell you is very important, so if you don't understand everything I say, just let me know. If now is a good time for you, I'll explain our new program and answer any questions that you might have.

[Wait—Continue only if you are not interrupting and he is not in a rush!]

That's great! The name of our institution is Thornewood University. We have no central campus. Our campus is the homes and offices of our students. We are not affiliated with or located in any country, but we do have a mailing address in the United Kingdom. We are fully recognized members of distance-learning organizations in Europe. Our original founders got together in 1983 and now we are part of a multinational group.

First of all, let me be honest with you. If you're looking for an accredited university, I suggest that you register at Harvard or Yale, pay the several hundred thousand dollars tuition, and study the many years required. Is this what you want?

[Wait—If "Yes," hang up!]

Or, would you rather have the benefits of an Ivy League education immediately with very little cost? **[Wait!]** Of course you would, so listen carefully! We don't give a damn about other universities, employers, professors, or anyone else. We only care about *YOU*! We will do anything legal, moral, and reasonable on your behalf. As your **[speak softly and fast]** nonaccredited "diploma mill," **[normal speech]** our job is to take care of *your* needs and wants by backing up *your* credentials. For example, we supply you with documents because of your work, private study, and life experience. Are we what you're looking for?

[Wait—If "No," hang up!]

Before I tell you more about our program, I want to tell you that I'm on your side 100 percent, and I am listening to everything you tell me. So that I can recommend the best program for you, please tell me, career wise, what you want out of your future.

[Wait!—listen closely to him, showing interest.]

In which field of study do you want your degrees?

[Wait!—You can recommend a field of study here if needed.]

Good choice! Now, let me ask two brief questions. Do you feel that you have the potential to be a qualified professional in your field? **[Wait!]**

Do you feel that you only lack documentation of your accomplishments. **[Wait!]** With your background, I feel that you can take advantage of a PhD in **[state the name of his field]** or an MBA—the price is the same so, which do you prefer, a PhD, MBA, or both? **[Wait!]**

Of course, we'll give you a bachelor's and master's for background, right, **[say his name.]**? **[Wait!]** You can comfortably use these diplomas to supply the documentation that you lack.

These nonaccredited diplomas should reflect your credentials so that you can use them for business, employment, and personal purposes. However, this program will be successful only if the degrees are in a field in which you are qualified.

In fact, the initial diplomas and transcripts that you receive are sample documents that we tailor make according to your instructions. These documents are free when you pay to register for the program. Of course, you cannot use sample diplomas for licensing or for transferring credits.

Now, before I tell you the low price of registration in our program, let's custom design your diplomas so that you know exactly what you are getting. Your diplomas will look exactly like those diplomas you've seen many times hanging on the walls of doctors, lawyers, and other professionals. Actually, most university diplomas look very much alike, but let's select a university and make your diplomas look like theirs. Of course, the diplomas will bear our university's name. What's your favorite university. **[Wait!]**

[If they can't think of one, suggest UCLA, if you must!]

That's a good choice because they have a very impressive diploma. What name do you want printed on the diplomas? **[Wait!]** Can we put on your diplomas that you graduated with top honors? **[Wait!]** As to the graduation dates, we want them to correspond to your age. What year were you born? **[Wait!]** We'll date the diplomas to **(dates—bachelor's, 2 years after DOS; master's, 4; MBA and PhD, 6.)**

You can assume any titles that come with your diplomas. For instance, when you get the PhD, or MBA, you can legally call yourself doctor or put "PhD" after your name. Do you plan to call yourself doctor? **[Wait!]**

In addition, to show what good students receive, there are custom-made transcripts and recommendation letters from professors at the university. Isn't this a great idea? **[Wait!]** We'll also issue laminated wallet-sized replicas of your diplomas so you can carry your credentials in your wallet to impress your friends. Do you understand? **[Wait!]**

Along with your materials, you'll receive our e-mail address, our UK mailing address, and our fax number for you to give to prospective employers or anyone checking your credentials. Naturally, when we receive an inquiry concerning your qualifications, we verify that you received your diplomas. We even send certified copies of transcripts when requested. You do want us to back you up when someone checks, don't you? **[Wait!]**

You have one full year to make any changes on your diplomas free of charge. The rest is up to you. You receive optional correspondence course lists and evaluation examinations so you can take the courses and get recognized degrees whenever you have time. Once your diplomas arrive along with their supporting materials, you're set for life. That's all there is to it. Isn't this perfect—[use his name]? [Wait!]

Excellent! Where do you want your diplomas and materials shipped? [Wait!] What is your daytime phone number? [Wait!] What is your evening/weekend phone number? [Wait!] What is your fax number? [Wait!] What is your e-mail address? [Wait!]

Now, [use his name], our program is perfect because you designed it yourself but, if I were you, I'd only be concerned about one thing.

[Wait for him to say "What's that?"] Will your friends and relatives be jealous of your newfound success? [Wait!]

Let me ask you this—If I were to give you $250,000 in cash right now, would you give me $10,000? [Wait!] Of course you would. Do you know that a person with a college degree can earn $25,000 more per year? [Wait!] That means over ten years, a degree can be worth more than $250,000 in extra earnings. In other words, I'm offering you the equivalent of maybe a quarter of a million dollars, right, [use his name]? [Wait!]

Moreover, we both know that I'm not going to ask you for $10,000. So now, how much are you willing to pay for $250,000 in cash? [Wait!]

<If he says $3,400 or more> Well, [his name], I have an additional surprise for you. If you can invest just [the price he said minus $500] in your future for the program—for signing up right now, on this call—I'll mark your account "Paid in Full." It can't get any better than that. Which is the easiest way for you to pay—cash, check, or credit card? [Wait!]

Go to "Wire," "Check," or "Credit Card"

<If "Negative">I'm a little confused, [his name]. You told me that you are willing to pay [the price he said], and I say the registration fee is only (the price he said minus $500.) What would you suggest? [Wait!]

<If anything else>

Well, I'll tell you what. If you can invest just twenty-nine hundred dollars ($2,900) in your future for the program—for signing up right now, on this call—I'll mark your account "Paid in Full." It can't get any better than that. Which is easiest. way for you to pay—cash, check, or credit card? [Wait!]

This is about a quarter of the telemarketing script. It continues in the same vein for another twenty pages. Our favorite bit is where the telemarketer is instructed to **[chuckle here]**.

C. COLUMBUS UNIVERSITY

We first became aware of this school in 1997 when a "faculty-wanted" advertisement for Colgate University in Louisiana appeared in the *Chronicle of Higher Education*. When the real Colgate University in New York complained, the Louisiana founder said he'd never heard of them and had named his school after the toothpaste. Under threat of legal action, he changed the name from Colgate to Columbus University.

Columbus University is a classic example of an institution that moves from one state to another as state laws or licensing requirements change, or as other circumstances dictate. It appears to have used various addresses in Alabama, Louisiana, Mississippi, and Tennessee. When its license was revoked in one place, it changed its address, not necessarily moving at all.

(Note: the Columbus University discussed here should not be confused with the legitimate Columbus University in Washington, DC, where, by chance, Allen Ezell's father earned his law degree at night school while employed at the FBI, later becoming a special agent.)

Ezell corresponded with and collected material from Columbus for several years, and turned it over to the FBI, which clearly made good use of it.

The first Columbus web pages, dated December 1998, can be found at http://www.archive.org, which shows an address in Metairie, Louisiana. The sales letter from President Harry J. Boyer refers to the institution as "an accredited distance learning . . . university." Accreditation came from the unrecognized World Association of Universities and Colleges, perhaps best known for accrediting the fake Edison University within weeks of its founding in the prison cell of convicted degree-mill operator James Kirk (LaSalle University).

Columbus calls itself "the established name in distance education," stating that "the principles of truth and honesty are recognized as fundamental to the University." They offered degrees in 128 subjects, from associate's through PhD, with a grand total, as it turned out, of one faculty member, herself with only a Columbus degree. Tuition ranged from about $2,000 to $4,000, with discounts for the military.

Within a year, Columbus had made the *Irish Times'* list of "12 famous diploma mills."

Columbus appears to have grown and prospered. Their February 2011 website can be read in French and Arabic, and features a large three-story brick building on a hill, which clearly has nothing to do with the small duplex apartment in New Orleans from which the university is run. Indeed, it was later identified as the main campus building of the Randolph-Macon Academy, a prep school in Virginia. And they list various affiliates in Africa, Asia, and the Middle East.

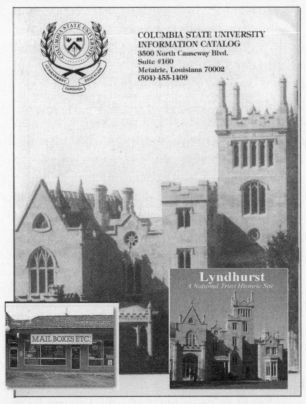

On the left is the campus of Columbus University, as depicted on their website. On the right is the main campus building of the Randolph-Macon Academy in Virginia. Is this not an amazing coincidence?

On May 10, 2004, *CBS Evening News* ran a story, arising from revelations during the congressional hearings, titled "Top Officials Hold Fake Degrees," which included Charles Abell, a senior assistant secretary of defense, with a master's degree from Columbus. Another well-known alumnus is "Dr." Brian McNamee, confessed provider of steroids to pitcher Roger Clemens.

Over the next few years, Columbus changed its address from Louisiana to a PO Box™ in Daphne, Alabama, to a PO Box in Picayune, Mississippi.

On February 23, 2010, following a criminal investigation of several years, the FBI filed a thirteen-page affidavit, and a search warrant was approved by a US magistrate. The following day, they executed the warrant on what apparently was the real office of Columbus, in a duplex on Hickory Street in New Orleans, seizing school files and computers. Newspaper accounts reported that three women worked in the office, including "Dr." Shannon O'Brien, identified as the sole faculty for all 128 degree programs.

This affidavit was to seek evidence that school officials are engaging in mail fraud and wire (telephone and Internet) fraud in violation of US Code Title 18, Sections 1341, 1343, and 1346, using the mails and Internet to obtain money, and depriving others of "the intangible right of honest services."

Unlike some of the earlier DipScam investigations, this time the FBI apparently did not purchase degrees from Columbus. Instead, they allege that during efforts to obtain state approval or accreditation, Columbus officials filed fraudulent and deceptive documents with state agencies in Louisiana, Mississippi, and Alabama. Further, Columbus is alleged to have made deliberate efforts to conceal its activities from education officials in Mississippi. Also, the various websites (columbusu.com, columbusu.net, columbusu.info, masterei.com) "are calculated to deceive prospective students as to the true nature of CU's fraudulent business practices. . . ."

The FBI verified that operators of CU issue diplomas that are sold by foreign partners and/or affiliates in the Middle East and elsewhere. The FBI learned that a Saudi partner sent a list of names to operators of Columbus, who then sent diplomas overseas.

The FBI confirmed that Columbus awarded doctoral degrees in

subjects including health service management, English, psychology, public administration, counseling, marketing, creative writing, and computer science. Columbus conceals the fact that they have no faculty qualified in any of these fields.

The FBI agent stated, "I have confirmed that operators of CU receive instructions concerning how to perpetrate these deceptive practices from an individual named Michael O'Keefe, Sr., who currently is incarcerated at a federal correctional facility in Butner, North Carolina, convicted of stealing from an insurance company. O'Keefe's instructions . . . include instructions on not telling students about the true nature of CU's operations in Mississippi and Alabama" (Martin was previously O'Keefe's accountant). O'Keefe served in the Louisiana State Senate for twenty-four years, and began a nineteen-year federal prison sentence in 1999. (A WWL-TV story ran on May 13, 2010, titled "Former State Senator Running School from Behind Bars.")

In summary, Columbus was a fraud from its inception, with an imprisoned former state senator (now in federal prison) allegedly pulling strings—possibly from inside prison. Columbus had no facilities per se, and it advertises unrecognized and worthless accreditation. The entire staff was three women, none of whom had ever been employed at a college or university.

The big question is: now what?

When the FBI has reviewed the seized materials and has conducted interviews with graduates to see what use they have made of their degrees, the lead FBI agent will prepare a summary investigative report for the United States Attorney's Office.

A member of the Assistant United States Attorneys (AUSA) will review this report, exhibits, charts, and so on, and render an opinion as to whether federal laws have been violated; if so, by whom, and if federal prosecution is warranted.

If prosecution is entertained, an indictment will be prepared and the matter will be presented to a Federal Grand Jury in the Eastern District of Louisiana. If a true bill of indictment is returned by the Grand Jury, then arrest warrants will be issued and served, followed by the prosecutive phase. Only time will tell what's next for officials of Columbus University.

Chapter 8

TIME BOMBS

People with Fake Degrees

In chapter 3, we wrote about the people who buy fake degrees, describing a few case histories. In this section, we're devoting a fair amount of space to these "time bombs"—cases of people with fake degrees—primarily because we have learned, in our many public talks and interviews, as well as in the responses to the earlier edition of this book, that this is a really good way to get people's attention and to drive home the significance of the problem in ways that charts, tables, and cumulative statistics cannot do so well.

It is one thing to read that there are many thousands of teachers and doctors with fake degrees; it is quite another to learn that *your* child's history teacher or *your* family doctor has a fake degree.

As you look at these examples from the hundreds of thousands, very likely millions, of cases out there, remember that these are more than impersonal statistics—every single one is a real person whose behaviors have had (or will have) significant impact on himself or herself, as well as employers, schools, churches, government agencies, and quite possibly the general public.

We have organized the list by the kinds of fake degrees involved: medical, business, political, therapist, and so on. Some are "time bombs" that have already exploded—having been reported on the Internet, through the media, or in court proceedings. And some are "time bombs" that are still ticking away, buried in peoples' resumes and employers' files. We know about these by searching online resume-posting sites (like Monster.com), the million-plus people described in the various *Who's Who* directories, as well as from press releases, articles, and websites where bad and fake schools are mentioned without apparent awareness of what they are.

In some cases, we are not using the names of these people, believing there is nothing to be gained by further embarrassing them, especially if they have already suffered legal and other consequences from their decision to use a fake or illegal degree or credential.

ACADEMIA

- One of the best-known and most outspoken admissions officers in the United States, the dean of admission at MIT, resigned after admitting she fabricated her academic credentials (three degrees) thirty years earlier. In her popular book on admissions anxiety, she warned against "making up information to present yourself as something you are not."
- In Canada, Ping Sun (also known as Randy) sold counterfeit degrees and transcripts from his real alma mater, York University: nearly $2 million worth from 2004 to 2008. When exposed by the *Star*, he fled to China.
- In Korea, Shin Jung Ah, professor at a major university, was criminally charged for forging and misusing a degree from Yale University.
- Following a massive recruiting drive in India, dozens of students flew to Fiji to enroll in University of Pacific International, only to find that it did not exist. At least fifty Nepalese were also scammed by this fake.
- A 951-page modern physics textbook called *Energy from the Vacuum* was written by Thomas E. Bearden, PhD, whose doctorate is from the bogus Trinity College and University.
- More than fifty Canadians teaching in Korea were arrested and deported after they were discovered to be using counterfeit Canadian diplomas.
- Robert "Dr. Bob" Miller was convicted eighteen times in fifteen years in Maryland for impersonating professionals of all kinds, from police officer to chiropractor. In 2008, he was caught operating three diploma mills selling degrees to Koreans. His "schools" were Louisiana Central University, Louisiana Capital University, and Washington Chiropractic College.

- The American Academy of Distance Education sold at least ten thousand fake credits to 750 Miami-area teachers to help them gain certification. Founder William McCuggle, a seventy-three-year-old retired teacher, pleaded guilty and was sentenced to two years.
- Prominent dancer Lan-Lan Wang, who had been on the faculty of three major universities, resigned when it became known that she did not earn either of her two claimed degrees.
- The Freehold, New Jersey, superintendent of schools was reimbursed for the $2,500 he paid for his bogus doctorate.
- In 2008, authorities in India's third-largest state, Bihar, fired fifteen thousand teachers who had used fake degrees to get their jobs. The Human Resources ministry suggested that an additional fifteen thousand were likely to be terminated as well.
- A University of Alabama administrator was dismissed because of his fake doctorate from the University of Beverly Hills. He went on to become curriculum/accreditation director for a county school system, where he was paid an additional $50,000 over ten years because of his doctorate.
- The president of the University of Toulon in France and two vice presidents were suspended in 2009 in the wake of a scandal in which more than two hundred Chinese exchange students purchased fake diplomas for about $4,300 each, a total of more than $800,000.
- The chief scientist in a study that led to new California policies on diesel fuel emissions, Hien Tran, falsely claimed a PhD from the University of California. He had purchased his degree for $1,000 from a diploma mill. The whistle-blower who exposed this information, Professor James Enstrom, was let go from his job at UCLA after thirty-four years.
- A Pensacola State College professor was fired when he was discovered to have a master's degree from an online diploma mill.
- In 2011, the vice president of China's preeminent agricultural university was found to have bought his master's degree from a California mill, California American University.
- A professor of psychology at Southwest Tennessee Community College has a fake PhD from Brighton University.

- A senior staff member at the University of Iowa had used two fake doctorates and three other fake degrees professionally for ten years, and was given a major postdoctoral grant from the National Institutes of Health. She was sentenced to thirteen years in prison.
- The president of Quincy University in Illinois claimed his master's was from the traditional LaSalle University in Philadelphia, but when it was revealed that it was from the fake LaSalle in Louisiana, he was invited to resign.
- The president of Toccoa Falls College, Georgia, resigned when the student newspaper reported that he had not received the master's degree listed on his resume.
- The former provost of Cheyney University, Pennsylvania, was forced to resign when her claim of an Oxford doctorate was found to be false.
- The CEO and principal of the state-approved Christa McAuliffe Academy in Washington received his MEd and PhD in educational leadership from the phony St. Regis University.
- The Chronicle of Higher Education website reported that "according to government statistics, six hundred thousand fake diplomas are circulating in China, although many government officials suspect that the actual number is much higher." Apparently most of them are counterfeit diplomas of real schools. "It seems insiders at real universities are selling diplomas for hefty prices."
- The Miami-Dade County Grand Jury determined that in one year, $345,000 of taxpayer money had gone to pay the salaries of four teachers with fake degrees and teaching credentials.
- William Kitchen, professor at Nashville State University, claims a PhD from the fake Cambridge State University.
- When human resource director Dr. Al Alt was named interim chancellor of the Yuba Community College District in California, a member of the Academic Senate said, "As human resources director, his expertise should be to identify diploma mills such as the Mississippi one where he got his PhD."
- In Asbury Park, New Jersey, a teacher/consultant was getting a $2,500 salary bonus based on her PhD from the fake Breyer

State University. She and three other district employees were ordered not to call themselves "Doctor."

- A professor at the University of Illinois Medical School has a real MD but has also used a fake PhD in public health from Columbia State University.

- Several school officials at Touro College, New York, a regionally accredited school, were found to be selling fake degrees and transcripts, as well as accepting bribes from students to change their grades. Touro founder and president Rabbi Bernard Lander was, in 2009 and at age ninety-three, the highest-paid college executive in the United States, at $4.8 million a year.

- A former student of York University, Canada, was found to be selling "near-perfect" copies of York diplomas for $3,000 and transcripts for $1,000 more.

- According to a Boston newspaper, the founder of the highly reputable Emerson College, Dr. Charles Wesley Emerson, feeling a need to appear credentialed, acquired his medical degree for $25 from a mail-order mill. The college librarian responded to a newspaper inquiry by writing, "given the nature of . . . his M.D. degree, let's just be happy that he founded an institution of higher education and not a hospital!"

- A full-time lecturer at University of California–Irvine received his PhD from the University Degree Program phony Devonshire University. When this became known, the School of Engineering thereupon decided not to recognize his degree, but "the university has no plans to reprimand or dismiss [him]."

BUSINESS AND MEDIA

- Celebrity chef Robert Irvine, host of the popular *Dinner: Impossible* program, lost his Food Network job when his degree turned out to be nonexistent, and when it was discovered that he didn't work at the White House or help design Princess Diana's wedding cake, as he had claimed.

- The cofounder of Zicam® nasal gel, a company that paid over $12 million to settle more than three hundred lawsuits related to their product, listed an MBA and doctorate in biopharma-ceutical project management from American University of Asturias, closed by Spanish authorities as a diploma mill.

- Bob Harris, who earned a big salary as meteorologist for CBS, the *New York Times*, and the Long Island Railroad, insisted on being called "Doctor Bob" because of his claimed PhD in geo-physics from Columbia University. He was fired when it was learned that he had lied about his doctorate and his other two degrees.

- Television station WSOC in Charlotte, North Carolina, reported that 1,400 airplane mechanics had acquired their cer-tification from "a diploma mill called St. George Aviation" in Florida, subsequently shut down by the Federal Aviation Administration. The FAA was apparently considering having them retested.

- A disaster-recovery executive for a major oil company has a degree-mill master's and doctorate.

- In 2010, the president of Microsoft China admitted that his PhD did not come from CalTech, as he had indicated in earlier writings, but that he had purchased it for $3,000 from an unac-credited California school. He is now the *former* president of Microsoft China.

- Jack Pelton, CEO of Cessna Aircraft, survived the national attention following a report on CBS television that he had received degrees in aeronautical engineering from Hamilton University, a diploma mill in Wyoming.

- One of the two public television networks in New Zealand hired a Canadian with a fake American MBA (Denver State University) as its chairman. When the fake was discovered, the Canadian was fired, indicted, convicted, imprisoned, and deported, all within a few months.

- There are, improbably, two computer experts writing under the pen name of Robert X. Cringely. The one who had also been a public television star turned out not to have the Stan-ford PhD he had been claiming. When challenged, he said, "[A] new fact has now become painfully clear to me: you don't say you have the PhD unless you really have the PhD."

- In a major 2010 court case, a computer services firm was successfully sued by British Sky Broadcasting, when the computer firm's leading expert, Joe Galloway, was shown to have a fake degree. Galloway spiritedly defended his degree and described his regular visits to the Virgin Islands to work on his Concordia degree. The prosecution thereupon introduced Lulu, a dog who had been awarded the same Concordia MBA but with better grades than Mr. Galloway. British Sky was awarded a judgment equivalent to $520 million.
- Bausch & Lomb chairman and CEO Ronald Zarella forfeited a bonus of $1.1 million for falsely claiming to have completed an NYU master's degree. The company stock dipped when columnist Herb Greenberg revealed this news.
- It was big news in Canada when investors in one of billionaire Richard Li's companies filed a class-action lawsuit claiming they were misled by his false Stanford degree.
- The chief financial officer of the very large Veritas Software company was fired when it was learned that he had neither the Stanford MBA nor the Arizona bachelor's degree that he listed on his resume. (*Veritas* means "truth" in Latin.)
- A large California engineering company demoted its president after learning he did not have the engineering degree he claimed. The company stock dropped 9 percent after that announcement.
- The FBI discovered a man with a fake mechanical engineering degree who had been working at the ill-fated Three Mile Island nuclear power plant.
- A man with a fake PhD in electrical aerospace engineering was discovered by the FBI working at the Johnson Space Center.
- An engineer responsible for airline safety at Lockheed NASA has a fake degree in manufacturing engineering.
- An engineer with responsibility for all his railroad's engineering work in a major industrial center has a fake engineering degree.
- Dr. Eric Gravenberg, a prominent motivational speaker and head of the African American Male Initiative, has his PhD from Columbus University, described by CBS as "a diploma mill Louisiana shut down."

- The *Orange County Register* withdrew a job offer to a Duluth journalist to become their publisher when they learned she did not have the bachelor's degree shown on her resume.
- Robert Irsay, who controversially moved his Baltimore Colts football team from Indianapolis in the middle of the night, claimed certain degrees and a distinguished military record. It turned out that he had neither.
- Radio Shack CEO David Edmondson resigned when a Fort Worth newspaper discovered he did not have the degrees listed on his resume. He did, however, get a one-million-dollar severance package.
- Ron Kagan, longtime director of the Detroit Zoo, admitted he did not have the PhD in zoology that he had claimed. He was docked $16,000 from his $192,000-a-year salary.
- The president and CEO of PepsiAmericas does not have the Michigan State University degree that has been listed in various SEC (US Securities and Exchange Commission) filings.
- The chairman and CEO of the huge MGM Grand casino empire abruptly resigned a job that had reportedly paid him $9 million a year after it became known that he did not have the MBA degree listed on his resume.
- Gregory Probert, CEO of Herbalife, resigned after it was discovered he did not have the MBA degree listed on his resume.
- The founder/principal of Camarda Financial, a large money-management firm in Florida, has his PhD from Louisiana degree mill LaSalle University.
- Seagate, which has sold over a billion hard drives, hired an engineer with a counterfeit Oxford degree. He was fired from the $95,000-a-year job twelve days later.
- A man who puts on stress-management workshops at corporations and universities has his PhD in psychology from the fake Columbia State University.
- The FBI discovered an engineer at Westinghouse Nuclear International with a fake PhD and two other fake degrees in mechanical engineering.
- The president and chief technology officer for Ecom Research Corporation, a software development company, lists an MBA

and PhD from Vernell, a fake university invented by the people at YourDegreeNow.com.
- The engineer responsible for nuclear deactivation activities at a large nuclear facility has a fake BA.
- High-profile lie-detector expert Edward Gelb, onscreen expert for *Larry King Live*, *Geraldo*, and others, involved with the O. J. Simpson and JonBenét Ramsey cases, and past president of the American Polygraph Association, has his doctorate from LaSalle University in Louisiana, acquired shortly before the FBI raid and the guilty pleas of its founders.
- The FBI discovered a Kennedy Space Center electrical engineer with a fake engineering degree on the customer list of an Arizona degree mill.
- The president of a company that screens potential jurors has a fake PhD in psychology.
- The head of training and education for a Fortune 500 company, responsible for more than fifty thousand employees, has a fake BA and MA.

GOVERNMENT AND POLITICS

- Charles Abell, who was Principal Deputy Undersecretary of Defense for Personnel and Readiness in the George W. Bush administration, responsible for human resource policies for several million people, uses a master's degree from the fake Columbus University in Mississippi.
- The Swedish Minister for Employment, Sven Otto Littorin, insisted his MBA from an unrecognized Louisiana school was valid, but when he refused to let anyone see his thesis, he was forced to stop using that degree.
- A male supervisor in the US Marshals Service was earning an additional $16,000 a year because of his degree from the fake St. Regis University. He was caught when someone noticed that his fake transcript included a course in self-defense for women.

- In Tanzania, eight senior cabinet members were found to have degrees, mostly PhDs, from American degree mills such as Washington International University and Commonwealth Open University.
- The city manager of Eagle Pass, Texas, was fired when his fake degrees came to light. He changed his name slightly and was then hired as city manager of Grantville, Georgia.
- A Government Accountability Office investigation found three National Nuclear Security Administration managers with top-level security clearances who received fraudulent degrees from diploma mills. Because their jobs did not require degrees, they were not disciplined.
- A Southern California custody evaluator, employed more than three thousand times by the family court system, with fees as high as $30,000 per case, was sued by a dissatisfied client, in part on the basis of questionable credentials.
- Florida House candidate Keith Richter listed a degree from a British degree mill. The ensuing bad publicity caused his employer, Hodges University, to lower his status from faculty to teaching assistant.
- Two Sacramento-area water district managers were sued for using public funds to buy diploma-mill degrees and then using those degrees to get pay raises and bonuses.
- The Interior Minister of Iran, Ali Kordan, was impeached when it was discovered he had a counterfeit degree from Oxford University. And an aide to President Mahmoud Ahmadinejad was fired after he attempted to bribe MPs to vote against the impeachment.
- 1995 World Fifa football player of the year George Weah lost his campaign for the presidency of Liberia after it became known that his degree was purchased from a Romanian-based degree mill. At press time, Weah was a candidate for the vice presidency of Liberia, with the election to be held in late 2011.
- It was page-one news when the Irish government's chief science adviser, Barry McSweeney, was found to be using a PhD from an unaccredited California school widely regarded as a degree mill.

- In 2009, the newly elected vice chairman of the North Carolina Republican Party, Dr. Timothy Johnson, refused to reveal the source of his PhD, but it was locally reported to have come from a Louisiana diploma mill.
- The chief technology officer for the Washington, DC, Board of Elections and Ethics did not have the American University degree she listed on her job application. She was suspended for sixty days.
- A Republican activist and veterans adviser in Florida claims a law degree from a Kansas diploma mill, Monticello University. Charley Price has sued four Korean War veterans who exchanged public e-mails about his law degree situation.
- Basketball star Dave Bing was elected mayor of Detroit in 2009 in spite of admitting that he did not have the MBA from General Motors Institute/Kettering University that he had claimed.
- The elected comptroller of the state of Tennessee has two legitimate law degrees and a Master's in Criminal Justice from a school widely identified as a degree mill.
- Even in Mongolia: the director general of the Mongolian Road Authority turned out to be a sheep herder and junior high dropout with fake diplomas from the National University of Mongolia.
- Cape Coral, Florida, councilman Mickey Rosado was fined $500 under a state statute outlawing false academic claims.
- Iraq's Justice Ministry launched an investigation following allegations that dozens of MPs may possess forged degree certificates.
- Pakistan's Oil and Gas Regulatory Authority (OGRA) chairman Tauqir Sadiq claimed to have acquired his law degree from the American Institute of London, which does not seem to exist in America or Britain.
- Delaware Tea Party senatorial candidate Christine O'Donnell misrepresented three different degrees in her campaign material. Her stint at Oxford University consisted of attending a course put on by a group that rented a room at Oxford.
- In 2011, the Virgin Islands Senate confirmed Elton Lewis as commissioner, Department of Planning. He had been police com-

missioner. Eight years earlier, he was found to have a degree from a diploma mill.

- In 2011, ten Pakistani legislators had been brought up on charges of using fake degrees.
- A high Ukrainian security official, Andriy Kislinsky, was fired for using a forged diploma from a prestigious university to further his career.
- The city manager of Sneads, Florida, was fired when it was learned he had a PhD from British degree mill Canterbury University.
- The European Union stopped sending aid to new member Bulgaria because of irregularities in handling funds. The woman brought in to solve the problems was hired on the basis of her German degrees, which were fake.
- Director of strategic planning for a Tampa-area city, earning $76,000, has a PhD from a school identified as a diploma mill.
- In response to a decree that all candidates must have a university degree, 160 people—more than 10 percent of the national candidates in Pakistan—either submitted a fake diploma, an illegible one, or none at all.
- The woman who heads the State of Tennessee codes-enforcement training program has a fake degree from Belford.
- Democratic congressional candidate David LaPere, in California, lost after his fake degree from Wexford University was publicized.
- Alicia "Chucky" Hansen, major candidate for governor in the US Virgin Islands, lost after claiming her fake St. Regis University degree was from the legitimate Regis University. She was later reelected to the legislature.
- Democratic state representative Gloria Schermesser had a bachelor's degree from the fake Columbia State University. She died in 2009, and the degree was mentioned in her obituary.
- The speaker of Nigeria's federal House of Representatives was disgraced and forced from office when it turned out that the degree he claimed from the University of Toronto was never earned. Now degree fraud in Nigeria, quite common, is known as "pulling a Toronto."

- North Dakota state senator Tim Flakoll is still in office, ten years after it was noted that his PhD was from a school whose degrees are a criminal offense in that state. That doctorate no longer appears in his official biography.
- California's Poet Laureate Quincy Troupe, also a popular professor at the University of California, San Diego, decided to retire from his $141,000-a-year job when state employees discovered he did not have the university degree he had long claimed.
- A board member of the Internet Crimes Against Children Task Force of the US Department of Justice has an MBA from a totally fake university.
- The $210,000-a-year president of the Houston-area transit authority was revealed by the *Houston Chronicle* not to have two claimed degrees. She was forgiven by the Metro board and kept her job.
- One of three finalists to head Oregon's Department of Environmental Quality withdrew when his degree from Missouri degree mill Northwestern College was revealed.
- In 2010, the new policy adviser to the mayor of Seattle lost his six-figure job after one week when the press discovered he didn't have his claimed PhD from the University of Washington.

LAW AND RELIGION

- The National Institute for Truth Verification sells voice-stress analyzers to police departments. Inventor and founder Dr. Charles Humble got his own PhD from Indiana Christian University, which *ABC News* identified as a degree mill.
- An East Indian attorney practiced for twenty-seven years with a fake law degree. Of eighty cases he tried in court, he actually won three of them.
- Gary Stocco, a burn-analysis expert who specialized in testifying against burn victims who were suing those they believed were responsible for their injuries, pleaded guilty to perjury when it was learned that his only degrees were from the fake University of San Moritz.

- Gene Morrison appeared as an expert forensic psychologist in more than seven hundred court cases and was paid more than $400,000 in taxpayers' money over twenty-seven years. All his degrees were fake, purchased from a website called affordabledegrees.com. Morrison's motto was "Exposing Unrighteousness for the Sake of Righteousness."
- Gainesville, Florida, immigration lawyer Finees Casado turned out to have no law degree. While on probation for this offense, he continued practicing law and was arrested again.
- A woman convicted of murder in Colorado appealed her conviction on the grounds that she had learned, correctly, that her lawyer had a fake law degree.
- An expert-witness engineer who testified in a court case involving a defective $300,000 motor home has all three of his degrees in engineering from the fake University of San Moritz.
- An expert witness for a major home retailer, sued by a man who fell and injured himself in the store, had a fake degree in safety engineering.
- Newly elected president Johnny Hunt of the large Southern Baptist Convention listed two doctorates that various media identified as coming from diploma mills.
- The pastor of the Lord's House in Buckeye, Arizona, was indicted on charges of having sex with teenagers during counseling sessions. He also had diploma-mill degrees and fake pastoral certification.

MEDICAL AND DENTAL

- Brian McNamee, who had been all-star pitcher Roger Clemens's personal trainer and who said he injected Clemens with steroids, called himself "Doctor McNamee" based on a PhD purchased from Mississippi degree mill Columbus University.
- A man with a fake medical degree examined and treated many patients in Lexington, Kentucky. Suspicion was aroused when he photographed his patients without clothing. It turned out he

had been convicted and imprisoned for the same offense years earlier in another state.

- In 2009, Spanish police arrested two sellers and twenty-five buyers of fake degrees, mostly medical degrees, from Peruvian universities.
- In Hong Kong, a practicing psychiatrist named Lam Chun-fai was found to be using a counterfeit medical degree from Cambridge University, England.
- Gary Lloyd was practicing pediatric medicine in Florida. His only medical diploma was a counterfeit from the University of Connecticut.
- In 2011, seven fake medical doctors were arrested in a South African sting operation. Residents from a town in the Eastern Cape said Dr. Valentine Zulu's untidy appearance and the way he dressed (flip-flops and baggy jeans) made them question his professionalism.
- In North Carolina, Laurence Perry, who bought his MD from the fake British Virgin Islands School of Medicine, was convicted after a child he took off insulin, in favor of an untested product, died.
- A well-known cardiologist/pilot turns out not to have a medical degree. As cardiologist and United Airlines captain, he put on expensive seminars for doctors and airline executives, and received millions in grants. He had been scheduled as a main speaker at an American Medical Association (AMA) convention when this news broke on CBS. The AMA simply changed their program to list him as *Captain* Hamman instead of *Doctor* Hamman (but later canceled the talk entirely).
- In 2011, a New York man with a fake Russian medical degree was convicted of raping women who came to him for cancer treatments. Some of Michael Sorodsky's patients died from lack of treatment. Indicted on 102 counts, he was sentenced to six years in prison, with half off for time served.
- A Tulsa chiropractor with two dubious naturopathic doctorates also falsely claimed to have an MD.
- Gregory Caplinger practiced medicine for more than twenty years in North Carolina and elsewhere with seven fake degrees,

including an MD he bought for $100. Finally indicted and convicted, he fled from the United States while on bail bond but was recaptured and imprisoned.

- A man with fake medical credentials was employed as a psychiatrist at a medical center. He was arrested after he prescribed a lethal medication to a woman with a history of suicide attempts who did, in fact, kill herself.
- A California heart surgeon with a fake medical degree stopped a patient's medication. When she died, it turned out she had left him half a million dollars.
- A man with bogus dental degree was employed at a New York clinic as a specialist in installing braces.
- A Florida man got staff privileges at two hospitals based on his counterfeit doctorates from Columbia and Stanford.
- An accountant in New York was employed as an emergency-room physician based on a fake medical degree. He was caught when a nurse noticed he referred to "sewing people up" instead of "suturing."
- An Illinois woman with a fake nursing degree was employed as a night supervisor at a Florida nursing home. After twelve deaths in two weeks, she was fired but not arrested.
- A surgery transplant administrator at an Ivy League university medical school has a fake PhD.
- The director of a major university's campus clinic has a diploma-mill MS and PhD in microbiology and genetics.

MILITARY

- More than one hundred military police in the central African nation of Cameroon were dismissed after the discovery that they had used fake certifications to get their jobs.
- Two dozen US Army National Guard and Reserve members faced disciplinary action over their use of fake degrees purchased from St. Regis University.
- When Admiral Donald Arthur retired as surgeon general of the US Navy, the chairman of the Joint Chiefs of Staff honored him

revelations that he did not have the University of Texas degree he claimed but rather a degree from the fake LaCrosse University.

- The former commissioner of the Mid-Eastern Athletic Conference did not become athletic director at Dartmouth when his false master's degree claim became known.
- Four small-college coaches all got in trouble for fake degrees around the same time: the Fayetteville State University men's basketball coach, the Campbell University women's soccer coach, the track and basketball coaches at Methodist College, and an assistant cross-country coach at St. Andrews.
- The head softball coach at the University of Tennessee–Chattanooga, a job requiring a bachelor's degree, has a fake bachelor's and master's from Western States University.

THERAPY AND PSYCHOLOGY

- A practicing clinical psychologist in Las Vegas, who evaluated and treated mentally ill children for Clark County, Nevada, had no advanced degrees other than the master's and PhD he bought from the phony Rochville University.
- Former stripper Lucy Wightman, known as Princess Cheyenne, bought a fake PhD from Concordia College and University, and posed as a licensed psychologist in the Boston area. She was convicted of fraud and larceny.
- A popular television personality known as the Love Doctor, who regularly reminded viewers that she had the answers to their problems because she was a doctor, lost her job after ABC determined that her PhD was fake.
- In upstate New York, police raided a sex therapy clinic run by a high school dropout who called himself "Doctor" based on a PhD purchased for $100 from the Universal Life Church. He drove a white Cadillac with the license plate "Doctor 1."
- A youth counselor for the Empowering Families Program in Culpepper, Virginia, bought his bachelor's, master's, and PhD from the fake Suffield University.
- The founder of a large marriage therapy center in Kennewick,

Washington, has his PhD in psychology from a Louisiana degree mill.

- Steven Feldman was indicted on four felony charges in Saratoga Springs, New York, for using a fake doctorate to obtain work as a psychologist for the county.
- The State of Washington suspended the license of chemical dependency counselor David Larsen, who purchased a doctor of psychology from the fake St. Regis University.
- A woman in Norwell, Massachusetts, was convicted of larceny and fraud for calling herself a doctor and a licensed psychologist based on her degree purchased from the fake Concordia College and University.
- In the molestation trial of a Pittsburgh school psychologist, it was discovered that he had been hired on the basis of his fake doctorate from Columbia State University.
- It was page-one news in St. Catharines, Ontario, when a school therapist with a doctorate from the fake LaSalle University in Louisiana was arrested for fraud.
- A Connecticut psychotherapist specializing in anxiety, depression, and panic has his PhD from the fake Columbia State University.

Chapter 9

···

ANIMALS WITH DEGREES

···

People often purchase degrees and other credentials for animals, either for fun or to make the point in a court case that the grantor of those degrees and credentials is not necessarily legitimate. Here are some of the "graduates" that got a fair amount of media attention.

Birdie August, budgie, doctor of aviation science. San Diego television producer J. W. August is a media pioneer in exposing diploma mills. In the course of one of his exposés on the huge diploma mill called Columbia State University, he demonstrated its fraudulence by purchasing an aviation doctorate for the office bird.

255

Maxwell Sniffingwell, bulldog, MD. In 2009, an Arkansas veterinarian, campaigning for strong laws against fake degrees, purchased a medical degree in reproductive science from Belford University for his pet English bulldog.

Colby Nolan, cat, MBA. The attorney general's office in Pennsylvania was apparently disappointed that their counterparts in Texas were not dealing with a Texas degree mill called Trinity Southern University, which was defrauding residents of Pennsylvania (and most other states). So they reached out and purchased a bachelor's degree for $299 and the proffered MBA for $100 more. After Pennsylvania sued, Texas got a restraining order against Trinity Southern. The owners were fined over $100,000 and ordered to cease and desist.

Henrietta Goldacre, cat, certified nutritionist. Best-selling British nutrition author Gillian McKeith has her doctorate from an unaccredited and now-closed American school and a diploma as a nutritionist from the American Association of Nutritional Consultants. In the course of investigating Dr. McKeith's credentials, British psychiatrist and writer Dr. Ben Goldacre, author of *Bad Science*, purchased the same nutrition diploma for his cat, Henrietta.

Kitty O'Malley, cat, high school diploma. A newspaper in Lakeland, Florida, obtained a high school diploma from "Washington High Academy" for "Kitty O'Malley," a cat also known as Spanky.

Oreo Collins, cat, high school diploma. A cat named Oreo C. Collins earned her diploma from Jefferson High School Online at the age of two, in a sting conducted by the Better Business Bureau of Central Georgia.

Tobias F. Schaeffer, cat, Certified Real Estate Appraiser. Tobias's owner obtained a Certified Real Estate Appraiser (CREA) designation for $75 from the National Association of Real Estate Appraisers (NAREA) for his cat, Tobias F. (for "Feline") Schaeffer. The certification diploma was hung over Tobias's litter box.

Zoe D. Katze, cat. For more information on this well-publicized story, do an Internet search on the cat's name. On her resume, Zoe was a consultant to the Tacayllaermi Friends School (spell it backward!).

Chester Ludlow, dog, MBA. In June 2009, a pug from Vermont named Chester Ludlow received an online MBA from Rochville University. The dog's degree was shipped from a post office box in Dubai just one week after the dog submitted $499 and his resume to the online school. Along with the MBA diploma, Chester received "two sets of college transcripts, a certificate of distinction in finance, and a certificate of membership in the student council." Chester is depicted at the start of this chapter, his graduation photo courtesy of the valuable Diploma Mill Police at www.geteducated.com.

John I. Rocko, dog, BS criminal justice. The defendants in an Ohio drug trial claimed their arrests were invalid because the police chief had a degree from a Belgian-run degree mill called Concordia College and University, which offers degrees in less than one day. A local radio station purchased a degree from the same place for a local police dog. The judge found "no similarity" between the dog's diploma and the chief's in acquitting the chief of wrongdoing.

Lulu Howard, dog, BA. In 2010, a large British broadcaster, British Sky, successfully sued a consulting company for misrepresenting their expertise. A key factor in the case was the claimed degree of a key witness, which had in fact been purchased from a notorious diploma mill. The witness made a spirited defense of all the work he had done to earn the degree, whereupon the prosecution revealed they had purchased the same degree for the prosecutor's dog, Lulu.

Sassafras Herbert, dog, certified nutritionist. In 1984, *Time* magazine reported that Sassafras, a female poodle belonging to a New York City physician, had received a diploma from the American Association of Nutritional Consultants. Her owner had bought the diploma for $50 to demonstrate that "something that looks like a diploma doesn't mean that somebody has responsible training."

Sonny Licciardello, dog, MD. In 2007, the popular Australian Broadcasting Corporation program *The Chaser's War on Everything* documented host Chas John Licciardello applying online and obtaining a medical degree for his dog, Sonny, from diploma mill Ashwood University. Sonny's "work experience" included "significant proctology experience sniffing other dogs' bums." The dog was fitted with a white gown and stethoscope, and walked through a large hospital (until he was evicted).

Wally Brancato, dog, AA. In 2004, Albany, New York, television station WRGB ran a report in which reporter Peter Brancato applied to Almeda University for, and received, an associate's degree on behalf of his dog, Wally. On the application, Brancato listed, "Plays with the kids every day . . . teaches them to interact better with each other . . . teaches them responsibilities like feeding the dog." Almeda University granted Wally a "life experience" associate degree in "Childhood Development." After the report aired, Almeda University protested that Brancato perjured himself by creating a false identity using a fabricated name and date of birth. In March 2008, Wally was featured in a Lake Geneva, Wisconsin, mayoral campaign, where one of the candidates had an Almeda degree. An opponent published a political cartoon showing the dog with a dialogue bubble reading "I graduated with Bill Chesen." Chesen took the cartoon to the police, who passed the defamation complaint to the district attorney's office, which declined to prosecute, since negative campaigning is legal, and Chesen had publicly "detailed his educational background in his campaign literature."

Chapter 10

....

THE LAURA CALLAHAN STORY

....

One of the biggest degree-mill stories in recent years is that of Laura Callahan, a senior director in the Department of Homeland Security's Office of the Chief Information Officer. Government Computer News *reported that Callahan had three degrees from a Wyoming degree mill. In our first edition, we invited Callahan to tell her side of the story in an essay titled "The Human Toll of Degree Mills: A Student's Perspective." In the ensuing seven years, Callahan has worked hard to leave these matters behind, earning a regionally accredited bachelor's degree and master's degree, and is well along the path to a regionally accredited doctorate. The man who ran the fake school that sold Callahan her degrees, Rudy Marn, was convicted of tax evasion relative to his degree-mill earnings and sentenced to federal prison. We invited Laura Callahan to reflect on the entire matter. Despite the clear evidence of hundreds, perhaps thousands of government employees with fake degrees, including a senior undersecretary of defense, no one else was treated this way by an employer or the media. Her story deserves to be told.*

SEVEN YEARS LATER
by Laura Callahan
This chapter © 2011, Laura Callahan

Seven years have passed since I became an unwitting victim of the shadow academic world where spurious degree issuing institutions, commonly known as diploma mills, operate their businesses. In the first edition of this book, I provided a detailed accounting of how I unsuspectingly became affiliated

259

with a diploma mill known as Hamilton University. Based upon the insight I have gained about the hazard that caught me not only by surprise but also wholly unprepared to understand the ramifications and implications of my circumstance, my objective in offering this retrospective is simple—to share my experience with the intent that my case may guide other diploma mill victims through their journey seeking restorative justice. The following is a brief summary of the events leading up to and surrounding my affiliation with Hamilton and the actions I took after I became aware that Hamilton University was identified as a diploma mill by government organizations.

To put all in its proper context, I hasten to emphasize some critical facts: My motivation for completing college was purely a personal desire and was in no way in response to a requirement for my employment or promotion potential, nor did I ever seek or use any financial assistance from my employer in my quest for a post-secondary degree. I was raised in a typical middle class family where love was plentiful and money sufficient to account for basic necessities. My mother was disabled and my stepfather worked for the United States Postal Service. My brothers and I knew the opportunity to attend college was not realistic given the family's financial situation, leading me to enlist in the military and subsequently become employed by the Federal government as a civil servant.

Typical of those who serve in the military, I attended college part-time during off-hours to broaden my knowledge. I found college rewarding because the opportunity to learn opened my mind to new ideas that complemented my work experience and helped shape me as a working adult. Over the years, I amassed a portfolio of over 250 semester hours of credit, including those required in bachelor's, master's, and doctoral level degree completion programs. However, even with the number and types of credits, I ran into the glass ceiling imposed by most colleges and universities known as the "residency requirement"—the minimum number of credit hours a student must take at the school in order to graduate. This criterion proved to be an impediment because my employer transferred me approximately every two to three years, making it difficult, if not impossible, to meet a school's residency requirement. Consequently, the residency matter added to the challenge because the requirement varied by school, ranging from thirty to ninety semester hours depending on the institution. Thankfully, while stationed in the Aleutian Islands, I learned of Thomas Edison State College, a regionally accredited school operating in Trenton, New Jersey. Thomas Edison State College was one of the early thought leaders in higher education seeking ways to support the academic needs of military personnel and their families. As such, Thomas Edison State College did not have a residency mandate. Leveraging their distance learning program, I transferred an initial trench of credits to Thomas Edison and received an associate's degree without having to take any additional courses at that school.

I continued to work and volunteered for increasingly challenging assignments to build my competencies. My work assignments included prolonged travel to install and upgrade computer systems at military installations around the world. When I was not traveling, I was on call twenty-four hours a day, seven days a week to support the operations of the computer systems I helped to install or upgrade. A forty-hour work week was a luxury and my scarce personal time was spent taking online or correspondence classes at night. Years passed in what seemed like an instant, and I was reminded by my mother of a promise I made years earlier. The promise was that I would finish college. I had a solid record of proven outstanding performance and the financial means to finish my education. My job did not require a degree, and the need for a degree for promotion considerations was moot because there was no higher rung on the ladder to climb. The years of hard work and numerous promotions I competed for based on my work results culminated in my final promotion to the Senior Executive Service in 1999. There is no other higher rank in the civil service, and I had no desire to become a political appointee.

With my career goal satisfied, I began searching for a college or university that would accept my mosaic of credits and had an online degree completion program that would enable me to work during the day and either take classes or do class work at night. Late one evening I happened upon the Academic Research and Referral Center (ARRC) while scanning websites containing information about colleges and universities and their distance learning programs. The ARRC offered a college matching service where they claimed to review your education and match you with those colleges best suited to your education goals. The ARRC's assertion that they were an independent entity not affiliated with or funded by any university gave me the clear impression I would receive an objective assessment. I completed the ARRC's application form, submitted my entire education portfolio and transcripts, and waited for a response. Shortly thereafter, the ARRC notified me that my education matched to the degree completion programs offered by Hamilton University.

I reviewed the prospective student package I requested and received. The package appeared professionally prepared with detailed descriptions about Hamilton's programs, faculty, student population, facilities, and accreditation. Hamilton University also offered a combined bachelor's/master's program allowing a student to complete both through one enrollment process. The combined approach rang familiar because I had heard of other universities advertising similar programs. Hamilton University also claimed to be accredited.

I checked with the Wyoming State Board of Education and confirmed Hamilton University was licensed to operate. Of equal importance, Hamilton claimed it was accredited by the American Council for Private Colleges and Universities (ACPCU). A check with the ACPCU confirmed Hamilton was accredited, its accreditation was current, and the next accreditation review was scheduled two years in the future.

Thus, with both a State of Wyoming and ACPCU confirmation as to Hamilton's accreditation and operational status under my belt, I submitted my prior learning experience package, complete with transcripts, to Hamilton University for review.

Hamilton University accepted my submission for entry into the bachelor's/master's degree completion program with one caveat; namely, Hamilton University advised me that while my general studies, business, mathematics, and computer science courses mapped to their degree requirements and would be accepted, I would still be short one class. Hamilton University had a requirement for all students, regardless of degree program, to complete their Natural Law course. Knowing I had not taken such a course, there was no reason for me to question this requirement. I enrolled in Hamilton University, completed their Natural Law course through their distance learning center, and received my bachelor's and master's degrees. The process was almost identical to what I experienced years earlier at Thomas Edison State College, with the exception that I had to take a class from Hamilton University. I subsequently advised the Human Resources Specialist at my US government employer of my degrees from Hamilton University and submitted my transcripts for inclusion in my personnel file to keep my training records up-to-date.

At no time either before, during, or after my interaction with Hamilton was I informed or advised that Hamilton was not what I had been led to believe—a fully accredited and valid post-secondary school licensed to operate in the State of Wyoming. Even more critically, the same held true for the ACPCU: I had no idea, nor did I have any reason to suspect, that the ACPCU was anything less than a credible and valid accrediting body. Thus, from my perspective, based upon the information provided by the State of Wyoming, the representations of the ACPCU and Hamilton University, and the response of the Human Resources office at my US government employer, I firmly believed I had enrolled in and had obtained academic degrees from an acceptable institution of post-secondary higher education.

Approximately a year later, I requested information from Hamilton University about their doctorate program. After reviewing the requested material, once again I submitted my prior learning experience and transcripts to Hamilton for evaluation. I received notification that those upper level courses not previously considered and applied towards my master's degree would be accepted for my doctorate. I was advised that the need to complete a dissertation was a requirement I would have to complete at Hamilton University. As I had done before, I enrolled in Hamilton's doctorate program and spent approximately a year researching and writing my dissertation. I submitted my dissertation as part of the degree completion requirement and waited for a response. Hamilton University notified me that my dissertation was accepted and awarded me my doctorate degree. As previously done, I advised my Human Resources Specialist of my Hamilton University degree and provided a copy of my transcript for inclusion in my personnel file to keep my training records up to date. The key elements of my dissertation were later used by the US Department of Labor in its E-Government Strategic Plan adding to my satisfaction knowing the research I completed was beneficial to someone else.

A few years passed before I received a telephone call late one Friday afternoon from a public affairs officer advising me about a story just released stating I had lied about my academic credentials. I felt this had to be some type of mistake because I had been open and candid about my academic background and, to my knowledge, did not misrepresent my credentials. Early the next Monday morning I immediately approached my supervisor, discussed the call, and sought guidance. I was advised that I should alert the security office handling personnel matters and follow their instructions. I was also reminded by my supervisor and security office personnel that as a civil servant, I was not authorized to interact with the media, and any inquiries were to be referred to public affairs. I abided by those directions and spent almost a year on administrative leave waiting for an outcome. During that period my family and I endured in silence the waves of media reports characterizing me in insulting and personally derogatory terms coupled with flippant comments from certain elected officials encouraging me to go to night school to learn a skill. Nowhere in the media coverage was one iota of consideration given regarding whether or not I knew of Hamilton University's questionable reputation. Basically, I was presumed guilty and, based on rules regarding interaction with the press, forced to remain silent, unable to defend myself.

When I was confronted with the harsh reality that Hamilton University was not a legitimate higher education institution, I immediately embarked on a search for guidance, instructions, and any other literature that could assist me through the process needed to exonerate myself from the negative connotations associated with diploma mills. My search proved futile because there was little, if any, help available for diploma mill victims.

A clergy member at my church told me a key testament to one's integrity is what that individual does to right a wrong. However, you cannot correct an error if you do not know the error exists. Based upon this one aspect of my experience alone, I urge government officials to include in their diploma mill investigations the need to obtain student enrollment records and use those records to warn students they may be the victims of education fraud. A positive approach for government investigators and oversight personnel would be to initiate litigation that would afford aggrieved students the opportunity to seek damages, if not reimbursement for money spent pursuing degrees at such institutions. How students chose to use this information will be telling as to their culpability in perpetrating fraud or being fraud victims.

After being cast aside for almost a year, I decided it was time to move on with my life, resigned my position as a career civil servant, and went to work in the private industry. With the horrific diploma mill incident behind me, I regained my self-esteem, and started back through the academic process to fulfill my long-standing promise to my mother. I completed a bachelor of science in business administration with a major in computer information systems at Thomas Edison State College. In accordance with the school's distance learning program, my credits were accepted through the transfer process leaving me short one course. The college had a requirement for a specific management course that I challenged by taking a proctored exam. I passed the exam, was awarded the three semester hours of credit, and received my baccalaureate degree.

Next I completed a master's of science degree in project management at the University of Wisconsin, Platteville. Again, following the school's process through their distance learning program, I transferred in the maximum number of credits allowed and took the required number of classes to fulfill their residency requirement. Having completed all course work, I am currently a doctoral candidate at a regionally accredited university with an expected graduation date planned for 2011.

The process of integrating back into the work force has been enlightening. First, it was intuitively obvious for me to recognize who was truly a friend versus those who associated with me for personal gain. It was disappointing to see colleagues, who had not seen or spoken to me in years, suddenly make derogatory statements about me in direct contradiction of their own written records where they previously attested to my professional acumen and technical competency. My experiences, both in dealing with my friends, business associates, and employer prompted me to research education fraud, where I learned of Wilfred Cude's book entitled *The Ph.D. Trap Revisited*.

Cude examines the evolution of universities, noting how changes in education reflected political, economic, and cultural influences. Cude uncovered various forms of inappropriate behavior and described in detail the political and ethical morass in higher education due to improper behavior and methodological confusion among academics. He further explained the positive outcomes of higher education and posited the notion that a second master's may be more beneficial than a PhD. Cude offered critical commentary of higher education leading one to wonder if diploma mills are merely the tip of the education fraud iceberg. One can only wonder why academics remain largely silent in the calls to stop diploma mill proliferation. Perhaps there is a level of concern that any probing or additional government oversight of this mainly self-regulated industry would open Pandora's box, revealing more than just diploma mill evils permeating higher education.

On the positive side, I have learned that the State of Wyoming undertook an investigation of Hamilton University. Review of the investigative record indicates students had filed complaints about Hamilton University with the Wyoming State Board of Education, but those complaints were not acted upon or published for public awareness. Counter to its claims, the entity that accredited Hamilton University, the American Council for Private Colleges and Universities, was actually affiliated with and operated by the same individual who ran Hamilton University. This person had a questionable past and was previously affiliated with diploma mills operating in other states. Hamilton University had not broken any laws per se, but its owner was eventually found guilty of tax fraud and sentenced to prison. In short, I have learned that not only was I victimized by a diploma mill, but that I was directed down the path to that entity by what I now have learned may also be termed an accreditation mill—an organization that lacks the same validity as the school that it supposedly accredits. Such was precisely the case in the ACPCU/Hamilton University axis.

To the best of my knowledge, I and other Hamilton University students have been left to figure out what to do regarding the worthless degrees issued by the school, beyond, of course, throwing them in the trash. As of this writing, I have not received any official communication from the State of Wyoming advising me of Hamilton University's deceptive practices and warning me about the legitimacy of degrees awarded by that school. I can only wonder what will happen to other Hamilton graduates, who like me, updated their personnel files to reflect degrees from Hamilton University. So too, there has been deafening silence from any government oversight personnel as to what steps should be taken to seek reimbursement or justice for the money spent, let alone personal and professional humiliation suffered as a result of such interactions.

In sum, my advice to those who believe they have become victims of diploma mills is to seek the assistance of federal and state agencies responsible for such oversight, including notifying proper employment officials of the circumstance to avoid accusations of intent to misrepresent any such educational activities. And, for those contemplating on-line or distance-enabled education, contact those very same entities for guidance and independent confirmation that the school and its accrediting body are valid and offer recognized and accepted degrees.

Chapter 11

···

EXISTING AND PENDING FEDERAL LEGISLATION

···

I n chapter 5, we described the way the decent anti-diploma-mill bill introduced by Congresswoman Betty McCollum was gutted and rendered almost useless by the time it was voted into law. We reported that a new bill was subsequently introduced (in 2011) by Congressman Tim Bishop, which would restore some provisions of the McCollum bill, address accreditation mills, and empower the Federal Trade Commission to act in degree-mill matters. Here is the text of the bill taken from the federal website http://www.govtrack.us, as introduced, before it went to various committees. In a year or two, in some form, it may reach a vote. We wish it well.

112TH CONGRESS 1ST SESSION 2011, H. R. 1758

To reduce and prevent the sale and use of fraudulent degrees in order to protect the integrity of valid higher education degrees that are used for Federal employment purposes.

In the House of Representatives, May 5, 2011

Mr. BISHOP of New York (for himself and Mr. COURTNEY) introduced the following bill; which was referred to the Committee on Education and the Workforce, and in addition to the Committees on Oversight and Government Reform, Energy and Commerce, and the Judiciary, for a period to be subsequently determined by the

Speaker, in each case for consideration of such provisions as fall within the jurisdiction of the committee concerned

A BILL

To reduce and prevent the sale and use of fraudulent degrees in order to protect the integrity of valid higher education degrees that are used for Federal employment purposes.

Be it enacted by the Senate and House of Representatives of the United States of America in Congress assembled,

This Act may be cited as the "Diploma and Accreditation Integrity Protection Act."

PURPOSE; DEFINITIONS

(a) PURPOSE.—The purpose of this act

is to protect institutions of higher education, businesses and other employers, professional licensing boards, patients and clients of degree holders, taxpayers, and other individuals from any person claiming to possess a legitimate academic degree that in fact was issued by a fraudulent or nonexistent school, by a non-educational entity posing as a school, or by any entity in violation of Federal or State law.

(b) DEFINITIONS.—In this Act:

(1) ACCREDITATION MILL

The term "accreditation mill" means an education or corporate organization that offers a form of educational recognition or accreditation, for a fee or free of charge, that—

(A) extends a permanent recognition or accreditation status to an institution with few or no requirements for subsequent periodic reviews;

(B) publishes a list of institutions and programs recognized or accredited by such organization that includes institutions and programs that did not apply for or otherwise request such recognition or accreditation by the organization; or

(C) lacks national recognition by the Secretary of Education or the Council for Higher Education Accreditation.

(2) DEGREE-GRANTING INSTITUTION

The term "degree-granting institution" means any entity that offers or confers an academic, professional, or occupational degree, diploma, or certificate, if such degree, diploma, or certificate may be used to represent to the general public that the individual possessing such degree, diploma, or certificate has completed a program of education or training beyond secondary education.

(3) DIPLOMA MILL

The term "diploma mill" means any entity that—

(A) lacks valid accreditation by an agency recognized by a Federal agency, a State government, or the Council for Higher Education Accreditation as a valid accrediting agency of institutions of higher education; and

(B) offers degrees, diplomas, or certifications, for a fee, that may be used to represent to the general public that the individual possessing such a degree, diploma, or certification has completed a program of education or training beyond secondary education, but little or no education or course work is required to obtain such a degree, diploma, or certification.

(4) INSTITUTION OF HIGHER EDUCATION.

The term "institution of higher education" has the meaning given such term in section 102 of the Higher Education Act of 1965 (20 U.S.C. 1002).

SEC. 3. ACCREDITING AGENCIES.

No accrediting agency or association may be considered to be a reliable authority as to the quality of education or training offered by a degree-granting institution for any purpose related to immigration, Federal employment and hiring practices, or for any other Federal purposes, unless the agency or association is a nationally recognized accrediting agency or association recognized by the Secretary of Education pursuant to part H of title IV of the Higher Education Act of 1965 (20 U.S.C. 1099a et seq.).

SEC. 4. FEDERAL EMPLOYMENT

For purposes of applying any civil service law, rule, or regulation that requires or takes into consideration a degree from an institution of higher education for purposes of appointment or promotion of, or improved pay for, a Federal employee, only a degree from a degree-granting institution that is accredited by a nationally recognized accrediting agency or association recognized by the Secretary of Education pursuant to part H of title IV of the Higher Education Act of 1965 shall be acceptable.

SEC. 5. UNFAIR AND DECEPTIVE ACTS AND PRACTICES REGARDING DIPLOMAS AND PROFESSIONAL CERTIFICATIONS.

(a) CONDUCT PROHIBITED.

Not later than 180 days after the date of enactment of this Act, the Federal Trade Commission shall initiate a rulemaking to define as an unfair and deceptive act or practice under section 18 of Federal Trade Commission Act (15 U.S.C. 57a) the following:

(1) The issuing of a degree, diploma, certificate, or any similar document by an entity that is not recognized as a legitimate postsecondary degree-granting institution by the Secretary of Education, if such degree, diploma, certificate, or similar document misrepresents, directly or indirectly, the subject matter, substance, or content of the course of study or any other material fact concerning the course of study for which such degree, diploma, certificate, or similar document was awarded.

(2) The offering or conferring of an academic, professional, or occupational degree if the entity offering or conferring the degree—

   (A) is not an institution of higher education; or

   (B) is not accredited by—

     (i) a nationally recognized accrediting agency or association recognized by the Secretary of Education pursuant to part H of title IV of the Higher Education Act of 1965 (20 U.S.C. 1099a et seq.); or

     (ii) an accrediting agency or association that is recognized as a legitimate accrediting agency or association for any purpose by any appropriate Federal agency or by the Council for Higher Education Accreditation unless the entity offering or conferring such a degree clearly and conspicuously discloses, in all advertising and promotional materials that contain a reference to such a degree, that the awarding of the degree has not been so authorized or that the entity offering or conferring the degree has not been so approved or recognized.

(3) The claiming or asserting in any advertisements or promotional material of an entity offering or conferring an academic, professional, or occupational degree, that such entity has—

(A) an accredited status unless it holds accreditation from an accrediting agency that is recognized by the Secretary of Education or the Council for Higher Education Accreditation, or is recognized for any purpose by any appropriate Federal agency; or

(B) an unaccredited, but approved status that misrepresents, directly or indirectly, the nature, extent, or credibility of such approval.

(4) The issuing of any accreditation, including institutional, programmatic, or specialized accreditation, to any degree-granting institution by any entity that is not recognized for accreditation purposes by the Secretary of Education, any other appropriate Federal agency, or the Council for Higher Education Accreditation.

(b) FINAL RULE

The Commission shall issue final rules under this section not later than 18 months after the date of enactment of this Act.

(c) REPORTING REQUIREMENT.—

(1) FEDERAL TRADE COMMISSION.

Inadministering and enforcing the rule required under subsection (a), the Federal Trade Commission shall report regularly to the Secretary of Education any information regarding entities which the Commission knows or suspects to be in violation of such rule.

(2) SECRETARY OF EDUCATION.—

The Secretary of Education shall make available to the general public, in paper and electronic forms, the information reported to the Secretary in accordance with paragraph (1).

Chapter 12

··

WHAT MAKES A DEGREE REAL?

··

Alan Contreras retired in 2011 as the head of Oregon's Office of Degree Authorization. During Contreras's administration, Oregon took the lead among the fifty states in confronting the problem of unrecognized and fake degrees. It was the first state to publish an official list of unacceptable degrees, and the first to pass a state law on that subject. Oregon was a pioneer in adopting the policy that acknowledges it will never eliminate out-of-state degree mills, but it can make it illegal to use those degrees in Oregon. Many other states have based their laws or policies on Oregon's, and Contreras has become a popular speaker and writer on these matters.

One of his recurring and very important themes is the problem caused by having fifty different sets of state school licensing laws, so that a school that is legal in one state may be illegal in another.

In this essay, condensed and adapted from a monograph he wrote for the State Higher Education Officers (SHEEO) in 2009, addresses the crucial issue of determining whether or not a given degree is real. Note: Contreras is also a lawyer, which is apparent from the extensive and detailed legal documentation he has provided.

WHAT MAKES A DEGREE REAL
by Alan Contreras
©2011, Alan Contreras

In order to understand why certain credentials are not valid college degrees, and why some degree-granters are called degree mills or diploma mills, it is necessary to know what

277

constitutes a valid degree. What this really means is that we need to know how a degree-granter obtains the formal authority to give someone a degree.

A degree is a type of public credential, an academic credential. A public credential is distinguished from other kinds of awards and recognitions in that it is used outside private life for a specific purpose. Legitimate degrees are given for certain accomplishments in fields of knowledge, within a structure that involves qualified teachers who evaluate student performance against a set of generally accepted norms.

A degree is valid if it is properly granted (that is, not fraudulently or mistakenly granted) by an entity that has the legal authority to do so. There are three sources of authority to issue college degrees in or from the United States. A college can obtain that authority from Congress, from a state government, or from a recognized sovereign Indian tribe.

The three-source theory derives primarily from the Tenth Amendment to the US Constitution, commonly referred to as the "Reserved Powers Clause,"[1] which recognizes that the Federal government's powers are limited to those granted by the Constitution; all other powers remain with the States or the people. Historically, education has been considered one of the most sacrosanct of these "reserved powers:" the states early acquired and have maintained a firm grip on education, about which the Constitution is entirely silent.

The baseline that can always be used to determine whether a US entity is a genuine college or a degree mill is therefore the answer to the question: which government authorized it to issue degrees? This chapter focuses on issues surrounding state authority to authorize colleges, as that is how almost all US colleges obtain their authority. But first, a very brief look at the other two sources of authority.

FEDERAL AUTHORITY

Congress rarely establishes degree-granting institutions. Examples are the military service academies and a small number of related institutions such as the Community College of the Air Force. In addition, the federal government has a unique relationship to certain colleges operating in the District of Columbia.

A few colleges operated by the Department of the Interior Bureau of Indian Affairs are, technically, federally authorized, though they also operate with tribal authority and therefore might be called "hybrids" in the tripartite taxonomy of approvals.

In general, federal authorization of degree-granting is not a significant factor in US education.

TRIBAL AUTHORITY

The right of federally recognized Indian tribes to charter degree-granting colleges without state approval is widely accepted by state authorities. It is worth mentioning that tribal chartering authority does not convey accreditation any more than federal or state authority does. State laws requiring that certain degrees be granted by an accredited institution or program in order to be used (e.g., for professional licensure) are not affected by the original source of degree authority, as any college can choose whether or not to become accredited, whatever the source of its initial charter or authorization.

STATE ACTION TO AUTHORIZE DEGREE-GRANTING INSTITUTIONS

By far the majority (over 98 percent) of US degree-granting institutions, amounting to about 4,200 colleges as of 2009, according to the Higher Education Directory, operate under the legal authority given them by state governments. State authorization is the normal method through which degree-granting colleges are established, although the nature of the legal basis for state degree-granting authority has rarely been discussed by courts or commentators. State-conferred degree authorization appears in three basic forms:

- public institutions actually owned or operated by the state or one of its subdivisions (such as a community college district),
- nonpublic institutions that have some kind of formal authorization to offer degrees, and
- schools formally exempt from state authorization requirements on religious grounds.[2]

This chapter focuses on one subspecies of degree-granter (nonpublic colleges) and one kind of state law and process (the process through which nonpublics obtain degree-granting authority) because this is the arena in which most of the issues surrounding degree mills and dubious degrees arise. It has also been the source of most litigation regarding degree-granting authority, and of much discussion in the unique legal situations that have caused problems in California and Texas, discussed below.

States claim to authorize nonpublic colleges to issue degrees in three ways:

1. Authorization by direct charter or some other kind of sui generis state action that approves specific schools by name. Many older charters were issued directly by legislative action or even, in their earliest form, by royal decree. Some California charters were issued by the state's Supreme Court.

2. Authorization via a system of statutes and regulatory standards under which a regulatory agency grants authorization through a letter or formal license.
3. Authorization by de facto delegation of state authority to a religious body via state "religious exemption" statutes. This approach is problematic and is not discussed in detail here.[3]

1. Degree Authorization by Charter

Direct approval by charter or school-by-school legislative action is rare today, although there is no legal barrier (and some advantages) to it being done. However, it is the source of degree-granting authority of many older schools like Harvard, Dartmouth, and William and Mary. The issue of degree-granting authority originating from charters has rarely been addressed by the courts; however, there are enough decisions to establish a solid and consistent baseline: degree-granting powers must be explicit.[4] A more recent opinion by the Pennsylvania Attorney General takes the same view.[5]

An alternate view by the Missouri Supreme Court in another very old case is something of an outlier, holding that degree-granting authority is implied when a college is brought into existence by formal state charter.[6]

2. Degree Authorization by State Agency Action

In addition to charters, there is the common, everyday process of state authorization[7] via an approval agency. Applying for state authorization and meeting state standards is the way that many US colleges (especially those established in the past 75 years) obtained their authority to issue degrees. State processes have engendered a number of disputes over the years, perhaps most notably the Nova University case,[8] but because these have not produced many cases dealing with the ways that colleges obtain their original degree authority, they are not discussed in any detail herein.

Courts have in some cases[9] held that state laws were insufficiently specific in how they established standards for private degree-granters, but that problem relates more to the execution of such laws than to their conceptual basis.

3. Religious "Exemptions" and Degree-Granting Authority

Many colleges began under the authority of churches or denominations. That is one of the traditional ways that colleges came to the US and to the states—indeed, it is one of the primary original mechanisms for the establishment of colleges.[10] Just as Harvard had to dance on the tightrope between a Royal charter and a legislative one, one commentator notes that early Catholic colleges "had to obtain special approval from the state before they could grant college degrees."[11]

This method of church-based degree-granting authority is, in effect, still used, but with only the most nominal state attention.[12] There are many so-called "religious exempt" colleges around the US, but in every case the exemption is expressly established by the state legislature. This is therefore a hybrid system under which the state delegates its degree authorization powers to churches that want to issue degrees.[13] Courts have consistently held that the issuance of degrees is not a religious act but one controlled by secular authorities.[14] The Attorneys General of Arkansas, Texas, Kentucky, and Nevada have expressed similar views as to degrees.[15]

A CAUTIONARY NOTE ABOUT INTERPRETING COURT DECISIONS

When a Florida federal court concluded in 1995 that the state's statute against the use of bogus credentials was in part unconstitutional, it concluded that because unaccredited

Pacific Western University held a California license to issue degrees, users of those degrees could not be barred from stating that they held the credential.[16] The court decided the case correctly, so far as it went, but the afterlife of the case has shown a troubling lack of attention to detail by those who have subsequently engaged with these issues.

A Florida prosecutor recently declined to pursue a case of falsely claiming a degree against police officers who were using fake degrees in part because he mistakenly thought Strang precluded the prosecution.[17] In fact, Strang only dealt with use of a genuine (albeit unaccredited) degree, while the police officers were using degrees that were fake, that is, they were sold by an entity that did not have the legal authority to issue degrees at all. Using such a credential is no different than using one run off on a home laser printer.

The Florida statute made it illegal to use an unaccredited degree as a credential, and this wording created some confusion when people used the term "unaccredited" to mean the same as "diploma mill." They are not the same. The court in Strang v. Satz came to the following perfectly reasonable conclusion:

"Commercial speech must be truthful and must relate to lawful activity in order to receive protection under the First Amendment. The parties do not dispute the fact that the speech at issue is both truthful and concerns lawful activity. The speech is thus protected commercial speech."

Readers of the case may read this language to mean that any claim of a degree from an unaccredited college is necessarily truthful and that all such claims carry a First Amendment protection. That is not a correct reading.

The entity from which Dr. Strang acquired his degree held a license to issue degrees from the State of California. That is what made Strang's degree claim truthful. Had his purported degree been from an entity such as "Redding University," which also claims to be located in California, the speech would not have been truthful because Redding University does not have a license to issue degrees—it is a mail-order degree mill.

It is therefore not possible for a degree claimant to truthfully state that he holds a degree from Redding University. Because it has no license to issue degrees, any claim of such degrees is by definition untruthful because they are not degrees. Only a claim of a degree issued by a school that has the legal authority to issue degrees can be truthful.

A SHORT NOTE ON NON-US DEGREES

In general, the requirements for degree legitimacy outside the US are similar to those for US degrees. There are certain basic standards that can always be applied to a degree issued in another country. One version of these standards is set forth in Oregon law:8

(3) A claimant of a non-U.S. degree issued by a degree supplier not accredited by a U.S. accreditor may submit to the Office information proving that the supplier issuing the degree has the following characteristics.

(a) The supplier is operating legally as a degree-granting institution in its host country.

(b) The host country has a postsecondary approval system equivalent to U.S. accreditation in that it applies qualitative measures by a neutral external party recognized in that role by the government.

(c) The supplier has been approved through the demonstrable application of appropriate standards by the host country's accreditor equivalent.

(d) All degrees issued by the supplier are legally valid for use and professional licensure within the host country.

Although there are other ways of approaching international validity, the standards set forth above are good ones that will screen out most bogus degrees.

···

Chapter 13

THE ETHICS OF USING FAKE DEGREES

···

Marina Bear, PhD, wife of coauthor John Bear, has been employed as an ethicist to help clients work through issues related to the use of fake degrees. This is a summary of her report in the case of a schoolteacher who bought a master's degree from an online degree mill in order to meet the job requirement for school principal. When another person who had been in line for the job of principal, a person with a legitimate master's degree, learned of the fake degree, she brought suit. The attorney for the plaintiff was troubled by the fact that the principal with the fake degree was well liked and, by all accounts, was doing a good job. What harm had been done? He asked Marina Bear for her analysis. This is an abridged version of the report, with personal references removed.

WHO DID WHAT TO WHOM:
AN ETHICIST LOOKS AT A CASE OF FAKE DEGREES
by Marina Bear, PhD

It is appropriate to begin by clarifying just what it is an ethicist does. Unlike a lawyer who works with facts of the case and such elements of the law as are, or might turn out to be, relevant, and whose aim is to bring about a successful outcome for his or her client, an ethicist brings together the facts of the case and the morals of the relevant society. By examining those, an ethicist aims to bring about as clear as possible a view of where things went wrong and what might be done both to rectify the situation and to make it less likely that things will go wrong in the same way in the future. In addition, the hope is to leave all parties concerned with an understanding of the consequences that have resulted, or most probably will result, from the case.

Our ethics are an expression of the society in which we live. Diverse as that society is, there are basic ethical principles that we hold in common, although how those principles are applied may vary.

Societies are divided into subgroups based on ethnicity, profession, special interests, and so forth. There are codes of ethics that guide the participants of those subgroups in their common activities. They identify what is expected of us and what we may reasonably expect of others, and they identify how breaches in the moral fabric may be mended. Sometimes those codes are written down.

Professional societies often publish them and their members display them as information whose very presence proclaims the moral character of the professional.

But many areas of human endeavor are not covered by such codes. Nonetheless, by appealing to more general principles widely held to be important for the health of our society, we can usually figure out the right thing to do using reason and common sense.

In the case of the principal, it is clear that there was some wrongdoing, but it is worthwhile to take a moment to figure out exactly what the wrong was and to whom the wrong was done.

As parents and citizens, we know that we want teachers of good character working with our children. Although many of us are unaware of the exact process by which teachers are hired, we place a certain amount of trust in those administrative bodies, which often include elected school boards, to see that teachers support the highest ethical standards in their classrooms, promoting such values as honesty and fairness, in addition to fostering a love of learning and conveying specific information.

We even expect that school administrators will behave with personal discretion, if not exemplary ethical behavior, in all aspects of their lives that may come into public view. And we have all heard of the high school counselor with unfortunate bouts of occasional kleptomania or the school superintendent whose personal life challenges community standards. Often they are simply strongly encouraged to leave public service and find employment in less sensitive areas, and that is the end of it.

One of the most basic of ethical principles is justice. That means that the rules apply to all concerned and that there is a dependable regularity to their application. It means that you and I are to be treated the same unless there is a clear and relevant difference between us that justifies differential treatment.

The school system had published clear qualifications for the job of principal. To meet that basic definition of justice, those qualifications should have been asked of *anyone* applying for the position. Meeting those requirements would have been a necessary, although not sufficient, criterion for further consideration. Choosing someone to lead an enterprise always involves judging the candidates' personal talents and skills and trying to predict the dynamic of the new working unit.

There is ample evidence that the principal had a good working relationship with members of the staff. If the selection committee had been free to hire without considering the master's degree, the principal may well have been the obvious choice based on experience and the already-present support of a number of her coworkers and, presumably, some satisfied parents of children in her classes.

But the requirement of an accredited master's degree was there, and it was ignored. By doing so, the school board was unjust, not only to all other candidates for the position who presented the technically minimum requirements for the job but also to other potentially interested members of the public who also did not hold accredited master's degrees but might have wished to be considered.

One of the most blatant and damaging forms of discrimination occurs when those responsible for hiring come to the process with unstated criteria that will narrow the field in ways the applicants for the job cannot predict and address. The most obvious example of this is the "foregone conclusion" interview process, where the main criterion for the position is that the candidate be the one the group has already agreed, openly or tacitly, will get the job.

It is usually impossible to determine whether this has gone on, since people often discover their consciences *after* committing an ethical blunder, and rarely does such behavior issue from groups with a strong moral fiber running through them that would lead to public confessions of inappropriate action.

What we do know in this situation is that the schools and the administrators' association set the standards, but somewhere along the line they were not followed.

How were these standards compromised, and what did this come to mean?

Here comes some of the common sense mentioned earlier. A job listing appears. If it looks interesting to me, I read the fine print. What do they say they want done? How much does it pay? What are the listed qualifications?

Since the principal had served as acting principal of the school, she probably had a better idea than most applicants of the tasks the job entailed.

The second question is not as simple as it looks at first glance. The principal was well aware of the fact that salaries in school positions are based on a formula that usually includes experience and level of certification, including the highest degree completed. Two teachers may instruct the same subject at the same grade level but receive widely different salaries for so doing if one has a master's degree in the relevant field and the other does not.

In fact, the second and third questions are interlinking in this case. To get the job, the candidate was supposed to present a master's degree from an accredited college or university; the salary was keyed to the presumption of that degree. It was not wrong of the principal to aspire to hold such a position, but it *was* wrong for her to claim it without holding the degree, unless some special accommodation had been made on her behalf. We'll get to that in the "What could they have done?" portion of this report.

If the principal is to be seen as innocent of any wrong-doing, she is guilty of a surprising level of ignorance regarding academic matters. That ignorance alone might bring one to question her fitness to operate as a school administrator, except that it is hard to imagine the situation in which damage could be done to students by her ignorance of how the world of higher education really works. An elementary school principal probably has little call to counsel people concerning university life. On the other hand, by presenting a degree-mill credential, she may well jeopardize the accreditation of her school in the eyes of whatever larger body is charged with reviewing its policies and procedures.

I have visited the website of the "university" from which [the principal] received her master's degree. One line was sufficient to throw into doubt the validity of the institution. It claims "a proprietary method of awarding equivalencies of work experience as substitutions for formal education requirements."

This is like suggesting that one can set up a private, proprietary way of issuing change for your hundred-dollar bills. Send in a hundred dollar bill and you'll get back eleven home-made ten-dollar bills—$110 for a $100 bill. It sounds like a good deal, but the chance that you could use them in the marketplace is small, and even if you did, you'd be setting yourself up for serious trouble.

The only way equivalencies make sense, whether of money or academic credits, is if most other relevant institutions will accept them as equivalent: that banks will accept the currency and reputable universities will accept the academic credits.

The principal simply e-mailed the "university" a short form that gave details of her experience and was immediately notified that she qualified for the master's degree.

First of all, anyone who believes that everything done on the Internet is legitimate and above-board suffers from that surprising level of ignorance mentioned above. Anyone who reads a newspaper or listens to the evening news has heard stories of scams involving the offer of items for sale that are never delivered or, if they are, turn out to be other than promised. Why do scams work? Because they seem to offer a good deal. The ["university"] degree sounds a lot like the "brand name merchandise" for sale at bargain rates on street corners in many major cities. Vuitton suitcase for $20? No problem.

Let us invoke another basic principle, common to every system of ethical thought: Do no harm. To be good people, we are expected to keep in mind the idea that in the light of the seeming capriciousness of fate, the power of nature, and the undependability of strangers, each one of us still has the capacity for advancing the good by, at the very least, not initiating harmful actions wherever possible.

Each time we further an unjust cause by colluding with it to our temporary advantage, we do wrong. The principal would probably not buy a shiny new car from someone who approached her in a parking lot and offered it to her for $2,000, no questions asked. Even if the car came with a legitimate-seeming bill of sale and registration, the very fact of its price and the way it was presented would suggest "hot car," and all the potential trouble that implies. And she'd probably agree that buying stolen merchandise put the buyer in the position of supporting the business of thievery.

The principal's situation is all too common, even if her search for a "good deal" may have less to do with money than with two other valuable commodities: time and pride. She needed the degree in a timely manner to appear to have the basic qualifications for the position of principal. No legitimate college or university can work as fast as the degree mills. The "university" didn't even need to examine her transcript. Why should she spend months applying to universities, having her qualifications evaluated by them, engaging in lengthy negotiations to get the most credit recognized for the courses she had already taken? The degree mill just takes your word for it.

Did a red flag go up in the principal's mind over this detail? Apparently not. Consider if she had walked into a shopping mall after refusing to buy that new-looking car from the man in the parking lot and had been confronted by a man in an academic robe who said to her, "Madam, you look like somebody in need of a master's degree. I can help." After she briefly recited her qualifications, he announced that she could have a master's degree as soon as her credit card was approved. The principal did the exact equivalent, and her Internet degree is worth as much as the shopping-mall degree.

There's a reason why pride was the first of the seven deadly sins.

Many people who fall into the hands of the proprietors of degree mills know that they *deserve* that degree. They've done the equivalent work. They may have more practical experience doing the very job for which the degree is a basic requirement than some young kid just out of college. They don't feel a need to present themselves to somebody in a university and ask for the rights and privileges that accrue from having that degree because they've already done the work.

The advertisements on the Internet and in the print media feed right into that syndrome. "You may have already earned your degree. Isn't it time you reaped the benefits?" "Your hard work and life experience deserve recognition."

But there's another basic ethical truth by which we operate in this society: We have a responsibility to learn the laws and rules under which we live and a duty to follow them. We have a responsibility to know the basic laws of nature if we're going to take on the care of another living thing. And if we're going to present ourselves as ready to work in a particular environment, we have a responsibility to understand the rules of that organization and a duty to follow them.

A cab driver needs to know the rules of the road and the

policies of his company regarding fares, care of his vehicle, treatment of customers, and the basic licensing he has to have to be a driver. He doesn't need to understand how getting a college degree works. And the principal didn't need to know how one becomes licensed to drive a vehicle that transports people.

But we all know there are standard ways to get what you think you need and there are often under-the-table ways to get the same thing, and it's a good idea to know which is the right one and which is the one that may get you into more trouble than it's worth.

Someone operating in the field of education has a responsibility to know how it works at any level in which she's likely to become involved and to have the common sense to distinguish the real coin of her realm.

Did the principal do wrong in "falling for" the diploma mill scam on the Internet? Yes. She is *not* an innocent victim because she had a responsibility to know how the world of higher education operates. She's not an innocent patient handing a prescription slip into a pharmacy and falling victim to the pharmacist's inattention or ignorance when she gets and takes the wrong medication. She surely would have heard the word *accreditation* during her tenure as a teacher. Most public schools, and many private ones as well, are subject to scrutiny by independent agencies to determine the standard of their operation from the cleanliness of their facility through the quality of their library as well as the evidence of learning that their students can demonstrate. Schools that fail such scrutiny may end up closing. Those who pass display their resulting certification proudly. To be unaware of the importance of accreditation is to have slipped up in responsibility to know.

There is, however, an all-too-human tendency to hope that details will work themselves out. It's a degree. It's not an accredited degree. Maybe it doesn't matter. So we use the dairy products that drifted to back of the fridge and are long past their expiration date and hope that nothing happens. We make that U-turn when there's no endangering traffic, even if there's a little sign that suggests it's not legal. We pay attention to the big stuff and hope that our overall goodness will count. Sometimes it works that way, sometimes it doesn't.

But what if the rule is wrong? If there's no traffic for blocks, shouldn't I be able to make that U-turn? Some cities try to accommodate variations: "No left turn between 7 and 9 a.m." But when there's no accommodation, you don't turn left unless you enjoy meeting your local law enforcement officers in adversarial situations.

Here we should take a moment to consider what a real school does that a diploma mill doesn't—a distinction that the principal did not consider in her deposition, although she uses the word *program* to describe what preceded the awarding of the degree. A master's program involves an array of learning experiences that are designed to produce in the student "mastery" of a body of knowledge.

Virtually all legitimate schools claim a right to administer a portion of that knowledge, since they believe that in awarding their degree they are giving the student the benefit of the school's prestige and reputation for the rest of that student's career, and that reputation, in part, rests, in turn, on their turning out students whose competence in their chosen field will bespeak the high standards of the school's instructional program. In fact, many schools insist on providing *all* the education at the graduate level.

In such cases, a student who applies with a significant amount of graduate credit is awarded equivalency in credits, but not in classes, so that when the student arrives at a final project, a thesis, dissertation, or other demonstration of achievement, the student can continue working independently without paying additional school fees until submitting the final work. Thus, the school retains the right to educate the student but allows the student some credit for time and work already accomplished.

Even when classes are accepted for transfer, most schools attempt to do so by finding actual equivalencies in their own program, since a graduate program is not just an accumulation of classes taken at random but an array of related studies within a discipline designed to produce just that mastery of the field. And the primary criterion for transfer of credits to an accredited college or university is that the credits presented, in turn, were done at an accredited institution. This implies some scrutiny by an impartial body of the quality of educational programs offered by the institution.

There is no sense whatever in which the degree mill offered a "program" to the principal.

Nonetheless, she may still feel that her qualifications should have been recognized under the rules of the schools and the administrators' association.

If a rule is wrong, obviously, we can try to change it. Here we come to the "What could we have done differently?" section of this report.

The school district seems to have some flexibility. While they require their administrators to earn three units of graduate credit every three years, their rules say that requirement may be waived or extended. What if the principal or a supporter proposed a plan whereby she might meet the degree requirement in an honorable and acceptable way?

Perhaps the school board was also suffering from "ignore the details and hope they will go away" syndrome. If so, that is unfortunate.

Or it may be the case that the current rules are set in stone, and changing them is impossibly difficult. In that situation, we may be facing an unjust law. If it is, indeed, an example of an ideal candidate who cannot be hired because the regulations prohibit it and the regulations cannot be changed, then a kind of courage not usually found in school boards and similar bodies is required.

We have no better teacher in the appropriate meeting of that situation than the late Dr. Martin Luther King Jr., whose "Letter from a Birmingham Jail" stands as a model for the intelligent person of good conscience who confronts an impossible law. He said, "One who breaks an unjust law must do so openly, lovingly, and with a willingness to accept the penalty." He wrote those words while suffering the penalty of imprisonment for breaking the segregation laws of the state of Alabama in 1963.

In our case, the fact that the principal may well have been the best candidate for the position implies that the law is inappropriate—even unjust to her and to those who would benefit from her service as principal. But the fact that the breach of that law had to be called to public attention by someone who felt wronged in that breach means it was *not* done openly. And there is no evidence that the principal even accepts the fact of her participation in the breaking of the rule, so she does not have the dignity of Dr. King's position.

Wrong was done by the hiring of this person to the position of principal.

The selection committee acted unjustly in not applying the stated criteria, thus wronging the applicants and probably some members of the public. The principal failed to exercise sufficient responsibility in determining the details of the requirements for the position and the appropriate way to meet the requirement for the master's degree. Presenting herself as holding a degree to which she is not entitled may endanger the reputation, and possibly the accreditation, of the institution that she leads.

It is often difficult to determine how to right ethical wrongs. It would be a shame if the principal's successful career as a teacher, mentor of teachers, and acting administrator were to end in embarrassment and result in her quietly disappearing like the kleptomaniac counselor.

It is entirely possible that she was the best candidate for the job, and her possession of an embarrassing master's degree is an obstacle that might be overcome by the school board granting her a period of time to research the acquisition of a legitimate, honorable degree in her field so that she may end her career in the way she, and her supporters, would prefer.

This presumes the capacity for recognition of her part in

the wrongdoing and her willingness to take further action toward legitimizing her employment. It is probably too much to address the question of repaying the school district for the increment in salary retained during the time she served without appropriate credential, although that may come up.

It is to be hoped that the basic values of honesty, responsibility, and justice will be upheld in the ultimate resolution of this case. By doing so, we do the best we can as individuals to maintain the moral strength of our communities.

PART 3

REFERENCE

Chapter 14

·····································

LIST OF UNRECOGNIZED SCHOOLS

·····································

For many years, we maintained a database of colleges and universities whose degrees were generally regarded as unacceptable in the worlds of business, government, and higher education. For two reasons, we did not include this database in the first edition of our book in 2005:

1. It was extremely time-consuming to keep the list up-to-date and correct.
2. While there was (and is) widespread agreement on the assessment of schools, it is by no means universal.

We acknowledge that such a list can have real value to readers of this book, so here is what we have done.

Among the states that maintain and publish their own list of schools whose degrees are not acceptable in that state, the states of Oregon and Michigan are especially thorough and diligent in keeping their lists up-to-date. But neither is perfect, so there are quite a few schools that appear on one list, but not on the other.

Rather than use our own list, then, we are instead offering our own "blending" of the Oregon and Michigan lists. These are institutions that, as Michigan describes it, grant degrees, that "will **not** be accepted by the Michigan Civil Service Commission to satisfy educational requirements indicated on job specifications."

In other words, these are schools and degrees that are not acceptable to the States of Michigan or Oregon. We have added a small number of schools from our own files as well: some older ones whose degrees still turn up from time to time, and some new ones that have not yet made it onto the Oregon and Michigan lists, but inevitably will.

This, then, is a place to start. If a school *is* on this list, it should at least be looked at more closely.

If a school is *not* on this list, and it is in the United States but not on the Council for Higher Education Accreditation's master list of accredited schools (http://www.chea.org), then it should *also* be looked at closely.

If a school is not on this list, and not in the United States, the task is harder. If it is listed in either of the two major reference books (*Europa World of Learning* and the *International Handbook of Universities*; many larger libraries will have at least one) on world schools, it is almost certain to be legitimate. But if it is not listed, then it also needs to be looked at closely. (Note: the above-mentioned CHEA list includes a very small number of non-US schools that happen to be accredited by US accrediting agencies: a total of sixty-three in Canada and fifty-six in the rest of the world.)

Here are the URLs for the four best state lists:

Michigan list: http://tinyurl.com/MichiganList

Maine list: http://tinyurl.com/MaineList

Texas list: http://tinyurl.com/TexasList

Oregon list: http://tinyurl.com/OregonList

THE LIST OF SCHOOLS UNACCEPTABLE IN MICHIGAN AND/OR OREGON

Note: the schools on the Oregon list that are not on the Michigan list, or schools where Oregon adds information to the Michigan list, or where the authors have added additional information, have a black dot following the listing: •

Abacus Academy

Abba Institute—TX

Aberdeen University, same as Alberdeen University •

Abingdon University, UK •

Academie Europeene d'Informationsation—Belgium; see World Information Distributed University •

Academy for Contemporary Research

Academy of Healing Arts

Academy of Health Sciences and Nutrition

Academy of Natural Therapies—HI, CA, WY, MT; closed by court order in HI; relocated to CA, then to either WY or MT •

Academy of Religious and Spiritual Studies

Accelerated Degree Programs

Acton Liberty University •

Acton University •

Adam Smith University—HI, NY, Liberia, Saipan; uses Acme Career Services, Las Vegas, for transcript and degree verification requests

Adams and WA University—England, SC

Adams Institute of Technology

Addison State University—Ottawa, Canada. This is not a state entity and has no Ontario authorization to issue degrees. •

Adjunct College—TX

Advanced Education Trust

Advanced Learning Network—VT; does not have Vermont authority to grant degrees; appears to be a conduit for converting nonacademic work to academic credits •

African Distributed University— possibly Nigeria; unrecognized; connected to the World Information Distributed University •

Akamai University—HI

AL Christian College—Montgomery, AL

Al Qasim University—Pakistan

Alberdeen University—NM

Albert University—SD

Alexandria University—NV; US online, not Egyptian

Al-Hurra University—Sweden, Netherlands, etc.; lacks degree-granting authority; sometimes spelled "Alhuraa" •

Al-Ishraw University—Saudi Arabia; lacks authority to issue degrees •

All Saints American University— Liberia

All-American University—NV •

Allen Maxwell University—WY, etc. •

Almeda College (University)—FL, ID

Almeda College and University— FL, ID, OR. Site "[c]losed by legal action in FL but may still be operating there. Operating illegally in ID." •

Almeda International University, same as Almeda University •

Al-Shurook University—Saudi Arabia; lacks authority to issue degrees •

Alston University—Stockton, CA

Ambai University—MA; has no degree-granting authority in Massachusetts •

Ambassador University Corporation

America West University •

American Androgogy University—
HI, Bolivia •

American Austin University

American Capital University—WY,
Liberia

American Central University—WY

American City University—WY

American Coastline University—HI,
LA, NY, CA, Russia

American College of Health Science—TX

American College of Metaphysical
Theology

American Columbus University—
CA

American Extension School of
Law—Chicago, IL

American Global International University—FL •

American Global Universities—WY,
IA, CA

American Global University School
of Medicine—OH; operating
without appropriate approval in
OH •

American HI University •

American Independent International University

American Institute of Management
Studies—HI, Indonesia

American Institute of Science—
Indianapolis, IN

American International Academy—
NY, WA

American International University
of Management and Tech-
nology—HI, CA; closed by
court order •

American International University—Canoga Park, CA; possibly Lebanon. Carries false
certification reading "ADA—
State of OR USA." Any degree
bearing this certification is
fraudulent.

American Legion University

American Liberty University—AL,
CA, also Greece, South Korea,
China, Taiwan, Malaysia, UAR,
according to their website •

American M&N University •

American Management Institute

American Medical College—ID

American National University—
Phoenix, AZ; HI, CA

American Open University

American Pacific University—
Vietnam; claims it offers Central WA University credits; faculty and programs in Vietnam
is false according to State of
Washington •

American PacWest International
University—HI; has filed suit to
close this entity •

American Pushington University •

American Scandinavian Academy—
Sweden, TX, AZ; IP address in
Netherlands; claims to be regis-
tered in TX; phone number is
Swedish •

American Scandinavian University •

American School of Metaphysics

American State University—HI;
relocated to WY as Hamilton
University; relocated to the
Caribbean as Richardson
University •

American States University—Honolulu, HI

American University for Humanities—MS, CO, Lebanon; new name for American University of HI, which was closed by court order; degrees issued from SD

American University of Asturias—Spain; closed by Spanish government •

American University of Athens, claims of SD authority and ACICS accreditation invalid since 2005 •

American University of Hawaii—MS, formerly HI, also India, Lebanon, Republic of Georgia; changed name in spring 2006 to American University of Humanities •

American University of HI—HI, MS, India, Republic of Georgia, Armenia, Lebanon, and others

American University of London—Saudi Arabia; lacks authority to issue degrees there •

American University of London—St. Kitts and Nevis, UK, Sri Lanka

American University of Mayonic Science and Technology—CO; lacks authority to issue degrees •

American University—HI, CA

American University—San Diego, CA (the one in Washington, DC, is accredited)

American West University

American Western University—AZ, OH

American Westpoint University •

Americana University—Liberia

Americus University—Washington, DC

Ameritech University—Liberia

Ames Christian University—FL

Amity University—India

Amorsolo Foundation—CA; also uses name CA University or CUFCE; no legal authority to issue degrees or transcripts •

Amstead University—NM

Anacrusis Institute—Greece, UK

Anderson University—CA

Anglo-American College of Medicine

Anglo-American Institute of Drugless Medicine

Anglo-American University—HI; closed by court order •

Apache University

Apostolic/Prophetic Bible College & Theological Seminary—Rochester Hills, MI

Aquinas University of Scholastic Philosophy—NY

Arabic Open University—Denmark •

Argus University—Fairplay, CO •

Aristotle University—CA

Armstrong University—CA; not accredited after mid-1990s •

Ashbourne—UK; not recognized by British authorities •

Ashburry University—MS •

Ashford University—UK (not to be confused with Ashford University in IA, formerly Franciscan University)

Ashington University—LA, British Virgin Islands

Ashwood University Fake, may also operate under "Universidad de las Palmas" •

Athenaeum U—Panama, UK

Athens Clark University

Atlanta Southern University—Atlanta, GA

Atlantic International University—FL, HI

Atlantic National University—CA

Atlantic Northeastern University

Atlantic Pacific University—Chengdu, China •

Atlantic Southern University—GA, WA

Atlantic University—NY (the one in VA is accredited)

Atworth University

Auberdeen University—ID; has no authority to issue degrees •

AZ American World University—CA, HI, IA, MS

AZ Midland University

Azaliah University—NM (lost accreditation in 2002), South Africa, Asia

Baden-Powell University of Scouting •

Baltimore State University (not to be confused with the University of Baltimore)

Bangalore Institute of Science, Technology, and Management—India

Bangladesh University

Barrington University—AL, NY (not to be confused with Barrington College in Rhode Island). Name changed to University of Atlanta, now has DETC accreditation. •

Barron University

Bavarian College of Science—Germany; unrecognized; no degree-granting authority •

Beacon Learning Center—Grand Rapids, MI; St. Joseph, MI

Bedford University •

Belford University—TX, NV, AZ

Beloved Community Seminary—OR, HI

Ben Franklin Academy and Institute for Advanced Studies—Washington, DC

Benchley State University

Benjamin Franklin Institute of Global Education

Bennington University—United States (not to be confused with Bennington College Vermont)

Benson University

Berean Community College

Berkeley International University of Southern CA

Bernadean University—Van Nuys, CA; used to give graduates a certificate absolving them of all sins •

Berne University—NH, PA, VA, St. Kitts and Nevis. Approval revoked by St. Kitts, February 2006; now operates as Bernelli University, VA. •

Bernelli University—VA

Bettis Christian University—AR, KS

Beulah College—Nigeria, TX

Bienville University—LA, MS; closed by state action in LA; not approved in MS •

Bircham International University—UK, Spain, Bahamas

Birkdale University •

Blackstone University

Bonavista University—WY

Bonneville University •

Bosdon Academy of Music

Boston City College (not to be confused with Boston College)

Bradford University (not be confused with Bradford College)

Brainwells University—US, Canada

Brantridge Forest School

Brantridge University—HI

Brentwick University

Bretton Woods University—NH

Breyer State University –AL, ID, CA, Liberia. Lost authority to issue degrees on June 3, 2007; not a state school. •

Bridgewater University—UK, Seychelles (not to be confused with Bridgewater State College in Massachusetts or Bridgewater College in VA)

Bright Way Technical University

Brighton University—HI, MO; closed by court order •

Britain College of Management and Science—UK

British American Business Institute

British West Indies School of Medicine •

Brixton University—BC, Canada; operating illegally, lacks authority to issue degrees •

Broadmore University •

Broadway Institute of Technology

Bronte International University— LA, Haiti, St. Kitts; new name for former Trinity College and University

Brown's International University •

Brownell University

Buckner University—TX

Buktronix University

Burkes University—Turks and Caicos •

Burnell College—UK

Burnett International University— FL, Haiti •

Business and Computer University College—Lebanon

Buxton University—UK

Byron University •

C&E American University Institute—Lebanon

Cal Southern University—TX; not a CA school; not the same as California Southern University; registered on South Pacific island of Niue

Calamus International University— British West Indies

Calgary College of Technology— Canada •

Calgary Providence University

California Christian College

California Institute for Human Science—CA, Japan •

California Institute of Behavior Sciences—CA

California Institute of Higher Learning

California Pacific University—CA

California Pacifica University—CA

California Technical University— CA; private high school in Los Angeles, no relationship to traditional "CalTech" in Pasadena, CA •

California University FCE, see Amorsolo•

California University for Advanced
Studies—CA •

California University of Management and Sciences—CA

California Valley State University

Calvary University—VA, OR, UK,
Netherlands, and others; has no
legal authority to grant degrees •

Cambridge Intercontinental University—SD •

Cambridge International University—South Africa; does not
have appropriate authorization
from South Africa •

Cambridge State University—
Shreveport, LA; Honolulu, HI;
not a state school

Cambridgeshire University—NY •

Camford University—AL •

Campile University—UK, Belize

Canada International Education
Centre—AB, Canada; lacks
degree-granting authority; lacks
Alberta approval •

Canadian School of Management—
Canada

Canbourne University—UK

Canterbury University—UK; not
associated with legitimate school
of same name in New Zealand •

Canyon College—ID, CA. All
degrees issued by the entity
should be considered invalid.
Continues to operate illegally in
Idaho. State of Idaho says,
"Idaho does not consider
Canyon College credits or
diplomas valid."

Capital American University—
Liberia

Capital City Religious Institute—
Baton Rouge, LA

Capitol University (not to be confused with Capital University in
OH)

Caribbean Medical University—
Curaçao

Carlingford University—UK •

Carlton University (not to be confused with Carleton College in
MN)

Carnegie Institute of Engineering

Carolina Institute of Human Relations—SC

Carolina University of Theology

Carrington University

Castlebridge University—HI •

Center College of Executive and
Professional Development—
India

Center of University Studies Graduate College

Center State University of Executive and Professional Development—Liberia

Central Pacific University—HI, SD,
Dubai

Central State Consortium of Colleges and Schools

Central State University—CA,
Canada (CSU in Wilberforce,
OH, is accredited)

Central States Research Center—
ON, Canada

Central University

Century University—Albuquerque,
NM (not to be confused with
Century College)

CETEC University—Santo Domingo

Chadwick University—AL

Chancery International University

Chapparal Western University—NV •

Charis School of Divinity—FL

Charitable University of SD

Chartwell University—Canada, Washington, DC •

Chase University

Chelsea University—UK; lacks authority to issue degrees in UK

Cherub College—Bahamas

Chicago Medical College—FL

Chillicothe Business College—OH

Chirological College of CA

Christian College

Christian Leadership University—NY

Christian University of HI •

Churchill College •

CIFAS University—Santo Domingo

City University Los Angeles—CA

Claremont University—Seychelles Islands; operated from IL by former St. Regis University degree-mill salesperson. No connection with genuine Claremont University in CA. •

Clayton College of Natural Health—AL. Degree holders ineligible for licensure in OR, other states. •

Clayton Theological Institute—CA

Clayton University—Hong Kong (not to be confused with Clayton College and State University in GA); operated legally in MO until about 1990

Clemson College (not to be confused with Clemson University in SC)

Clermont College (not to be confused with University of Cincinnati–Clermont College).

Clermont College of Business—MT; appears to be an offshoot of Prescott College, closed by HI

Cleveland University (not to be confused with Cleveland State University)

CliffPort University •

Clinton University—Livonia, MI

CO University of Naturopathic Medicine—Spain, British Virgin Islands

Coast University

Colgate College (not to be confused with Colgate University)

College of Applied Science—London

College of Franklin and Marshall (not to be confused with Franklin and Marshall College of Lancaster, PA)

College of Hilton Head

College of Homeopathy—MO

College of Journalism—WV

College of Life Science—TX

College of Life—FL

College of Medical and Health Science—St. Lucia

College of Natural Therapeutics

College of Naturatrics—MO

College of Nonsense—NV

College of Universal Truth—Chicago, IL

Colony University—Liberia

Columbia Commonwealth University—MT, WY, Malawi, Africa

Columbia Pacific University—CA

Columbia School

Columbia State University—LA (not to be confused with Columbia University in NY or Columbus State University in

GA); closed by court order, owner imprisoned

Columbus University—LA, MS (not to be confused with Columbus State University in GA); closed by state action in LA

Commonwealth Open University— Virgin Islands

Commonwealth School of Law—WA

Commonwealth University—CA

Communion of Saints Seminary— OR; operating illegally in OR; degrees invalid •

Concordia College and University—Spain, Dominican Republic, Indonesia, Belgium; St. Johns, VI ("registered by the government" of Liberia)

Concordia Ivy College—HI, Taiwan

Continental University—Liberia, Philippines

Continuing Career Institute—TX

Cook's Institute of Electronics Engineering—Jackson, MS; note: now DETC-accredited •

Corlins (or Corllins) University— CA, MI; no authority to issue valid degrees •

Cornerstone University—LA (not to be confused with Cornerstone University in MI, which is accredited)

Cornwall Independent University— UK •

Cosmopolitan University, headquarters may be in Chile; offices in other countries and in MO, FL •

Cranston University—NV, Singapore

Crestmont College—LA •

Cromwell College of IT and Management—UK

Cromwell University

Crossworld Institute of Professional Studies—Kenya; related to the Bircham University degree mill •

Crown Church College and University

Crown College of the Bible—TN

Cultural International Center—CA, Lebanon

Culture University—HI

Culverton College—Malaysia •

Dallas State College—Dallas, TX

Darthmouth College (not to be confused with Dartmouth College in NH)

Dartley University—SD; lacks authority to grant degrees •

Dartmouth University (not to be confused with Dartmouth College in NH)

Darton University Degree.com—TX, FL, Mexico

Del Sur Christian College—TX

Denmark College of Management and IT—Denmark

Denver State University

DePaul University—France •

Devonshire University

Diamond Head University

Diplomatic State University

Diplomatic University

DiUlus Institute and University— NM, Italy

Dixon Bird Medical University—St. Kitts •

Donsbach University—CA

Dorcas University

Drake College (not to be confused with Drake University in IA or Drake College of Business in NJ)

Dream Institute

Dublin Metropolitan University— Ireland

Dukson University •

Earlscroft University—UK, Seychelles

Earlstown University; sells degrees outright •

Earthnet Institute—HI; closed by court order 2005

East Point University

Eastern American University—NM •

Eastern Caribbean University—TX, St. Kitts

Eastern MO Business College—St. Louis, MO

Eastern State University

Eastern University—Albuquerque, NM

Ecole Superieure Internationale de Bruxelles—Belgium

Eden University—HI?

Edenvale University—TX, NY, UK

Edison University—HI (not to be confused with Thomas Edison State College in NJ)

Eire International University— Pakistan •

Ellington University

Elysion College—CA

Emerson University—CA (not to be confused with Emerson College in MA)

Empire University—HI •

Esoteric Theological Seminary—TX

Euclid University—Belgium, Chad, Central African Republic, Pakistan

Eula Wesley University—Ruston, LA

European American University— Dominica

European Carolus Magnus University—Belgium

European College of Medicine—UK; division of unaccredited St. Luke College of Medicine

European Continental University— SD, UK; lacks degree-granting authority •

European Graduate School—NY, Switzerland

European Management University International—Denmark, Sweden, US, China; degree mill •

European University of Ireland— Ireland

European University of Ireland— Ireland; does not have authority to issue Irish degrees •

Eurotechnical Research University—TX, Hilo, HI

Evergreen University—Reston, VA

Excelsior University (not to be confused with Excelsior College in Albany, NY)

Expressive Psychology Association

Fairfax University—LA, MT, SD, UK

Fairmont International University (formerly Preston University)

Farington University

Felix Adler Memorial University— North Carolina

Felton University

Firelake University—Finland; not a

Finnish college; lacks authority to issue degrees •

FL Atlantic Southeastern University—(not to be confused with FL Atlantic University in Boca Raton, FL)

FL Green University—Pakistan? •

FL State Christian College—FL

Forest Park University—Chicago, IL

Fort Young University—Liberia

Foundation for Economic Education—Irvington-on-Hudson, NY

Foundation University—Netherlands; does not have valid approval from government of the Netherlands to issue degrees •

Four States Cooperative University —TX

Frederick Taylor International University Ruston—LA, HI, CA; closed by court order in HI •

Frederick Taylor University—Moraga, CA

Free Swiss University of St. George—Switzerland •

Freiburgh University—Belgium •

Friends International Christian University—HI, CA

Full Gospel Christian College—Pontiac, MI

Garfield Technical College

Gemini College—UK

Generale University—Canada •

Geniversity—Quebec, VA; lacks authority to issue degrees •

Geo-Metaphysical Institute—NY

George Washington State College

George Washington University—CA (GWU in Washington, DC, is accredited)

Georgia Christian University—GA

Georgia South Technical Institute

German-American Dental College—Chicago, IL

Gestalt Institute of New Orleans—New Orleans, LA

Glamount University—TX •

Glamshier University—WY, etc. •

Glencullen University—UK

Glendale University—UK

Glenford University—LA

Global Church Theological Seminary

Global Church University

Global Open University—SD, Uganda, Netherlands, Zambia, India; lacks appropriate degree-granting authority •

Global University School of Nursing—Jamaica

Global Virtual University (not to be confused with Global University in Springfield, MO)

Goa University

Gold Coast University—HI

Golden Pacific University—HI, CA

Golden State University—HI (not to be confused with Golden State College in CA; may be multiple entities, one of which became Honolulu University of the Arts, Sciences, and Humanities) •

Gordon University—IL, FL •

Graduate College

Graduate University

Grandview International University—MO; does not have degree-granting authority according to state of MO •

Great Lakes University—MI (not to be confused with Great Lakes Christian College)

Greenleaf University—MO; degrees banned for use in Sweden •

Greenwich University—CA, HI, Norfolk Island

Gulf Southern University—LA

Halifax University—WY

Hamilton College—Clinton, NY

Hamilton State University—AZ

Hamilton University—WY, HI, Bahamas; see American State University. Moved to Bahamas as Richardson University. •

Hamline State University (not to be confused with Hamline University in Minnesota)

Hampton Bay University—Liberia

Hampton College—NV (not to be confused with Hampton University in VA)

Hancock University—TN

Harmony College of Applied Science—Los Altos, CA

Harrington University—UK

Hartford Technical Institute

Hartford University—Vanuatu (claims of Minnesota location are false)

Hartland University—Liberia

Hartley University—UK

Hawaii American University—HI; closed by court order •

Hawaii International University—HI •

Hawthorn University—CA, NY, FL •

Hawthorne University—UT

Heed University—FL, WI, Caribbean

Hegel International University—CA, HI, Japan •

Herguan University—CA •

Heritage International University— UK? FL? •

Heritage University •

Hill University, degree mill; probably sells from the UAE •

Hilton Head University •

His Majesty's University of Polytechnics—Sacramento, CA

Hollywood College—CA

Hollywood Southern University

Holos University—MO, SD, Norfolk Island

Honolulu University of the Arts, Sciences, and Humanities—Honolulu, HI, Thailand, Pakistan

Honolulu University—Honolulu, HI, SD •

Honolulu USA—Thailand, Pakistan

Hoover University—SD •

Horizons University—France, VA •

Humberman University College

Huntington Pacific University

Hyles Anderson College—Crown Point, IN

Illawarra College—NH, VA, Australia

Illinois College of Physicians and Surgeons

Independence University—MO

Indiana Northern University— IN •

Information University of America

Institute for Creative Process

Institute for Human Dynamics

Institute for Science in Mind

Institute for the Management of Information Systems—UK

Institute of Excellence—FL

Institute of Executive and Professional Development—Liberia

Institute of Global Education—OR; has no authority to issue degrees or credit •

Institute of New Media and Technology

Instituto Biblico Ebenezer—MI

InTech University—Liberia

InterAmerican University—CA, NY, NV (not to be confused with the InterAmerican University of Puerto Rico)

Intermountain Institute of Natural Health—ID

International Academy for Planetary Planning

International Academy of Education University—NY, Japan

International American University—Nepal, CA; formerly Management Institute of America •

International Bible University

International Career Academy

International College of Associates in Medicine—TX

International Earth Environment University—SD, Japan

International East-West University —HI

International Further Studies Institute

International Graduate Center—VT, St. Croix

International Institute for Advanced Studies—MO, HI •

International Institute for Specialised Education and Research; UK, TN •

International MBS—Liberia

International Medical School of America—TX

International Mid Pac College—HI

International Open University— Baton Rouge, LA

International Organization for Nontraditional Distance Education—HI, Japan, Philippines

International Seminary—Plymouth, FL

International Theological University—CA

International Universities Consortium—MO

International University for Graduate Studies—St. Kitts and Nevis

International University of Fundamental Studies

International University of Nursing—St. Kitts

International University—Austria

International University—MO, LA

IOND University—HI, Japan, Philippines, Ireland; degree mill closed in HI by court order •

Irish International University— Seborga, Italy; Ireland, UK, Cambodia, Malaysia, Kenya, Switzerland; the Irish government has requested that Malaysia close this entity on the grounds that it is neither Irish nor a university. All degrees should be considered invalid. Claim of affiliation with University of Lodz in Poland is denied by University of Lodz. •

Irish University Business School— Ireland; not accredited by HETAC in Ireland; Oregon does not recognize any of these operators •

Isles International University, St. Kitts, Malaysia •

ITECOPAM—Haiti; not a recognized Haitian college •

Ivory Carlson University—MN; degree mill; apparently based in India

Jackson State University—Los Angeles, Nashville, Reno, Chicago (JSU in MS is accredited)

James Cook Medical School—TX, Cook Islands

James Monroe University—Liberia, AZ, ID, WA

Jefferson United University—HI •

Jenzabar University

JLF University—FL •

Johann Keppler School of Medicine—NY, Zurich

John Hancock University

John Quincy Adams College—Portland, OR

John Thomas—MO

Johnson Davies University—Liberia; British Virgin Islands •

Jose Bernardo Gutierrez Medical School—TX •

Kalinga University—India (not to be confused with Kalinga University in the Philippines)

Kardan Institute of Higher Education—Afghanistan; affiliated with Preston University, AL •

Karma University—CA

Kendall University—Dominica •

Kennedy-Western University—CA, WY, ID; name changed to Warren National University, 2006 •

Kensington University—HI, CA (not to be confused with Kensington College in CA); closed by court order •

Kent College—LA

Kentucky Christian University—Ashland, KY (Kentucky Christian College in Grayson, Kentucky, is accredited)

Keystone University—FL

Kincaid Academy of the Arts

Kingdom College of Natural Health—LA, WY, Guam, Russia

Kingsfield University—UK

Kingsley University

Kingston University—SD •

Knightsbridge University—Denmark; does not have appropriate legal authority to issue degrees in Denmark •

Knoxville College—TN (only degrees obtained prior to December 1996 are accepted)

Korey International University—HI •

LA International University—New Orleans, LA

Lacrosse University—LA, MS

LaCrosse University—LA; closed by state action, relocated to MS •

LaHaye Global University of Journalism and Media •

LaJolla University

Lamberhurst University—UK

Lambert University—HI; formerly Newport Asia Pacific University •

Lamp Beacon University

Landegg International University—Switzerland; lacks appropriate authority to issue degrees •

Landford University

Landsfield University—Seychelles

Langley University

Lansbridge University—BC, Canada; closed by court order •

LaSalle University—LA (not to be

confused with LaSalle University in PA)

Laureate University—Canada, UK? No evidence of authority to issue degrees. Not related to Laureate Education Inc., which operates accredited Walden University. •

Laurence University—HI

Lawford State University—MD

Leal University—Hazelwood, MO

Lee Community College—Singapore

Leibniz—NM, Italy

Leiland College of Arts and Sciences—HI

Leland Stanford University—Baton Rouge, LA

Leugenia University—SC

Lexington University—online, NV (not to be confused with Lexington College in IL)

Liberty International University •

Life Science College—CA, OK

Limburg University—Sweden, Greece; lacks degree-granting authority •

Lincoln International University, Inc.—HI; closed by court order •

Lincoln University—NM, Italy (not to be confused with Lincoln College in IL or other accredited Lincolns)

Lincoln-Jefferson University—IN, NY, possibly IA. Registrar arrested in NY, 2010 •

Lion Investigative Academy—PA

Logos Bible College—TX, FL

Logos Christian College

London College of Technology—UK

London Institute for Applied Research, "LIAR" •

London University Colleges

Lorenz University

Los Angeles State University

Los Angeles University—North Hollywood, CA

Louisiana Capital University—Kenner, LA

Louisiana Central University—LA •

Louisiana Christian University—Lake Charles, LA

Louisiana International University—LA •

Louisiana Pacific University—LA •

Loyola State University—IL and LA (not to be confused with Loyola University)

Madison State University—NY

Madison University—MS

Management Institute of Canada—ON, Quebec; not a Canadian degree granter •

Manhattan University—BC, Canada; HI

Manitoba University of Science and Arts

Marcus Tullius Cicero University San Francisco—CA

Marlborough University—HI

Marlowe University—NJ, FL

Marmaduke University—CA

Martin College—FL

Marylebone University—Seychelles, UK •

Maxipoint University—SD •

McKinley University—UT •

McPherson Institute of Technology

Medical College of London—St. Lucia, West Indies; UK, Montserrat

Medical University of the Americas—Belize; not the same as same-name school in Nevis, which is approved by NY

Mellen University—Lewiston, NY

Meridan University

Meta Collegiate Extension—NV

Metropolitan Collegiate Institute—UK

Metropolitan University of FL

Miami Christian University—Miami, FL

Miami State University (not to be confused with Miami University, Oxford, OH)

Middle Tennessee University (not to be confused with Middle Tennessee State University in Murfreesboro, TN)

Midwest Missouri University—MO

Midwestern University—MO (not to be confused with Midwestern University in AZ or IL or Midwestern Baptist Theological Seminary in MO)

Millard Fillmore Institute •

Miller University—Philadelphia, PA

Milton University—MD, NY

Miranda Internal University—TN, WA, Italy

Mishigan International College—Pakistan •

Miura Marina Institute—Japan •

Mole Ltd. University—River Ridge, LA

Monterrey Institute for Graduate Studies—TX, FL; claimed to be a branch of a Mexican institution with authority to operate in the US, but did not have that authority •

Monticello University—HI, KS, SD, West Indies; another name for Thomas Jefferson University. Closed by court order in HI. •

Montserrat University—CA

More University—Lafayette, CA

Morris Brown College—Atlanta, GA (only degrees obtained prior to December 2002 are accepted)

Must University

Myers College Online (not to be confused with Myers University, Cleveland, OH)

Nassau State Teachers College

Nasson University

Nation State University—HI

Nation University—HI; closed by court order •

National Christian University—TX

National College of Arts and Sciences

National College—KS, OK

National Consortium Staff College—MO

National Graduate University

National Stevens University—CA

National University of Colorado—Denver, CO

National University of Dakota—SD

National University of Hawaii—HI

Naturopathic Institute of Therapies and Education—Mt. Pleasant, MI

Nebraska College of Physical Medicine

Netherlands, Nepal

New Horizons University

New Manhattan University

New Tribes Bible Institute—Jackson, MI

New World College—Baton Rouge, LA

New York City University (not to be confused with the City University of NY: CUNY)

New York State College
Newbridge University •
Newburgh Theological Seminary—
    IN
Newport Asia Pacific University—
    HI, CA
Newport University—CA, HI,
    Lebanon
Newton University—BC, Canada;
    HI; closed by court order •
Newyorker University—SD •
Nightingale University—Panama;
    lacks degree-granting authority •
Nobel University—South Korea
Nonprofit Management University
North American College of the
    Artsy
North American University—
    Scottsdale, AZ
North Lexington University—MA;
    degree mill; has no authority to
    grant degrees •
North Norway University—Norway,
    Panama, UK; not a Norwegian
    degree granter •
North United University
Northern American College
Northern Michigan State University
    (not to be confused with
    Northern Michigan University
    in Marquette, MI).
Northern New England University
Northern Utah University/Northern
    UT Management Institute
Northern Washington University
Northfield University
Northland Open University—
    Yukon, Canada
Northridge State University

Northwest Florida University
Northwestern Californian University
Northwestern College of Allied
    Sciences—OK
Northwestern Graduate School—
    MT
Northwestern International Univer-
    sity, Ltd.—Cyprus, Denmark
Norway University—Norway,
    Panama, UK
Notre Dame de Lafayette Univer-
    sity—Long Prairie, MN
Notre Dame University (not to be
    confused with the University of
    Notre Dame in South Bend, IN).
Nova College—Calgary, Canada
Novus University—MS
Oaklands University—UK (not to be
    confused with Oakland Univer-
    sity in Rochester, MI)
Oceania University of Medicine—
    Samoa, FL, PA; operating ille-
    gally in FL •
Ohio Central College
Ohio Christian College
Ohio Saint Mathew University—OH
Oklahoma A&M University
Olive Branch University—Belgium? •
Omega University—NH •
Omniversity—AL •
Open University of America—MD,
    Puerto Rico (not to be confused
    with the Open University of
    Lincoln, NE)
Open University of America—
    Puerto Rico •
Open University of Lincoln—NE
Orienta University
Oriental University—Washington, DC

Orion University or College—LA

Oxford College of Applied Science •

Oxford International University—
UK (not to be confused with
Oxford University)

Oxford Trent University—TX

Pacific Basin University—TX,
Mexico, Micronesia

Pacific Buddhist University—HI,
Japan

Pacific Coast University—CA

Pacific International University—
Springfield, MO

Pacific National University and
Theological Institute—Los
Angeles, CA

Pacific Southern University—HI;
closed by court order •

Pacific Western University—HI,
China, Hong Kong; not the
same as Pacific Western
University, CA •

Pacific Yale University—HI, CA,
South Korea

Panama Canal University

PanAmerican University—Liberia

Paramount University of
Technology —WY

Parkhurst University

Parkwood University—US, UK

Pass Christian University •

Patriot University—CO

Pebble Hills University—Seborga,
Italy; Hutt River, Australia •

Pennington University •

Pensacola Christian College—
Pensacola, FL

Personal Therapy Institute

Pickering University—HI; closed by
court order •

Pigeon Hill University •

Port Rhode University

Prescott College of Business and
Leadership Studies—HI

Prescott University—New Zealand
(not to be confused with
Prescott College in AZ)

Preston University—AL, CA, WY,
Pakistan, Dubai,

Prixio Southern University

Promis University of London—UK,
Belize

Pylon University—HI, CA, South
Korea

Queens University of Brighton—
MO, CA

Queens University—CA

Queenston University—UT,
Australia, Vanuatu

Rai University International—SD,
Australia, UK; lacks degree-
granting authority •

Raighlings University •

Randford University—DC, FL, VA

Ratchford University

Ravenhurst University

Ravenscroft University •

Redding University—United States?
Falsely claims to be a CA
degree granter.

Regency College Rhode Island
School of Law

Regent International University—
Australia?

Regus University—CA, DC, TX

Revans University—Vanuatu •

Rhode Island State University

Richardson University—WY,
Caribbean; formerly Hamilton
University •

Richfield University—HI •

Ridgewood University—Israel, US; fake •

Robert de Sorbon—ME, FL, France, Switzerland, Comoro Islands

Robert Kennedy University—Switzerland; approved by its canton, but degrees not accepted by other Swiss universities •

Robertstown University—Liberia, AZ, ID, WA

Rochdale College •

Rochelle University; associated with Rochville University; no connection with College of New Rochelle in NY or Université de la Rochelle in France •

Rochfort College

Rochville University

Rockfield College of Management—Zurich, Switzerland; not recognized by Swiss Confederation nor accredited by Swiss University Conference •

Rockford Community College

Rocklands University—UK

Romano Byzantine University—MN, VA

Rosebud University

Royal Canadian Institute of Technology—BC, Canada; no legal authority to issue degrees •

Royal College of Science

Royal Open University

Royal Orleans College—LA •

Royal University of Copenhagen—Denmark •

Rumson University •

Rushmore University—SD, WY, GA, Cayman Islands, British Virgin Islands

Rutherford University—BC, Canada; WY, Swaziland; formerly Stratford University •

Sacramento International University

Sacramento Regent University—CA

Sacramento Theological Seminary—CA •

Saint Ambrose College—Anguilla, PA •

Saint Andrews Correspondence College

Saint Augustin University—FL

Saint Augustine School of Medical Assistants—GA

Saint Augustine University

Saint Charles University—LA •

Saint Christopher's College of Medicine—Senegal, UK, Belize; UK stopped accepting degrees in March 2006 •

Saint Clements University—Australia, Turks and Caicos, Niue, Botswana, Ghana, Namibia, Uganda, Zambia

Saint George University International—Saint Kitts, Grenada

Saint James University West

Saint John's University College of Medicine—Montserrat

Saint John's University—Springfield, LA

Saint Joseph University—NY (not to be confused with St. Joseph's College in Brooklyn, NY)

Saint Lourdes University

Saint Lucia College of Medicine—Saint Lucia

Saint Luke School of Medicine—CA, KY, Ghana, Liberia

Saint Martin's College and Seminary—Milwaukee, WI

Saint Mary's College of Medicine—HI

Saint Mary's School of Medicine—HI, TX, Cook Islands

Saint Marys Universities (not to be confused with Saint Mary's College in MI, Saint Mary's University of Minnesota, or St. Mary's University in TX)

Saint Matthew's University—FL, ME, NY, Grand Cayman

Saint Michael University—BC, Canada; CA, NY, FL, DC

Saint Paul's College & Seminary

Saint Regis University—Washington, DC; Dominica, Liberia; closed by court order July 2005 •

Saint Renoir University

Saint Stephen's Educational Bible College—Los Angeles, CA

Saint Theresa Medical School—Saint Kitts

Saint Theresa's Medical University—Saint Kitts; associated with unrecognized Warnborough College or University •

Saint Thomas Institute—India

Saint Thomas University (not to be confused with St. Thomas University in FL)

San Diego Pacific University

San Francisco College of Music and Theater Arts

San Francisco International University—CA

Sands University—Yuma, AZ

Scandinavian Academy—Sweden, TX; see American Scandinavian Academy •

Scarsdale University—CA, UK

SD Law School

Sedona University—AZ •

Senior University—BC, Canada

Sequoia University—CA •

Shaftsbury University—UK?

Shelbourne University—PA

Shelterglen University—OH •

Shepperton University

Sierra University—Costa Mesa, CA (not to be confused with Sierra College in Rocklin, CA)

Smith Gaither Christian University—KS

Solsbury University—ON, Canada

Somerset University—UK •

South Atlantic University

South Eastern University—UK •

South Pacific School of Medicine—TX; originated on Cook Islands •

South Pacific University—HI, CA

Southcoast International University •

Southeastern University—SC •

Southern California University for Professional Studies—Santa Ana, CA; later accredited by DETC •

Southern California University—CA

Southern Eastern University—UK •

Southern Graduate Institute—KY

Southern Indiana Baptist College—Dupont, IN

Southern Institute of Technology

Southern International University—New Orleans, LA

Southern Pacific University—HI, Malaysia; closed by court order •

Southland University—CA

Southwest International University—Bayside, NY; HI, NV

Southwestern State University (not to be confused with Southwestern University in Georgetown, TX)

Southwestern University—Tucson, AZ; St. George, UT

Spartan Health Sciences University—TX, NM, Mexico, St. Lucia

Spartan University of Health Sciences—TX, NM, Mexico, St. Lucia; operating illegally in NM •

Stafford University

Stamford University—NY •

Standford University—FL, TX (not to be confused with Stanford University in CA)

Stanley State University

Stanton University—TX, HI, LA, MO, SD

Stefan International University, Inc.—HI, CA

Stensan International University, Inc.—CA

Stetson College (not to be confused with Stetson University in DeLand, FL)

Stonebridge Associated Colleges—UK •

Stonington University •

Strassford University—UK

Success Seminary—OR; operates illegally in Oregon •

Suffield College and University—CT, ID (In 2010, Allen Ezell bought a backdated Suffield degree for $140, paid by certified check. When they realized who he was, they returned his money in cash—old bills, sent by courier—a first in Ezell's experience.) •

Summerset University—UK

Summit University of LA—LA, TX

Summit University—LA, Japan

Sunshine Community College

Sussex College of Technology aka Copen Labs

Sutherland University

Swiss European University—Switzerland; not recognized by Swiss government •

Synergystics—Rochester, NY

Taiken Wilmington University—United States, Japan?

Taurus International University—CA

Taylor University of Bio-Psycho-Dynamic Sciences—Chattanooga, TN

Tecana International Universita—South America

Technopole University

Temple Bar College

Templeton University—NV, Singapore

Tennessee Christian University—TN

Texas Christian Bible University—TX (not to be confused with Texas Christian University)

Texas Theological University—TX

Texas University (not to be confused with the University of Texas, Texas State University, or Texas Tech University)

Theological University of America—LA •

Thierry Graduate School—Belgium •

Thomas A. Edison College—FL and AR (not to be confused with Thomas Edison State College in NJ)

Thomas Bilney Theological
Seminary—OH •

Thomas Jefferson University—MO
(Thomas Jefferson University
in Philadelphia, PA, is
accredited)

Thomas University—PA

Thornewood (or Thornwood) University—UK

Thornhill University—London, UK;
Brooklyn, NY

Thornwood University—
Netherlands, UK

Toronto Metropolitan University
(not to be confused with the
University of Toronto)

Trident University of Technology—
NJ, WI, Singapore

Trinity College and University—SD,
Pakistan, Venezuela, Netherlands, Canada?, Caribbean?

Trinity College of Natural Health—IN

Trinity College of Science and Management of Southwest International University

Trinity College of the Bible and Theological Seminary—IN

Trinity International University
College—WY, SD, France (not
to be confused with Trinity
International University in IL)

Trinity Southern University—TX,
FL

Tuit University—GA

Tulsa College

Two Dragon University

Udex University—Egypt, Dominica

UK University of Doncaster—
England

Union University—Los Angeles, CA

(Union University of Tennessee
is accredited)

United American Medical College—
ON, Canada

United Nations University

United Pacific University—HI

United States Global University •

United States Open University—HI,
CA, SD

United States University of
America—DC, FL

Universal Bible Institute—
Birmingham, AL

Universal Ecclesiastical University

Universal Life—CA

Universidad de las Palmas; association with Ashwood University •

Universidad Eugenio Maria de
Hostos (UNIREMHOS)—
Dominican Republic

Universidad Federico Henriquez y
Carvajal—Dominican Republic

Universidad Hispana—UT

Universidad Hispanica de America

Universitas 21—Channel Islands, UK

Universitas Sancti Martin—OK

Université de Wallis—Wallis and
Fortuna Islands, South Pacific

Université Libre Internationale—
Belgium

Universiteit Russell Hobbes—
Netherlands?

University College for Advanced
Studies—India

University College of Hospitality and
Care—SD, UK

University de la Romande—UK

University Degree Program (1)—
US, UK, Ireland, Israel, Cyprus,
Romania

University Degree Program (2)—WA?

University for Integrative Learning—CA

University for Professional Studies

University High School—Miami, FL; operated by Stanley Simmons (a defendant during Operation DipScam), exposed by *NY Times* sports writer Pete Hamel as selling high school diplomas and transcripts to talented high school athletes whose grades were not good enough to get into college or for NCAA eligibility •

University of Aberdeen International—SD •

University of Advanced Research—CA, HI, Pakistan, Thailand; closed in HI by court order •

University of America—New Orleans, LA

University of Beford

University of Berkley—MI, PA, possibly OH (not to be confused with the University of California, Berkeley).

University of Beverly Hills—CA, SD •

University of Boston (not to be confused with Boston University, Boston College, or University of Massachusetts–Boston)

University of Canterbury—UK •

University of Cape Cod

University of Central Europe—MS

University of Central Kentucky

University of Columbia

University of Corpus Christi—Reno, NV

University of Devonshire—UK

University of Doncaster—UK •

University of Dorchester

University of Dublin—CA; no connection to legitimate Irish university •

University of Dunham

University of East Carolina

University of East GA—GA

University of Eastern FL—Chicago, IL

University of East-West Alternative Medicine—HI, South Korea

University of Ecoforum for Peace—HI, Belgium, Switzerland

University of England at Oxford—UK, IL, CA

University of Esoterica and the Esoteric Theological Seminary—TX

University of Esoterica—MD and other locations

University of Health Science Antigua—Antigua

University of Health Science—HI

University of Honiara—Solomon Islands, New Zealand?

University of Honolulu USA—UT, Thailand, Pakistan; no connection with HI •

University of Honolulu—HI, China; closed by court order •

University of Honorius—New Zealand; degree mill •

University of Independence

University of James—CA •

University of Metaphysical Studies—NM; illegal in NM •

University of Metaphysics—CA, NV?

University of Middle Tennessee—TN

University of Natural Medicine—NM

University of New Castle—OR, WA, DC, Ireland, UK, South Pacific Islands

University of Newcastle (or New Castle)—OR

University of Newlands—New Zealand; lacks ability to issue degrees •

University of North America—MO

University of Northern Washington—HI, WA, Vancouver, UK; operating illegally in Oregon •

University of Northwest—LA, NJ, WY, India, Pakistan, Afghanistan •

University of Palmers Green—UK

University of Pittsburg (University of Pittsburgh is accredited)

University of Ravenhurst—UK

University of Saint Bartholomew •

University of San Gabriel Valley—CA

University of San Moritz—UK, Cyprus

University of San Rafael

University of Santa Barbara—CA (not to be confused with the University of California–Santa Barbara)

University of Santa Monica—CA; later accredited by DETC •

University of Science at Berkeley— Japan

University of Science, Arts, and Technology (USAT)— Montserrat

University of Sciences in America— Baton Rouge, LA

University of Sealand

University of Sheffield •

University of Sint Eustatius— Caribbean; denied license in FL •

University of Southern Minnesota

University of Sulgrave •

University of Sussex at Brantridge

University of Switzerland

University of Teesside

University of the American Republic •

University of the Americas •

University of the Bahama Islands

University of the Eastern United States

University of the Holy Land—OR, Israel

University of the New World—AZ

University of the President—UT

University of the Rockies—Denver, CO

University of the Science of Man— UK •

University of the United States

University of Walla Walla—CA (Walla Walla College in WA is accredited)

University of Wexford—UK

University of Winchester •

University of WY—London, England

USA International University—HI

UTESA University—Santo Domingo

VA International University—VA •

Valde University—IL

Van Ives University

Vancouver University Worldwide— BC, Canada; Singapore

Verity Education—IL, IN, MI

Vernell University—NV

Victoria Brooke University •

Victorville International University •

Vital Connection University—CO, NJ, AZ •

Von Epstein University—NV, Argentina, Ireland, UK, Germany; not recognized by Bavaria •

Wakefield International University—St. Kitts and Nevis

Walton University •

Warnborough College—TX, WA, UK; Washington, DC

Warnborough University—Ireland, UK

Warren National University (formerly Kennedy-Western University)—WY

Washington American Governors University—SD •

Washington American Open University—HI

Washington Institute for Graduate Studies—UT

Washington International Academy—NY

Washington International University—King of Prussia, PA; HI, British Virgin Islands

Washington School of Law—Salt Lake, UT

Washington School of Theology—OR

Weimar College—Weimar, CA

Wellington University—NJ

Wesleyan International University

West American University

West Clayton University

West Coast University—Australia, Panama, UK, Dubai, India; no connection with legitimate school of same name in Los Angeles •

Westbourne University—UK

Westbrook University—CA, NM, NY (formerly licensed in NM; not to be confused with Westbrook College in Maine) •

Western Cascade University—CA

Western College

Western MI Bible Institute—Muskegon, MI

Western Pacific University—HI •

Western States University for Professional Studies—MO

Western States University—Doniphan, MO; TX; originally Yuma, AZ

Western University—CA

Western Washington International University—HI

Western Washington State University

Westgate University—SD?

Westhampton University—UK

Westminster University—HI •

Westmore College or University—Singapore

Weston Reserve University—Canada, Kuwait, Seychelles

Westport University •

Wexford University •

Weybridge University—Gibraltar •

WI International University—Ghana, Ukraine, and other locations

William Bradford University

William Tucker University—Seborga, Italy; DC •

Williams College—ID (Williams College in Massachusetts is accredited)

Williamsburg (or Williamburg) University—NY, Saudi Arabia, UK

Williamstown University •

Wilson State University, Inc.—NJ, HI

Windsor University •

Wittfield University—HI

Worcester (or Worchester) University —Panama

World Information Distributed University—Belgium, Switzerland, Russia; not recognized in Belgium •

World Pacific University—Guam, Ascension Island

World University—Santo Domingo

WY College for Advanced Studies •

Yorker International University— NY, SD

Youngsfield University—NY, UK •

Youngstown College (not to be confused with Youngstown State University in OH)

YUIN/American University—HI, CA

Zenith University—HI; connection with Pickering and Brighton •

Zoe University—FL •

Chapter 15

....

LIST OF UNRECOGNIZED ACCREDITING AGENCIES

....

In most countries, degree-granting institutions are either run by or approved by the national government, so there is no need for a separate, independent agency to say that a given school is OK. But the US Constitution does not mention the concept of education, and things have evolved so that school evaluating and licensing is done by the states and by private entities called accrediting agencies. The main federal role is to ensure that the accrediting agencies deal properly with federal matters such as guaranteed student loans.

Accreditation in America, then, is a process in which an accrediting agency, comprising persons who are, theoretically, impartial experts in higher education, looks at a given school, or department within a school, and determines whether it is worthy of approval.

There are six regional accreditors (representing six regions of the country), as well as professional accreditors (representing specific areas of study: chemistry, music, psychology, etc.), and national ones (for distance learning, continuing education, etc.).

And there are a great many accrediting agencies that were set up by less-than-wonderful schools or groups of schools for the purpose of accrediting themselves and thus fooling well-meaning potential students, who know enough to *want* accreditation but don't realize there can be *useless* accreditation.

Who "accredits" the accreditors? In the United States, there are two sources: the US Department of Education, which recognizes accreditors who follow the guidelines for federal loans, and the Council for Higher Education Accreditation (CHEA), a private agency with more than three thousand schools as members. It is safe to say that every accreditor whose accreditation principles and procedures are generally accepted in the academic, government, and business world are recognized by one or, in nearly all cases, both of these. About sixty recognized accreditors are listed on the CHEA website (http://www.chea.org).

Among the nearly three hundred unrecognized accrediting agencies, there are a very small number that are either too new or too nontraditional to be recognized. But many of the other agencies, even those that operate quite legally (very few jurisdictions have laws regulating accreditors), will typically accredit a new school within days, even minutes, of its coming into existence. Indeed, many unrecognized accrediting agencies are just another button on the telephone of the school that set them up.

Many of these unrecognized agencies exist only on the Internet. Some use mailing service addresses. Some have been formed in or by other countries generally to accredit schools either in the United States or schools controlled by Americans that would be unlikely to qualify for generally accepted accreditation.

Some accreditors use the ploy of accrediting Harvard, Yale, and Princeton (without their knowledge) along with a bunch of bad or fake schools.

A few unrecognized accrediting agencies may have limited acceptance in certain situations; most do not.

Here is a list of nearly three hundred accrediting agencies that, as of 2011, are *not* recognized either by CHEA or by the US Department of Education. Inclusion on this list does not mean that the accreditor is good or bad, real or fake, but *only* that it not recognized by either of those two entities. As always, people will need to make their own decisions as to where to draw a line on their own continuum.

By "unfindable" on the following list, we mean that despite our best efforts at Internet and other searches, we were not able to locate the accreditor or any independent reference to it. And by "state law," we mean that the accreditors are either mentioned on various states' official lists of agencies they don't recognize, or that they accredit schools whose degrees are illegal in those states. (These include Oregon, Texas, Maine, and Michigan.)

Finally, before getting to the list, there is a category of membership organizations representing or advocating aspects of higher education and distance learning, which some bad or fake schools have been able to join as members by disguising their true intentions and fraudulent nature. Once they have joined (or sometimes even if they have been denied membership), they promote the membership as if it were accreditation. This is especially deceptive if the organization offers both membership categories (almost anyone willing to pay to join) and legitimate accreditation as well.

This has happened in the past, for instance, with the highly reputable American Association of Collegiate Registrars and Admissions Officers (AACRAO), which was not monitoring its membership rolls as carefully as they do now.

Once a fraudster gains membership, they promote that fact to enhance their credibility.

Another example of this is the prestigious AACSB, the Association to Advance Collegiate Schools of Business. On one hand, they accredit schools such as Harvard and Stanford. And on another hand, they offer paid memberships for $1,000 to $10,000 to for-profit and nonprofit organizations such as IOPCA, the International Organization of Professional Cultivation and Accreditation, not recognized by CHEA, which in turn is affiliated with DETCA, the Distance Education and Training Congress of Accreditation, also not recognized by CHEA. No matter how reputable IOPCA may be, there may still be people who confuse "membership" with "accreditation."

The following entities, among others, offer "membership" in lieu of, or in addition to accreditation:

- American Association of Collegiate Registrars and Admissions Officers
- American Association of Independent Colleges and Universities
- American Association of International Medical Graduates
- Commission on Medical Denturitry Accreditation
- Council on Higher Learning
- North American Liberty Party
- Online Christ Centered Ministry
- United States Distance Learning Association

- Washington Higher Education Coordinating Board
- World Online Education Association

UNRECOGNIZED ACCREDITING ORGANIZATIONS

Academy for Contemporary Research. Accreditor claimed by various now-defunct schools.

Academy for the Promotion of International Cultural and Scientific Exchange. Switzerland, Hawaii. Associated with people who were a part of La Jolla University in California and Louisiana, Irish International University, and others. Has accredited the fake Monticello University.

Accreditation Agency for European Non-Traditional Universities. Its slogan is "Knolwedge [sic] is Power." Registration is claimed in Republic of Ireland, the only telephone number listed is in New York. Has accredited the possibly defunct Ballmore Irish University.

Accreditation Association of Ametrican [sic] College [sic] and Universities. Has accredited American University of Hawaii.

Accreditation Association of Christian Colleges and Seminaries. Had been in Morgantown, Kentucky, and now cannot be located.

Accreditation Commission International. See Accrediting Commission International for Schools, Colleges and Theological Seminaries

Accreditation Council for Distance Education

Accreditation Council for International Education

Accreditation Council on Medical Denturitry

Accreditation Distance Education Council (connected to the operator of St. Regis University; not to be confused with the legitimate Distance Education Council recognized by the Indian Department of Education)

Accreditation Governing Commission of the United States of America. The chief accrediting commissioner is associated with schools that claim Liberian accreditation and others. Has accredited American Coastline, Breyer State, University of Northern Washington, and others.

Accrediting Association of Christian Colleges and Seminaries. Sarasota, Florida.

Accrediting Commission for Colleges and Universities. Cannot locate. Claimed by Intercultural Open University.

Accrediting Commission for Specialized Colleges. Gas City, Indiana. Established by George Reuter and "Bishop" Gordon DaCosta on DaCosta's dairy farm. The only requirement for candidacy was a check for $110. Reuter went on to start the International Accrediting Commission, which closed after a "sting" operation in which the state attorney general established a one-room fake school and purchased their accreditation.

Accrediting Commission International for Schools Colleges and Theological Seminaries. Beebe, Arkansas. They started up right after the International Accrediting Commission was closed down by the Missouri attorney general following a clever sting operation. Despite the written denial of founder Dr. John Scheel, they offered immediate and automatic accreditation to IAC members. (We have Scheel's letter making the offer.) ACI does not make a list of accreditees public, but more than two hundred schools have been identified that claim their accreditation, more than two-thirds of them religious.

Accrediting Commission of Independent Colleges and Schools. Bald Knob, Arkansas. This religious accreditor has a name nearly identical to the recognized Accrediting Council for Independent Colleges and Schools, and both use the "ACICS" acronym.

Accrediting Council for Colleges and Schools. Unfindable accreditor of Intercultural Open University.

Advanced Online Business Education Society. The only schools they accredit are associated with the American Management and Business Administration Institute, such as AMBAI University.

AF Sep. The unfindable accreditor claimed by Beta International University.

Akademie fuer Internationale Kultur und Wissenschaftsfoerderung. See Academy for the Promotion of International Cultural and Scientific Exchange.

Alternative Institution Accrediting Association. Washington, DC. Has accredited several fake schools.

American Accrediting Association of Theological Institutions. Rocky Mount, North Carolina. The Christian Bible College is at the same address. Used to charge $100 for accreditation.

American Alternative Medical Association. See American Association of Drugless Practitioners.

American Association of Accredited Colleges and Universities. Unfindable accreditor claimed by Ben Franklin Academy.

American Association of Bible Colleges

American Association of Drugless Practitioners. Accreditor of Clayton College of Natural Health, Southern College of Naturopathy, and so forth. Had been at same residential address as the American Alternative Medical Association.

American Association of Independent Colleges and Universities. In late 1970s and early 1980s, officials of Ricks College and Biola University served on the board of directors for AAICU.

American Association of Independent Collegiate Schools of Business. Unfindable accreditor once claimed by Rushmore University.

American Association of International Medical Graduates

American Association of Nontraditional Colleges and Universities

American Association of Nontraditional Colleges and Universities. Accreditor claimed by short-lived Southeastern Internet University.

American Association of Nontraditional Collegiate Business Schools. Unfindable accreditor once claimed by Rushmore University.

American Association of Nontraditional Private Postsecondary Education. Listed as a "suspect accreditor" by the New Brunswick Department of Education.

American Association of Schools. Temple City, CA. It maintains a list of "recommended institutions" composed mainly of legitimate schools plus one unrecognized school, which has shared an ISP with the accreditor.

American Association of Specialized Colleges. Previously operated by Gordon DaCosta, Gas City, IN, at same time he also ran Northern Indiana University and Indiana Northern Graduate School.

American Bureau of Higher Education. Claimed to be in Nevada; claimed by the fake Concordia College and University.

American Council for Freedom and Excellence in Higher Education. Unfindable accreditor claimed by the fake Regency University.

American Council of Colleges and Universities. St. James University, Danville, VA, and Chapel Hill, NC, claimed accreditation by ACCU.

American Council of Home Study Colleges. Swartz Creek, Michigan. Apparently nonexistent accreditor claimed by the short-lived Prescott College of Business.

American Council of Private Colleges and Universities. Unfindable accreditor set up by Hamilton University, Wyoming.

American Council on Post-Secondary Accreditation

American Council on Private Colleges and Universities

American Education Association for the Accreditation of Schools, Colleges and Universities. Unfindable accreditor claimed by the University of America.

American Educational Accrediting Association of Christian Schools. Dothan, Alabama.

American Educational Association of Non-Traditional Christian Schools. Dothan, Alabama.

American Federation of Christian Colleges and Schools. Lakeland, Florida.

American Federation of College and Schools

American Federation of Colleges and Seminaries. Lakeland, Florida.

American Federation of Colleges and Universities

American Institute of Healthcare Professionals. See Central States Consortium of Colleges and Schools.

American Institution Accrediting Association

American International Commission for Excellence in Higher Education. Fake accreditor used by Les Snell's fake Amherst University.

American International Council for Assessment Universities, Colleges and Schools. Unfindable accreditor claimed by Wittfield University.

American Naprapathic Association. Unfindable accreditor claimed by Chicago National College of Naprapathy.

American Naturopathic Certification Board

American Naturopathic Medical Certification and Accreditation Board. Accreditor claimed by Westbrook University. Its accreditation letter is identical to that written by the National Board of Naturopathic Examiners.

American Naturopathic Medicine Association

American Notable Universities and Colleges Association. Washington, DC. It accredited legitimate schools (without their consent or knowledge) as well as spurious ones.

American Psycotherapy [sic] Association. Katy, Florida.

APIX Institute. Unfindable accreditor claimed by Horizon University, France.

Arizona Commission of Non-Traditional Private Postsecondary Education. The accreditor set up by Southland University when it moved from California to Arizona. After a protest from the real Arizona Commission, the name was changed to the Western Council.

Asia Theological Association

Assessment and Qualifications Convention. Established by a school operator to offer accreditation.

Association for Distance Learning

Association for Distance Learning Programs. ADLP, aka National Academy of Higher Education and Association of Distance Learning Programs; accredited Lacrosse University in Mississippi.

Association for Online Academic Accreditation. It accredits MacArther University, Ratchford University, and many others. It claims that it has tried to become recognized but that US laws prohibit this.

Association for Online Academic Excellence. Wales.

Association for Online Distance Learning. The single-page website lists among its accredited members Almeda College and University and Bond College and University. It also accredited Chase University, which has the same domain registration details.

Association for Promotion of International Cultural and Scientific Exchange. Supposedly had offices in Canada and Switzerland.

Association Internationale des Educateurs pour la Paix Mondiale. At least three unrecognized universities have claimed this accreditation.

Association of Accredited Private Schools. Unfindable accreditor claimed by City University Los Angeles and others.

Association of Career Training Schools. Its literature said, "Have your school accredited with the Association. Why? [It] could be worth many $$$ to you."

Association of Christian Colleges and Theological Schools. Paducah, Kentucky. They say they are "an accreditor for Christian schools that do not wish to deal with a professional accreditor."

Association of Christian Schools and Colleges. Unfindable accreditor claimed by Pickering University.

Association of Christian Schools International, Colorado Springs, Colorado. Seems to have some acceptance in the world of religious schools.

Association of Distance Learning Programs. Accreditor of schools that have also claimed Liberian and/or Russian accreditation, including the International College of Homeland Security, International University of Fundamental Studies, Irish International University, and others.

Association of Distance Learning Programs. See National Academy of Higher Education.

Association of Fundamental Institutes of Religious Education. AFIRE was active in the '80s; now it cannot be located.

Association of International Colleges and Universities. Unfindable accreditor claimed by Wittfield University.

Association of International Educational Assessors. Associated with the fake St. Regis University.

Association of Open and Distance Education. Accreditor claimed by Burkes University.

Association of Private Colleges and Universities. Established by a founder of Trinity College and University. It originally said it was a nonprofit entity but changed that claim when challenged. It says that it is set up to "annihilate illegal degree mills."

Association of Reformed Theological Seminaries

Association of Virtual Universities, Colleges, and Schools. Unfindable accreditor claimed by Julius Caesar University.

Association of World Universities and Colleges. Apparently established in Switzerland by the president of the University of Asia. Accredits the University of Asia.

Australian Universities Association. Accreditor previously claimed by the University of Asia. Website registered to proprietor of the University of Asia.

Board of Online Universities Accreditation. New Orleans, Louisiana. Claimed by Rochville University and Ashwood University.

British Learning Association

British Public University System. Claims to be licensed by the British Honduras Higher Education Policy Commission (British Honduras changed its name to Belize in 1981). It seems to act as an umbrella organization for a group of schools (Croxley Heritage University, London Sanford University, Victoria Brooke University, etc.) that claim accreditation from Euro American Accreditation Council for Higher Education.

Central Orthodox Synod. Unfindable accreditor claimed by International Reform University.

Central States Consortium of Colleges and Schools. Warren, Ohio. Affiliated with the American Institute of Healthcare Professionals, which accredits some schools on the state list.

Central States Council on Distance Education. Address in Washington, DC; associated with Distance Graduation Accrediting Association.

Centre of Academic Excellence

Christhomas Consortium London. Accreditor claimed by International University (Missouri), which calls it "the recognized official body of accreditation in the U.K."

Christian Accrediting Association

College for Professional Assessment. Unfindable accreditor claimed by Thomas Jefferson Education Foundation and others.

Commission for the Accreditation of European Non-Traditional Universities. Accreditor claimed by the University de la Romande.

Commission on Medical Denturitry

Commonwealth Universities Association. Accreditor claimed by the University of Asia. Site is registered by the president of the University of Asia.

Congress for the Accreditation of Educational and Training Organization. Accredits Dublin Metropolitan and Calamus International universities. Formerly Non-Traditional Course Accreditation Board.

Correspondence Accreditation Association. Accreditor created by and claimed by Trinity College and University in the United Kingdom.

Council for Distance Education Accreditation. Murfreesboro, Tennessee.

Council for International Education Accreditation. Accreditor for Almeda University, American University, Ashworth College, and dozens of others.

Council for National Academic Accreditation. Cheyenne, Wyoming. It wrote to schools offering accreditation for $1,850.

Council for the Accreditation of Correspondence Colleges. Louisiana. Accreditation claimed by several otherwise unrecognized schools.

Council on Higher Learning

Council on Post Secondary Accreditation. Unfindable accreditor claimed by South Atlantic University.

Council on Postsecondary Alternative Accreditation. Unfindable accreditor claimed by Western States University.

Council on Postsecondary Christian Education. Nonexistent accreditor claimed by the owners of LaSalle University and Kent College in Louisiana.

Distance Education and Training Congress of Accreditation

Distance Education Council of America. Delaware. Clearly designed to be confused with the recognized Distance Education and Training Council. Sold accreditation for $200, $150 extra for an "excellent" rating.

Distance Graduation Accrediting Association. Accreditor claimed by St. Regis University, Capitol University, Orienta College and University, and others.

Distance Learning Accreditation Board. Boston, Massachusetts.

Distance Learning Council of Europe. Accreditor claimed by Wexford University; its site is almost identical to that of the European Council for Distance and Open Learning.

Eastern Christian Accrediting Association of Colleges, Universities and Seminaries. Cannot be located.

Educational Accreditation Association. Idaho.

Educational Quality Accrediting Commission. Created by Bircham International University; accredits American Coastline, Irish International, and many others.

Euro American Accreditation Council for Higher Education. Accredits schools affiliated with the misleadingly named British Public University System (located in Belize), Croxley Heritage University, London Sanford University, Victoria Brooke University, etc.

Euro-American Accreditation Agency. Cyprus. Formed by an accreditor of Northwestern International University.

European Committee for Home and Online Education. Accreditor of University of Dorchester, University of Dunham, Strassford University, Shaftesbury University, Stafford University, and so forth.

European Council for Distance and Open Learning. For a long time, the world's largest degree-mill scam—the University Degree Program based in Romania—avoided any mention of accreditation when pitching the phony degrees from the University San Moritz, University of Palmers Green, Harrington University, and dozens of others. In 2001, the program established the website for this accreditor and began mentioning it in its sales pitches.

European Council for Home and Online Education. Unfindable accreditor claimed by Renshaw's College.

European Quality Improvement System. Brussels, Belgium.

Examining Board of Natural Medicine Practitioners. Scarborough, Ontario, Canada

Expressive Psychology Association

Global Accreditation Commission. Unfindable accreditor once claimed by Adam Smith University and others.

Global Accreditation for Christian Schools. Unfindable accreditor claimed by Dayspring University.

Global Accreditation Organization for Life Experience and Education. South Africa. Accreditor for Cambridge International University, the fake University of Palmers Green, and others.

Government Accreditation Association of Delaware. Unfindable accreditor claimed by Yorker International University and Albert University.

Higher Education Accrediting Commission. Their mission is to accredit other accrediting agencies: the Board of Online Universities Accreditation, the Universal Council for Online Education Accreditation, the International Accreditation Agency for Online Universities, and the World Online Education Accrediting Commission, which are all affiliated with the same schools: Ashwood, Belford, and Rocheville universities.

Higher Education Services Association. The accreditor for a group of schools including Ellington University, Garfield Technical College, Lexington University, Stanton University, and others. It will accredit only schools "sponsored" by its members.

Integra Accreditation Association. It sent out a mailing in 2000 inviting schools to apply; it's now unfindable.

InterAmerican Association of Postsecondary Colleges and Schools. Unfindable accreditor of Universitas Sancti Martin.

Inter-Collegiate Joint Committee on Academic Standards. Controlled by affiliates of College Services Corporation, it accredits Vernell University and Alexandria University, as well as names that appear on the diplomas sold by the yourdegreenow.com and degrees-r-us.com websites.

Interfaith Education Ministries Association of Academic Excellence. Washington, DC. Accreditor of St. Regis University, Dorcas University, Bircham International, Advanced University, and others. It also does foreign credential evaluation.

International Academic Accrediting Commission. Has a fax number near Tacoma, Washington. Accredits "Mave University."

International Accreditation Agency. Chesterfield, Derbyshire, United Kingdom.

International Accreditation Agency for Online Universities, associated with the fake Ashwood, Belford, and Rochville universities; address is a mailbox service in Humble, Texas.

International Accreditation and Recognition Council. Nerang, Australia. Accredits Warnborough, Southern Pacific, and Queens University of Brighton, among others.

International Accreditation and Recognition Council. Robina, Australia. Members include Bircham International University.

International Accreditation and Registration Institute. Accreditor claimed by the apparently defunct Nation University.

International Accreditation Association

International Accreditation Association. Claimed accreditor of University of North America; now it cannot be located.

International Accreditation Association of Nontraditional Colleges and Universities. Claims to be in British West Indies. Website in Niue.

International Accreditation Association of Universities and Colleges

International Accreditation Commission for Post Secondary Education Institutions. Claimed accreditor of University of the United States and Nasson University, both operated from a convenience address in Mobile, Alabama.

International Accreditation for Universities, Colleges, and Institutes. Accredits Wittifield University in Hawaii and University of Honolulu (whose address is in Delaware).

International Accreditation for Universities, Colleges, Institutes, Organizations and Professionals. Had been listed as accreditor for Trinity International University, University of Honolulu–Hawaii, and Chase University. Address is in Houston, Texas; domain registration was in Bellevue, Washington.

International Accreditation Society. Its list of accredited schools includes real ones (Harvard, Stanford) as well as many on the "illegal in Michigan" list.

International Accrediting Agency for Private and Post Secondary Institutes. Accreditor claimed by CliffPort and Glanmount universities, apparently in Pakistan.

International Accrediting Association for Colleges and Universities

International Accrediting Association of Ministerial Education. Accreditor claimed by Valley International Christian Seminary; now it cannot be located.

International Accrediting Association of Nontraditional Colleges and Universities. British West Indies. Accreditor claimed by Postsecondary Education Institute. Now it cannot be located.

International Accrediting Association of Universities and Colleges

International Accrediting Association. Accreditor for the Universal Life Church and its $100 PhDs.

International Accrediting Commission

International Accrediting Commission for Postsecondary Institutions. Accreditor once claimed by Adam Smith University.

International Accrediting Commission for Schools, Colleges and Theological Seminaries. Holden, Missouri. More than two hundred schools, many of them Bible schools, were accredited by this organization. Following the state attorney general's clever "sting" operation, setting up a fake school that it instantly accredited, they were closed. See "Accrediting Commission International for Schools, Colleges and Theological Seminaries."

International Association of Colleges and Universities. Accreditor claimed by the dubious University of America.

International Association of Educators for World Peace. Fairfax, California. Accreditor claimed by European Union University.

International Association of Fake Universities. It admits it is a fake accreditor, but some of the fake schools it accredits have realistic names; also, it will print a diploma with the university name of your choice.

International Association of Monotheistic Schools. Accreditor claimed by Alan Mitchell School of Psychology. It cannot be located.

International Association of Non-Traditional Schools. Accreditor claimed by some British degree mills, now it cannot be located.

International Association of Schools, Colleges and Universities. Antwerp, Belgium. Accredited at least four unrecognized schools including Newport University, Vision International University, and American Pacific University.

International Association of Universities and Schools. Geneva, Switzerland. Incorporated by Robert K. Bettinger, President of Barrington University, it accredited Barrington for three years, but no longer.

International College and School Accreditation Association. Listed many legitimate schools plus Pennington University. It cannot be located.

International Commission for Excellence in Higher Education. Accreditor established by and claimed by the fake Monticello University.

International Commission for Higher Education; members include Breyer State University and Lacrosse University.

International Commission for the Accreditation of Colleges and Universities. Gaithersburg, Maryland. Accreditor established and claimed by the United States University of America.

International Commission of Open Post Secondary Education. Possibly in Ireland; their accreditation is claimed by Westcoast University.

International Commission on Academic Accreditation. Unfindable accreditor claimed by Freedom Bible College.

International Commission on Distance Education. Madrid, Spain

International Council for Accreditation and Academic Standards. It cannot be located. Accreditor of Adams University, Kendall University, MacArther University, Ratchford University, and Ross College, among others.

International Council for Accrediting Alternate and Theological Studies. India.

International Council for Accrediting Alternative and Theological Studies; accreditor of Scofield Graduate School & Seminary and Trinity Graduate School and Theological Seminary.

International Council for Open and Distance Education

International Council of Assessment Universities. Accreditor claimed by Wittfield University and Darton University. It cannot be located.

International Council of Colleges and Universities. Was in Lebanon, Tennessee. It cannot be located.

International Council of Higher Education. Switzerland. Accreditor claimed by Trident University of Technology.

International Council on Education. Elmhurst, New York. Many links don't work, and bits are cut and pasted from other sites, but it asks $5,500 for an application. Inter-American University claims accreditation from ICE.

International Distance Education and Training Council (IDETC) (not to be confused with the recognized Distance Education and Training Council). It lists all the DETC schools as ones it accredits and one more, American Central University.

International Distance Learning Accreditation Council. Accredits many legitimate schools, also Americus University (which shares a phone with the council), South Pacific University, International University for Professional Studies, and others.

International Distance Learning Accrediting Association

International Education Ministry of Accreditation Association

International Online Accreditation Association. Accredits Westmore College where buyers can pay $10 per point to raise their grade point average from the standard 3.2 GPA.

International Organization of Professional Cultivation and Accreditation

International University Accreditation Foundation. Apparently established by Chief Alexander Swift Eagle Justice of the Cherokee Western Federation. It has accredited Swift Eagle's International Theological University and others.

International University Accrediting Association. California.

Internet University Accreditation Association. Although it claims to accredit fifty-six Internet universities worldwide, only three are listed: Alcott University, University of the Islands, and Western Ohio University, the last being the only one we can find.

Kingdom Fellowship of Christian Schools and Colleges

Korean Royal Association of Professors. Accredits the nonexistent Aardvark University, apparently created by pranksters to get a school listed first in some directory.

Life Experience Accreditation Association. Accreditor claimed by Earlscroft University, now it cannot be located.

Louisiana Capital Education Foundation. Accreditor claimed by Louisiana Capital College, now it cannot be located.

Mid States Accrediting Agency. Listed as a "suspect accreditor" by the New Brunswick Department of Education, Canada.

Middle States Accrediting Board. Accreditor claimed by Thomas University, now it cannot be located.

Midwestern States Accreditation Agency. Claimed accreditor for Tony Geruntino's fake schools in the 1980s: American Western, National College of Arts and Sciences, and so forth.

National Academy for Higher Education, accreditor of the fake Concordia College and University as well as Lacrosse University and the American University of London.

National Academy of Higher Education. Accredits many unrecognized schools.

National Academy of Higher Learning

National Accreditation Association. Riverdale, Maryland. Associated with the fake American International University, it offered accreditation to many fake schools.

National Association for Prior Learning Assessment Colleges. Run by, and accredits only, Trinity Southern University.

National Association for Private Nontraditional Schools and Colleges

National Association for Private Post Secondary Education. Washington,

DC. Listed as a "suspect accreditor" by the New Brunswick (Canada) Department of Education.

National Association for Schools and Colleges. See National Association of Private Nontraditional Schools and Colleges.

National Association of Alternative Schools and Colleges. Accreditor claimed by Western States University, now it cannot be located.

National Association of Open Campus Colleges. Springfield, Missouri. Claimed as accreditor by the fake Southwestern University.

National Association of Private Nontraditional Schools and Colleges. Established in Grand Junction, Colorado, in the 1970s by people associated with Western Colorado University. It has seemed to make sincere efforts but has been repeatedly rejected by the US Department of Education. At its peak it had several dozen accreditees, just before its demise, only four.

National Association of Private Theological Institutions. New Albany, Indiana. While it once accredited a University of Indiana that was not the real U of I, it now accredits five Bible schools and a Christian martial arts university.

National Association of State Approved Colleges and Universities, Inc. Operated in the 1980s by the founder of Andrew Jackson University, Louisiana.

National Board of Education. For several years, the claim was made that this was an official Liberian organization, and its accreditation was sold for $50,000. Disappeared at the time of the closure of the fake St. Regis University.

National Board of Naturopathic Examiners. Shares its address with Matt's Health Foods, whose owner is a faculty member of a school it accredits and is chair of the accrediting agency.

National Commission on Higher Education

National Council for the Accreditation of Private Universities and Schools of Law. Accreditor claimed by the fake Monticello University.

National Council of Schools and Colleges. Accreditor claimed by International University in Louisiana and California, now it cannot be located.

National Diet and Nutrition Association. Accreditor claimed by Universitas Sancti Martin, now it cannot be located.

National Distance Learning Accreditation Council. Accreditor claimed only by Suffield College and University and Redding University.

National Educational Accrediting Association.

National Federal Accreditation Assembly. Accreditor claimed by Laureate University and others.

National Learning Online Council

National Private Schools Association Group. We chose not to pay the $750 it charges to see its database of 130,000 schools, so we are not sure what it does, but it seems to involve accreditation.

Naturopathic National Council

New Millennium Accrediting Partnership For Educators Worldwide. Founded by "the enlightened staff" of the University of Berkley, which is the only school it accredits.

Nontraditional Course Accreditation Board. Former name of Congress for the Accreditation of Educational and Training Organisation. Accreditor claimed by Calamus University and Dublin Metropolitan University.

North American Association of Unaccredited Colleges and Universities. The irreverent site candidly admits that the schools it accredits are as fake as the accreditor and include Central University of Natural Therapy, Prairie Institute of Social Science, and Switzer United College of Kansas.

North American College and University Accreditation. Claims to currently serve fifty-five institutions throughout the region but names none. Possible connection with Western Ohio University.

North American Regional Accrediting Commission. Accreditor claimed by International University (Los Angeles, California), now it cannot be located.

Northwest Regional Accrediting Agency. Listed as a "suspect accreditor" by the New Brunswick (Canada) Department of Education.

Online Christ Centered Ministries

Oxford Educational Network. Claims to operate under a Royal Charter granted by King Charles I of England in the year 1640. Run from a post office box in Fort Worth, Texas. Affiliated with the Most Rev. Patriarch Dr. Chief Alexander Swift Eagle Justice.

Pacific Association of Schools and Colleges. Serious effort started in 1993 by a former California state education official but did not last.

Parliamento Mondiale per la Sicurezza e la Pace. Accreditor claimed by Senior University, Wyoming. It awards titles of nobility from an address in Palermo, Italy.

Private World Association of Universities and Colleges

Professional Board of Education. West Lebanon, New Hampshire. Accreditor claimed by Concordia College and University and others.

Regional Education Accrediting Commission

Society of Academic Recognition. Accreditor claimed by the spurious University of Corpus Christi, now it cannot be located.

Southeast Accrediting Association of Christian Schools, Colleges and Sem-

344 PART 3: REFERENCE

inaries. Milton, Florida. Accreditor claimed by Evangelical Theological Seminary and others.

Southern Accrediting Association of Bible Colleges and Seminaries. Accreditor claimed by Logos Christian College and Covenant Life Christian College; cannot be located.

Southern Accrediting Association of Bible Institutes and Colleges

Southern Association of Accredited Colleges and Universities. Listed as a "suspect accreditor" by the New Brunswick (Canada) Department of Education.

Southern Cross International Association of Colleges and Schools. Accreditor claimed by Cambridge Graduate School, Kelvin College, and others, now it cannot be located.

Southwestern Association of Christian Colleges. Accreditor claimed by St. Thomas Christian College, now it cannot be located.

Tennessee Association of Christian Schools

Transworld Accrediting Commission. Siloam Springs, Alaska. Accreditor claimed by Cumberland University.

United Colligate [sic] College Association. Accreditor claimed by Earlscroft University, now it cannot be located.

United Congress of Colleges. Ireland, United Kingdom. Accreditor claimed by Earlscroft University, Canterbury University, others, now it cannot be located.

United National Universities. An "accreditational organization" associated with the operator of an unaccredited school, apparently defunct.

United Nations Convivium for International Education. Associated with the operator of an unaccredited school, it had listed hundreds of traditional schools along with some others.

United States Commission of Colleges. Claims to be an official military accreditor and accredits only Armed Forces University.

United States Distance Education and Training. After a brief hiatus in 2003 when the real DETC complained, the US-DETC's website is back and as misleading as ever, listing a great many real schools and a few others less real.

United States Distance Learning Association, Boston, MA. Per website, they have twenty thousand members worldwide.

Universal Accrediting Association. Accreditor claimed by the Universal Life Church and University.

Universal Accrediting Commission for Schools, Colleges and Universities. Athens, Greece. Accreditor claimed by Romano Byzantine College, now it cannot be located.

Universal Council for Online Education Accreditation. Accreditor claimed by Belford University and Rochville University.

Uniworld Association Incorporated. Accreditor claimed by International University of Fundamental Studies, University of Northwest, and others. See also International University Accrediting Association.

Virtuous Universal Accreditation Commission

West European Accrediting Society. Liederbach, Germany. Established by the later-imprisoned owners of a group of degree mills including Loyola, Lafayette, and Cromwell universities.

Western Accrediting Agency. Listed as a "suspect accreditor" by the New Brunswick (Canada) Department of Education.

Western Association of Private Alternative Schools. Claimed as accreditor by Western States University, now it cannot be located.

Western Association of Schools and Colleges. This is the name of the legitimate regional accreditor. A fake one was established by the later-imprisoned operators of many degree mills (Loyola, Roosevelt, Cromwell, etc.).

Western Council on Non-Traditional Private Post Secondary Education. Established by the founder of Southland University. See also Arizona Commission of Non-Traditional Private Postsecondary Education.

World Association of Universities and Colleges. Established in 1992 by Dr. Maxine Asher, founder of American World University, and run from a secretarial service address in Nevada. Accredits many schools in the United States and elsewhere. When James Kirk was imprisoned for LaSalle University, he started Edison University from his Texas prison cell, and it quickly got WAUC accreditation. When the Louisiana attorney general closed down Cambridge State University as a degree mill, it moved to a mailbox service in Hawaii and has WAUC accreditation. In 1999, William Howard Taft University, formerly a WAUC accreditee (and now with recognized accreditation) brought suit against WAUC. Highlights of the action from a Taft press release: WAUC was "not able to provide any documented evidence that it had ever conducted a site visit at any member institution," and although it had "consistently promoted itself as a nonprofit corporation," it acknowledged in writing that "WAUC is a for-profit corporation."

World Council of Excellence in Higher Education. Claimed as accreditor by Intercultural Open University, now it cannot be located.

World Council of Global Education. See World Council of Postsecondary and Religious Education.

World Council of Postsecondary and Religious Education. Part of the World

Natural Health Organization. Accreditor once claimed by Bernadean University. Accredits a small number of religious schools.

World Counsel (Council) of University Academic Accreditation

World International Medical Association, operated by the owner of the fake United American Medical College.

World Online Education Accrediting Commission. Accreditor claimed by Ashwood University.

World Online Education Association, a California membership organization, which says that due to constant abuse of their logo, they want to make clear that they are *not* an accrediting agency for any institution that purports to offer higher-education qualifications. They say that any claims of accreditation or membership in the WAOE by a university are fraudulent.

World Organization of Institutes, Colleges and Universities. Accreditor claimed by Omega University.

World-Wide Accreditation Commission of Christian Educational Institutions. Richmond, Virginia. It says that "in accordance with the Inspired teaching of the Bible, [we have] chosen not to seek endorsement with either the EAES or CHEA." Affiliated with the Spirit of Truth Institute, which sells honorary doctorate degrees.

Worldwide Accrediting Commission. Cannes, France. Set up by later-imprisoned owners of a group of degree mills (Loyola/Paris, DePaul, etc.) to accredit their own schools.

Chapter 16

··

COUNTERFEITING SERVICES

··

Well over a hundred counterfeiting services have operated on the Internet in the last few years. They change their names, locations, and services offered even more often than the fake schools. This is a representative sample of ones in business at this time. New ones can always be found by doing an Internet search for "counterfeit diplomas" or "counterfeit degrees." The topic is discussed in detail in the book *Counterfeit Diplomas and Transcripts* that Allen Ezell wrote for AACRAO, the registrars' association, in 2008. Here are some that were active recently or currently.

A Bogus PhD (http://www.bogusphd.com). It claims that its degrees "look official and real" and "may even closely resemble a genuine degree from some actual college or university," but it has only one design. Diplomas are $39.95 and come with any university name, date, degree, and specialty, including medical, dental, and law.

AAAardvark University (http://www.boxfreeconcepts.com/aaardvark .html). Billing itself as the world's first fake university (alphabetically, that is), it offers a wide variety of bachelors', masters' and doctoral degrees to individuals meeting the criteria of IAFU, the International Association of Fake Universities. AAAardvark issues its degree through BoxFree Concepts.

Back Alley Press (http://www.backalleypress.com). A part of Shun Luen Co., closed down in Ottawa, Canada, and now in China. Back Alley points out that US counterfeits are of low quality because of strict US laws, but in China the government is lenient about high-quality "novelty items," whether watches, software, or diplomas. Authentic-looking diplomas from more than one thousand universities, with transcripts, for $137 to $700.

BestFakeDiploma.com (http://www.bestfakediploma.com). This wording is identical to that of SuperiorFakeDegrees.com, and like it, BestFake-Diploma.com links to, and is a front for, DiplomaServices.com.

Black Market Press (http://www.blackmarket-press.net). Custom-designed transcripts and diplomas. It also offers a do-it-yourself option that provides customers with templates and supplies, including seals and security holograms that allows them to create their own transcripts and degrees. Information on lock picking, identity theft, and bank fraud is also available.

BoxFreeConcepts.com (http://www.boxfreeconcepts.com/fake/diplomas .html#). Three fake diploma design templates are sold, with others available for more schools, transcripts, and so forth. See also Magic Mill.

Closed University (http://www.closeduniversity.com/ecommerce). This claims to offer "safer" diplomas because they are from closed schools, but most of the hundreds of authentic designs offered are from currently operating schools, from Arizona State to Wichita State. Diplomas and authentic-looking transcripts are about $120 each. Affiliated with Replicadiploma.com.

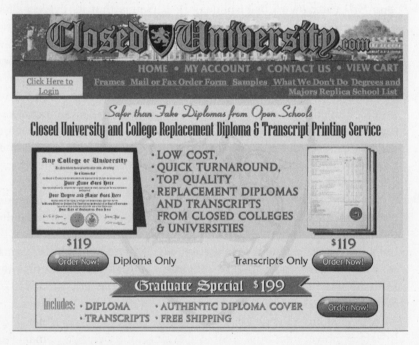

The "Closed University" company claims to specialize in the diplomas of actual universities that are no longer in business.

Closedcollege.com (http://www.closedcollege.com). Diplomas and transcripts from several hundred genuinely closed schools, although sometimes only a closed branch campus of a still-thriving school (such as Antioch University, San Francisco). The convenience address in Washington is also used by the bogus accreditor of Hartford University and others.

Cooldegree (http://www.cooldegree.com). Although it invites you to "Impress your friends and colleagues with a diploma from a well-known University, in any field of study that you desire," most of its diplomas feature the name of fictitious schools, such as Denver State University. They once offered verification services for an additional fee, but no longer.

Counterfeit Library (http://www.counterfeitlibrary.com). This fascinating site was the discussion forum for the degree-counterfeiting industry. It is now closed, but archives can still be read on the "Wayback Machine" at http://www.archive.org.

Degree Now (http://www.degree-now.com). See Degrees-R-Us.

Degrees-R-Us (http://www.degrees-r-us.com). This became the poster child for counterfeiting services when the Government Accountability Office (GAO), at the request of Sen. Susan Collins, bought Lexington University degrees in her name. The GAO learned that the business is run from his Las Vegas home by a disbarred attorney, and it also operates as University Services Corp. and College Services Corp. Diplomas were sold from a wide range of schools, including Chapparal Western University, Columbia Western, Cranston, Hampton, Vernell, and Lexington, through half a dozen nearly identical websites.

Digital Products (http://www.fakeid.cwc.net). This British outfit offers fake diplomas, drivers' licenses, computer certifications, and printing equipment.

Diploma Collection (http://www.diplomacollection.com). You can choose any high school for a diploma, but the higher degrees, including a doctorate in medical science, all come from the fake Cambridge State.

Diploma Masters (http://www.diplomamasters.com). This offers a long list of schools, customized transcripts, and a "third party" verification service. This claims to be "an official distributor for a third party 'Record Verification' provider," apparently affiliated with counterfeiters Fantasy Diplomas and DiplomasForLess and degree mills Lexington and Ellington universities and Global Church Theological Seminary and University, their accreditor (the Higher Education Services Association), and Verification Services.

Diploma Replacement Services (http://www.diplomareplacementservice
.com). Fakes sold from virtually any school for $124 to $370. It requires
a notarized statement affirming you have earned the degrees you're
buying, but it reminds you that notaries don't know if you're telling the
truth. It claims that a competitor named DiplomaServices.com has
stolen its business plan.

DiplomaMakers.com (http://www.diplomamakers.com). This claims to be
the largest supplier of novelty online degrees in the world, with
diplomas in three sizes from any university on earth, from $70 on up,
"Guaranteed to fool even your professor!" It was shut down by Canadian authorities in 2001 and moved to Nevada, but there is another
counterfeiter, ReplacementDiplomas.com, at the same mailbox service
address in Canada.

Diplomaone.com (http://www.diplomaone.com). It says that its "documents
will pass the test when it comes to authenticity" and "will fool the most
suspecting individuals." Any school, degree, and date for $99 and $200
more for a verification service.

Diplomas and More (http://www.diplomasandmore.com). It markets its
products extensively on eBay. The diplomas do not purport to be exact
replicas of the originals, but Diplomas and More allows you to choose
the degree (except medical), the name of the school, and the grades
shown on the transcript.

Diplomas for Less (http://www.diplomasforless.com). Counterfeit diplomas
for $100 ($50 more for overnight delivery) from most US high schools
and universities, except the University of Phoenix, University of
Houston, University of California, Syracuse University, or from any
institution in Illinois or Connecticut. Affiliated with various other counterfeiters, fake schools, and verification services.

DiplomaServices.com (http://www.diplomaservices.com). Medical, dental,
law, and all other diplomas from almost any school for $100 and up. It
charmingly calls its competitors' products "garbage."

Diplomaville.com (http://www.diplomaville.com). It seems to specialize in
"extremely detailed reproductions" of University of California
diplomas, with raised seals, for $250. Stanford, Johns Hopkins,
Columbia, and more than one hundred others cost a bit less. High
school diplomas, GED certificates, and fake computer certifications are
sold as well.

Documents and Such (http://www.documentsandsuch.com). For $49.95,
this website allows you to select from four different templates, the name

of the school, the type of degree, the major (no restrictions), and the graduation date.

Espionage Unlimited (http://www.espionage-store.com/cert.html). Diplomas and everything from military credentials to drivers' licenses for $30 and up, $10 more for Gothic lettering.

Fake Diplomas (http://www.fake-diplomas.com). Curiously, despite the name, there is information only on real schools. Perhaps it is hoping to sell space to the fakes.

Fakedegrees.com (http://fakedegrees.com). For $50 you join for six months and use the software and templates to create your own diplomas. Curiously, the site offers Harvard, Oxford, and Cambridge but not Yale or Princeton. Transcript and letter of reference capabilities are promised.

FakeDiplomas.com. (http://www.fakediplomas.com). Probably the same as fakedegrees.com. If you send in a good picture of a diploma, you get free membership.

Fantasy Diplomas (http://www.fantasydiplomas.com). Virtually identical to Diplomas for Less and Diploma Masters.

Graduate Now (http://www.graduatenow.com). See Degrees-R-Us.

Home School Diplomas (http://members.tripod.com/~deed). This amateurish site on a free server piously states it will not make diplomas for accredited schools. The samples displayed are for a fictitious school (Southern University of Theology) and a degree mill (Metropolitan Collegiate). Fifty dollars for a diploma, more for a transcript.

I Need a Diploma.com (http://www.ineedadiploma.com). Diplomas for most schools in most subjects for around $100. Extra for transcripts, honors degrees, and "security holograms."

Ideal Studios (http://www.idealstudios.com). This low-tech company, which has been around forever, sells paper, ribbon, gold seals, and a sheet of press-on letters for $29.

Magic Mill (http://www.boxfreeconcepts.com/magicmill/index.html). Although it offers silly diplomas from such institutions as Flatulence University and Innuendo State, other names, such as Carolina Coast University and Southern States University, lend themselves to abuse, and you can order a diploma, including medical and dental, with any school name you like.

Make Your Own Degree (http://www.myodegrees.com). Formerly an all-purpose counterfeiter, now it provides only links to, and serves as a front for, Fakedegrees.com.

If you call this company by four in the afternoon, you can have your diploma hanging on the wall the following morning.

Novelty Diploma Center (http://www.nd-center.com). All degrees from almost any school for $400, $200 more for a custom seal. It claims that it has "the most extensive list of colleges and universities in the world," and "no one will ever doubt of your degree."

Peter Leon Quinn (http://www.peterleonquinn.com). The self-styled designer of impressive authentic-looking certificates used to display samples, but now they must be requested by e-mail.

Phony Diplomas (http://www.phonydiploma.com). Document Printing Services, LLC, operating under the name Phony Diplomas, sells both customizable in-house designs and actual replicas selectable from a list of about 150 actual diplomas. No medical or dental degrees, and no sales to the state of Connecticut, even though they are located in Virginia.

Premier Degrees (http://www.premier-degrees.com). See Degrees-R-Us.

Real Diploma Printers (http://diplomareplication.andmuchmore .com). "100 percent Replicated and Authentic" diplomas from most US, Canadian, and British universities, "guaranteed to fool anyone." Mysteriously priced at $300 for one degree, $500 for two, and $1,200 for three.

ReplacementDiplomas.com (http://www.replacementdiplomas.com). Medical, dental, law, and other degrees, both from closed schools and existing ones. Orders mailed to Laval, Quebec, Canada.

Secretknowledge.com (http://www.secretknowledge.com). Rather crude-looking fake from this British site for about $5, "guaranteed to work or your money back."

Superior Fake Degrees (http://www.superiorfakedegree.com). Apparently a front for DiplomaServices.com.

Virtual Diploma (http://www.boxfreeconcepts.com/download/ degree.html). The "Virtual Diploma Mill" is another entry to the BoxFreeConcepts site.

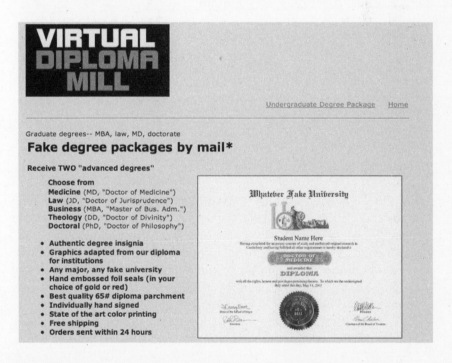

Virtual Diploma is one of the relatively few businesses that not only sell diplomas from any university but also sell medical and dental degrees.

Wall Candy Degrees (http://www.boxfreeconcepts.com/download/degree .html). Simple diplomas from four fake schools for about $10: Canterbury College, St. Charles University, Michigan Institute of Technology, and Southwestern Christian College.

Your Degree Now (http://www.yourdegreenow.com). See Degrees-R-Us.

Chapter 17

....

THE MEDIA PROFESSIONAL'S GUIDE TO FINDING PEOPLE WITH FAKE DEGREES

....

W e are often asked by media professionals—newspaper, magazine, radio, and television reporters, editors, and producers—if we know of any people using fake degrees in their geographical area or in their area of special interest (military, teachers, clergy, etc.). While the answer sometimes is yes, our more common response is to give advice on how to find such people on their own. Often it is all too easy. Here are the four ways that regularly work for us and for many others. Asking us is still an option, via our website at http://www.degreemills.com.

INTERNET SEARCH OR LEXISNEXIS/GOOGLE NEWS SEARCH

The search needs to be made for a specific degree-mill name and, typically, either a geographic area and/or a job specialty. Such a search will find articles that have already appeared regarding people and those degrees. In addition to articles about "time bombs" that have already exploded, there will also be articles in which a person's bogus degree is referred to in either a positive context ("Local Principal Completes PhD at Columbia State University") or simply as a routine mention in an article about another aspect of the person's life entirely, or as just a listing in a school's catalog, a church's board of directors, a company's annual report, and so on.

The next question, of course, is for which schools to search. There is not a simple answer, since even a smaller or older school with only a few findable alumni may still produce the politician, sheriff, principal, or business leader one hopes to find.

A good starting place often are some of the larger and more enduring names such as Columbia State University, LaSalle University (Louisiana), each of the thirty-or-more schools in the University Degree Program (see chapter 7), and the Sussex College of Technology.

Many other school names can be found on the consolidated Oregon-Michigan list in chapter 14.

While LexisNexis is almost always the best media search, Google, which searches forty-five hundred publications, works well, although only for recent stories.

RESUME SERVICES

There are two very large online services, and many others, in which people in the job market can post their resume at no cost, and then employers pay a fee in order to search through those resumes. Because all services have fast and accurate search capabilities, it is possible, for instance, to search for the name of a degree mill and either a geographical area or specific set of ZIP codes, various job categories, or both. For instance, it is possible to search for "Harrington University" and "US Army" and a given set of ZIP codes.

Monster (http://www.monster.com) is the industry leader, with over one hundred million resumes online.

CareerBuilder (http://www.careerbuilder.com) is another major one. The formerly huge HotJobs was merged into Monster.

There are many different pricing plans offered, ranging from a subscription of a few weeks, with a limited number of "views" to annual subscriptions with unlimited numbers of views. A "view" means actual inspection, and printing, of a resume. Often, however, it is possible to search for a certain school and other criteria and read brief overviews of the resumes found, without being charged for a view.

Costs run from $400 or $500 for a subscription of several weeks to $5,000 and up for an annual full-service subscription. Pricing plans seem to vary often, and each service has its own unique set of plans.

Monster.com, for instance, offers geographical searches, covering only those clients living within a certain radius, for instance, a hundred miles, of any given ZIP code.

What can one expect to find in such a search? We had the opportunity for a short "test drive" at one of the smaller services. In the time available, we did a search for five "schools" that we regard as degree mills and found 170 "hits" for the least popular, on up to 754 for the most.

Bear in mind that these resume services represent only a tiny fraction of American workers, and, of course, only include those people who choose to mention their "alma mater" on their resume; many people don't. They also tend to be people in lower-paying and less responsible jobs, although many media people tell us they have readily found teachers, sheriffs, clergy, therapists, and so on.

SOCIAL NETWORK SEARCHES

A great many people mention their alma mater on various social networking pages, even including the bad and fake schools. As an example, the fake Almeda College and University has (when we checked in mid-2011) 2,869 hits on LinkedIn and more than three hundred on Facebook®. Even the fake Columbia State, out of business for fifteen or more years, has several hundred hits.

Among the sites to check, in addition to LinkedIn and Facebook, are MySpace (over 100 million), MyLife (51 million), Tagged (100 million), Black Planet (20 million), ClassMates (50 million), Bebo (120 million), Hi5 (60 million), and scores of others in the millions, easily findable via an Internet search.

WHO'S WHO SEARCH

Marquis, the publisher of twenty *Who's Who* biographical directories, offers a searchable database of, as the publisher describes it, "over 1 million of the most accomplished individuals from all fields of endeavor including: government, business, science and technology, the arts, entertainment and sports." The flagship volumes are *Who's Who in America* and *Who's Who in the World*. The rest are either geographical (such as *Who's Who in the East*) or demographic (law, medicine, finance).

Most biographies include information on academic degrees earned. While the cost of a year's subscription (there are no shorter ones available) is $1,600, more than a few newspapers and magazines already have subscriptions to facilitate research on breaking news stories, obituaries, and such (http://www.marquiswhoswho.com). When we expressed interest in doing research with the database, we were given a free five-day, one-hundred-search trial run.

ASK ON A NEWS FORUM

There are two very active Internet news forums where some members are eager to help locate both fake schools and the people who use their degrees. When a major network was seeking people using the degree of just one particular fake school, a request at http://www.degreeinfo.com led to reports on several dozen people using that degree. Six of these people, including a college professor, a popular television personality, a man with a responsible job at a nuclear power plant, and an inspector at a controversial tire plant, were interviewed on the air.

While most replies one gets at DegreeInfo are reliable, it is a lightly moderated forum, and there are some spokespeople for some of the dubious schools that may respond, defending their school, typically without revealing their affiliation.

A comparable, but smaller forum, with a moderate number of overlapping members, is found at http://www.degreediscussion.com.

SEARCH THE ST. REGIS UNIVERSITY CUSTOMER LIST

This is a one-time opportunity, but it is a big one. In every instance but one of a degree mill being closed or raided or sued by authorities, their customer list, the people who bought and are using those degrees, remains private.

The lone exception is the huge international phony, St. Regis University, which the Secret Service was instrumental in bringing down (the full story is in chapter 7).

The complete list of St. Regis customers has been made available via the Freedom of Information Act, thanks to the diligent efforts of Spokane *Spokesman-Review* reporter Bill Morlin. That list of 9,612 degree purchases is available online at http://www.spokesmanre-view.com/data/diploma-mill/. It lists the name, state or country of residence, degree(s) purchased, and which of the St. Regis people's dozen-or-so fake schools issued the diploma.

Many reporters have benefited from using this list to find local people with, of course, the usual precautions that accuracy is not guaranteed.

REFINING ONE'S SEARCH

While there are well over a thousand degree-granting schools that have been called degree mills, we suspect that the twenty or thirty that are most active at any given time probably account for well over half the degrees, although there have been two very large ones—LaSalle University and Columbia State University, with at least fifteen thousand "graduates" each—that were closed in the late 1990s.

LaSalle exemplifies one of the problems that can occur. There is a very real and traditional LaSalle University in Philadelphia, as well as the fake in Louisiana. In chapter 3, we offer advice on how to rede-fine one's search in the section on how to check out a school. (In this instance, in order to find the *fake* LaSalle, one might search for

["LaSalle University" + Louisiana – Philadelphia]: the school name as a single phrase, plus the word *Louisiana*, and *not* including the word *Philadelphia*.) The fact that the real LaSalle has very few doctoral programs, while the fake LaSalle specialized in PhDs, can be helpful in a search.

Columbia State University, while a rich source of fake degree buyers (our Monster.com and other database searches found about a thousand), also has its challenges. There are, of course, many legitimate entities using the word *Columbia*, but even putting the full name in quotation marks, as good search protocol suggests, can have errors. For instance, we found that about 5 percent of "hits" in a "Columbia State University" search were, in fact, really for the legitimate "Columbus State University" but had been mistyped in the original source documents.

That kind of problem, plus the fact that people do change their names, whether on marriage or at other times, is just a reminder to use all appropriate due diligence before "going public" with a degree-mill accusation.

Chapter 18

···

ACCREDIBASE

···

There has long been a need for a reliable service that not only keeps track of the never-ending array of degree mills, but that also evaluates new arrivals on the scene and consults with the people who can benefit from this information: human resources personnel, students and would-be students, educators, reporters, regulators, and others.

People who have tried—Vicky Phillips with her Diploma Mill Police™ (http://www.geteducated.com) and John Bear with his Degree Consulting Services, sold many years ago to Peter Proehl (http://www.degreeconsult.com)—discovered the immense amount of work required to keep lists accurate and up-to-date, and now focus on working with individual clients.

The huge United States Information Services (USIS), the privatized investigative arm of the Office of Personnel Management, announced a major plan to go into this business in 2004 but later veered off in other directions. And when Barry Minkow got out of prison after his $100 million Ponzi scheme at ZZZZ Best carpet cleaning service, he announced that he had found God, earned a religious degree from Liberty University, and would devote himself to exposing degree mills and degree fraud through his Fraud Discovery Institute. He did this for a while in 2010–2011, "outing" seven major corporate executives with fake degrees (including the president of Herbalife) before himself pleading guilty to stock manipulation and quite possibly heading back to prison.

And so we come to a company called Verifile, which has arisen in the last few years as a major and reliable background screening service for employers and, through their Accredibase™ database of thousands of fake institutions and accreditors, a valuable source of information on the credential fraud industry, available on a subscription basis. Subscribers who mention that they learned about it here will be offered a nice discount for their first year's subscription. Please visit Accredibase at http://www.accredibase.com.

THE ACCREDIBASE 2011 ANNUAL REPORT

We are grateful to Accredibase and its managing director, Eyal Ben Cohen, for giving us permission to reprint some major excerpts from their 2011 annual report. While some of the information duplicates information or advice elsewhere in this book, there is enough that is new, or enhanced, to make it worth reading. Here is their introduction and the first two of seven chapters. The entire report is available free online.

Diploma and Accreditation Mills:
New Trends in Credential Abuse
© 2011 by Accredibase Ltd., all rights reserved.
by Eyal Ben Cohen and Rachel Winch

Overview

Verifile Limited's second annual Accredibase™ report into diploma and accreditation mill activity has revealed an astounding 48 percent increase worldwide in the number of known diploma and accreditation mills in the last year. As the Internet is the primary home for these bogus education and accreditation providers, little action is taken to stop them from helping unscrupulous candidates deceive unsuspecting employers.

According to the 2011 report, the USA remains the world's fake college capital. This year has seen a 20 percent increase in known diploma mills in the US, with the number rising from 810 to 1,008. While more than 40 percent of the diploma mills operate in California, Hawaii, Washington and Florida, the report reveals that District of Columbia has seen the sharpest increase among US states with 74 percent, rising from 19 to 33 mills over the past year.

The UK remains Europe's bogus university capital with 57 percent of European diploma mills claiming to operate from its shores. This year has seen a 25 percent increase in known diploma mills in the UK, with the number rising from 271 to 339, whilst in Europe as a whole the total number has risen from 454 to 593, an increase of 31 percent.

Introduction

A doctor is someone to be trusted, a person who has studied for years to earn his title, has gone through rigorous testing and peer review, and is an expert in his field, right? Wrong. The title can be bought online from a diploma mill for a few hundred pounds or dollars—your pet rabbit can get those prestigious letters before its name. Wikipedia even publishes a list of animals with fraudulent diplomas. Despite the light-hearted nature of these stories about pets with degrees, they demonstrate a serious point. Some unscrupulous operators will award a diploma or degree in exchange for money without carrying out any checks on the applicant, and without requiring any actual study—and people are really using these fake degrees to gain employment, trust and prestige.

Accredibase™, Verifile Limited's database of diploma and accreditation mills, keeps track of the credential fraud industry that exploits the anonymity and ever-widening reach of the Internet to sell its wares.

After a busy year of research, Accredibase™ reveals a huge increase in the number of known diploma and accreditation mills. The database now includes 2,615 known bogus education and accreditation providers—an increase of 48 percent in just one year. In addition to the huge number of confirmed mills known to Accredibase™, new suspect institutions are discovered on a daily basis—more than 2,000 are under investigation by Accredibase™ for inclusion in the database. There can be no doubt that bogus degrees are a real and worrying problem in today's society, given the number of sellers in the market. As Stephen Fry said on a recent edition of the BBC's QI, "pseudo-credentialing is a big issue."

In this report, we examine the current status of the diploma mill problem, revealing the global diploma mill hotspots. We investigate the new generation of bogus universities, taking a closer look at University Degree Program and Belford University networks, the involvement of bogus colleges in immigration scams and the phenomenon of online high school diploma mills. We also look back at the year's developments in terms of legislation to combat bogus education providers and discuss what can be done to protect employers, educators and the general public from bogus degrees.

1. So, What Are Diploma and Accreditation Mills?

Diploma mills are mostly online entities that offer substandard or bogus degrees in exchange for payment and not much else. Often these entities will grant a "degree" based on the submission of a résumé detailing life experience, and will even let the applicant choose his own subject and year of graduation. Others might require the student to do some work, but because of the lack of recognised accreditation or authorisation to grant degrees, the certificates are worthless.

Systems of higher education recognition and accreditation vary greatly across the globe, making it easier for diploma mills to confuse and deceive. In the United States, authorisation to operate and grant degrees is usually issued by the state; however, accreditation is granted by private accreditation agencies. Accreditation agencies are considered "recognized" if they have recognition from either the U.S. Department of Education or the Council of Higher Education Accreditation (CHEA). Some states will only license institutions with recognised accreditation; others allow unaccredited universities and colleges to operate. The United Kingdom does not operate the same system of accreditation by private organisations. In order to grant UK-recognised degrees, UK universities must be given degree-awarding power by a Royal Charter or Act of Parliament. This does not apply to foreign universities operating in the UK; they can offer their own awards in the country as long as they do not claim to be a UK institution.

Diploma mills should not be confused with companies producing fake certificates in the names of genuine, respected institutions. Forgeries have become so sophisticated that it can often be impossible to tell a fake certificate from a real one. Counterfeit documents are a huge issue for prospective employers and educators, but fake certificates can soon be spotted by checking directly with the university or college in question, who will be able to confirm whether or not the individual is on the graduation roll. Bogus universities, on the other hand, will readily verify their customer's credentials, so an extra level of diligence is required to weed out these degrees.

Telltale signs of a diploma mill include poorly made Web sites, offering a degree at a very low cost and in a very short space of time, and the opportunity to choose your own graduation date. Some diploma mill operators go to extraordinary, and sometimes bizarre, lengths to attempt to give their "universities" credibility. Hillmax University is one such example. Hillmax appears to be a clone of the notorious Rochville University. It is not, unsurprisingly, authorised to offer or advertise degree programs in Ontario, Canada, where it claims to be located.

We noticed that the university was using an image of Brian May, guitarist for the rock group Queen, upon receipt of his doctoral degree from the recognised UK University Liverpool John Moores!

Diploma mills often surround themselves with other dubious organisations in an attempt to gain credibility.

These include accreditation mills and even micronations acting as "recognition mills." An accreditation mill is a bogus accrediting agency that is not recognised by the authority responsible for governing education provision in its country of operation. They offer accreditation for a fee and will carry out little or no investigation into the quality of education provided by the institutions they claim to accredit. They often choose names similar to recognised accrediting agencies, and will even falsely add recognized schools to their lists of accredited members. Accreditation mills are often fabricated by the owners of diploma mills who are trying to deceive people into thinking their schools are legitimately accredited. Accreditation mills have been found to operate from the same address, and even have their Web site hosted at the same IP as schools they claim to accredit.

We use the term "recognition mill" to refer to an entity such as a micronation, or individuals purporting to represent a micronation, that grants meaningless recognition to diploma and accreditation mills. Examples include Hutt River Province in Australia, and the Principality of Seborga in Italy. Several diploma mills claim to be approved by Hutt River Province, a self-styled state in Western Australia, which is not recognised in any way by the Australian Government

The Principality of Seborga is a micronation located in northwest Italy, which covers an area of 15 km2 with a population of less than 400. A group of diploma mills including Pebble Hills University claimed to be located in Seborga and to be recognised by the Principality's Department of Education. In fact, Seborga is administered by the Italian government and the "Principality" only has symbolic value. After a police investigation, the address used by Pebble Hills and 10 other institutions was found to be a room used as a cellar.

2. What's the Big Problem?

The sheer number in existence indicates that selling degree certificates is big business for diploma mill operators, and that bogus degrees present real risk for prospective employers, educators and the general public. Bogus degree holders not only lack the qualification and associated experience they purport to have, but also demonstrate a clear lack of honesty and integrity.

Many high profile examples exposing bogus degree users hit the media in 2010. Take the case involving EDS (a division of HP), who was ordered to pay damages to BSkyB for making fraudulent representations when bidding for a £48 million project. The *Times* reported that former EDS managing director, Joe Galloway, lied in court about the origins of an MBA degree. He was exposed when BSkyB's barrister purchased the same degree on the Internet from Concordia College and University for his dog, Lulu. The dog even managed to obtain higher marks for her Concordia degree than the EDS executive.

For every high profile case, there are many, many more bogus degrees used by ordinary people, exposing potential employers to risk. Verifile's CV screening team regularly finds dubious qualifications popping up in its background checks. Recent examples involved a couple of blue chip financial service providers. The first was an applicant for a role managing sensitive functions in relation to the company's product line. The discovery of a degree from the bogus Rochville University on this candidate's CV was a real cause for concern for this bank.

When Verifile first received the applicant's details, a degree from New Rochelle University was listed. At first glance, this might have been the recognised College of New Rochelle in New York. The applicant later told Verifile that the degree was from Rochelle University, an unfindable entity thought to be related to Rochville University. It was finally revealed that the BSc in Computer Technology was actually from Rochville when Verifile asked the candidate to supply a certificate.

Another example involved an applicant for a role in the IT department of a London-based mortgage company that had a BSc in Computer Science from the unrecognized University of NorthWest. In addition to having an entry in Accredibase™, University of North-West has also been blacklisted in four U.S. States—Texas, Oregon, Michigan and Maine.

According to Oregon's Office of Degree Authorization, University of NorthWest was actively selling invalid degrees in Afghanistan in the summer of 2010. This particular candidate had also lied about A-Levels grades on his CV, which made Verifile's report regarding his bogus education even harder to ignore.

If someone is prepared to use a degree from a diploma mill in a job application, he may well be prepared to fabricate or omit other parts of his past, as the above example demonstrates, or to deceive in the future. This kind of deception is a clear warning sign of a lack of honesty and integrity, even if a degree is not essential for the role, and exposes the potential employer to real risk.

Diploma Mill Credentials on Display

A quick search on the professional networking site LinkedIn reveals just how easy it is to find professionals flaunting diploma mill degrees. There are almost 2,500 hits on the networking site for

"Almeda"—referring to the notorious online diploma mill Almeda University; and 734 hits for "Belford"—relating to Belford University and Belford High School.

It seems incredible that bogus degree holders would want to advertise their credentials so publicly, and even more incredible that they might not be aware of the bad press surrounding these online "universities." Bogus degree holders rely on the fact that many do not know that bogus universities even exist, and that a lot of prospective employers do not conduct thorough background checks. It is worthless to simply verify someone has a degree at a university if steps are not taken to ensure that the institution is not a diploma mill.

The Rest of the Accredibase Annual Report

Subsequent chapters address the huge University Degree Programme, fake high schools, immigration and visa mills, an in depth look at one major fake (International University of America), other global issues, and matters of enforcement.

PART 4

WHAT WE CAN DO ABOUT DEGREE MILLS

Chapter 19

∙∙

SOLUTIONS AND SUGGESTIONS

∙∙

What can be done? What can *we* do?

Those are the questions that we hear most often from law enforcement professionals, from government regulators, from educators, from journalists, from human resources professionals, from degree-mill victims, and from the general public.

There is no one single answer, but there are many possibilities that we discuss in this chapter.

Despite the gloomy state of affairs with regard to the proliferation of fake-degree sellers and users, we really feel there is hope of making a major dent in their activities. As discussed in chapter 1, we came so very close to eliminating degree mills in the 1980s, and maybe, just maybe, the time is right once again in this decade to try again to make a significant dent in the problem. It is possible that a combination of effective laws, effective enforcement, and effective publicity could increase the size of the dent.

The problem is vastly bigger than it was in 1991 when Allen Ezell retired from the FBI and DipScam ended. But there are many things that can and, we feel, *should* be done to address the problem today. Every phony that is closed, every scam artist who decides *not* to open a school, every company and government agency that improves its credential-checking activities, and every citizen who decides *not* to buy a degree is a step in the right direction.

This is the longest section in the book because there are so many things to suggest in the hope that even one might attract the attention and interest of each reader. We have identified more than one hundred things that could be done to address the problem.

371

And before we get to them, we need to acknowledge a few things that *are* being done as we go to press, which represent a situation very much in process.

In 2004, a diploma-mill summit was convened in Washington, with representatives from the Department of Education, the FBI, the FTC, the Office of Personnel Management, the Government Accountability Office, and some investigators acting on behalf of the House of Representatives. Their announced goal was to protect the federal workforce from the scourge of degree mills. To this end, the Government Accountability Office has conducted a "degree audit" at the Pentagon along with a similar audit of six government agencies that had been previously requested. The depressing results of this audit are discussed on page 159.

The first summit discussed the notion of putting out an "official" list of properly accredited schools. While it could do no harm to collect this information in one well-publicized and easily accessible official location, there are already such lists readily available in various published directories as well on the websites of the various accrediting agencies and others.

At least two significant problems arise about such a list, however.

One problem is the matter of the federal government suggesting that state-licensed schools are not acceptable, since they would apparently *not* be on such a list.

Should the federal government be in a position of saying that, for instance, a California-approved degree—one that qualifies its holder to sit for the bar exam and various state licensing exams—is unacceptable?

Can the federal government say, as *we* are happy to do, that some states' school laws are good ones, and others are terrible?

The even bigger problem is that of schools based in other countries that make their programs available to US students. The public would turn to such a list hoping to learn about the legitimacy of a given school. Presumably neither the venerable Oxford University nor the totally fake Harrington University would be on such a list, nor would any of the degree mills run from the United States but making use of registration or a mailbox in another country.

Far more useful, we suggest, would be an official list of schools that do *not* meet generally accepted accrediting principles.

Here now our thoughts on the many things that could be done to deal with degree mills.

WHAT THE FEDERAL GOVERNMENT COULD BE DOING

Federal Bureau of Investigation

The FBI has two ways of functioning with regard to potential crime: reactive and proactive.

Reactive

For many matters, the FBI waits until a crime has been committed or a complaint has been received. At that time, with FBI-HQ permission, a regional field office will open a case and assign it to a special agent to investigate. If the investigation is of sufficient magnitude and involves other agencies, then a task force can be formed that includes investigators from the other agencies.

This task force can then deal with the matter locally, regionally, or nationally, with the nature of the crime most likely governing the scope of the investigation.

Proactive

When a problem is felt to be of sufficient importance, the FBI can be aggressive in addressing the matter, not necessarily waiting for a complaint to be filed. An agent writes a report for his or her supervisor. With authority from FBI-HQ, a new case is opened.

Thus, the FBI can become involved in the investigation and discovery of *potential* crimes. This is what is done, for instance, with terrorism, child pornography, Internet stalking, and so on. And, for ten years (1980 to 1990), it was done with diploma mills. During this time, Allen Ezell and colleagues, based in North Carolina and, later, Florida, developed their own leads, pursued information submitted by the public, and worked closely with other agencies, grand juries, and federal prosecutors.

With Allen Ezell's retirement, DipScam was also retired. Now the FBI treats degree mills on a case-by-case basis, in the reactive model, as earlier described. There is little or no investigative work leading to the discovery of degree mills.

While this approach has resulted in a few significant accomplishments in the post-DipScam era—LaSalle University in Louisiana, Columbia State University in California, the fake MD, "Doctor" Caplinger in North Carolina, and the ongoing case of Columbus University, described in chapter 7—activities in the field have been drastically curtailed in the last decade and a half.

Here are four suggestions for the FBI:

1. Best of all, of course, would be a revival of DipScam or something comparable, as a national priority. FBI people have suggested that in the post-9/11 world, new issues unrelated to terrorism must take a backseat. Well, even the backseat gets to wherever the car is going. And there are these two matters as well:

    - clear evidence that some unaccredited and possibly fake schools have somehow gotten permission to issue H-1B student visas, permitting foreign nationals to enter the country, and
    - clear evidence that one of the largest degree mills ever—generating hundreds of millions of dollars in revenues—is owned by an American living overseas, whose demographic profile suggests at least the possibility of a concern with terrorist matters.

2. A nationally designated specialist in degree fraud who can work with FBI regional offices, advise other law enforcement people, and be a liaison with the media.

3. A hotline and/or a website where people could learn about degree fraud and fake schools and leave information on potential abuse.

4. In a recent FBI raid on Internet gambling websites, the websites involved were also seized. That could well be considered for Internet degree mills.

Secret Service

In addition to protecting officials and pursuing counterfeiters, the US Secret Service is charged with investigation of major fraud. When the huge St. Regis University fraud was under way, and no other enforcement agency seemed willing or able to do anything about it, the Secret Service stepped in. They determined that degree fraud can be closely linked to homeland security matters, by showing how easily a likely terrorist could get a fake degree which could lead to a student visa to enter the United States. This case is described in detail chapter 7. While the Secret Service did good work in the St. Regis case, in the ensuing seven years, they have declined to get involved again in these matters, despite strong encouragement from experts in the field.

Federal Trade Commission

The Federal Trade Commission's (FTC) Bureau of Consumer Protection is mandated, as it says on its website (http://www.ftc.gov), "to protect consumers against unfair, deceptive or fraudulent practices. The Bureau enforces a variety of consumer protection laws enacted by Congress, as well as trade regulation rules issued by the Commission."

There was a time, half a century ago, when the FTC was on the front lines in dealing with fake degrees and the schools that issued them. But in the last few decades, the FTC has done little, even though some senior administrators there have knowledge of, and concern for, degree mills.

As with so many government agencies, the FTC operates in a triage model. With limited budget and investigative staff, the agency has decided to focus on claims for foods, drugs, dietary supplements, and other products promising health benefits; health fraud on the Internet; weight-loss advertising; marketing directed to children; performance claims for computers; tobacco and alcohol advertising; protecting children's privacy online; and claims about product performance. But with a few notable exceptions, there has been nothing related to fake degrees and their sellers.

In the mid-1990s, the FTC did a terrific job in the initial investigation that led to the closing of Columbia State University by the FBI and the postal service. The FTC maintains a "spam database"—spams forwarded by the public at http://www.ftc.gov, which the FTC monitors for themes of abuse and fraud. That database contains tens of millions of spams, of which a tiny fraction, .05 percent, relate to degree and driver's license fraud, mostly from the same American-owned, Romanian-based operation. Working with British authorities, the FTC secured temporary, then permanent, restraining orders to close down the websites and domestic voice mail and message drops, and, with British authorities, enjoined the entities involved from sending out these spams.

Sadly, this was only a temporary roadblock in the path of the Romanian juggernaut, which, undeterred, promptly moved them to service providers in other countries. (The FTC action is described at http://tinyurl.com/SpamAction.)

The good news is that the FTC has provisions for priorities, enforcement, and rules in place to strike a major blow to the degree mills.

The bad news is that it hasn't exercised those priorities or enforced those rules. Here are the details.

Priorities

The stated priorities of the FTC's Division of Marketing Practices, available on its website (http://www.ftc.gov), include "shutting down high-tech Internet and telephone scams that bilk consumers out of hundreds of millions of dollars annually" and "halting deceptive telemarketing or direct mail marketing schemes that use false and misleading information to take consumers' money." Such as, may we suggest, fake-degree schemes bilking Americans out of many tens of millions of dollars a year.

Enforcement

The FTC's enforcement division has the power to enforce "federal consumer protection laws by filing actions in federal district court on behalf of the commission to stop scams, prevent scam artists from repeating their fraudulent schemes in the future, freeze assets, and obtain compensation for scam victims."

Rules

Most significantly, the FTC already has a rule in place dealing with false claims made by schools about the nature of their degrees and their accreditation.[1] The reason the word *rule* has a capital R is that rules are a very specific aspect of what the FTC can do. But the kicker is that the FTC has a bit of a Pollyanna philosophy: the FTC hopes and expects that everyone will do the right thing. And so it depends heavily on "voluntary compliance" with its rules. This is a little bit like leaving your store unlocked at night and hoping that the crooks will practice "voluntary compliance" with burglary laws and leave you alone.

Rule § 254.3 is extremely clear and unequivocal. It says that "an industry member should not . . . represent, without qualification, that its school is accredited unless all programs of instruction have been accredited by an accrediting agency recognized by the US Department of Education."

Our recommendations for the FTC could hardly be clearer or simpler.

1. Enforce your own Rule 254.3! It would have a dramatic and instantaneous effect as early as tomorrow morning. Every one of the dozens of unaccredited schools that advertise in *USA Today*, the *Economist*, and other major publications is in violation of this rule. If they couldn't make their useless accreditation claims, these unaccredited schools would get far fewer customers. And if they made the claims on the Internet, or through mail or telemarketing, it's time for your enforcement division to act.
2. Add degree mills to your enforcement priorities.
3. Put up a warning on your otherwise excellent website at http://www.ftc.gov. The site provides useful consumer advice on automobiles, investments, credit privacy, diet, products

and services, e-commerce, scholarship services, energy, tele-marketing, franchise opportunities, telephone services, tobacco, identity theft, and travel. Information on degree and credential fraud would be a fine addition. Now, a search of the FTC site for *diploma mill* finds one hit (and that, only slightly helpful), while *telemarketing* and *identity theft* yield thousands of hits.

Congressman Tim Bishop's bill, introduced in 2011, and described in chapter 5, would go a long way toward empowering the FTC in these matters.

Internal Revenue Service

The IRS is always interested in criminals and scam artists: people who, in addition to their ill-gotten gains, don't always pay their taxes. But there have been situations in which the IRS inadvertently helped out some fake schools and agencies by being remiss in the matter of monitoring their nonprofit status.

When a school or an accrediting agency identifies itself as non-profit, there is a certain marketing advantage. The public, rightly or wrongly, sees a nonprofit as more legitimate, less likely to be raking in huge profits for greedy owners. When the IRS allows a for-profit entity to call itself nonprofit, it is contributing to the deceit.

To be tax exempt, an organization, as described in section 501(c)(3) of the Internal Revenue Code, must be set up so that none of the earnings or profits go to any individual, and if the organization goes out of business, all its assets must go to other nonprofit causes or to the government.

Several mills actually reproduced a copy of a 501(c)(3) nonprofit IRS form as part of their literature, but apparently they never had that status or even applied for it.

The IRS participated in the search of LaSalle University in Louisiana, ostensibly run by a nonprofit church, because of these concerns. The concerns were valid, and tax fraud was one of the many counts on which LaSalle's owner was later indicted. He had taken a "vow of poverty," and so the tiny "church" he founded owned his sports cars, his million-dollar riverfront mansion, and so on.

And the unrecognized accreditor called World Association of Universities and Colleges attracted member schools in part by featuring their nonprofit status. But a successful legal action brought against WAUC by a disenchanted member school determined that the association was, in fact, a for-profit organization.

We appreciate that the IRS cannot do a detailed investigation of every 501(c)(3) applicant to be certain each is a true nonprofit. But we hope the IRS will pay close attention to some of the multi-million-dollar mills that may be hiding their profit-making status and under-reporting or not reporting their ill-gotten gains, sometimes through banking chicanery involving off-shore or other foreign accounts.

And there is always the "Al Capone" approach, in which the arch criminal was finally sent away for simple tax fraud. This happened recently when Rudy Marn, never charged for his major degree-mill activities with Hamilton and other universities, was nabbed, convicted, and imprisoned for failure to pay taxes on his fake degree sales.

United States Postal Service and the Postal Inspection Service

Both the USPS in general and the Postal Inspection Service in particular have had a modest role in dealing with degree-mill issues.

The Postal Inspection Service is the primary law enforcement arm of the United States Postal Service (http://www.usps.com/postal-inspectors). Postal inspectors are federal law enforcement officers who carry out investigations, make arrests, and serve federal search warrants and subpoenas. But there are only about two thousand postal inspectors for the entire United States, and with the huge increase (and high profile) of identity-theft crime, and a recent focus on Internet chat room predators, there has been little focus on degree mills.

Perhaps there is also the factor of overlap with other law enforcement agencies, as well as the fact that many degree mills specifically avoid using the postal system in order to escape the jurisdiction of postal inspectors, resorting instead to the unpoliced Internet and the even more anonymous overnight delivery services.[2]

Like the Federal Trade Commission, the Postal Inspection Service generally does not deal with individual cases of mail fraud, but, as its website says, "it can act against a company or individual if there is a pattern of activity suggesting a potential scheme to defraud."

The postal service can, however, stop delivery of mail to a given customer when there is ample evidence that the customer is behaving in an illegal manner. The postal inspector prepares an affidavit in which he or she describes probable cause of illegal activity through the US mail. The inspector then appears before a US magistrate in the US District Court. If the magistrate feels there is probable cause, a temporary restraining order (TRO) is issued. The TRO enables the inspector to stop mail delivery. Mail is returned to the sender with a notice that mail service has been suspended for illegal activity.

This very relevant tool has been applied to diploma mills only rarely, and even then, not necessarily permanently. While mail to the phony John Quincy Adams University was permanently stopped in the 1970s, mail to the currently active University of Berkley was temporarily stopped in the late 1990s but was later resumed, and the operator made many more millions of dollars.

The USPS website suggests that the main current concerns of the Postal Inspection Service are identity theft, senior sweepstakes victims, spam, home-improvement schemes, phony inheritances, unsolicited merchandise, prison pen pal money-order fraud, and fraudulent health and medical products. There is nothing said about degree-mill fraud. It would be an appropriate addition to this site.

There have been a small handful of occasions in the last decade when the Postal Inspection Service *was* the lead agency in a degree-mill issue, most notably in the cases of Gold Coast University (also known as Coast University) in Hawaii, John Quincy Adams University (address in Oregon, actually run from Illinois), and the fake medical degrees sold by a man in Virginia representing two Caribbean frauds, CETEC and CIFAS. In these cases, the postal inspectors did the investigation and prepared the brief to secure the search warrants that led to the "raid" on the premises. They also worked with the FBI and the IRS in collecting evidence in several other cases, including participating in the execution of search warrants.

While dealing with degree mills themselves is a matter that can be handled by a number of different law enforcement agencies—local, state, or federal—there are two degree-mill matters that are solely related to the United States Postal Service, and both, unfortunately, have had recent law and policy changes that immeasurably benefit the fake schools.

Private mailboxes

There are more than ten thousand private mailbox services, about a third of them UPS stores (formerly Mail Boxes Etc.) at which individuals and businesses can rent a box to receive their mail. Many degree mills receive their mail in this fashion, in the United States, Great Britain, and elsewhere. They wish to fool their customers and potential customers into believing they have a campus, or at least offices, and so they wish to have an address that cannot be clearly identified as a mailbox service.

For many years, private mailbox services permitted their customers to use the street address plus almost any sort of number, which actually identified their rented box.

123 Main Street, Suite 23 (or Apartment 23), 123 Main Street, Building 23, 123 Main Street, 23rd floor

Then, in 2002, the postal service passed a consumerist regulation, which required businesses using a private mail box to use "PMB" and a number for their address:

123 Main Street, PMB 23

While not everyone knew what a PMB was, many did, and it certainly waved a major red flag for anyone checking out a school.

As the Federal Trade Commission's Shirley Rooker wrote when this PMB regulation went into effect, "Recent amendments to postal regulations will make it harder for criminals to victimize innocent consumers by using mail drops. . . . The second line of the address block on mail going to mail drops must carry the designation PMB, which stands for private mailbox. It also must be on the return address of outgoing mail. These changes are significant because crooks, hiding behind private mailboxes, have ripped off seniors, traded in child pornography, operated lottery scams, and conducted a host of other frauds."

But a year later, the postal service was ordered by the Bush administration to end this requirement, since it was felt by the government to be hostile to small businesses: it prevented them from having a "presence" as an actual business with real offices. The degree-mill operators (and, presumably, the child pornographers) could not have been more pleased with this decision.

A few years after this, the "PMB" rule was reinstated, but private box holders were now permitted to use a number sign, #, instead of PMB. So now an address of "123 Main St., #17" is still a red flag, but not as clear a one as "PMB."

The Freedom of Information Act and PO boxholders

A great many degree-mill and unaccredited-school operators have used post office boxes (as contrasted with private mailboxes) as their primary or sole address. It is important for people checking out a school, whether as a potential student or as an investigator, to learn where the school is *really* located. It has been not uncommon for a school to have a box in one state but to be located in another state or even in the home of the owner.

For many years, the Freedom of Information Act was specifically made applicable to the postal service (39 USC 410(b)(1)), requiring any local postmaster to make available to any member of the public the actual physical location of any holder of a commercial post office box as the customer reported it on Form 1583. On many occasions, important information was learned about a degree mill's real location, its real owner, and links with other businesses through this use of the Freedom of Information Act.

In 2002, this all changed. It is no longer possible for an individual, whether student, potential student, journalist, or other interested party, to learn the real location of the holder of a post office box rented for business purposes. Postal Bulletin 22018 states that "information contained in Form 1583 will be disclosed only to a government agency upon written certification of official need or pursuant to a subpoena or a court order. . . . USPS will ignore civil subpoenas."

Once again, the degree-mill operators and child pornographers could not have been more pleased.

(Note: few years later, the rule was changed, so that process servers, but not members of the general public, could request this information via a special Process Servers Application available from the USPS.)

Even when the postal service was required to give the street address of commercial box holders, the system was abused by degree mills, since the postal service either did not confirm that the street address provided on Form 1583 was a real one or that the business in question was actually there. For instance, when a colleague, using the Freedom of Information Act, got the street address provided by a New Orleans "university" that was heavily advertised, he found nothing but a totally empty and apparently abandoned room in a small office building. The institution seems to have lied in filling out Form 1583, itself a federal crime.

The use of private mailboxes by degree mills does have its amusing moments. When one currently operating wonder (then run from Connecticut, now claiming to be in Moscow or possibly in Liberia) was using a private mailbox in South Dakota, it insisted that its multi-thousand-volume university reference library was located at their South Dakota "campus."

Summary of recommendations for the USPS

- Include degree-by-mail fraud information on the USPS website.
- Require any entity calling itself "college" or "university" to identify its address as a private mail box (PMB).
- Make the actual addresses of any post office box renters calling themselves "college" or "university" available to the public under the Freedom of Information Act.

- Make more active use of the power to stop mail delivery to
  degree mills.

Office of Personnel Management

The Office of Personnel Management (OPM) calls itself "the Government's personnel agency" (http://www.opm.gov). As such, it is very
much interested in and concerned with the matter of degree mills, fake
credentials, and resume fraud. In 1998, we were invited to put on a two-
hour workshop on degree mills for an OPM conference in Pittsburgh.

Five years later, in 2003, OPM, under pressure from Capitol Hill,
convened two half-day workshops where we had the pleasure of
speaking to nearly five hundred senior federal human resources executives and investigative officers. This event was repeated a year later.
People seemed really determined to do something. Over a two-year
period, four press releases were sent out from OPM with these titles:

August 2003: "Director Challenges Agency to Stop Use of Diploma
Mills"
May 2004: "Director Sets Aggressive Agenda for Bogus Degree Training"
January 2005: "Stricter Guidelines Regarding Diploma Mills"
February 2005: "Steps Being Taken to Combat the Use of Diploma
Mills"
Number of press releases on degree mills between 2005 and 2011: zero
Number of mentions of the terms "diploma mills" or "degree mills"
on the OPM website between 2005 and 2011: zero

These zeroes are not because the problem has been solved; it is
probably worse than ever.

In 2008, John Bear was keynote speaker at the big every-three-
years Department of Defense Education Conference, speaking on
degree mills. After the talk and the question period, a general came
up to Bear and said, "I never knew the problem was so severe. No one
told me. I have just ordered 1,500 copies of your book, and will give
one to every key personnel officer in my command."

It has been suggested in the press that OPM may bear some
responsibility for this lack of information and for not having sufficiently clear guidelines in place for the military and the hundreds of

other federal agencies. But in fact there *are* such guidelines in print, and they were given to participants in our various workshops.

The problem seems to lie in the area of encouragement and motivation to *use* these guidelines, since the kinds of comments we heard from well-meaning HR people are ones like:

- I didn't appreciate the scope of the fake degree problem.
- I didn't realize there were fake accrediting agencies.
- I didn't know how easy it is to get counterfeit diplomas and transcripts.

The process of checking people out seems remarkably informal. When a federal agency, whether NASA headquarters or a remote Bureau of Indian Affairs field office in Arizona, has a question about the school claimed by a job applicant, it can ask the OPM Investigative Services Office in Pennsylvania whether such-and-such a school is legitimate. Often, the diligent and hardworking staff members will know. On rare occasions they ask us.

But there are problems with this system.

- The various federal HR departments may not see a red flag and may not even ask OPM.
- The system does not directly address employees with counterfeit credentials bearing the names of legitimate schools.
- The system does not address people who simply falsify their resumes.
- With around two million federal employees, there are bound to be some, perhaps many, who have slipped through the net.

Since "the Director of OPM is the President's principal advisor in matters of personnel administration . . . and for the improvement of human resource management and human capital practices," there is ample opportunity to make information on fake degrees and credentials available not only to federal agencies but also to others who may come to the OPM website (http://www.opm.gov) and archives to gain information on how "the government's personnel agency" deals with these issues.

But no information is to be found there. A search of the large and well-designed website for the terms *degree*, *diploma*, *credential*, or *resume* comes up with nothing. The site index, with more than five hundred listings, from "Access America" to "Zipped File Help," has nothing. A search of the OPM's list of hundreds of publications, periodicals, operations manuals, CDs, and videotapes yields nothing.

It could be very helpful, both to federal agencies and the human resources world in general, if the OPM made its clear guidelines on checking out schools and credentials available.

The OPM maintains millions of personnel records at its investigative center, deep in a limestone mine in eastern Pennsylvania. An investigative reporter in Washington has told us that he has fantasies about the number of "time bombs" that may be ticking away there, but he acknowledges they are just about as inaccessible as the gold in Fort Knox.

Government Accountability Office

The Government Accountability Office (GAO) is the audit, evaluation, and investigative arm of Congress. Its mission, as stated on its website, is to "ensure the accountability of the federal government for the American people." The tools of the GAO are financial audits, program reviews and evaluations, analyses, legal opinions, and investigations. The GAO has had two significant involvements in the world of fake degrees.

In 2003, Sen. Susan Collins of Maine was concerned about the proliferation of degree mills on the Internet. Contact was made with GAO's investigators, who then purchased two degrees for $1,500 from the fake Lexington University, in the name of Susan M. Collins.

Further testing the system, these investigators then established their own fake school, the Y'Hica Institute for the Visual Arts, ostensibly in London, England. ("Y'Hica" stood for "Yes, Here it comes again!") Then they made application to the Department of Education for authority to obtain federal student loans. They were all too successful. As the Associated Press reported, the GAO had little trouble gaining US certification of the school by the Department of Education and obtaining loan approvals for three students (including Susan

M. Collins) from two of three major lending institutions contacted (Nellie Mae Student Lending Inc. and the Sallie Mae Servicing Corp.) Only the Bank of America became suspicious and did not offer the more than $50,000 in requested loans.

Under instructions from the Senate Committee on Governmental Affairs, the Government Accountability Office conducted a "degree audit" of eight federal agencies, looking for employees at the GS-15 level and above who had degrees from unrecognized schools. GS (General Schedule)-15 is quite a high-level position, with salaries typically over $100,000 a year.

The GAO found twenty-eight senior-level employees with highly dubious degrees. Further, in records obtained from three unrecognized California and Wyoming schools, the GAO found 463 federal employees at all GS levels, at least 14 percent of them paid for by the agency (and, thus, by the taxpayers).

The GAO requested data from four schools. The one that refused to cooperate, quite possibly the largest, was never subpoenaed and never suffered for this refusal. One wonders why. And, remarkably, the head of GAO Special Investigations, Robert Kramer, commented on the difficulty of getting federal agencies to cooperate with his investigation. "We had more luck going to the schools than to the agencies," he said.[3]

Further, there is the matter of retirement benefits for these hundreds, perhaps thousands of people with fake degrees. The degrees got them higher pay, and the higher pay gets them higher retirement benefits, paid for, of course, by the taxpayers.

In connection with those three California and Wyoming schools, the GAO uncovered another widespread scam. Since the federal government will pay for courses (but not degree programs) from unrecognized schools, representatives of every school contacted by undercover investigators offered to bill for individual courses (even though no courses were actually offered), and then to apply the federal payment for these nonexistent courses to the degree program and award the degree.

Some responses to the GAO findings suggest that the numbers were small enough not to be alarming. Consider, however, the following: The GAO audit looked at only eight agencies, fewer than 5 percent of the total number. The GAO looked only at people with a

GS-15 rating and above, fewer than 5 percent of the total number of people. And the GAO looked for a limited number of dubious schools, again probably fewer than 5 percent.

These three "fewer than 5 percent" categories suggest that if the GAO had looked at the full categories, it would have found more than one hundred thousand government employees with unrecognized degrees.

And even that number does not take into account the very large number of people who have bought counterfeit diplomas with the names of real schools or who have simply lied on their resumes. Small wonder that Senator Collins described this finding as the "tip of the iceberg."

The Disappointing Aftermath of the Collins Hearings

After all those revelations of fake degree use, of naming the names, what happened? In two words, almost nothing. There was no public disclosure of the fake degree users, either by government agencies or investigative reporters. There wasn't even any action taken against the degree mill that sold Sen. Collins her fake degree and transcript, http://www.degrees-r-us.com.

The official government position seemed to be that as long as the fake degree was not used to meet a job requirement, there was no harm done

The tax-paying American people might well benefit from more action by the GAO. If the Department of Education itself could be duped by a not-too-elaborate fake school, then how many other government agencies have inadequate defenses against this sort of thing? More "sting" operations would help us learn.

And considering the very modest degree audit turned up all those "time bombs," how many others might there be among the more than four million federal employees, civilian and military? Wouldn't it be extraordinary if those four million resumes were matched against the names of the one hundred largest mills?

A concerned or angry enough Congress could order the GAO not only to find out but also to tell us what it learned.

Finally, of all the schools and people identified at the various congressional hearings, only two were ever prosecuted: a medical degree "expediter" for a CETEC University, a Caribbean medical school that sold MDs, and Ronald Pellar of Columbia State University (who was already in prison for an earlier scam, teaching people to tattoo "permanent" make-up on clients by having them learn with ballpoint pens and cantaloupes!).

Department of Education

The US Department of Education is in an awkward and ambivalent place when it comes to degree mills. On one hand, the department is the place that many people, businesses, and organizations think first of telephoning, writing, or e-mailing to find out more about mills and to learn whether any given school is legal.

On the other hand, as the secretary of education wrote in 2003, "the Department of Education has no oversight or regulatory authority over institutions that do not participate in the programs included in the Higher Education Act. Thus we have no independent authority or ability to determine if such a school is a diploma mill."[4]

Hey, let's play that one again. The Department of Education says that it does not have the ability to figure out if a given school is a degree mill or not.

The secretary of education goes on to say that the decision as to whether any given school is a mill "is best made by appropriate regulators in the State in which the school is located."[5]

The huge problem with this suggestion is that we are talking about fifty very different sets of state laws and, in the world of distance education, people in one state regularly dealing with a school in another state. Therefore, we have the common situation in which a school may be completely legal in one state (for instance, California approved, Alabama approved, or Wyoming licensed) and yet be regarded as illegal and, indeed, a cause for prosecution in another state.

This said, the good news is that some very useful information on degree mills can be found, with only a bit of difficulty, online. A search for *degree mill* at ed.gov finds absolutely nothing. Not even a cross-reference to *diploma mill*. But a search for *diploma mill* gets a couple dozen hits, most of them related to high schools, two old ones on colleges, and, happily, one pretty good new one, with the unwieldy address of http://www2.ed.gov/notclamped/students/prep/college/diplomamills/index.html. (Here's a suggestion: why not "ed.gov/diploma mills" instead.)

Here, then, are four suggestions for the Department of Education:

1. The secretary of education wrote that the problem of degree mills "is serious and requires careful consideration by the Department [of Education] as to whether a federal response is appropriate."[6]

   We suggest that a federal response is appropriate. In 1960, for the first and only time, the then Office of Education published what was called an "Official List of Diploma Mills." There is no reason this could not be done again, avoiding the problem of state differences by including only those places that are phony beyond any reasonable doubt—perhaps, for instance, those chosen unanimously by a committee of experts in the field.

2. A more user-friendly website (although the current one is fairly good). On the opening page, there is a "quick click" menu for more than fifty major topics, from accreditation to student loans, but there is nothing on degree mills. Adding a section on degree mills would be a good thing.

3. A consumer information site, directly linked to the opening page and supported with in-print and telephone services. The generally helpful Office of Accreditation and State Liaison within the Department of Education has been considering actions in this direction, and we think this should be encouraged, supported, and financed.

4. An ombudsman office. The Department of Education already has such an office to deal with mediating and resolving problems related to financial aid. Such an office could also deal with school and degree matters, including problems of acceptance of degrees by employers and schools, problems of schools misrepresenting themselves, and so on.

The US Congress

Because our country's founders chose not to give any control over education to the federal government, the subject has largely been a matter dealt with by the states, with the major exception of federal loan issues.

Every five or six years, when the nation's Higher Education Act is rewritten, and every special interest group, from school bus safety to naturopathic physician licensing, is focused on Washington, there are those who hope that Congress will address the matter of fake schools and degrees.

In our first edition, published in 2005, we urged passage of a law that would make degree mills a federal issue. Well, we got one in 2009, but it is quite minimalist, and much of the heart of it was gutted between its introduction and its eventual passage. Thanks for trying. Now our wish is that you'll go back and try a little harder.

US State Department

The Apostille is the degree mill operator's most popular tool. It is used to fool people in one country into thinking a fake diploma issued in another country is legitimate. The implications are significant for higher education, immigration systems (visas), and commerce (jobs, promotions, pay raises)

The Apostille is, simply, an international notarization or documentation. Authorities in one location certify that the signature and seal on a document from another location is an authentic copy. The Apostille Convention in The Hague makes clear that, "the effect of an Apostille does not extend to the content of the public document to which it relates."

One can take any document to a local notary service, located almost anywhere. The notary compares the signature on the document with the signature on a passport or driver's licence, and if they are the same, the notary will stamp and seal the document. The notary does not read the document; it is irrelevant. A person can type out a document stating that he has won the Nobel Prize for Chemistry, is owed $1,000,000 by a major corporation, or has been elected pope of the Roman Catholic Church.

HOW THE APOSTILLE IS MISUSED BY DEGREE MILLS

United States of America

DEPARTMENT OF STATE
To all to whom these presents shall come, Greetings:
I Certify That the document hereunto an-
nexed is under the Seal of the State of
California, and that such Seal is entitled
to full faith and credit.*

In testimony whereof, I, Colin L.
Powell, Secretary of State, have
hereunto caused the seal of the Department of State to be affixed and
my name subscribed by the Assistant
Authentication Officer, of the said
Department, at the city of Washington, in the District of Columbia,
this 30th day of September, 2004.

Colin Powell's Signature
Secretary of State
Someone Else's Signature
Assistant Authentication Offier

* For the contents of the
annexed document, the
Department
responsibili

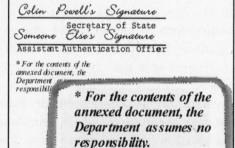

* *For the contents of the
annexed document, the
Department assumes no
responsibility.*

ANNEXED DOCUMENT

Allen Ezell
and John Bear
have been
awarded the
Nobel Prize
for Physics.
Dr. Ezell
earned his
Ph.D. from
Harvard Uni-
versity. Mr.
Bear has been
elected
Governor of
Nebraska.

The Apostille is one of the most common tools used by degree mills. It consists of a notarized document (which can say anything at all) and a certificate from the Department of State acknowledging the notarization is authentic. This Apostille "certifies" that the authors of this book have won the Nobel Prize.

In the United States, the notarized document is taken to a state agency to be authenticated, which simply means that the original notary really is a licensed notary. Again, the content is irrelevant and not read by the notary. Then the document goes to the State Department, which acknowledges the state authentication and issues the Apostille.

In most other countries, the Apostille is granted by various agencies: the Foreign and Commonwealth Office in the United Kingdom, the Ministry of External Affairs in India, and so on.

The crucial thing is that at no point does anyone read the document.

Scores of degree mills have used the Apostille process to fool students. They type out a statement that says they are licensed, accredited, approved, and internationally recognized. That statement is locally notarized, then they get the Apostille and say, for example, "We are fully accredited and recognized by the government of the United States, as attested in a document signed by Secretary of State Hillary Clinton." (The same claim was earlier made about Henry Kissinger and Colin Powell. In fact, the secretaries *never* sign Apostilles. As is made clear on the document itself, they designate a clerk to sign for them.)

There is hope that things could change.

The Permanent Bureau of The Hague Conference on Private International Law has recently acknowledged that "degree mills are a problem that goes well beyond the scope of the Apostille Convention itself."[7] They have recommended "the issuance of an Apostille only for legitimate diplomas issued by public or similarly approved, regulated, or controlled institutions. . . ."[8] It will not be easy to implement this rule, but at least there is hope. And, of course, the US Department of State could act independently and deny Apostilles for this kind of use. But even if they do, all the existing phonies that have their Apostille will continue to use them to fool people.

WHAT INTERNATIONAL ORGANIZATIONS COULD BE DOING

Interpol

Interpol is not a police force itself, but it facilitates the police of each of its 188 member-nations, working and cooperating with the police of other countries in crimes that involve two or more countries. In other words, it is a communication service that can smooth the progress of interaction between any of the twenty thousand federal, state, and local law enforcement agencies and their counterparts in other parts of the world.

The Interpol office typically can be found inside an existing agency. In the United States, the US National Central Bureau for Interpol can be found in the Department of Justice in Washington and has, not unexpectedly, a connection with the Department of Homeland Security.

Like so many agencies, Interpol operates in a triage mode and must decide, for any given case, if it has staff, budget, knowledge, and interest in helping. It seems logical that Interpol should have interest in international degree fraud, since it fits in Interpol's priority areas of interest: money laundering, financial and high-tech crime, and public safety.

In reality, degree matters seem not to be a priority. We have heard from people who told us they were unable to obtain information through ordinary Interpol channels. For instance, a US attorney in New York, checking on a psychotherapist using a degree from the fake Romanian "University Degree Program," tried without success to get information on them. And an English county weights-and-measures investigator who was asked to learn more about a local mailbox service that was receiving mail for a Belgian degree mill ran into a dead end when he asked Interpol for help in communicating with Belgian authorities.

We wish Interpol would at least take international degree fraud more seriously and provide information on its website (http://www.interpol.int). One can currently find useful material on issues from counterfeiting to football hooliganism, but a search for the words *degree, school, diploma,* or *certificate* came up empty. Given the interest in counterfeiting, the addition of counterfeit diplomas to Interpol's website would be a logical fit, if they chose to do so.

International Organization for Standardization

The International Organization for Standardization (abbreviated ISO in the United States) was established to develop an international system of standards so that, for instance, a Norwegian flange (made to ISO standards) would fit onto a Malaysian furnace, or a South African chemical compound could be used in a Brazilian laboratory.

Within the ISO, there used to be a subdivision, ISO 9002 (now merged into ISO 9001), to cover organizations that produce, install, and service products. One of these "products" is education, leading to degrees.

More than twenty years ago, an unaccredited school in California began marketing the fact that they had "achieved" ISO certification. When we asked its founder, Theron Dalton, how this had happened, he was unusually candid. "The first one through the door gets to write the standards," he said in a personal communication to John Bear. "You could write standards for a cement life preserver, and as long as you make them to that standard, you'll get your ISO certification."

The encouraging news is that there has been no flood—indeed, there has barely been a trickle—of other schools following this approach. In 1999, Eastern Michigan University's website (www.emich.edu) announced it was "the only accredited university in the northern hemisphere to be ISO 9002 certified." In subsequent years, a very small number of schools have advertised their ISO license, ranging from the traditional University of Wolverhampton in England to the unaccredited Southern Pacific University of St. Kitts.

It might be appropriate for the International Organization for Standardization to revisit the matter of certifying degree-granting universities, both to weed out the less-than-wonderful ones and as a boon to transnational acceptance of schools and degrees.

The United Nations

Bad and fake schools love to claim that they are in some way affiliated with or approved by the United Nations. The UN is so huge and complex and bureaucratic that there is often no one there who knows or frets about the flea who claims to have captured the elephant on which it lives. Nor does it seem practical to expect the UN to notice when a degree mill claims to be UN-approved because it made a small donation to a charter school sponsored by large corporation that was a private-sector partner of UNESCO.

There are, however, two things the UN might address.

Foremost is the matter of the International Association of Universities, self-described on its website (http://www.unesco.org/iau) as "the UNESCO-based worldwide association of universities." The IAU maintains a list of schools it calls the World Higher Education Database (WHED), and it publishes a huge book called the *International Handbook of Universities*.

While rules for being listed in the WHED must have seemed straightforward when originally formulated, they become much less clear in a world where, for instance, complications like the following can occur:

- One UN member-nation can accredit a university not recognized in its own country (for instance, St. Kitts and Nevis for a university that at the time was run from New Hampshire, or the Republic of Malawi for an unaccredited university based in Wyoming).
- A US company can make a deal with an accredited university in another country to offer doctoral degrees in the United States with little oversight from the home university. For instance, a doctorate-granting institute that was run briefly from Florida, Monterrey Institute for Graduate Studies, claimed a link to a traditional Mexican university that seemed to have no idea what was being done in its name.
- People claiming to represent a UN member-nation can sell the accreditation of that country to schools in another country (for instance, the offer made by the St. Regis University people to sell Liberian accreditation for fees that grew quickly from $1,000 to $50,000).

In each of the above cases, and others, the schools in question either were listed in the *International Handbook of Universities* or made the claim that they would be.

It would be good if IAU's UNESCO European Centre for Higher Education, based at UNESCO House in Paris, were crystal clear on the rules for inclusion and exclusion from the *International Handbook of Universities*. Some of the above-mentioned cases dragged on for a year or more, causing much public confusion.

It would also be nice to have relevant information readily available, perhaps on the IAU's website at http://www.unesco.org/iau/.

Finally, the estimable United Nations University, based in Tokyo, is an international community of scholars serving as a "think tank" on matters of global concern. It is presumptuous to think that international degree fraud should be on the same page with issues of poverty, war, human rights, famine, security, and AIDS. But among the hundreds of conferences, seminars, and workshops that UNU holds or sponsors each year, perhaps one might look at (and help increase awareness of) the degree-fraud problem.

STATE AGENCIES

Every state has one or more state agencies that deal with approving or licensing new schools in the state and regulating schools that already operate in the state. A few have laws specifically relating to the use of degrees by people in the state.

With fifty sets of state laws, and with enforcement attitudes and policies ranging from strict to negligible, the situation is complex and often unclear. There are many anomalies, which make trying to "get a handle" on the state situation even harder. Here are some examples.

- Montana had a decent school-licensing law but intentionally chose not to enforce it.
- California had a reasonable school-licensing law, but it expired and was not renewed for several years, during which time many bad and fake schools rushed to California (or at least took out convenience addresses), knowing they would be safe

from regulation. California once again has modest regulation, but chooses to ignore the many unaccredited schools that are really run from California although they have a token office or just a mailbox in another state or country.

- Louisiana exempted religious schools from the need for state licensing but then agreed that religious schools could offer degrees in nonreligious subjects, since God created everything.
- Wyoming also fails to regulate religious schools and allows them to offer nonreligious degrees. And Wyoming's nearly automatic licensing of unaccredited nonreligious schools made that state a haven for the "bad guys."
- New Mexico enacted a reasonable school licensing law but then grandfathered in all the unaccredited schools that could never have qualified under the new law.
- Idaho properly regulates schools but intentionally ignores some dreadful Idaho-based schools as long as they do not enroll students living in that state.

The Eight Questions a State Should Ask

We are not going to get into detailed recommendations for each state; that could fill an entire book. These are eight questions that any state might well ask on the occasion of considering new laws or revisiting old laws relating to schools and degrees, with some short comments on each.

1. *Academic quality and/or consumer issues.* Some states look closely at curriculum. The state of New York is the only state that is actually a recognized accrediting agency. Some states have little or no interest, as long as the public isn't defrauded. Indeed, in the late 1990s, California took the unusual step of moving school licensing from the Department of Education to the Department of Consumer Affairs.

The question is: for schools in our state, are we concerned with the academic quality of schools, the consumer issues (not making misleading claims or taking money under false pretenses), or both?

2. *Actual presence in the state.* Are we concerned about schools

that have token offices (or mailboxes) outside the state but that really are run from within our state? This is, for instance, a significant issue in California, where some very large unaccredited schools are almost entirely run from offices in California, despite claiming their authority to operate from Wyoming, Hawaii, New Mexico, and elsewhere.

3. *Out-of-state schools.* Are we concerned with schools that have no connection with our state but offer programs and degrees to state residents? Some states, such as Minnesota, have made the claim that they have the right to restrict out-of-state schools that do not meet their standards from offering correspondence or online programs to people in their state. Schools that were notified that they were in violation simply changed their rules by saying that all diplomas would be awarded only in the state where they were located and that graduates would have to travel there, or make private shipping arrangements, to receive their diplomas. A California school that received the Minnesota warning hired a constitutional lawyer, who told them she felt Minnesota was on shaky ground based on precedents for interstate commerce.

4. *Procedures for starting a new school.* Do we want to encourage people to start new and innovative schools in our state? A few states encourage this, a few tolerate it, and many discourage it. California and Indiana, for instance, encourage innovation through a meaningful but not excessively rigorous procedure of state licensing called State Approval in California, and State Accreditation in Indiana. Other states, such as Louisiana and South Dakota, have adopted what is called the "up or out" approach. New schools are permitted to operate for a fixed period of time with little oversight (two years is typical), but if they have not achieved recognized accreditation, or cannot show they are close to it, then they can no longer operate.

5. *Regulating degree use.* Are we concerned about the degrees used publicly by citizens of our state or visitors to our state, regardless of where the degrees were issued? In the 1990s, Florida enacted a law making the use of unaccredited degrees illegal. The law was badly written—not taking into account non-US schools, for instance—and was found to be unconstitutional, although the *state*

Supreme Court said it might be approved if rewritten. Since that time, there has been a small trend toward regulating degree *use* rather than degree *granting*. Oregon, Illinois, New Jersey, Nevada, and North Dakota have passed such laws. The challenge is to be extremely clear in defining what is illegal and to have enforcement procedures in place.

6. *Clarity of the law.* Are our laws (or proposed laws) clear, unambiguous, and sensible? Florida's law badly defined eligible schools. Iowa's "up or out" law had no time provisions. Other states have suffered from intentional ambiguity—something happening "when it is felt that" certain circumstances have occurred. And a few have referred to "accredited colleges and universities" without taking note of the fact that there are many unrecognized accreditors. Hawaii has a law that makes it extremely easy to be a legal school there: in effect, having little more than one employee in the state and a small number of Hawaii residents enrolled. But even that is more than many fake schools do, and Hawaii has been aggressive in pursuing violators.

7. *Fairness and uniformity.* Are the laws enforced fairly, uniformly, and strictly, or *would* they be? We hear from regulators and enforcers that because of budget cuts, staff shortages, and lack of direction from management, they are limited—and frustrated—in their pursuit of bad schools. Hawaii, as just mentioned, has been the most aggressive in bringing legal actions against violators—more than fifty to date—largely due to the efforts of one attorney in the Department of Consumer Affairs, who operates in triage mode, due to the number of possible cases.

8. *Nature of penalties.* Are the penalties meaningful, or are wrists being slapped? Large fines are common, imprisonment is increasingly rare, and enforcement is a real problem. The state of Kansas won a million-dollar-plus judgment against degree-mill operator Les Snell and his Monticello University, but Snell moved to Colorado and was not pursued. Hawaii has won numerous million-dollar judgments, but mostly against perpetrators living elsewhere, and collections are rare. Is prison a deterrent? Sometimes. Some major perpetrators (Tony Geruntino, the Fowler brothers) never went back into the business after prison. Some (Ernest Sinclair, James Kirk) actually ran their

next phonies from within prison. And others (Edward Reddeck, Ronald Pellar) went back into business as soon as they were freed.

Each of these questions is worthy of lengthy analysis and discussion, and indeed such discussions have gone on in many states over many years, sometimes harmoniously (or at least collegially), and sometimes acrimoniously.

One expert who writes often and well on these matters is Alan Contreras, who retired in 2011 as the administrator of Oregon's Office of Degree Authorization. One of his short essays on these matters comprises chapter 12 of this book, and his long, scholarly 2009 white paper, "The Legal Basis for Degree Granting Authority in the United States," written for SHEEO, the State Higher Education Executive Officers (http://www.sheeo.org), is available free, online, at http://tinyurl.com/ContrerasPaper.

Other Government Agencies

Noneducational or consumer-related agencies at the state, county, and city level have, from time to time, been relevant in the fight against degree mills in matters as ordinary as sales tax (fake schools may not be collecting and paying it), zoning violations (doing business from a home), business and insurance violations (employees not being paid minimum wage or provided with workers' compensation insurance), as well as health and safety violations. (Columbia State University had sixteen people, many of them undocumented aliens, working in a small, poorly ventilated, and generally unsafe building, with no business license and numerous other violations, ignored, sadly, for years by the city of San Clemente, Orange County, and indeed the state of California.)

PRIVATE AGENCIES

There are hundreds of organizations and agencies that are concerned with one or more aspects of colleges and universities, accreditation, degrees, and credentials. And the issues that occur with these organizations are twofold.

First, many of them have open membership. Anyone can join. And so degree mills often say (correctly but irrelevantly) in their literature that they "are members of the American Council on Education, the International Council on Education, the Society for University Planning," and so on.

Our recommendation here is that these organizations restrict their institutional memberships to schools with recognized accreditation (or its counterpart in other nations) and that they pay attention to the use of their name by both members and nonmembers.

The second issue is that of improving public awareness of bad and fake schools. Of the myriad acronymic groups out there (AACSB, AAACE, AAHE, AAPICU, AAUA, ACBA, and so on—and that's just a small portion of the As), almost none has any public awareness or information on these matters. One significant exception is the Council for Higher Education Accreditation (CHEA), which *does* have a lot of useful degree-mill information on its website (http://www.chea.org).

An example from a few years ago shows how valuable such organizations *could* be. There was an interesting phony university operating from Miami using the name of a legitimate university in Peru (Villarreal) and claiming to be its "international office." Nonresident PhD degrees were offered through aggressive advertising. As many as a thousand US academics signed up, at $10,000 each, making it a $10 million business. As things began to shred (phone calls unanswered, mail returned), more and more people began writing and calling the American Council on Education, which told us at the time that it was concerned and looking into the matter. But to the best of our knowledge, the ACE never said or did anything publicly, either in the way of a warning or advice to the victims. The fake Villarreal University simply faded away, and no refunds were ever made. Today, if one searches the ACE website (http://www.acenet.edu) for *diploma mill* or *degree mill*, one comes up empty-handed.

Human Resource Policies

Shortly before the FBI "raid" on the phony LaSalle University in Louisiana, LaSalle's literature listed hundreds of large companies that they said accepted and, in most cases, paid for their degrees. When we started checking on that claim by calling the companies listed, we discovered that LaSalle's claim was correct but for the wrong reasons. Based on ten completed phone calls, we learned that four of the companies had confused the fake Louisiana LaSalle with the real Pennsylvania LaSalle. And the other six said that their policy was to accept and often pay for *all* accredited schools. They didn't know that there was such a thing as unrecognized or fake accreditation.

The lack of knowledge and skill among many corporate human resources and personnel officers was clearly determined by a comprehensive survey of them, done as part of Richard Douglas's 2003 doctoral dissertation research through the Union Institute and University.[9]

Douglas had more than 250 HR executives with major companies fill out a long and detailed questionnaire, in which they were asked to rate the acceptability of various schools when considering employees for hire, promotion, and tuition reimbursement purposes. The list of schools included everything from traditional regionally accredited institutions to out-and-out degree mills.

Douglas determined that human resource professionals often did not understand the differences between real and fake schools, and they often did not check. Many of these professionals responded that they accepted, for hiring, promotion, and tuition reimbursement, degrees from schools they did not know were degree mills.

Further, a significant subset of them ranked completely phony schools (for example, Columbia State University) ahead of regionally accredited schools (for example, Capella University).

In his dissertation, Douglas concluded that "human resources professionals require training regarding degree acceptance and recognition."

We concur and suggest that the problem is immense and one of great urgency.

Online Resume Services

One of the major marketing phenomena of the Internet era is the growth of online resume services. People looking for jobs, or thinking about changing jobs, put their resumes or CVs online, where they can be read by potential employers. Typically, there is no charge to make your resume available, and then companies and other potential employers pay a monthly fee for the privilege of searching through these resumes.

One company, Monster.com, has, through internal growth and through acquisitions, grown phenomenally to dominate this field. There are more than 150 million resumes online, representing more than half of the entire American workforce. Using its fast and efficient search engine, employers can quickly find job seekers sorted by location, by skills, by salary . . . and by degrees claimed.

Monster.com and its two main competitors (CareerBuilder.com and indeed.com) do not investigate or verify any of the statements or claims made on these resumes. It is the case that many thousands of people list degrees from degree mills.

Once, at the request of ABC's *Good Morning America*, John Bear conducted a detailed search of the entire Monster.com database. (At the time, it was possible to search all their millions of resumes; more recently, the search is limited to a few hundred or so.) Since ABC was looking for only a handful of people with fake degrees to interview, the searching was stopped after five thousand people with responsible positions *and* fake degrees had been found. Clearly, there could have been a great many more. And goodness only knows how many others—a far larger number, we suspect—list degrees from legitimate schools that they did not happen to earn or for which they had purchased a counterfeit diploma.

Of course, people should not list fake degrees on their resumes. But many do. And of course, employers should use due diligence to check on these degrees. But many don't.

And so Monster.com (and the others) could perform a very helpful service simply by declining to post resumes that list degrees from bad, fake, or simply unaccredited schools. How would they choose which ones? They could either develop their own list, or they could use a publicly available list, such as the Michigan/Oregon list in this book.

Sadly, this is not done, and it seems unlikely to be done. A colleague of ours, who believed he had a good personal relationship with one of the founders of Monster.com, approached that person with ample evidence of some of the dangerous fakes with resumes on Monster (the doctors, lawyers, sex therapists, teachers, nuclear engineers, and so on), with the idea that Monster could not only do a lot of good in the world but also gain an edge on its competition by weeding out these thousands of imposters.

Despite several follow-up inquiries, he never got an answer. But a few months later, the press reported that a top executive of Monster.com itself had been falsely claiming to have an MBA.

The Media

The media (newspapers, magazines, radio, and television) have played the role of both hero and villain in the fight against degree mills. On one hand, a superb four-day page-one series on degree mills in Arizona's largest daily paper was instrumental in the passage of tough new state laws and the closing or departure of dozens of fake schools operating there. The series ran from March 5 to March 8, 1982. On the other hand, for many years, virtually every weekly issue of the prestigious *Economist* magazine had several, sometimes many, advertisements for totally fake schools. The good and the bad were ironically juxtaposed when *USA Today* ran a long and good degree-mill warning front-of-section article . . . and five pages further along were advertisements for some of the bad and fake schools about which the article warned.[10] The Internet version of the article was accompanied by paid banners for some of the worst offenders.

The message to these media outlets is simply this: stop running ads for unrecognized and fake schools. It is doing a terrible disservice to your readers, as well as giving added credibility to the phonies. Often we hear from an aggrieved victim, "But I saw the ad in the *Economist*. Surely the *Economist* wouldn't accept ads from fake schools." Yes, it would, plus it has been doing it for years, including the notorious Columbia State University "PhD in 27 Days" ads and others of its ilk.

We estimate that the more than thousand bad and fake school ads that have run in the *Economist* have cost their readers many millions of dollars, as well as planted time bombs in countless resumes. The "hall of shame" of major media that have run such ads include the *Economist*, *USA Today*, *Psychology Today*, *Utne Reader*, *Army Times*, and *Navy Times* (think how many servicemen and servicewomen are being fleeced by their own trade publication), the *International Herald Tribune*, many of the airline in-flight magazines, *Investor's Business Daily*, non-US editions of *Time* and *Newsweek*, and all too many more.

Frequent Publicity

The media generally have little interest in the fake schools, but they do pay erratic attention to people caught using fake degrees. While the case of the past executive director of the Moral Majority, identified during congressional hearings as holder of a degree from a diploma mill, got a lot of coverage, the discovery of a questionable degree held by an undersecretary of defense got almost no media attention.

Of course, we wish there were more substantial coverage, as this is one of the few ways to warn people about buying fake degrees. But we've gotten quite discouraged tugging on sleeves in the hope that the media will pay attention. Both authors were both involved in the federal trial of a flamboyant and colorful family from Chicago, the Fowler brothers, on trial in Charlotte, North Carolina, for running a string of a dozen or more fake schools and accrediting agencies. Allen Ezell describes this case in chapter 6.

As it happened, the trial involving Jim and Tammy Faye Bakker and Jessica Hahn was going on in the same building, so the lobby was awash in reporters and photographers. We could not interest a single one of them in the multi-million-dollar degree-fraud case that went on there for three and a half weeks. To the best of our knowledge, not a word about the Fowler brothers ever appeared in a newspaper or magazine.

As long as we are addressing the media, there is one more issue. Quite a few of the consumerist articles that do appear regarding degree mills caution the readers to deal only with accredited schools. But they often fail to go the crucial next step and warn the readers that there is such a thing as fake accreditation; that there are hundreds of fake accrediting agencies. So we get the sad letters from victims saying, "But they were accredited; I checked it out."

Registrars and Admissions Officers

College registrars are faced every day with the need to make decisions on which degrees and transcripts to accept, which to question, and which to reject.

Their professional association, the American Association of Collegiate Registrars and Admissions Officers (AACRAO, http://www.aacrao.org), has been on the front lines of the fake-degree battle for a long time.

- The organization frequently has workshops on degree fraud at its national and regional conventions, conducted by Allen Ezell and other experts.
- It has an Internet forum where professionals can ask questions and exchange information.
- It sells two helpful publications dealing with these matters: a twenty-five-cent brochure and a $25 workbook, both listed in the bibliography. It has also published and sold two helpful books by Allen Ezell, one on fake accreditors and one on counterfeit diplomas.
- It offers, for a fee, the service of evaluating academic credentials. While the service is comparable to that performed by independent credential evaluation firms (discussed in this section), AACRAO's opinion tends to have more "clout" because of the organization's reputation. As a result, it could be more proactive and perhaps a bit faster in identifying and evaluating degree mills.

At the time when a dozen or so American-run unrecognized schools paid up to a $50,000 fee and made the claim of Liberian accreditation, many eyes turned to AACRAO to see what it would have to say. Many months passed, because AACRAO was apparently waiting for someone to formally request and pay for an evaluation of one of these Liberian accreditees. Finally this happened, and AACRAO issued a policy statement saying that recent Liberian accreditation did not meet its standards. Prompter action might have impeded the growth of some of the dreadful schools in question.

Guidebook Publishers

The public tends to rely on the information found in published directories and guidebooks, especially when they come from large and well-known publishers. Unfortunately, in the world of college guides, this confidence is problematic. Dreadful and fake schools have been listed or advertised in major directories, from the once-preeminent *Lovejoy's* to the popular *Which MBA?* Several publishers of college directories—including Peterson's and Princeton Review, two of the largest—"sell space in their books to admissions offices that want to add their own messages. . . . Critics call such tactics highly misleading to students and parents."[11]

Educause

Educause is a large nonprofit association "whose mission is to advance higher education by promoting the intelligent use of information technology" (http://www.educause.edu/). In November 2001, the US Department of Commerce gave Educause the sole authority to dispense the ".edu" Internet suffix, which is widely (but incorrectly) regarded as a measure of legitimacy.

The problem is that more than fifty bad and fake schools have already been given, and regularly use, the ".edu" suffix. This was done through a combination of clerical error and lack of clear policy, mostly by the company called VeriSign, which used to be in charge. VeriSign mistakenly gave out more than four hundred ".edu" suffixes during its tenure.

The problem now is that "Educause has decided that because there are so many hundreds of unaccredited users, they don't want to deal with revoking them, so there will be *no* effort made to limit use of the .edu suffix only to legitimate schools."

The State of Oregon's website (http://www.oregon.gov/) correctly states that the extension ".edu" is in essence a random, meaningless arrangement of letters that does not confer any kind of legitimacy on any entity, nor is it ever likely to do so.

This regrettable situation could be solved if Educause were to make the current rules retroactive, and if it were also to apply them accurately to new applicants. Educause is *still* giving the ".edu" extension to bad and fake schools.

If Educause continues to stonewall in this matter, perhaps some of its 1,800 institutional members, virtually all of them properly using their ".edu" extension, might have something to say.

Another solution lies in the fact that even though the US Department of Commerce gave the "franchise" to Educause, it still retains final say on the way Educause handles ".edu" matters. That responsibility lies with the National Telecommunications and Information Administration within the Department of Commerce, which could invite Educause to shape up, or give the ".edu" franchise to someone else.

Colleges and Universities

A few years ago, John Bear wrote an article for *University Business*, a magazine for university presidents and financial officers. The title was "Diploma Mills: The $200-Million-a-Year Competitor You Didn't Know You Had" (online at http://tinyurl.com/UniversityBusiness). The main point was that the huge phonies were not only demeaning the whole world of higher education but were also diverting students who might have attended the legitimate school.

The article encouraged universities to speak out actively on the problem, to aggressively protect their own good name when a fake school used the same or a comparable one, and to refuse to advertise in publications where their own ad would run alongside ads for fake schools.

After the article ran, there were perhaps a dozen letters to the editor from university presidents, all of them of the "*They* should do something!" variety.

There have been rare exceptions. The real Washington University in St. Louis, Missouri, got an injunction against the dubious Washington University in Pennsylvania—but the dubious one simply changed its name to Washington International University. The real Thomas Edison State in New Jersey got an injunction requiring the fake Edison (run from a prison cell in Texas) to give up its name. And then there was the fake Western Washington State University, complete with its own ".edu" suffix (http://www.wwsu.edu), run from Norcross,

Georgia. The real WWSU, in Bellingham, Washington, got an injunction, but the Georgia-run phony merely changed its name slightly to Western Washington International University, did not change its website, and rolled merrily along. More recently, the real American University won a domain registration dispute with the less-real Americus University, which simply disappeared.

For the most part, universities do not protect their own good name. There is a charming display at the World of Coca-Cola museum in Atlanta showing all the would-be competitors the company was able to stop: Boca-Cola, Roca-Cola, Koka-Cola, and so on. Would that some of that same attitude carried over to Berkeley, Cambridge University, and the University of Wyoming, for instance, each of whom have been told about the dubious University of Berkley (a shed in Pennsylvania), Cambridge State University (a mailbox service in Hawaii), and the fake University of Wyoming (run from Switzerland) but have done nothing.

Even worse are the counterfeiting services, routinely selling well-made copies of the diplomas and transcripts of hundreds of legitimate schools. In addition to the fraud perpetrated by the sellers and buyers of these products, and the degrading of the real school's good name, there is also the matter of both trademark and copyright violation.

Credential Evaluation Services

One of the very complex issues in higher education is the matter of international equivalencies. Is a British "honours" degree equivalent to an American bachelor's, master's, or in between? What about a Mexican "Bachilerato" or a Japanese "Gakushi"? To help resolve these questions, the US Office of Education used to offer a credential evaluation service. But this was discontinued in 1974, giving rise to the growth of independent and unregulated evaluation services—more than thirty at this time.

About half of these services belong to a trade association, the National Association of Credential Evaluation Services (http://www.naces.org), and while they may differ somewhat in some of their evaluations, they are unlikely to report that a degree mill or unrecognized school is equivalent to a properly accredited American university. However, because the field is unregulated and unlicensed, anyone can hang out a shingle as a credential evaluator, including people who also run degree mills. Indeed, this has already happened. As educational philosopher Bill Dayson once wrote on DegreeInfo.com, "Credential evaluation could very easily become the next new frontier of 'degree-mill-science.' Perhaps it already has. We have had phony universities, then spurious accreditation, so why not some corrupt evaluators? Unlike universities and accreditors, evaluators are faceless and work in the shadows. You can search for schools and accreditors, but evaluators remain mysterious and hidden."[12]

Since anyone can open a spurious credential service on the Internet, there is no way this practice can be stopped. Short of the Department of Education returning to the business of credential evaluation (extremely unlikely), we can only wish that NACES will do its best to be militant in policing its members and applicants and that registrars and HR professionals will give extra care to scrutinizing reports from evaluators with which they are not familiar.

In 2004, eleven teachers in Georgia lost their jobs after buying master's and doctoral degrees from the spurious St. Regis University, ostensibly in Liberia. As the *Atlanta Journal-Constitution* (March 13, 2004) reported,

> Georgia recognized degrees from St. Regis, because it was affiliated with the American Association of Collegiate Registrars and Admissions Officers, a nonprofit voluntary organization that includes a foreign education credential service. But officials with [AACRAO] said they offer membership to anyone who pays. . . . Dale Gough, the organization's director of international education services said if Georgia officials had called his association about St. Regis, he would have told them, as he has told other states, that St. Regis was a diploma mill.

Georgia was also duped by a bogus credential evaluation agency, apparently financed by St. Regis, and run by a woman in Florida (using an assumed name) who had been involved with fake schools in the past.

Better Business Bureau

In the mid-1990s, Columbia State University was the biggest degree mill in the United States. It was also a member in good standing of the Better Business Bureau, which reassured many people who went on to buy a fake degree. When experts complained about this policy, the BBB response was to say that it could not adjudicate differences of opinion.

The BBB is a corporation where a great many consumers turn to check out a company or organization. But it does a considerable disservice to the public by accepting as members in good standing quite an array of unrecognized schools that may operate legally in their own jurisdictions (Idaho, Mississippi, Wyoming, and so on) but whose degrees would subject the holders to criminal action in various other states.

A search of the BBB site for *degree mills*, *degree fraud*, *fake degrees*, or *credential fraud* found nothing. A search for *diploma mills* found one article, but it focused entirely on fake high schools—and unfortunately did not mention that fake high schools are often operated by people who also grant fake college degrees, using the high schools as a feeder to higher degrees.

We'd like to see the BBB restrict membership to schools with recognized accreditation and help publicize the problem of fake schools.

Headhunters

More than a few executives and administrators with fake degrees have been recruited and recommended by executive search firms, commonly known as headhunters. When this happens, not only are the headhunters doing a major disservice to their clients but they also may be putting their own firms in jeopardy.

Following a well-publicized fake degree scandal in New Zealand, the headhunter firm that recruited the senior government executive with the fake degree, Millennium People, went out of business after all the bad publicity. The company had claimed that "extensive reference checks" had been done, and it was "defeated by a sophisticated international fraudster," but the simple fact was that three minutes of Internet research or a call to the registrar of any local university would have produced the information that the school in question was a fake.

Other recruitment firms in comparable situations have survived, albeit with a diminished reputation, as in the case of the superintendent of schools for California's second-largest school district whose headhunting firm failed to discover his fake doctorate claim.

The best advice here is that one should perform due diligence and not rely on earlier results. The California superintendent's spurious doctorate had been missed in each of his three previous top jobs, with each headhunting firm possibly assuming that earlier searches had verified the degree.

Internet Service Providers and Search Engines

This may be a little bit like making a wish that there would be no more war, famine, or floods on our planet. We have four wishes here. The first may be on its way to coming true; the second at least is a possibility, but we hold little hope for numbers three and four.

1. *Regulate spam.* It would be nice if the big companies that offer e-mail services could do more about the millions of spam messages sent every week to their customers by the degree mills and other bad schools. They have gotten better in recent years, but more than a few phony schools still get most of their students through spam messages.

2. *Responsibility for site content.* This second wish has a chance of coming true, albeit probably not through the industry developing a conscience (some providers will, but there will always be rogues) or through government regulation (there will always be rogue nations as well).

The matter of who is responsible for the content of websites is very much unresolved in the courts: Is it the site owner? The Internet service provider? No one? And does it matter if people knew it was illegal content?

In the best of worlds, it would be nice if Internet service providers stopped providing services to fake schools.

3. It would also be nice if the major Internet search engines (Google®, Yahoo!®, Bing®, etc.) did not provide the names of fake schools in searches, or, if they do, they might consider adding a warning to those results.

4. And as long as we're wishing, what if the search services did not sell banner and pop-up advertising to fake schools and degree counterfeiting services?

Academic Research

Given the importance of degree mills in the academic world, as well as in the public arena where the fake degrees are used, it is surprising how little research has been done on the topic. Indeed, we could find only two doctoral dissertations (out of over a million done since 1861) specifically on the topic: a 1959 historical look at the subject and a 2001 experimental study of the factors people take into account in choosing a degree mill. One other, in 2003, included degree mills in research on how HR executives evaluate schools.[13]

Frustrated by the lack of information on how college registrars deal with unaccredited and fake degrees, John Bear spent several thousand dollars of his own money to send a detailed questionnaire to a large number of registrars. The findings, reported at the registrars' national convention in 2000, suggested that while they are much more knowledgeable and vigilant than the typical corporate HR person, many of them still have a lot to learn.

With thousands of graduate students each year casting about for topics for term papers, master's theses, and doctoral dissertations, we would hope that degree-mill-related issues will be increasingly addressed.

The Public

It goes without saying that if people did not buy fake and useless degrees, the huge number of degree mills would be out of business overnight. But, realistically, that is like saying that if no one drank and drove, the number of traffic deaths would be dramatically reduced. If no one wanted to pay for sex, prostitution would be eliminated. If no one gambled or used drugs, then organized crime would be in big trouble. If no one fudged on their taxes, the federal budget would be balanced in a year.

So-called victimless crime has, of course, victims.

It seems to us, however, that the crime of degree fraud can have much broader, far-reaching effects than many other crimes. Of course, we do not wish to diminish the anguish of armed robbery, physical assault, kidnapping, and murder. But the perpetrators of these crimes typically have a relatively small number of victims. Contrast this smaller group of people with, for example:

- the viewers who followed the advice of a popular TV personality with a fake doctorate
- the victims of a man with a fake dental degree employed at a New York clinic
- the more than one hundred thousand students affected by the policies of a big-city school superintendent with a fake doctorate
- the readers who followed the financial advice of a popular business columnist for a major magazine who had a fake business degree
- even the listeners who got caught in the rain following the forecasts of a popular network weatherman with a fake meteorology degree

Our best advice to the public in general can be expressed in these two words: be careful. Or in these two words: due diligence. Or these two: be skeptical.

Perform due diligence before dealing with a doctor, lawyer, accountant, therapist, and so forth. Where did they get their degrees? The diploma on the wall is not enough evidence; there are so many degree-counterfeiting services.

And do due diligence before choosing a school for yourself. Ask whether the degree you will earn will meet not only your immediate needs but also those in the future, as best you can predict. People move. People change jobs. Employers change policies with regard to degrees. Something that seemed reasonable now (or seemed to be a risk worth taking) might prove to be a problem later on.

As reported in chapter 3, John Bear once testified in the trial of a state psychologist who had purchased a degree-mill doctorate and had been earning doctoral pay for six years. The man claimed he didn't know the school was illegal and said that he was not troubled by the school's lack of a telephone, its mailing service address, or its willingness to grant the degree based on life experience and to back-date the diploma.

During his closing argument, the prosecutor turned to the jury and said, "There sits a man who clearly spent more time deciding which candy bar to buy from the vending machine than he did in choosing his university."

In summation, we suggest that the proliferation of degree mills can only be stopped (or slowed down) by a concerted effort in these five categories:

- *Demand.* Devalue the degrees purchased by prosecuting the users and publicizing the prosecution. Embarrass the "gradu-ates."
- *Supply.* Outlaw degree mills in the states where they operate and all locations where they maintain their offices.
- *Prosecution.* Prosecute the operators under state or federal statutes.
- *Pressure.* Increase pressure on publications to refuse to accept their advertising.
- *Awareness.* Increase public awareness of degree mills and the harm done to society.

And at all times, remember those three two-word mottoes:
Be careful. Be skeptical. Due diligence.

NOTES

INTRODUCTION

1. His name has been changed for this otherwise-accurate account.

2. Following an indictment on eighteen counts of mail fraud, tax evasion, and money laundering, James Kirk, also known as Thomas McPherson, pleaded guilty to one count and was sentenced to five years in federal prison.

3. The cost of a fake degree can range from under $100 to more than $5,000, and prices are usually negotiable.

4. We are grateful to Dr. Robin Calote for sharing her alarmingly large collection of degree-mill articles from the 1920s.

5. Press release, US Office of Education, April 11, 1960.

6. Bear was invited back to do two more of these workshops the following year.

7. Many more of these "time bombs" are described in chapter 8.

8. Robert H. Reid, "Degree Mills in the United States (PhD diss., Columbia University, 1963).

9. David W. Stewart and Henry A. Spille, *Diploma Mills: Degrees of Fraud* (New York: American Council on Education, 1988). Both were employed by the American Council on Education when this was published.

10. See Steve Levicoff, *Name It and Frame It* (Ambler, PA: Institute on Religion and Law, 1993), which looks primarily at Christian degree mills.

11. This is very similar to the process of fingerprint identification, in which each examiner has his or her own number of "points of identification" required to make a match. It is called a floating standard.

12. Accreditation is explained in some detail in chapter 14. The three schools that award bachelor's degrees based on prior learning are Excelsior College in New York, Thomas Edison State College in New Jersey, and Charter Oak State College in Connecticut.

13. John Bear and Mariah Bear, *College Degrees by Mail and Internet* (Berkeley, CA: Ten Speed Press, 2001).

CHAPTER 1

1. J. M. Wallace-Hadrill, *The Barbarian West: The Early Middle Ages A.D. 400–1000* (New York: Hutchinson's University Library, 1952), p. 93.

2. Hastings Rashdall, *The Universities of Europe in the Middle Ages* (Oxford: Oxford University Press, 1895).

3. Carlo Finocchietti, Claudia Checcacci, Luca Lantero, *How to Spot and Counter Diploma Mills* (Rome: Cimea-Naric Italia, 2010).

4. Barbara Tuchman, *Distant Mirror: The Calamitous 14th Century* (New York: Knopf, 1978).

5. We are grateful to Vasco Dones for telephoning a scholar in Italy to get to the bottom of the "two hams" matter.

6. Edwin Wooton, *A Guide to Degrees in Arts, Science, Literature, Law, Music, and Divinity* (London: L. U. Gill, 1883), pp. viii–x.

7. Robert H. Reid, "Degree Mills in the United States" (PhD diss., Columbia University, 1963), pp. 82–83.

8. US Senate, *Hearings*, 68th Congress, 1st Session, pursuant to Senate Resolution 61, March 1924.

9. Walter Wienert, "Doktorfabriken," (unpublished manuscript, 1958), cited by Reid.

10. Benjamin Fine, *New York Times*, February 7, 1950.

11. Reid, "Degree Mills in the United States," p. 29.

12. Reid, undated personal communication, late 1970s.

13. Nothing was ever done to attempt to close this institution or to prosecute its people.

14. US Congress, House, "A Joint Report by the Chairmen of the Subcommittee on Health and Long-Term Care and the Subcommittee on Housing and Consumer Interests of the Select Committee on Aging: Fraudulent Credentials," 99th Congress, December 11, 1985, Comm. pub. no. 99 (Washington, DC: US Government Printing Office, 1986).

15. Ibid.

16. Fraud by wire (telephone, etc.) must be interstate. Mail fraud does not need interstate action, since the US mail is involved.

17. It came with a cover letter stating, "You have been a credit to our institution and to our country." He was very perceptive indeed.

CHAPTER 2

1. Bob Jones University, a totally legitimate school that did not believe in secular accreditation, is an often-cited example of this category. But even they finally pursued and achieved accreditation through a recognized religious accreditor.

2. The university in question claims that the thirty-day residency is mandatory, but we have three letters sent to potential students who said that they were unable to come to St. Kitts. (Two of them were a pair of two-year-old twins. But that's another story.) The letters assure them that visitation was not necessary.

3. For instance, "Major university seeks adjunct faculty in business, psychology, and engineering for high-paying part-time assignments."

4. The question often arises, "Why not sue people like this?" Apart from the time and cost, there is the tiny likelihood of collecting. In this instance, an assets trace revealed that the man had considerable assets—all banked in a tax-haven country.

CHAPTER 3

1. He does.

2. You can read a portion of the telemarketing "script" of a very successful degree mill in chapter 7. It is enlightening to read the text as if you were an honest person in search of a degree to see if you might be persuaded. One out of three people who received this call ended up buying a degree.

3. Sinclair was convicted of mail fraud and sentenced to Federal Correctional Institution, Terminal Island, California. While there, he started and ran his next phony school, Hollywood Southern University, selling degrees to inmates, guards, and the general public. Then he signed up for a "work furlough" program to attend a cake-decorating class. He walked in the front door of the school and out the back door, and he has never been heard from again.

4. The research was published as a master's thesis by George M. Brown, "Are Virtual Universities in Australia a Guise for Degree/Diploma Mills to Thrive?" Flinders University of South Australia, 2001.

CHAPTER 4

1. There are more than a few people who believe that credentials are irrelevant, that skill or knowledge is the only relevant consideration. Long-time Louisiana state senator Woody Jenkins opposed *any* school licensing in his state for this reason. He put his career where his mouth was. Even though he graduated from law school with high honors, he refused to take the bar exam, claiming that the state had no right to decide who could give legal advice and who couldn't.

2. *Hofstra Labor & Employment Law Journal* 23 (2006), Ohio State Public Law Working Paper Series no. 79.

3. John Bear consulted with the attorneys for the company, who were trying to decide if they should take any action in the matter.

4. For instance, Supreme Court of the United States, *Faragher v. City of Boca Raton*, 524 US 775 (1998).

5. Originally published in 1974, it was revised and updated in 2003; things hadn't changed all that much.

CHAPTER 5

1. *Federal Criminal Code and Rules* (Eagan, MN: West Group, 2000), pp. 423, 489, 663, 730.

2. Title 18, part 1, chap. 63, sect. 1343.

3. Eventually we did. It had come from Kensington University, an unaccredited school at one time approved by the state of California, which later lost that approval.

CHAPTER 12

1. The Tenth Amendment reads: "The powers not delegated to the United States by the Constitution, nor prohibited by it to the States, are reserved to the States respectively, or to the people."

2. Religious exemption is controversial, raises a variety of legal and policy issues, and is allowed in fewer than half of the states.

3. See Contreras (2009), *Legal Basis, supra* and see also Contreras, "Why Are Religious Diploma Mills Always Neo-Protestant? *Free Inquiry*, June, 2009.

4. See the following: *National Assn. of Certified Public Accountants v. United States*, 53 App. DC 391, 292 F. 668 (1923), *cert den.* Oct. 6, 1923; *Townshend v. Gray*, 62 Vt. 373, 19 A. 635 (1890), *The Medical College of Philadelphia Case*, 3 Whart. 445 (1838); Regents of University of Maryland v. Williams, 9 Gill and J. 365, 31 Am. D. 72 (1838); *In re Duquesne College Charter* (Com. Pl.) 12 Pa. Co. Ct. R. 491, 2 Pa. Dist. R. 555 (1891); *Kerr v. Shurtleff*, 218 Mass. 167, 105 N.E. 871 (1914).

5. Opinion of Attorney General Packel to John C. Pittenger, Pennsylvania Secretary of Education, issued Dec. 18, 1973, 63 Pa. D. & C.2d. 436, 1973 WL 41066, Pa. Dept. of Justice. The Attorney General made clear that degree-granting authority had to be explicit in law, and also embarked on a short informative history of the meaning of the words "diploma" and "degree" and how they had diverged in the past hundred years.

6. *State ex rel. Granville v. Gregory*, 83 Mo. 123, 53 Am. Rep. 565 (1884). In this case the college was established by express state charter that simply didn't mention degree-granting, rather than starting itself as a corporation.

7. States use various terms such as licensure, authorization, approval, and the like. Although these sometimes have slightly different meanings, I use the term *authorization* to encompass all formal state conferral of degree-granting authority by a non-legislative body.

8. *Nova University v. Board of Governors of the U. of N. Carolina*, 267 S.E.2d. 596, (NC Ct. App 1980), *aff'd*, 287 S.E.2d. 872 (NC 1982). This case also reaffirmed the states' basic authority over education. See also *Nova University v. Educational Institution Licensure Commission*, 483 A.2d 1172 (DC 1984).

9. *Packer Collegiate Institute v. University of the State of New York*, 81 N.E.2d. 80 (NY 1948) noted a lack of sufficient standards and what subjects they should cover; *State v. Williams*, 117 S.E. 2d. 444 (NC 1960) dealt with similar issues.

10. An excellent look at the underpinnings of mainstream religious college authority from a Catholic perspective is Peter J. Harrington, "Civil and Canon Law Issues Affecting American Catholic Higher Education 1948–1998: An Overview and the ACCU Perspective," *Journal of College and University Law* 26, no. 67 (1999).

11. Ibid. at 70.

12. See Alan L. Contreras, *Rendering unto Caesar: Do Religious Exemption Laws Produce an Ungodly Number of Diploma Mills?* In prep., 2012.

13. An alternate view is that the law recognizes that churches have an

innate right to train their leaders and this right necessarily includes degree-granting authority. This view is more difficult to support on historical grounds, as degree-granting authority was effectively a royal monopoly for so long prior to colleges coming to American shores.

14. *New Jersey State Board of Higher Education v. Board of Directors of Shelton College*, 90 NJ 470, 448 A.2d 988 (1982). It was really two cases decided 15 years apart, but the key case for degree authority is the 1982 case. See also *State ex rel. McLemore v. Clarksville School of Theology*, 636 S.W.2d. 706, 5 Ed. Law Rep. 1294 (1982); *State Board of School and College Registration v. Ohio St. Matthew University of St. Matthew Church of God*, Case No. 72-AP-130, Court of Appeals for Franklin County, Ohio (1972), unpublished. One case that reached a different conclusion is an outlier and was not well considered by the court: *HEB Ministries Inc. et al. v. Texas Higher Education Coordinating Board et al.*, 235 S.W. 3d 627, 226 Ed. Law Rep. 348, 50 Tex. Sup. Ct. J. 1094.

15. Arkansas Atty. Gen. letter opinion 2001-163, July 31, 2001, issued to State Sen. Ed Wilkinson; Op. Tex. Att'y Gen No. JC-0200 (2000), cited at 661 by the Texas Supreme Court in the HEB Ministries case but not reviewed in full for this article; 1988-91 Ky. Op. Atty. Gen 2-533, Ky. OAG 91-14, 1991 WL 53810 (Ky. A.G.), letter opinion of January 23, 1991, to Gary S. Cox, Executive Director, Kentucky Council on Higher Education; Nevada Atty. Gen. letter opinion issued Sep. 7, 1973, to Merlin Anderson, Administrator, Commission on Postsecondary Institutional Authorization. The date on the Arkansas letter may be erroneous in the original.

16. *Strang v. Satz*, 884 F.Supp. 504.

17. Press release from Stephen B. Russell, 20th Judicial Circuit of Florida, August 11, 2006, accessed on the web on April 6, 2010.

18. OAR 583-050-0014(3)

CHAPTER 19

1. Mike Lambert, executive director of the Distance Education and Training Council (a recognized accreditor), was instrumental in getting this rule on the books. He, too, has been frustrated that it hasn't been enforced.

2. Some of the biggest degree mills send their diplomas and other materials by Federal Express. By virtue of going to a FedEx office, paying in cash, and putting a false return address on the envelope, the packages seem to be untraceable. Other mills use overnight delivery services in the mis-

taken belief that this exempts them from mail fraud charges. However, in 1989, Congress recodified the mail fraud statutes, adding private or commercial interstate carriers (title 18, section 1341, USC).

3. "Bogus Degrees and Unmet Expectations: Are Taxpayer Dollars Subsidizing Diploma Mills?" United States Senate, 108th Congress, 2d Session, May 11–12, 2004 (Washington, DC: US Government Printing Office), p. 16.

4. Letter from secretary of education Rod Paige to Senator Susan M. Collins, October 9, 2003, archived at www2.ed.gov/policy/highered/guid/secletter/031009.html.

5. Ibid.

6. Ibid.

7. "The Application of the Apostille Convention to Diplomas Including Those Issued by Diploma Mills," Hague Conference on Private International Law, Special Commission of February 2009 on the practical operation of The Hague Apostille Service, Preliminary Document No. 5. 2008, The Hague, the Netherlands.

8. Ibid.

9. John Bear was one of five members of Douglas's doctoral guidance committee.

10. "Money" section, *USA Today*, September 28, 2003.

11. *Chronicle of Higher Education*, June 6, 2000.

12. http://www.degreeinfo.com, March 23, 2001.

13. Robert H. Reid, "Degree Mills in the United States" (PhD diss., Columbia University, 1963); Robyn Calote, "Diploma Mills: What's the Attraction?" (EdD diss., University of LaVerne, 2002); Richard Douglas, "The Accreditation of Degree-Granting Institutions and Its Role in the Utility of College Degrees in the Workplace" (PhD diss., Union Institute and University, 2003).

SELECT BIBLIOGRAPHY

BOOKS

Bear, Mariah, and John Bear. *Bears' Guide to Earning Degrees by Distance Learning*. 15th ed. Berkeley, CA: Ten Speed Press, 2002. While most of the book focuses on legitimate ways to earn degrees online and by distance learning, there is a long chapter on degree mills, describing several hundred of the worst in more detail than this book provides. Out of print but readily available for $5 or less on http://www.bookfinder.com.

Berg, Ivan. *Education and Jobs: The Great Training Robbery*. New York: Percheron Press, 2003. Reprint, New York, HarperCollins, 1971. Addresses the issue of whether degree requirements make sense in hiring practices.

Burke, Jeanne M., ed. *Higher Education Directory*. Falls Church, VA: Higher Education Publications, 2012. Until 1983, the US Department of Education published an annual directory of detailed information on every school with recognized accreditation and on the recognized accreditors. When the department stopped, Higher Education Publications (www.hepinc.com) was formed to carry on the work, producing this valuable reference work, which appears annually. Originally it listed California-approved schools but stopped that practice in 1988.

Europa Publications. *Europa World of Learning, 62nd Edition*. London: Routledge, 2012. More than three thousand large pages (and very small type) describing in some detail every college and university on earth, plus thousands of educational organizations. While the new edition costs more than $1,000, last year's edition typically sells on the Internet for under $30—quite a bargain.

Ezell, Allen, *Accreditation Mills*. Washington, DC: AACRAO Publications, 2007. A more detailed look at the problems identified in this book and how they can be dealt with.

———. *Counterfeit Diplomas and Transcripts*. Washington, DC: AACRAO Publications, 2008. Gives readers the tools needed to protect the legitimacy of their documents, recognize counterfeit documents, and explore relief against injury done by the counterfeiters.

International Association of Universities. *International Handbook of Universities*. 22nd ed. New York: Palgrave Macmillan, 2011. More than fifteen thousand schools described in detail in three volumes with more than three thousand pages (at a cost of more than $700).

Levicoff, Steve. *Name It and Frame It: New Opportunities in Adult Education and How to Avoid Being Ripped Off by "Christian" Degree Mills*. 4th ed. Ambler, PA: Institute on Religion and Law, 1995. While the focus is on religious schools, there is much valuable advice on the world of degree mills in general. Out of print.

Reid, Robert H. *American Degree Mills: A Study of Their Operations and of Existing and Potential Ways to Control Them*. Washington, DC: American Council on Education, 1959.

Stewart, David W., and Henry A. Spille. *Diploma Mills: Degrees of Fraud*. New York: American Council on Education/Macmillan, 1988. Originally announced in 1982 as a "hard-hitting" book on the problem, when it finally emerged six years later, the lawyers had marched in, and it turned out a rather soft-hitting look at the problem and a then-useful but now-obsolete look at the relevant laws in each state.

Walston, Rick. *Walston's Guide to Christian Distance Learning*. 6th ed. Longview, WA: Xulon Press, 2012. The Rev. Dr. Walston covers mostly the legitimate schools, but he pulls no punches in his descriptions of many "Bible" schools with misleading accreditation claims, sometimes following his description with a thundering, "Shame!"

DISSERTATIONS AND A THESIS

Brown, George. "Academic Qualification Acceptability and Authenticity: A Comparative Risk Assessment of Approaches Employed by the Recruitment and Higher Education Sectors of Australia." PhD diss., University of Adelaide, 2007. Brown used the theoretical framework of risk assessment and management to look at providers of fake degrees and credentials to the Australian market.

———. "Are Virtual Universities in Australia a Guise for Degree/ Diploma Mills to Thrive?" MEdMgt thesis, Flinders University of South Australia, 2001.

Calote, Robin Joyce. "Diploma Mills: What's the Attraction?" EdD diss., University of LaVerne, 2002. Calote looked at the variables in how degree mills present themselves that seemed to be of particular interest to potential customers.

Douglas, Richard. "The Accreditation of Degree-Granting Institutions and Its Role in the Utility of College Degrees in the Workplace." PhD diss., Union Institute and University, 2003. Douglas's research focused on large corporation human resources executives and how they make their decisions on which schools to accept or recognize or pay for. His findings suggest that the majority of HR people do not know nearly as much about accreditation and about bad and fake schools as one might wish.

Reid, Robert H. "Degree Mills in the United States." PhD diss., Columbia University, 1963.

FOUR CONGRESSIONAL REPORTS

US Congress, House. A Joint Report by the Chairmen of the Subcommittee on Health and Long-Term Care and the Subcommittee on Housing and Consumer Interests of the Select Committee on Aging. Fraudulent Credentials, 99th Congress, December 11, 1985, Comm. pub. no. 99. Washington, DC: US Government Printing Office, 1986. This is one of the two reports that came from Rep. Claude Pepper's subcommittee and focuses more on health fraud.

US Congress, House. A Joint Report by the Chairmen of the Subcommittee on Health and Long-Term Care and the Subcommittee on Housing and Consumer Interests of the Select Committee on Aging. Fraudulent Credentials, 99th Congress, December 11, 1985, Comm. pub. no. 99-551. Washington, DC: US Government Printing Office, 1986. This is the second report that came from Rep. Claude Pepper's subcommittee and focuses more on federal employees.

US Senate. Bogus Degrees and Unmet Expectations: Are Taxpayer Dollars Subsidizing Diploma Mills? Hearings before the Committee on Governmental Affairs, United States Senate. Washington, DC: US Government Printing Office, 2004. Covers the two-day hearings conducted by Sen. Susan Collins and others.

US Senate. Hearings before a Subcommittee of the Committee on Education and Labor, United States Senate, Diploma Mills. 68th Congress. January and March 1924. Washington, DC: Government Printing Office, 1924. This was the first time the US Senate looked at the degree-mill problem. The focus was on fake medical degrees.

AACRAO

The American Association of Collegiate Registrars and Admissions Officers (www.aacrao.org) produces many valuable publications on the educational systems of various countries; it also offers two useful publications to help spot fake schools and credentials.

"Fraudulent Academic Credentials: Bogus US Institutions; How to Avoid Fake Schools and Fake Degrees." A somewhat dated (1988) brochure from the National Liaison Committee on Foreign Student Admissions, priced for distribution in larger quantities at thirty cents each.

Misrepresentation in the Marketplace and Beyond: Ethics under Siege, ed. Peggy Askins. A sixty-four-page booklet on how to spot false schools and transcripts.

WEBSITES

http://www.degreeinfo.com and http://www.degreediscussion.com. These two forums are the main Internet locations for discussions of bad and fake schools (as well as good and real ones). There is much overlap, but some experts post in both places. They have good search engines linked to more than a hundred thousand postings covering hundreds of schools—good, bad, and fake. The forums are lightly moderated, so the proponents of unrecognized schools—either individual ones or of the concept in general—have their say as long as they are not aggressive or dishonest in what they write.

http://www.degreemills.com. This site has been set up by the authors of this book, Allen Ezell and John Bear, to update the information contained in the book, to report on relevant news and developments from the world of higher education, and to offer an opportunity for questions, responses, and the exchange of ideas.

http://www.degree.net. Caution: this was John Bear's site, but the publisher let the registration lapse, and it was "hijacked" by someone on the island of Vanuatu in the South Pacific. It is now in the hands of an anonymous owner. John Bear has nothing to do with this site.

SUBJECT INDEX

NOTE: Many more unrecognized accrediting agencies are listed on pages 330 through 346 of this book.

Christa McAuliffe Academy CEO
and principal, 238
Chronicle of Higher Education, 14,
194, 230, 238
Chun-fai, Lam (psychiatrist), 249
church. *See* religious
church-based degree-granting
authority, 282
church-operated schools, 48
church-state situations, 48–51
Clark, Charles ("Boobie"), 40
CLEP. *See* College Level Evaluation
Program (CLEP)
coaches of two major university
sports teams, 22
co-conspirators, 80, 82
Cohen, Eyal Ben, 362–68
College Level Evaluation Program
(CLEP), 26
Collin, George
"Bruning St. Regis," 174–233
"Information about the 'National
Board of Education,' Saint
Regis University, and Amer-
ican Coastline University,"
199
Collins, Grant, 217, 220
Collins, Oreo (cat), 256
Collins, Susan (Maine senator), 14,
19–20, 349, 386–88
Columbia State University (CA)
accrediting agency and, 70
Austen Henry Layard and, 82
aviation doctorate for office bird,
255
bank deposits of $72 million, 17
biggest degree mill in US, 412
California warehouse, 91
Connecticut psychotherapist and,
254

degrees, twenty-seven-day, 106
Economist and ads from, 405
FTC investigation of, 376
Gloria Schermesser and bachelor's degree, 246
"graduates," fifteen thousand,
359
guides to distance learning, 79
human resource professionals
and, 403
local principal and PhD degree,
355
Monster.com and other database
searches, 360
PhD degrees, 17, 239, 242, 254,
355, 405
Pittsburgh school psychologist
and, 254
in post-DipScam era, 374
Ronald Pellar and, 61–62, 389
undocumented aliens and no
business license, 401
unrecognized school, 307, 356
Commission on Medical Denturitry
Accreditation, 329
Congress. *See* US Congress
Congressional committee, 11, 177
Connecticut psychotherapist, 254
consumer protection
action, 215–16
agencies, 129
laws, 53, 375–76
See also law enforcement and
legal/ethical issues
Consumer Protection Act, 196
Contreras, Alan, 216, 277–84
Copeland, Royal (New York sen-
ator), 37
Copen, Bruce, 170–71
Cosell, Howard, 40

INDEX OF SCHOOL NAMES

NOTE: Many more unrecognized schools are listed on pages 299 through 325 of this book.

Geneseo State University of New
York, 180
Georgia Christian University (GA),
95, 310
Glencullen University (UK), 224, 310
Global Church Theological Semi-
nary, 310, 349

Hamilton University (WY), 49, 240,
260, 262–68, 302, 311
Hampshire University, 224
Hampton College (NV), 311, 349
Harrington University (UK), 224,
311, 356, 372
Hartford University (Vanuatu), 311,
349
Hartland University (Liberia), 183,
311
Harvard, 70, 76, 86, 96, 120, 157,
226
Hillmax Universityy, 364–65
Hodges University (England), 244
Holmes University, 180
Holy Acclaim University, 178–79
Hutt River University, 72

Innuendo State University, 351
Interfaith Education Ministries
Association of Academic Excel-
lence, 182
Interfaith Education Ministry, 192
International Alliance of Universi-
ties, The, 76
International College of Homeland
Security, 197, 334
International University (LA), 169,
472
International University of
Advanced Studies (New
Utopia), 72

International University of
Advanced Studies (TX), 72
International University of Funda-
mental Studies, 182, 312, 334

Jackson State University (CA), 130,
313
James Monroe University (Liberia),
188–89, 206, 313
Jefferson High School Online, 256
Johann Keppler School of Medicine
(NY), 151, 313
John Quincy Adams University
(OR), 130, 380
Johns Hopkins University, 350
Johnson Davids University, 72

Kennedy-Western University
(CA/WY), 52, 65, 313, 324
Kingsfield University (UK), 224, 313
King's University, 72

LaCrosse University (LA), 253, 313,
333, 340–41
Lafayette University, 224
Landford University, 224, 313
LaSalle University (LA). *See subject
index*
Lexington University (NV), 115,
314, 349, 386
Livingston University of America,
36
Louisiana Central University (LA),
236, 314

Madison University (MS), 251, 314
Marquis University, 72
Metropolitan Collegiate, 351
Michigan Institute of Technology,
354